CORPORATE ENVIRONMENTAL RESPONSIBILITY IN INVESTOR–STATE DISPUTE SETTLEMENT

This book explores the potential of the current investor–state dispute settlement (ISDS) mechanism to materialise the responsibility of foreign investors through the states' counterclaims and defences at the jurisdictional, merits, and quantum phases. In doing so, it seeks to incorporate the recent developments of ISDS in both international and domestic laws of certain jurisdictions on corporate responsibility, including the parent company's due diligence and legal effects of corporations' voluntary commitments. The book also reflects the interests and perspectives of the victims who suffered loss and injury due to investors' conduct. The author demonstrates that the current system does have the inherent potential to advance responsible investment, even though reforms are needed to overcome its limitations. Fully utilising this potential to reflect investor responsibility in the international investment agreement–based dispute settlement mechanisms will help to develop practices based on greater due diligence and responsible business conduct.

TOMOKO ISHIKAWA is a professor at Nagoya University in Japan. She is a member of the ICSID Panel of Conciliators, appointed by the ICSID Administrative Council. Her professional experiences include serving as an associate judge at Tokyo District Court and holding the position of deputy director at the Ministry of Foreign Affairs of Japan.

CORPORATE ENVIRONMENTAL RESPONSIBILITY IN INVESTOR–STATE DISPUTE SETTLEMENT

The Unexhausted Potential of Current Mechanisms

TOMOKO ISHIKAWA
Nagoya University

CAMBRIDGE
UNIVERSITY PRESS

CAMBRIDGE
UNIVERSITY PRESS

Shaftesbury Road, Cambridge CB2 8EA, United Kingdom

One Liberty Plaza, 20th Floor, New York, NY 10006, USA

477 Williamstown Road, Port Melbourne, VIC 3207, Australia

314–321, 3rd Floor, Plot 3, Splendor Forum, Jasola District Centre, New Delhi – 110025, India

103 Penang Road, #05–06/07, Visioncrest Commercial, Singapore 238467

Cambridge University Press is part of Cambridge University Press & Assessment,
a department of the University of Cambridge.

We share the University's mission to contribute to society through the pursuit of
education, learning and research at the highest international levels of excellence.

www.cambridge.org
Information on this title: www.cambridge.org/9781009077033

DOI: 10.1017/9781009076425

First published 2023
First paperback edition 2024

A catalogue record for this publication is available from the British Library

Library of Congress Cataloging-in-Publication data
Names: Ishikawa, Tomoko (Lawyer), author.
Title: Corporate environmental responsibility in investor-state dispute settlement :
the unexhausted potential of current mechanisms / Tomoko Ishikawa, Nagoya University, Japan.
Description: Cambridge, United Kingdom ; New York, NY : Cambridge University Press, 2023. |
Includes bibliographical references and index.
Identifiers: LCCN 2022013564 (print) | LCCN 2022013565 (ebook) | ISBN 9781316513972
(hardback) | ISBN 9781009077033 (paperback) | ISBN 9781009076425 (epub)
Subjects: LCSH: International business enterprises–Law and legislation–Environmental aspects. |
Social responsibility of business–Law and legislation–Environmental aspects. | International
commercial arbitration–Environmental aspects. | Investments, Foreign (International law)–
Environmental aspects.
Classification: LCC K1322 .I845 2023 (print) | LCC K1322 (ebook) |
DDC 346/.066–dc23/eng/20220801
LC record available at https://lccn.loc.gov/2022013564
LC ebook record available at https://lccn.loc.gov/2022013565

ISBN 978-1-316-51397-2 Hardback
ISBN 978-1-009-07703-3 Paperback

CONTENTS

FIGURES

ACKNOWLEDGEMENTS

My appreciation goes to many people for their support with this book project. First and foremost, I would like to thank Yarik Kryvoi, Elizabeth Whitsitt, Ondřej Svoboda, Rajesh Sharma, and Geraldine Rebeca Fischer for their invaluable comments and suggestions on chapters of and issues discussed in the manuscript. I thank the anonymous reviewers who provided immensely helpful advice on the book proposal and the first draft of several chapters. Valuable research assistance came from Arjun Solanki, Hotaru Tokunaga, Abhay B. Bhandari, Li Yingru, Abdoul Koanda, and Marie N'Guessan. Responsibility remains solely with the author. I also thank the editorial team at Cambridge University Press, especially Joe Ng and Gemma Smith, for their support and guidance. This project was funded by the Japan Society for the Promotion of Science (grant number 18K01275), without which the production of the book would not have been possible.

In-class discussions with my students, who shared stories and experiences concerning transnational corporations' activities in their home countries including Nigeria, Côte d'Ivoire, Burkina Faso, Mozambique, Mongolia, and Sri Lanka, were a great source of inspiration. Some arguments of this book were shared and tested in conferences and a study group meeting, and I thank Wang Guiguo, CIArb YMG, and Professor Takashi Uchida (who was my supervisor for Japanese civil law at Tokyo University) for giving me these opportunities in spite of the disruptions caused by the pandemic.

Stone walls do not a prison make, as Lovelace said, and I am indebted to friends in many parts of the world for reminding me of this and for their encouragement and support. Among them, Miriam Embury in England for helping me keep in good spirits during the more trying times of the pandemic. Lastly, I thank my loving family for their encouragement and a constant reminder of what is important in life (Naoki Ishikawa), continued belief in me (Coe), understanding for the reduction in movie nights (Kan), and making me smile (all).

TABLE OF CASES

Investor–State Arbitrations

Occidental Petroleum Corporation and Occidental Exploration and Production Company v. Republic of Ecuador, ICSID Case No. ARB/06/11, Award, 5 October 2012. 130, 192, 193, 196, 198

Occidental Petroleum Corporation and Occidental Exploration and Production Company v. Republic of Ecuador, ICSID Case No. ARB/06/11, Dissenting Opinion of Professor Brigitte Stern, 20 September 2012. 129, 196

Oko Pankki Oyj, VTB Bank (Deutschland) AG and Sampo Bank Plc v. Republic of Estonia, ICSID Case No. ARB/04/6, Award, 19 November 2007. 161

Ortiz Construcciones y Proyectos S.A. v. People's Democratic Republic of Algeria, ICSID Case No. ARB/17/1, Award, 29 April 2020. 174

Oxus Gold plc v. Republic of Uzbekistan, the State Committee of Uzbekistan for Geology & Mineral Resources, and Navoi Mining & Metallurgical Kombinat, UNCITRAL, Final Award, 15 December 2015. 89, 103, 105, 161

Pac Rim Cayman LLC v. Republic of El Salvador, ICSID Case No. ARB/09/12, Award, 14 October 2016. 129

PAO Tatneft (formerly OAO Tatneft) v. Ukraine, PCA Case No. 2008-8, Partial Award on Jurisdiction, 28 September 2010. 159

PAO Tatneft (formerly OAO Tatneft) v. Ukraine, PCA Case No. 2008-8, Award on the Merits, 29 July 2014. 134

Parkerings-Compagniet AS v. Republic of Lithuania, ICSID Case No. ARB/05/8, Award, 11 September 2007. 168

Penwell Business Limited (by MegaCom) v. Kyrgyz Republic, PCA Case No. 2017-31, Award, 8 October 2021. 165

Perenco Ecuador Ltd. v. Republic of Ecuador and Empresa Estatal Petroeleos del Ecuador, ICSID Case No. ARB/08/6, Interim Decision on the Environmental Counterclaim, 11 August 2015. 66, 118, 125, 128, 131, 150

Perenco Ecuador Ltd. v. Republic of Ecuador and Empresa Estatal Petroeleos del Ecuador, ICSID Case No. ARB/08/6, Decision on Claimant's Application for Dismissal of Respondent's Counter-Claims, 18 August 2017. 117

Perenco Ecuador Ltd. v. Republic of Ecuador and Empresa Estatal Petroeleos del Ecuador, ICSID Case No. ARB/08/6, Award, 27 September 2019. 117, 133

Perenco Ecuador Ltd. v. Republic of Ecuador and Empresa Estatal Petroeleos del Ecuador, ICSID Case No. ARB/08/6, Decision on Annulment, 28 May 2021. 58

Peter A. Allard v. Government of Barbados, PCA Case No. 2012-06, Award on Jurisdiction, 13 June 2014. 11, 131, 160

Philip Morris Brands Sàrl, Philip Morris Products S.A. and Abal Hermanos S.A. v. Oriental Republic of Uruguay, ICSID Case No. ARB/10/7, Award, 8 July 2016. 11, 129, 172, 176, 177

Phoenix Action, Ltd. v. Czech Republic, ICSID Case No. ARB/06/5, Award, 15 April 2009. 11, 166

Ping An Life Insurance Company of China, Limited and Ping An Insurance (Group) Company of China, Limited v. Kingdom of Belgium, ICSID Case No. ARB/12/29, Award, 30 April 2015. 82

Other Investor–State Dispute Documents

International Court of Justice and Permanent Court of International Justice

Application of the Convention on the Prevention and Punishment of the Crime of Genocide (Croatia v. Serbia) (Judgment) (Preliminary Objections) [2008] ICJ Rep. 412. 74

Application of the Convention on the Prevention and Punishment of the Crime of Genocide (Croatia v. Serbia) (Judgment) (Merits) [2015] ICJ Rep. 3. 74

Application of the Interim Accord of 13 September 1995 (FYRM v. Greece) (Judgment of 5 December 2011) [2011] ICJ Rep. 644. 82

Application of the International Convention on the Elimination of All Forms of Racial Discrimination (Qatar v. United Arab Emirates) (Judgment of 4 February 2021). 74

Armed Activities on the Territory of the Congo (Democratic Republic of the Congo v. Uganda) (Order) (Decision to Obtain an Expert Opinion) [2020] ICJ GL No 116, ICGJ 547 (ICJ 2020). 130

Arrest Warrant of Apr. 11, 2000 (Democratic Republic of the Congo v. Belgium) (Judgment of 14 February 2002) [2002] ICJ Rep. 3. 163

Barcelona Traction, Light and Power Co., Ltd. (Belgium v. Spain) (New Application: 1962) (Judgment of 5 February 1970) [1970] ICJ Rep. 3. 2

Case Concerning Application of the Convention on the Prevention and Punishment of the Crime of Genocide (Bosnia & Herzegovina v. Yugoslavia (Serbia & Montenegro)) (Order) (Provisional Measures) [1993] ICJ Rep. 3. 74

Certain German Interests in Polish Upper Silesia (Germany v. Poland) (Merits) (1926) PCIJ, Series A, No. 7, 19. 121

Certain Iranian Assets (Islamic Republic of Iran v. United States of America) (Judgment) (Preliminary Objections) [2019] ICJ Rep. 7. 163

Certain Phosphate Lands in Nauru case (Nauru v. Australia) (Judgement) (Preliminary Objections) [1992] ICJ Rep. 240. 82

Certain Questions of Mutual Assistance in Criminal Matters (Djibouti v. France) (Judgment of 4 June 2008) [2008] ICJ Rep. 177. 79

Corfu Channel case (United Kingdom of Great Britain and Northern Ireland v. Albania) (Order) (Expert Opinion) [1948] ICJ Rep. 124. 130

Delimitation of the Maritime Boundary in the Gulf of Maine Area (Canada v. United States of America) (Order) (Appointment of Expert) [1984] ICJ Rep. 165. 130

East Timor (Portugal v. Australia) (Judgment of 30 June 1995) [1995] ICJ Rep. 90. 82

Elettronica Sicula S.p.A. (ELSI) (United States of America v. Italy) (Judgment of 20 July 1989) [1989] ICJ Rep. 15. 128

Factory at Chorzów (Germany v. Poland) (Jurisdiction) (1927) PCIJ, Series A, No. 9. 93

Gabcíkovo-Nagymaros Project (Hungary v. Slovakia) (Judgment of 25 September 1997) and (Separate Opinion of Judge Weeramantry) [1997] ICJ Rep. 7. 7

Jurisdiction of the Courts of Danzig (Advisory Opinion) [1928] PCIJ, Series B, No. 15. 31

Jurisdictional Immunities of the State (Germany v. Italy) (Order) (Counter-Claims) [2010] ICJ Rep. 310. 90

Maritime Delimitation in the Caribbean Sea and the Pacific Ocean (Costa Rica v. Nicaragua) (Order) (Decision to Obtain an Expert Opinion) [2016] ICJ Rep. 235. 130

Inter-American Court of Human Rights

Inter-American Commission of Human Rights

Iran–United States Claims Tribunal

European Court of Justice and Court of Justice of European Union

European Court of Human Rights

Other International Cases

Domestic Cases

Canada

Ecuador

France

India

The Netherlands

Norway

United Kingdom

United States of America

TABLE OF TREATIES, LEGISLATION, AND OTHER DOCUMENTS

Treaties (Other than International Investment Agreements)

United Nations Documents

Other Documents

European Commission, 'Q&A: Commission Launches Comprehensive European International Investment Policy', 7 July 2010, European Commission Memo/10/303, available at: https://ec.europa.eu/commission/presscorner/detail/en/MEMO_10_30. 220

European Parliament, *European Parliament Resolution of 10 March 2021 with Recommendations to the Commission on Corporate Due Diligence and Corporate Accountability*, 2020/2129(INL), available at: www.europarl.europa.eu/doceo/document/TA-9-2021-0073_EN.html. 28, 112

ICSID, 'History of the ICSID Convention: Documents concerning the Origin and the Formulation of the Convention on the Settlement of Investment Disputes between States and Nationals of Other States', 1970, Vol. I, Vol. II-1, and Vol. II-2. 57, 90, 91, 94

Institut de Droit International, 'Eighteenth Commission on Equality of Parties before International Investment Tribunals, Mr Campbell McLachlan, Rapporteur', 31 August 2019, 18 RES EN, available at: www.idi-iil.org/app/uploads/2019/09/18-RES-EN.pdf. 10

International Bar Association, IBA Rules for Investor-State Mediation, Adopted by a Resolution of the IBA Council on 4 October 2012. 209

International Bar Association, IBA Rules on the Taking of Evidence in International Arbitration 2020, Adopted by a Resolution of the IBA Council on 17 December 2020. 129, 132

International Chamber of Commerce, International Organisation of Employers, Business at OECD, and Business Europe, 'Business Response to the Zero Draft Legally Binding Instrument to Regulate, in International Human Rights Law, the Activities of Transnational Corporations and Other Business Enterprises ("Zero Draft Treaty") and the Draft Optional Protocol to the Legally Binding Instrument ("Draft Optional Protocol") Annex', October 2018, available at: https://iccwbo.org/content/uploads/sites/3/2018/10/icc-joint-business-response-zero-draft-2018.pdf. 36

International Commission of Jurists, 'Maastricht Guidelines on Violations of Economic, Social and Cultural Rights', 26 January 1997. 68

International Council on Human Rights and Policy, 'Beyond Voluntarism: Human Rights and the Developing International Legal Obligations of Companies', International Council on Human Rights and Policy, February 2002, available at: https://papers.ssrn.com/sol3/papers.cfm?abstract_id=1551200. 78

International Finance Cooperation and Multilateral Investment Guarantee Agency, Independent Accountability Mechanism (CAO) Policy (2021), 28 July 2021, available at: www.ifc.org/wps/wcm/connect/d3e7f1c4-fd6b-40fd-ae76-fb028916611d/IFC-MIGA-Independent-Accountability-Mechanism-CAO-Policy.pdf?MOD=AJPERES&CVID=nFDGwP2. 40

International Law Association Study Group, 'Draft Report on The Use of Domestic Law Principles for the Development of International Law', 10 August 2016, available at: www.ila-hq.org/images/ILA/DraftReports/DraftReportSG_DomesticLawPrinciples.pdf. 75

International Mediation Institute, 'IMI Competency Criteria for Investor-State Mediators', 19 September 2016, available at: https://imimediation.org/about/who-are-imi/ism-tf/. 216

International Seabed Authority, 'Regulations on Prospecting and Exploration for Polymetallic Sulphides in the Area', 7 May 2010, Doc. No ISBA/16/A/12/Rev.1. 36

International Seabed Authority Council, 'Regulations on Prospecting and Exploration for Cobalt-Rich Ferromanganese Crusts in the Area', 22 October 2012, UN Doc. ISBA/18/A/11, Doc. No ISBA/18/A/11. 36

OECD, 'Annual Report on the OECD Guidelines for Multinational Enterprises', 2008, available at: www.oecd.org/daf/inv/mne/employmentandindustrialrelations-2008annualreportontheoecdguidelinesformultinationalenterprises.htm. 44

OECD, 'Codes of Corporate Conduct: Expanded Review of Their Contents', May 2001, OECD Working Papers on International Investment 2001/06. 155

OECD, 'Due Diligence Guidance for Responsible Business Conduct', 2018, available at: www.oecd.org/investment/due-diligence-guidance-for-responsible-business-conduct.htm. 46

OECD, 'G20 Guiding Principles for Global Investment Policymaking', available at: www.oecd.org/daf/inv/investment-policy/G20-Guiding-Principles-for-Global-Investment-Policymaking.pdf. 220

OECD, 'National Contact Points for Responsible Business Conduct: Providing Access to Remedy: 20 Years and the Road Ahead', 2020, available at: http://mneguidelines.oecd.org/NCPs-for-RBC-providing-access-to-remedy-20-years-and-the-road-ahead.pdf. 40

OECD, 'OECD Guidelines for Multinational Enterprises', 2011, available at: www.oecd.org/corporate/mne/48004323.pdf. 34, 44, 46, 55, 213, 218

OECD, 'Policy Framework for Investment 2015 Edition', available at: www.oecd.org/investment/investment-policy/Policy-Framework-for-Investment-2015-CMIN2015-5.pdf. 44

European Union Laws and Regulations

Directive 2014/95/EU of the European Parliament and of the Council of 22 October 2014 amending Directive 2013/34/EU as regards disclosure of non-financial and diversity information by certain large undertakings and groups Text with EEA relevance, OJ 2014 No. L330, 15 November 2014. 44

Directive 2014/24/EU of the European Parliament and of the Council of 26 February 2014 on public procurement and repealing Directive 2004/18/EC (1), OJ 2014 No. L94, 28 March 2014. 45

Regulation (EC) No 864/2007 of the European Parliament and of the Council of 11 July 2007 on the law applicable to non-contractual obligations (Rome II), OJ 2007 No. L199, 31 July 2007. 27, 28, 110

Regulation (EU) 2017/821 of the European Parliament and of the Council of 17 May 2017 laying down supply chain due diligence obligations for Union importers of tin,

Domestic Laws

France

Germany

India

Indonesia

Japan

Malawi

Mauritius

Peru

United Kingdom

United States of America

ABBREVIATIONS

ATS	Alien Tort Statute
BIT	bilateral investment treaty
CAO	Compliance Advisor Ombudsman
CSR	corporate social responsibility
ECOWAS	Economic Community of West African States
ECtHR	European Court of Human Rights
ESG	environmental, social, and governance
FDI	foreign direct investment
FET	fair and equitable treatment
FTA	free trade agreement
GRI	Global Reporting Initiative
IACtHR	Inter-American Court of Human Rights
IBA	International Bar Association
ICC	International Chamber of Commerce
ICCPR	International Covenant on Civil and Political Rights
ICESCR	International Covenant on Economic, Social and Cultural Rights
ICJ	International Court of Justice
ICS	Investment Court System
ICSID	International Centre for Settlement of Investment Disputes
IEA	International Environmental Agreement
IFC	International Finance Corporation
IIA	international investment agreement
ISDS	investor–state dispute settlement
MIC	Multilateral Investment Court
MIGA	Multilateral Investment Guarantee Agency
NCP	National Contact Point
OECD	Organisation for Economic Co-operation and Development
PCA	Permanent Court of Arbitration
PCIJ	Permanent Court of International Justice
PRI	Principles for Responsible Investment
SASB	Sustainable Accounting Standards Board
SCC	Stockholm Chamber of Commerce

SLO	social licence to operate
TNC	transnational corporation
UNCESCR	United Nations Committee on Economic, Social and Cultural Rights
UNCITRAL	United Nations Commission on International Trade Law
UNCTAD	United Nations Conference on Trade and Development
UNDRIP	United Nations Declaration on the Rights of Indigenous Peoples
UNEP	United Nations Environmental Programme
UNGP	United Nations Guiding Principles on Business and Human Rights

1

Introduction

Corporate Responsibility and the 'One-Sidedness' of Investment Law

1.1 Introduction: Protection of Transnational Corporations in International Law

Transnational corporations (TNCs) are dominant driving forces in the global economy. By the early 1970s, they 'had come to play a central role in the world economy',[1] and currently occupy roughly one-third of world GDP.[2] The number of TNCs has dramatically increased due to the internationalisation of small and medium-sized enterprises' (SMEs) business activities since the late 1970s.[3] Meanwhile, large-scale TNCs have assumed as much economic and political power as many states.[4] TNCs have thus become predominant providers of foreign direct investment (FDI). While sharply contrasting views exist on the relationship between FDI and economic growth in capital-importing countries,[5] it remains a

[1] United Nations Centre on Transnational Corporations, *The New Code Environment* (1990) ST/CTC/SER.A/16, at 3. See also Hedley, 'Transnational Corporations and Their Regulation', 216–218.

[2] Organisation for Economic Co-operation and Development (OECD), 'Multinational Enterprises and Global Value Chains: New Insights on the Trade-Investment Nexus' (2018) available at: https://doi.org/10.1787/18151965 (accessed 15 December 2021).

[3] Jaworek and Kuzel, 'Transnational Corporations in the World Economy', 58.

[4] Dumberry, 'Entreprise, sujet de droit international?', 104–105; Steinitz, *Case for an International Court of Civil Justice*, 3; Karavias, *Corporate Obligations Under International Law*, 2.

[5] There are a large number of empirical studies on this subject that produce inconclusive results. The results differ depending on many factors, including the industrial sectors in which FDI is made, geographical areas, a country's income levels, and institutional quality. Recent studies include: Baiashvili and Gattini, 'Impact of FDI on Economic Growth'; Thi-Huyen Dinh, Vo, Vo and Nguyen, 'Foreign Direct Investment and Economic Growth'.

fact that FDI has become the second largest external source of capital for developing countries, following personal remittances.[6]

In tandem with the dramatic growth of TNCs and FDI, international law has begun to offer strong protection to foreign investors. Traditionally, diplomatic protection was the primary mechanism by which an injury done to a foreign investor could be pursued on the international plane.[7] Only states could institute the claim, and it was understood that in those claims a home state was asserting its own, rather than the affected investor's, rights.[8] The protection offered under this mechanism was considered insufficient for foreign investors for a number of reasons. A claim is admissible only when the investor has exhausted the local remedies in the host state.[9] It is up to the home state of the injured investor to take up its claim,[10] which it may be unwilling to do 'for reasons which have nothing to do with its [the case's] merits'.[11] This could also make it unlikely that disputes of concern to SMEs, who have less political influence than large companies, are pursued by the home state.[12] The investor generally has no control over the proceedings,[13] and the home state may compromise the case for diplomatic or

[6] OECD, 'Non-ODA Flows to Developing Countries: Foreign Direct Investment', OECD, available at: www.oecd.org/dac/financing-sustainable-development/development-finance-standards/beyond-oda-fdi.htm (accessed 15 December 2021).

[7] See Vandevelde, 'Sustainable Liberalism', 379–380. There were also claims commissions that authorised individuals to file claims on the international plane, such as the Iran-United States Claims Commission and the United Nations Compensation Commission. However, such tribunals are distinguished from investment treaty arbitration, in that their authority was granted 'only after the fact, and that authority was limited to disputes arising from a distinct period, series of events, or subject matter'. Van Harten and Loughlin, 'Investment Treaty Arbitration', 129.

[8] *Mavrommatis Palestine Concessions (Greece v. U.K.)* (Objection to the Jurisdiction of the Court) (1924) PCIJ Series A, No. 2, 12.

[9] Crawford, *Brownlie's Principles of Public International Law*, 690; International Law Commission, 'Preliminary Report on Diplomatic Protection by Mohamed Bennouna, Special Rapporteur', 4 February 1998, UN Doc. A/CN. 4/484, para. 40; Douglas, *The International Law of Investment Claims*, 29, 98; *Emilio Agustín Maffezini v. Kingdom of Spain*, ICSID Case No. ARB/97/7, Decision on Jurisdiction, 25 January 2000, para. 22.

[10] *Barcelona Traction, Light and Power Company, Limited (Belgium v. Spain) (New Application: 1962)* (Preliminary Objections) [1970] ICJ Rep. 3, para. 78.

[11] Brierly, *The Law of Nations*, 277. See also Kaufmann-Kohler and Potestà, *Investor-State Dispute Settlement and National Courts*, 18–19.

[12] Puig and Shaffer, 'Imperfect Alternatives', 394; Bronckers, 'Is ISDS Superior to Litigation', 659.

[13] Dolzer and Schreuer, *Principles of International Investment Law*, 212; Brower and Schill, 'Is Arbitration a Threat or a Boon', 480.

other reasons.[14] Significantly, when the home state is awarded compensation from the defendant state, the home state does not have an international obligation to pass it to those who suffered loss.[15]

The advent and rapid development of international investment agreements (IIAs) and investor–state dispute settlement (ISDS) mechanisms (collectively, 'the IIA regime')[16] remedied these issues. Under this regime, states submit to investment promotion and protection obligations under IIAs. When a dispute arises between a foreign investor and the host state, the investor, under the majority of the IIAs,[17] may file a case against the host state before an investment arbitration tribunal and (once operational) investment court(s) (collectively, 'IIA-based dispute settlement mechanisms'), alleging a breach of the IIA and other obligations by the host state. The requirement of exhaustion of local remedies is typically waived in the IIA regime. Investment arbitration liberated investors from international politics and governmental bureaucracy, which had been considered a major flaw in the mechanism of diplomatic protection.[18]

Where the host state is found to be liable under the applicable law to the dispute by the tribunal, in the vast majority of cases compensation is ordered as a remedy. The winning party then benefits from the strong enforcement mechanism for pecuniary damages under the Convention on the Settlement of Investment Disputes between States and Nationals of Other States (ICSID Convention)[19] or the Convention on the

[14] Toope, *Mixed International Arbitration*, 89.

[15] Article 19 of the Draft Articles on Diplomatic Protection provides that the state 'should' '[t]ransfer to the injured person any compensation obtained for the injury from the responsible State subject to any reasonable deductions'. United Nations General Assembly, 'Draft Articles on Diplomatic Protection with Commentaries', 1 May–9 June and 3 July–11 August 2006, 61st Session, Supplement No. 10, 2006, UN Doc. A/61/10. For a criticism of this soft approach, see Gaja, 'Position of Individuals in International Law', 13; Pellet, 'Projet d'articles de la C.D.I.', 1154.

[16] This study adopts the following definition of the concept of a regime: 'implicit or explicit principles, norms, rules and decision-making procedures around which actor expectations converge in a given issue-area'. Krasner, 'Structural Causes and Regime Consequences', 1. See also Haas, 'Why Collaborate?', 358.

[17] An increasing number of IIAs do not provide investment arbitration. UNCTAD, 'Taking Stock of IIA Reform: Recent Development, UNCTAD IIA Issue Note', June 2019, available at: https://unctad.org/system/files/official-document/diaepcbinf2019d5_en.pdf (accessed 15 December 2021).

[18] Franck, 'Legitimacy Crisis in Investment Treaty Arbitration', 1538.

[19] The Convention on the Settlement of Investment Disputes between States and Nationals of Other States, Washington, DC, 18 March 1965, in force 14 October 1966, 575 UNTS 159.

Recognition and Enforcement of Foreign Arbitral Awards (New York Convention).[20] These benefits for investors also generally apply to the investment court system (ICS)[21] which, in this study, refers to both the mechanisms for investment courts in the recent European Union (EU) IIAs and a Multilateral Investment Court (MIC) that is currently discussed in the ISDS reform discussions in the United Nations Commission on International Trade Law (UNCITRAL) Working Group III (UNCITRAL ISDS reform discussions).[22]

The IIA-based dispute settlement mechanism has largely replaced diplomatic protection.[23] Although the increase in the number of IIAs has slowed down recently, reflecting the trend of reviewing IIA policies by many countries,[24] the dispute settlement mechanism remains the primary forum for investor–state disputes.

1.2 Environmental and Human Rights Impact of TNC Activities

TNCs, thus, enjoy protection from the IIA regime. Meanwhile, the activities of TNCs have impacted the countries in which they operate. The impact of TNC activities varies depending on a range of factors, including the political and social status of the host state,[25] types of

[20] The Convention on the Recognition and Enforcement of Foreign Arbitral Awards, New York, signed on 10 June 1958, entered into force 7 June 1959, 330 UNTS 38.

[21] The enforceability of the 'awards' produced by investment courts through the ICSID Convention remains controversial. See e.g. Kaufmann-Kohler and Potestà, 'Can the Mauritius Convention Serve'; Reinisch, 'Will the EU's Proposal Concerning'; Calamita, 'Challenge of Establishing a Multilateral Investment Tribunal'.

[22] The EU aims to merge the existing plurilateral investment courts into an MIC. Dimitropoulos, 'Investor-State Dispute Settlement Reform', 544. For an overview of the ICS, see in particular Bungenberg and Reinisch, *From Bilateral Arbitral Tribunals and Investment Courts*; Kaufmann-Kohler and Potestà, 'The Composition of a Multilateral Investment Court'.

[23] *CMS v. Argentina*, ICSID Case No. ARB/01/8, Decision on Jurisdiction, 17 July 2003, para. 45. For a list of the diplomatic protection cases in the field of international investment law, see Vandevelde, 'Sustainable Liberalism', 379–380. Once an investor has instituted investment arbitration proceedings, the ICSID Convention (Article 27(1)) and many IIAs require the home state of the investor not to exercise diplomatic protection or bring an international claim concerning the same issue against the host state.

[24] UNCTAD, 'The Changing IIA Landscape: New Treaties and Recent Policy Developments', UNCTAD IIA Issue Note, July 2020, at 1, available at: https://investmentpolicy.unctad.org/publications/1230/the-changing-iia-landscape-new-treaties-and-recent-policy-developments (accessed 15 December 2021).

[25] Giuliani and Macchi, 'Multinational Corporations' Economic and Human Rights Impacts', 487–492.

technology traded,[26] and the sector in which FDI is targeted,[27] but none of these factors individually fully explain the impacts they have.[28] In many cases, they bring certain benefits to the host state, including greater tax revenue, creation of employment opportunities and skills development, scientific development, transfer of new technologies, and sound management practices through linkages with local firms.[29] In the environmental context, it is observed that the prosperity brought by FDI enables the pursuit of 'higher societal expectations for environmental quality of life',[30] and technological advancement and good practices brought by TNCs may contribute to better environmental protection in the host state.[31] In the human rights context, it is also argued that TNCs, in particular consumer product firms that are concerned with the cost of negative publicity and consumer protests, can be 'a powerful lever for improving local human rights conditions'.[32]

Conversely, TNCs' activities have also caused serious environmental degradation and violation of human rights in host states,[33] as illustrated by ample publicised cases.[34] The following factors strongly suggest that

[26] Zomorrodi and Zhou, 'Impact of FDI', 4.

[27] Blanton and Blanton, 'Sectoral Analysis of Human Rights and FDI', 469–493.

[28] Giuliani and Macchi, 'Multinational Corporations' Economic and Human Rights Impacts', 500. See also Al Faruque, 'Mapping the Relationship', 551; OECD, *FDI Qualities Policy Toolkit: Policies for Improving the Sustainable Development Impacts of Investment*, OECD, 4 November 2021, at 12–13.

[29] See e.g. Kusek and Silva, 'What Matters to Investors in Developing Countries', 31–33; Kordos and Vojtovic, 'Transnational Corporations', 153.

[30] Wälde and Kolo, 'Environmental Regulation, Investment Protection', 815.

[31] UNCTAD, 'Environment, Series on Issues in International Investment Agreements', United Nations Publications, 2001, UNCTAD/ITE/IIT/23. For the so-called environmental Kuznets curve theory, which posits that economic growth actually and eventually improves host states' environmental conditions, see e.g. Stern, Common and Barbier, 'Economic Growth and Environmental Degradation'; Nahman and Antrobus, 'The Environmental Kuznets Curve'. For the critiques of this theory, see e.g. Andreoni and Levinson, 'Simple Analytics of the Environmental Kuznets Curve'; Dasgupta, Laplante, Wang and Wheeler, 'Confronting the Environmental Kuznets Curve'; Deacon and Norman, 'Does the Environmental Kuznets Curve Describe'.

[32] Spar, 'Foreign Investment and Human Rights', 69. See also Fry, 'International Human Rights Law', 106; De Schutter, 'Transnational Corporations', 403–444.

[33] See e.g. Jägers, *Corporate Human Rights Obligations*, chapter I; Weiler, 'Balancing Human Rights and Investor Protection', 433; Cazala, 'Le respect des droits de l'homme', 334; Márquez, 'Legal Avenues for Holding Multinational Corporations', 59–60.

[34] For these cases, see e.g. Steinitz, *Case for an International Court of Civil Justice*, chapter 2; Kaeb, 'Emerging Issues of Human Rights Responsibility', 327–353. See also UN Human Rights Council, 'Report of the Special Rapporteur on the Rights of Indigenous Peoples', 11 August 2016, UN Doc. A/HRC/33/42, para. 26.

the risk of adverse effects caused by TNCs' activities remains high. Well-financed TNCs often invest in large-scale projects that have grave environmental and human rights implications in areas such as waste management, exploration, and exploitation of natural resources and mining. TNCs have also become increasingly involved in the provision of essential infrastructure systems, which was once in the public domain, such as electricity and gas, water and sewage management.[35]

Amongst various public interest issues concerning TNCs' activities, environmental degradation has attracted particularly significant public attention both within and outside the context of investor–state disputes. The following factors underscore the particular importance of addressing environmental values in the business context. First, environmental degradation caused by TNCs' activities may produce particularly long-term, intergenerational, large-scale, and irreversible damage to the ecosystem of the host state, which may lead to a loss of 'the conditions for a decent, healthy, and secure life'[36] and result in 'breakdown of the economic, social and political framework of civilization'.[37]

Secondly, regardless of whether the emphasis is put on human or non-human aspects of the ecosystem,[38] it is undeniable that environmental degradation such as the contamination of water, air, and land; deforestation; pollution; and the destruction of natural resources often has serious human rights implications. Environmental protection and human rights share overlapping societal values, common interests and objectives and are heavily interlinked.[39] As Judge Weeramantry stated in

[35] Addo, 'Human Rights and Transnational Corporations', 7; Kriebaum, 'Human Rights of the Population of the Host State', 654.

[36] Millennium Ecosystem Assessment Board, 'Living Beyond Our Means: Natural Assets and Human Well-being (Statement from the Board)', Millenium Ecosystem Assessment, March 2005, at 3, available at: www.millenniumassessment.org/en/Reports.html# (accessed 15 December 2021). See also Anton and Shelton, *Environmental Protection and Human Rights*, chapter I.

[37] World Charter for Nature, G.A. Res. 37/7, UN GAOR, 37th session, Supplement No. 51, 1982, UN Doc. A/37/51, para. 3(a), at 17. See also Millennium Ecosystem Assessment, *Ecosystems and Human Well-being*, 26–27; European Commission et al., 'System of Environmental-Economic Accounting 2012: Experimental Ecosystem Accounting', United Nations, 2014, UN Doc. ST/ESA/STAT/Ser.F/112, at 2.

[38] See e.g. Redgwell, 'Life, The Universe and Everything'; Shelton, 'Human Rights, Environmental Rights'; Taylor, 'From Environmental to Ecological Human Rights'.

[39] Anderson, 'Human Rights Approaches to Environmental Protection', 2–4; Shelton, 'Human Rights, Environmental Rights', 105; Anton and Shelton, *Environmental Protection and Human Rights*, 119; Morgera, *Corporate Accountability in International Environmental Law*, 49–50.

his separate opinion in the *Gabcíkovo-Nagymaros Project* case, environmental protection is 'a *sine qua non* for numerous Human Rights'.[40] The link between environmental protection and human rights is recognised in the Stockholm Declaration,[41] various international human rights treaties,[42] works by United Nations bodies,[43] a factsheet of case law recently published by the European Court of Human Rights (ECtHR),[44] and in the context of investment arbitration.[45]

The long-term, intergenerational, large-scale, and irreversible nature of environmental damage and its serious human rights implications underscore the importance of addressing corporate environmental responsibilities. In investment arbitration, host states have alleged, in many cases, investors' misconduct concerning environmental threat or degradation in defence and/or counterclaims.[46]

40 *Gabcíkovo-Nagymaros Project (Hungary v. Slovakia)* (Merits) (Separate Opinion of Judge Weeramantry) [1997] ICJ Rep. 7, 111.

41 United Nations, 'Declaration of the United Nations Conference on the Human Environment', UN Doc. A/Conf.48/14/Rev.1 (1972) (principle 1).

42 For example, Organization of African Unity, African Charter on Human and Peoples' Rights, 27 June 1981, CAB/LEG/67/3 rev. 5, 21 I.L.M. 58 (1982); Council of Europe, European Convention for the Protection of Human Rights and Fundamental Freedoms, as amended by Protocols Nos. 11 and 14, 4 November 1950, ETS 5; Organization of American States, American Convention on Human Rights, 22 November 1969, in force 18 July 1978, 1144 UNTS 123, OASTS 36; Convention on Access to Information, Public Participation in Decision-Making and Access to Justice in Environmental Matters, Aarhus, 28 June 1998, in force 30 October 2001, 2161 UNTS 447.

43 UN General Assembly, 'Human Rights and the Environment', 19 April 2012, UN Doc. A/HRC/RES/19/10. The reports by the Independent Expert and the Special Rapporteur (since March 2015) are available at: www.ohchr.org/EN/Issues/Environment/SREnvironment/Pages/MappingReport.aspx (accessed 15 December 2021). See also UN Human Rights Council, 'Analytical Study on the Relationship between Human Rights and the Environment', 16 December 2011, UN Doc. A/HRC/19/34; Office of the United Nations High Commissioner for Human Rights and United Nations Environment Programme, 'Human Rights and the Environment Rio+20: Joint Report OHCHR and UNEP', 2012, available at: https://wedocs.unep.org/bitstream/handle/20.500.11822/9970/JointReport_OHCHR_HRE.pdf?sequence=1&isAllowed=y (accessed 15 December 2021).

44 European Court of Human Rights, 'Environment and the European Convention on Human Rights', European Court of Human Rights, July 2021, available at: www.echr.coe.int/documents/fs_environment_eng.pdf (accessed 15 December 2021).

45 Kinnear, 'ICSID in the Twenty-First Century', 424.

46 Recent cases include *Burlington Resources Inc. v. Republic of Ecuador*, ICSID Case No. ARB/08/5; *Perenco Ecuador Ltd. v. Republic of Ecuador and Empresa Estatal Petroeleos del Ecuador (Petroecuador)*, ICSID Case No. ARB/08/6; *David R. Aven and Others v. Republic of Costa Rica* (*Aven v. Costa Rica*), ICSID Case No. UNCT/15/3; *Adel A Hamadi Al Tamimi v. Sultanate of Oman* (*Al Tamimi v. Oman*), ICSID Case No. ARB/11/33; *South American Silver Limited v. Plurinational State of Bolivia*, PCA Case

1.3 IIA-Based Dispute Settlement as a Forum to Examine States' Responsibility

However, the current IIA-based dispute settlement mechanism is not structured as a system to hold TNCs accountable for their conduct. This is not surprising, given that the IIA regime has developed as a way to redress the imbalance in the bargaining power between host states and foreign investors. This imbalance arises from the fact that in many cases the investor has sunk substantial capital into the host state, which makes it difficult to withdraw or write off a small loss,[47] and that the state can change 'the playing field on which the investor is operating'.[48] IIAs have thus developed as instruments that restore the parity between them, by typically providing the host states' obligations without reference to investor obligations (Chapter 2, Section 2.3.2) and by granting investors the right to file their claims against states before IIA-based dispute settlement mechanisms, without according the state the corresponding right (Chapter 3, Section 3.1).

In this sense, the IIA-based dispute settlement mechanism is structurally similar to international human rights courts such as the ECtHR[49] and the Inter-American Court of Human Rights (IACtHR).[50] However, investment disputes are distinguished from human rights cases for the following reasons.[51] While human rights treaties, as well as national

No. 2013-15; *Copper Mesa Mining Corporation v. Republic of Ecuador* (*Copper Mesa v. Ecuador*), PCA No. 2012-2.

47 Reisman, 'International Investment Arbitration and ADR', 190–191; Brower and Schill, 'Is Arbitration a Threat or a Boon', 478; Kurtz, 'On Foreign Investor "Privilege"', 315.

48 Bjorklund, 'The Role of Counterclaims', 462. See also Foster, 'Investors, States, and Stakeholders', 370–371.

49 The European Convention on Human Rights grants corporations the access to the court in cases of violation of their human rights (Article 34). See Motte-Baumvol, 'Le comportement de l'investisseur', 199; Kriebaum, 'Is the European Court of Human Rights an Alternative', 220–228 (also noting the limitation that the ECtHR does not offer protection for indirect damages of shareholders).

50 Article 1(2) of the American Convention on Human Rights provides that 'For the purposes of this Convention, "person" means every human being'. In *Titularidad de Derechos de las Personas Juridicas en el Sistema Interamericano de Derechos Humanos*, Advisory Opinion OC-22/16, 26 February 2016, the IACtHR held that only certain legal entities, that is, 'trade unions, federations and confederations' have rights under the Convention and have the right to petition the Inter-American system in defense of their own rights. van der Heijden et al., '3 Inter-American Court of Human Rights', 38.

51 Discussion on investment protection and human rights is often made in relation to the question of the nature of investors' rights under IIAs, i.e. whether they are 'derivative' (or 'delegated') or 'direct' rights. See e.g. Douglas, 'Hybrid Foundations of Investment Treaty

constitutions and human rights acts, provide 'obligations of "integral" character, not dependent on a corresponding performance',[52] obligations concerning investment promotion and protection under IIAs are accepted by contracting states as a *quid pro quo* of attracting foreign investments with the expectation that foreign investments bring benefits to their society.[53] The Inter-American Court of Human Rights, in *Sawhoyamaxa Indigenous Community v. Paraguay*, noted the difference in nature between the American Convention on Human Rights which 'stands in a class of its own and that generates rights for individual human beings' and the relevant IIA (Germany–Paraguay bilateral investment treaty) which 'depend[s] entirely on reciprocity among States'.[54] Likewise, in *Theodoros Adamakopoulos and Others v. Cyprus*, Arbitrator Kohen recognised the difference by stating that investors 'do not have "inherent rights". . . . Investors' rights are exclusively based on the will of the Parties of having a mutual exchange of investor protection'.[55]

Given this reciprocity, the expectation on the part of the host state 'concerning the behaviour of foreign investors within their economies'[56] should be acknowledged as an element of the protection offered by IIAs. This nature of investors' rights, together with the potentially grave implications of investor activities for the public interest of the host state justify the approach seeking to materialise investor responsibility in the IIA-based dispute settlement mechanism.

1.4 The Asymmetry Concern: Call for Reform of the Current IIA Regime

The one-sidedness of the IIA-based dispute settlement mechanism has been subject to increasing criticism.[57] There is a growing body of researches that suggests policy reform of the IIA regime to address this

Arbitration'; Paparinskis, 'Investment Treaty Arbitration'; De Brabandere, *Investment Treaty Arbitration*, chapter 2.

52 Gourgourinis, 'Nature of Investor's Rights under Investment Treaties'.

53 Roberts, 'Clash of Paradigms', 71–72.

54 *Sawhoyamaxa Indigenous Community v. Paraguay*, Judgment of 29 March 2006 (Merits, Reparations and Costs), IACHR Series Case No. 146, para. 140.

55 *Theodoros Adamakopoulos and Others v. Republic of Cyprus*, ICSID Case No. ARB/15/49, Statement of Dissent of Professor Marcelo Kohen, 3 February 2020, para. 59. See also Puma, 'Human Rights and Investment Law', 240–241.

56 Sauvant and Ünüvar, 'Can Host Countries Have Legitimate Expectations?', 1.

57 See e.g. Amado, Kern and Rodriguez, *Arbitrating the Conduct of International Investors*, 10–19; Popova and Poon, 'From Perpetual Respondent to Aspiring Counterclaimant?',

issue.[58] Several countries, in their submissions at the UNCITRAL ISDS reform discussions, raised the issue of imbalance in the current IIA-based arbitration system and called for the incorporation of the principle of the protection of responsible and sustainable investment in the reform process.[59] Outside UNCITRAL, institutions and intergovernmental organisations have expressed support for the equality of parties in international investment tribunals[60] and the incorporation of 'development-oriented investor obligations' in future IIAs.[61]

Overall, the one-sidedness of the current IIA-based dispute settlement mechanism has increasingly been recognised as a major issue in the current backlash against the IIA regime that needs to be addressed. There is growing momentum to incorporate and reflect the concept of 'responsible investment', which is defined for the purposes of this study as an investment approach that explicitly acknowledges and incorporates environmental, social, and governance (ESG) factors,[62] in the regime.[63]

223–224; Schreuer, 'Why Still ICSID?', 1; Mbengue, 'Les obligations des investisseurs étrangers', 297.

58 For example, Arcuri and Montanaro, 'Justice for All?'; Ho and Sattorova (eds.), *Investors' International Law*; Gaillard, 'L'avenir des traités'.

59 For example, UNCITRAL, 'Possible Reform of Investor-State Dispute Settlement (ISDS) Submission from the Government of Morocco, Note by the Secretariat', 4 March 2019, UN Doc. A/CN.9/WG.III/WP.161, para. 4; UNCITRAL, 'Possible Reform of Investor-State Dispute Settlement (ISDS) Submission from the Government of South Africa, Note by the Secretariat', 17 July 2019, UN Doc. A/CN.9/WG.III/WP.176, paras. 34–35; UNCITRAL, 'Possible Reform of Investor-State Dispute Settlement (ISDS) Submission from the Government of Mali', 17 September 2019, UN Doc. A/CN.9/WG.III/WP.181; UNCITRAL, Report of Working Group III (Investor–State Dispute Settlement Reform) on the Work of Its Thirty-Sixth Session (Vienna, 29 October–2 November 2018), 6 November 2018, UN Doc. A/CN.9/964, para. 16.

60 For example, Institut de Droit International, 'Eighteenth Commission on Equality of Parties before International Investment Tribunals, Mr Campbell McLachlan, Rapporteur', 31 August 2019, 18 RES EN, available at: www.idi-iil.org/app/uploads/2019/09/18-RES-EN.pdf (accessed 15 December 2021).

61 For example, UN Economic Commission for Africa, the African Union, the African Development Bank and UNCTAD, 'Next Steps for the African Continental Free Trade Area', September 2019, available at: https://euagenda.eu/upload/publications/aria9_report_en_4sept_fin.pdf (accessed 15 December 2021). AfCFTA has fifty-four signatories (out of fifty-five member states of the African Union) and entered into force on 30 May 2019.

62 Principles for Responsible Investment, 'What Is Responsible Investment?', available at: www.unpri.org/an-introduction-to-responsible-investment/what-is-responsible-investment/4780.article (accessed 15 December 2021); Cambridge Institute for Sustainability Leadership, 'What Is Responsible Investment?', available at: www.cisl.cam.ac.uk/business-action/sustainable-finance/investment-leaders-group/what-is-responsible-investment (accessed 15 December 2021).

63 Nowrot, 'Obligation of Investors', 1160.

It should be noted that, since the beginning of the twenty-first century, the IIA regime has experienced a shift towards greater recognition of the regulatory power of the host states and international fields of law outside the regime (external international norms)[64] in both IIA-making (see Chapter 2, Section 2.3.1) and investment arbitration cases.[65] It has been observed that this shift was necessary 'for its survival', amidst growing concerns and discontent over the impact of the current IIA regime on public interests,[66] which was caused by dramatic increase in the number of investment arbitration cases, including some high-profile cases involving environmental and human rights issues.[67]

Currently, as discussed above, the issue of investor responsibility has also attracted growing criticism and concern. States and scholars increasingly see the protection and promotion of foreign investment not as the end itself, but as a means to realise the objectives of sustainable

[64] In this study, the term 'norms' refers to a broad concept that operates at a high level of generality, covering both legally binding and non-binding laws, rules and principles. See Toope, 'Formality and Informality', 107.

[65] For example, *Desert Line Projects LLC v. Republic of Yemen*, ICSID Case No. ARB/05/17, Award, 6 February 2008, para. 106; *Phoenix Action, Ltd. v. The Czech Republic*, ICSID Case No. ARB/06/5, Award, 15 April 2009, para. 78; *Peter A. Allard v. The Government of Barbados*, PCA Case No. 2012-06, Award, 27 June 2016, para. 244; *Chemtura Corporation v. Government of Canada*, UNCITRAL, Award, 2 August 2010, paras. 137–138; *Philip Morris Brands Sàrl, Philip Morris Products S.A. and Abal Hermanos S.A. v. Oriental Republic of Uruguay*, ICSID Case No. ARB/10/7, Award, 8 July 2016, paras. 301–307 (Arbitrator Gary Born dissented); *Aven* Award, paras. 423, 441–446, 585. See also Viñuales, *Foreign Investment and the Environment*, 9–23 (explaining the signs of changing relationship between environmental law and investment law); Joshi and Gurpur, 'The Silent Spring of Human Rights', 561–563; Baltag and Dautaj, 'Investors, States, and Arbitrators', 13–45; McLachlan, 'The Principle of Systemic Integration'; French, 'Treaty Interpretation and the Incorporation'.

[66] Danic, 'Droit international des investissements', 533. See also Rolland and Trubek, 'Legal Innovation in Investment Law', 381–431; Simma, 'Foreign Investment Arbitration'; McLachlan, 'Investment Treaties and General International Law'; Langford and Behn, 'Managing Backlash'.

[67] For example, *Metalclad Corporation v. United Mexican States*, ICSID Case No. ARB(AF)/97/1; *Chevron Corporation and Texaco Petroleum Corporation v. Republic of Ecuador*, UNCITRAL, PCA Case No. 2009-23; *Philip Morris Brands Sàrl, Philip Morris Products S.A. and Abal Hermanos S.A. v. Oriental Republic of Uruguay*, ICSID Case No. ARB/10/7; *Vattenfall AB, Vattenfall Europe AG, Vattenfall Europe Generation AG v. Federal Republic of Germany*, ICSID Case No. ARB/09/6; *Vattenfall AB and others v. Federal Republic of Germany*, ICSID Case No. ARB/12/12; *Gabriel Resources Ltd. and Gabriel Resources (Jersey) v. Romania*, ICSID Case No. ARB/15/31. According to Langford and Behn, among the 389 finally resolved investment arbitration cases (as of 1 August 2017), 84 are classified as 'cases raising public interest concerns or arousing public interest'. Langford and Behn, 'Managing Backlash', 576–577.

development,[68] for which responsible investment is a necessary element.[69] This suggests that the issue of investor responsibility in the IIA regime must also be addressed for its sustainable operation. However, as discussed in Chapter 2, Section 2.3.2, recognition of investor responsibilities in the text of IIAs remains exceptional. Although there are recent cases where environmental and human rights concerns relating to the investor's conduct have resulted in a loss of protection or discounted compensation,[70] the host state's counterclaims raised in *IIA-based* arbitration cases have rarely succeeded (see Chapter 5, Section 5.1).

1.5 Aims and Scope of This Study

1.5.1 Exploring the Unexhausted Potential of the Current Framework

Against this background, this study aims to explore ways of materialising investors' environmental and human rights responsibilities in the current framework of the IIA-based dispute settlement mechanism. As noted, environmental degradation almost always affects the local people, and therefore has serious human rights implications. Based on this recognition, this study stands on the premise that the act of placing and reflecting environmental responsibility on investors in the IIA regime should be grounded in the need of those who have allegedly incurred damages due to a TNC's conduct (the victims), yet have neither standing nor the right to intervene in the proceedings.

Nevertheless, this study does not offer direct solutions for redressing harm done to the victims of the investor's misconduct. It does not provide a comprehensive analysis of the means to regulate and enforce TNC responsibility in international and domestic fora, nor does it present a reform proposal for the IIA regime to enable victims to directly sue

[68] For example, UNCITRAL, 'Possible Reform of Investor-State Dispute Settlement (ISDS) Submission from the Government of South Africa, Note by the Secretariat', 17 July 2019, UN Doc. A/CN.9/WG.III/WP.176, para. 16; van Aaken and Lehmann, 'Sustainable Development and International Investment Law', 330–333; Muchlinski, 'Towards a Coherent International Investment System', 415–418; Schill and Djanic, 'International Investment Law and Community Interests', 232.

[69] Principles for Responsible Investment, 'Investing with SDG Outcomes: A Five-Part Framework', 2020, available at: www.unpri.org/download?ac=10795 (accessed 15 December 2021).

[70] For example, *Aven v. Costa Rica*; *Copper Mesa v. Ecuador*; *Al Tamimi v. Oman*. For further cases, see Chapter 6.

investors in the IIA-based dispute settlement mechanism (this issue is discussed in Chapter 7, Section 7.5).

Rather, this study is based on the following premises. First, to the extent that the dispute settlement mechanism under existing IIAs continues to be utilised by investors, there is considerable demand to explore ways in which the current mechanism can operate as a system to advance responsible investment. Although several countries have begun to terminate or withdraw from IIAs,[71] the existence of a constituency with an interest in investment arbitration in private legal practices and arbitration institutions may make it difficult for many governments to utilise this option.[72]

Second, establishing perfect symmetry as well as a mechanism in which victims may directly pursue their claims by drastic reform of IIA-based dispute settlement mechanisms remains a distant possibility. Notably, neither the existing IIAs that provide the structure for investment courts nor the current discussions on the MIC[73] have taken concrete steps to address the asymmetry issue,[74] even though this issue is recognised by Working Group III.[75] Nor do they accord legal standing

[71] In their 2017 work, Haftel and Thompson observed that close to 200 IIAs, among nearly 3,000, have been renegotiated since the 1990s. Haftel and Thompson, 'When Do States Renegotiate Investment Agreements?', 26. For the states that began to terminate their IIAs, see Lim, Ho and Paparinskis, *International Investment Law and Arbitration*, 478–479; Schill, 'Reforming Investor-State Dispute Settlement', 653; Gathii, 'Understanding Tanzania's Termination'. Following the *Achmea* judgment (Case C-284/16, *Slovak Republic v. Achmea BV* [2018] ECLI:EU:C:2018:158), the EU member states started terminating their intra-EU BITs (Agreement for the Termination of Bilateral Investment Treaties between the Member States of the European Union, SN/4656/2019/INIT, OJ L 169, 29.5.2020, pp. 1–41). On the other hand, Ecuador re-signed the ICSID Convention on 23 June 2021.

[72] St John, *The Rise of Investor-State Arbitration*, 240–241.

[73] UNCITRAL, 'Initial Draft on Standing Multilateral Mechanism: The Selection and Appointment of ISDS Tribunal Members and Related Matters, Note by the Secretariat', September 2021, available at: https://uncitral.un.org/sites/uncitral.un.org/files/media-documents/uncitral/en/standing_multilateral_mechanism_-_selection_and_appointment_of_isds_tribunal_members_and_related_matters__0.pdf (accessed 15 December 2021). This identifies 'counterclaims' as one of the reform solutions that the Working Group 'may wish to consider incorporating' in the discussions about 'procedural rules reform' (para. 67).

[74] See Perrone, 'Taking Local Expectations Seriously', 125; Porterfield, 'Exhaustion of Local Remedies', 12; Kang, 'Innovative but Insufficient?'.

[75] UNCITRAL, 'Possible Reform of Investor-State Dispute Settlement (ISDS) Multiple Proceedings and Counterclaims, Note by the Secretariat', 22 January 2020, A/CN.9/WG.III/WP.193, paras. 38–41; UN General Assembly, 'Report of Working Group III

to third persons so that they may participate in the proceedings, despite the fact that the EU, in its submission on 24 January 2019 at the UNCITRAL ISDS reform discussions proposing the MIC, stated that 'third parties, for example representatives of communities affected by the dispute, [should] be permitted to participate in investment disputes'.[76] Therefore, South Africa, in her submission at the UNCITRAL ISDS reform discussions, claimed that while the establishment of the MIC 'may bring institutional improvements', such improvements do not solve 'the systemic issues', including the absence of corresponding investor-responsibility obligations.[77] State attitudes towards this issue will vary depending on several factors, including the degree of confidence in their own judiciary and the prospect of enforcing domestic judgments against investors' assets.[78] Fundamentally, whether the creation of an international forum to pursue the responsibility of TNCs should be sought through ISDS reform discussions is a contested question (see Chapter 7, Section 7.5). Finally, any consideration for reforming the current regime towards more symmetry should be based on a careful assessment of what can be done within the current framework of IIA-based dispute settlement mechanisms.

Therefore, it is time to reconsider the potential of the current regime. This study is motivated by the belief that methods to pursue and reflect investor responsibility in the current IIA regime exist but have not been fully utilised. At the same time, an examination of the potential in the current regime will also reveal what remains as its insurmountable limitations, which will inform the directions for reforming the current IIA-based dispute settlement mechanism.

(Investor-State Dispute Settlement Reform) on the Work of Its Thirty-Seventh Session (New York, 1–5 April 2019)', 9 April 2019, UN Doc. A/CN.9/970, paras. 35–36.

[76] UNCITRAL, 'Possible Reform of Investor-State Dispute Settlement (ISDS) Submission from the European Union and Its Member States', 24 January 2019, UN Doc. A/CN.9/WG.III/WP.159/Add.1, para. 29. See also UNCITRAL, 'Possible Reform of Investor-State Dispute Settlement (ISDS) Standing Multilateral Mechanism: Selection and Appointment of ISDS, Note by the Secretariat', para. 67, available at: https://uncitral.un.org/sites/uncitral.un.org/files/media-documents/uncitral/en/standing_multilateral_mechanism_-_selection_and_appointment_of_isds_tribunal_members_and_related_matters__0.pdf.

[77] UNCITRAL, 'Possible Reform of Investor-State Dispute Settlement (ISDS) Submission from the Government of South Africa, Note by the Secretariat', 17 July 2019, UN Doc. A/CN.9/WG.III/WP.176, para. 78. See also Arcuri and Violi, 'Human Rights and Investor-State Dispute Settlement', 590; Choudhury, 'Investor Obligations for Human Rights', 83.

[78] For a general observation of the states' positions, see Roberts, 'Incremental, Systemic and Paradigmatic Reform', 411–423.

1.5.2 *Investors' Environmental and Human Rights Responsibilities*

This study primarily focuses on situations in which investors' conduct results in environmental threat or damage in the host state's territory. However, the inseparable link between environmental protection and human rights protection, as discussed in Section 1.2, makes it necessary to examine human rights that are affected by environmental degradation.[79] It would be impossible to provide an exhaustive list of human rights that are affected by environmental degradation. Rights that are frequently raised and discussed in connection with environmental harm include the right to life; the right to health,[80] which extends to the right to safe and potable water, adequate nutrition, and sanitation;[81] property rights;[82] and the rights of indigenous peoples.[83] Environmental degradation, in itself, may be understood as constituting a violation of 'a right to a healthy environment', which was recently recognised in a UN Human Rights Council resolution.[84] Civil and political rights[85] can be equally

[79] The other dimension of the link between environmental and human rights protection, i.e. human rights as a means to achieve environmental ends, falls outside the scope of this study. For this dimension, see UN General Assembly, 'Report of the Special Rapporteur on the Issue of Human Rights Obligations Relating to the Enjoyment of a Safe, Clean, Healthy, and Sustainable Environment, Submitted to the 37th Session of the Council (26 February–23 March 2018)', 24 January 2018, UN Doc. A/HRC/37/59, para. 4; De Jonge, *Transnational Corporations and International Law*, 189; Anderson, 'Human Rights Approaches to Environmental Protection', 2.

[80] For example, Constitution of the World Health Organization, signed 22 July 1946, entered into force 7 April 1948; Article 12 of the International Covenant on Economic, Social and Cultural Rights (International Covenant on Economic, Social and Cultural Rights, 16 December 1966, in force 3 January 1976, 993 UNTS 3, OASTS 36).

[81] See United Nations, Committee on Economic, Social and Cultural Rights, UN ESCOR, 22nd session, 'The Right to the Highest Attainable Standard of Health', UN Doc. E.C.12/2000/4, ICESR General Comment 14 (2000); Kinney, 'The International Human Right to Health', 1468.

[82] For example, Article 17 of the Universal Declaration of Human Rights (UN General Assembly, Universal Declaration of Human Rights, 10 December 1948, 217 A (III)).

[83] For example, UN General Assembly, 'United Nations Declaration on the Rights of Indigenous Peoples', 2 October 2007, UN Doc. A/RES/61/295 (UNDRIP).

[84] UN Human Rights Council, 'Resolution on the Human Right to a Safe, Clean, Healthy and Sustainable Environment', 8 October 2021, UN Doc. A/HRC/48/L.23/Rev.1. For the unsettled status of the right to a healthy environment in international law, see e.g. Knox and Pejan, 'Introduction', 1–2; Knox, 'Human Rights, Environmental Protection', 519–524; Ong, 'Locating the "Environment"', 192; Merrills, 'Environmental Rights'; Loucaides, 'Environmental Protection'; Boyle, 'Human Rights and the Environment', 626–633; Churchill, 'Environmental Rights in Existing Human Rights Treaties'.

[85] International Covenant on Civil and Political Rights, 16 December 1966, in force 23 March 1976, 999 UNTS 171.

affected, as serious environmental degradation often causes conflict between project operators and the affected community,[86] and is 'frequently accompanied by repression of activists and denial of access to information'.[87] When examining investors' environmental responsibility in investor–state disputes, the pertinent question is whether the right is recognised and potentially actionable under the international and domestic laws relevant to the dispute.[88]

1.5.3 Conceptual Clarifications: TNCs, Investors, and FDI

Some clarifications on the scope of this study need to be made. First, definitional issues concerning TNCs need to be clarified. As Ruggie observes, there is 'no legally precise and universally accepted definition of the multinational enterprise'.[89] TNCs are sometimes distinguished from multinational corporations in that while the former are 'enterprises owned and controlled by entities or persons from one country but operating across national borders', the latter are 'those owned and controlled by entities or persons from more than one country'.[90] Despite the lack of precision in meaning,[91] it is clear that both terms involve an element of control of entities by foreign nationals,[92] and this element is crucial for the purposes of this study, which focuses on FDI, rather than

86 Cotula and Perrone, 'Investors' International Law and Its Asymmetries', 83 (observing that many investment disputes arise from 'tensions between foreign investors and local communities').

87 Anderson, 'Human Rights Approaches to Environmental Protection', 5. Cf. Ratner, 'Corporations and Human Rights', 492–493 (identifying the rights whose protection is 'within the unique province of states' such as the presumption of innocence).

88 For example, In *South American Silver v. Bolivia*, Bolivia asserted that the development of the claimant's mining project was a threat to the indigenous communities' right to a healthy environment, citing Articles 25 and 29(1) of the UNDRIP. *South American Silver Limited v. Bolivia*, Respondent Counter-Memorial, 31 March 2015, paras. 320–324.

89 Ruggie, 'Multinationals as Global Institution', 318; Kerbrat observes that the absence of a precise definition of multinational enterprises is a result of an intentional choice to avoid stalemate of negotiations in search of a definition. Kerbrat, 'Manifestations de la notion d'entreprise multinationale', 62–65.

90 Muchlinski, *Multinational Enterprises and the Law*, 6. See Weissbrodt and Kruger, 'Norms on the Responsibilities of Transnational Corporations', 90; Sauvant, 'Negotiations of the United Nations Code of Conduct', 16.

91 Dubin, 'Entreprise multinationale', 15.

92 Baez, Dearing, Delatour and Dixon, 'Multinational Enterprises and Human Rights', 191; Bantekas, 'Corporate Social Responsibility in International Law', 312; Vagts, 'The Multinational Enterprise', 792; Wildhaber, 'Some Aspects of the Transnational Corporation', 80–81.

foreign portfolio investment (FPI) (see below). Therefore, in this study, it suffices to adopt a brief and general (i.e. regardless of legal forms) definition of TNCs given by the United Nations Conference on Trade and Development (UNCTAD): TNCs are 'incorporated or unincorporated enterprises comprising parent enterprises and their foreign affiliates'.[93]

Secondly, throughout the text, the term 'investors' refers to all kinds of foreign investors including, but not limited to, TNCs. Nevertheless, some parts of this study offer analyses that apply specifically to TNCs when discussing, for example: (a) particular difficulties of regulating TNCs within the domestic legal framework (Chapter 2, Section 2.1.1); (b) jurisprudence of the US Alien Tort Statute (ATS) on the treatment of TNCs (Chapter 2, Section 2.1.3); (c) legal implications of internal regulations, global codes of conduct and non-financial reports published by TNCs (Chapter 2, Section 2.2.3 and Chapter 5, Section 5.4); and (d) admissibility of counterclaims against a parent company (Chapter 4, Section 4.4.2).

Thirdly, foreign investment takes the form of both FDI and FPI. However, given that the principal focus of this study is investor responsibility for environmental and human rights harm caused in the territory of the host state, the analyses focus on FDI, which 'usually involve [s] a control position by the foreign investor',[94] rather than FPI, which is a short-term investment seeking the maximum return for a given level of risk.[95]

1.6 Structure of the Book

This book consists of six chapters. This introductory chapter sets the background of this study. Chapter 2 examines the current situation concerning the codification, recognition, and implementation of corporate responsibility both in and outside the IIA regime, focusing on environmental and human rights responsibilities. The first part of Chapter 2

[93] UNCTAD, 'World Investment Report 2002: Transnational Corporations and Export Competitiveness', 12 June 2003, UNCTAD/WIR/2002, 291.

[94] Goldstein, Razin and Tong, 'Liquidity, Institutional Quality'.

[95] See UNCTAD, 'Comprehensive Study of the Interrelationship between Foreign Direct Investment (FDI) and Foreign Portfolio Investment (FPI): A Staff Paper Prepared by the UNCTAD Secretariat', 23 June 1999, UNCTAD/GDS/DFSB/5; Evans, 'Foreign Portfolio and Direct Investment'; Goldstein and Razin, 'Foreign Direct Investment vs Foreign Portfolio Investment', 3.

discusses certain challenges in regulating and pursuing the responsibility of TNCs' conduct in domestic legal orders. It then proceeds to note a general lack of international mechanisms for holding TNCs responsible for their conduct. This is done through the examination of: (a) the paucity of international (both customary and treaty) law that provides binding obligations of juridical persons as well as a lack of enforcement mechanisms; (b) the recent developments towards establishing binding international human rights obligations of corporations; and (c) the development of 'soft law' instruments to advance the concept of corporate responsibility, including those developed by private initiatives. The second part of this chapter examines the recognition of investor responsibility in the text of IIAs and model IIAs. The examination relies on a dataset of 1,000 randomly selected IIAs and model IIAs (IIA dataset, see Section 1.7). The analysis reveals that, while there is a clear tendency in IIAs that have been signed or adopted since the first decade of the twenty-first century for a greater recognition of sovereign rights to regulate, the number of IIAs that incorporate the concept of investor responsibility is still limited. However, it also reveals that in the recent IIAs that were signed or adopted in the second decade of the twenty-first century, there has been an observable trend to include provisions on investor obligations and corporate social responsibility (CSR).

Chapters 3–5 discuss counterclaims by the host state. Chapter 3 first examines the benefits and obstacles of the use of counterclaims by comparing their use with the option of pursuing investors' legal responsibility through the host state's own courts. It then proceeds to address a question which has been relatively unexamined: Given the existence of the interests of victims as third persons to the dispute, is the host state in the right position to pursue compensation for damages suffered by victims? Based on the assessments of (a) the state's obligation to protect against human rights abuses by private persons and (b) the *parens patriae* doctrine developed in international and certain domestic jurisprudence, it is concluded that the host state has the right to pursue investors' responsibility in its own right and on behalf of victims. Reflecting the premise of this study that any attempt to materialise environmental responsibility of investors in the IIA-based dispute settlement mechanism should consider the interests of victims, it then proceeds to examine whether there are circumstances in which the admissibility of such counterclaims should be denied in light of the victims' due process rights. This question is answered in the positive, and the factors that make the counterclaim inadmissible on this ground are identified.

Chapter 4 clarifies the requirements of jurisdiction and admissibility for filing counterclaims. After arguing that the determinative element for the parties' consent to counterclaims is the scope of investment disputes given in the relevant IIA, it confirms, through the analysis of the IIA dataset, that the content is actually given under the majority of IIAs. It then examines questions of admissibility, focusing on the requirement of a close connection between the principal claim and the counterclaim and the issue of a parent company's liability under a counterclaim that is based on alleged damage caused by its local subsidiary.

Chapter 5 addresses the application of domestic laws, international norms, voluntary standards, and CSR commitments to the determination of merits and remedy of counterclaims, as well as the consequences of such application. It starts by examining certain controversies over the application of domestic law in investment arbitration to conclude that none of these constitutes an obstacle to its application for the determination of counterclaims. It then argues for an approach that respects domestic jurisprudence on legal questions and the use of experts to address the concerns over the lack of expertise of the tribunal in domestic law. The chapter then proceeds to examine counterclaims based on the investor's international responsibility. Based on the examination of recent cases in which such counterclaims did not succeed on their merits,[96] it is concluded that the host state's failure to identify 'secondary rules' that determine the consequences of the investors' asserted breach of international law has been an obstacle to such counterclaims. It then examines the role of domestic law in this situation. Referring to the analysis of the case law of certain jurisdictions, particularly that under the US ATS, it demonstrates that domestic law may determine a remedy for the violation of international environmental and human rights law by corporations, even in the absence of implementing legislation in the host state. Lastly, the chapter examines the potential role of CSR commitments in pursuing counterclaims, which has significant implications in situations where there is a gap between stated voluntary commitments by the investor and local standards. It discusses the possibility that the investor's breach of the former may give rise to legal responsibility in the framework of domestic law, in particular through civil tort law, thereby providing a ground for a counterclaim.

96 *Urbaser S.A. and Consorcio de Aguas Bilbao Biskaia, Bilbao Biskaia Ur Partzuergoa v. Argentine Republic*, ICSID Case No. ARB/07/26, Award, 8 December 2016; *Aven* Award.

Chapter 6 discusses ways of reflecting investors' environmental and human rights responsibility in the assessment of the investor's principal claims. It examines the grounds on which investors' environmental misconduct during the operation of its investment (performance-phase misconduct) leads to a limitation of investment protection in the jurisdictional and merits phases, as well as a reduction in the amount of compensation awarded to the investor. First, it argues that, although it is possible for the host state to contest the admissibility of the investor's claim based on its performance-phase misconduct in limited circumstances, the assessment should be done at the merits phase, where the impact of such conduct is considered together with the host state's conduct and other circumstances of the case. In the merits phase, it discusses the impact of the investor's performance-phase misconduct on an assessment of the protection of the investor's legitimate expectations. The analysis seeks to reflect the interests of victims in this assessment by examining the role that the concept of 'social licence to operate' (SLO), which is based on the perceptions of local stakeholders, may play in this context. Specifically, it argues that the loss of an SLO brought about by the investor's conduct may, in certain circumstances, reduce the grounds for protecting the investor's legitimate expectations. It then discusses ways to address the risk of abusing the SLO in balancing this context. At the remedy phase, this chapter examines contributory fault as a concept that may reflect investor misconduct in a direct and value-based manner, and discusses selected questions on its application.

As noted, the examination of the potential in the current regime also reveals its limitations. On this basis, Chapter 7 concludes this study by examining how the analysis presented in this text may inform discussions on the reform of the IIA regime. To incorporate the interests of victims in the dispute settlement mechanism, it specifically proposes a mechanism for encouraging third parties' participation in investor–state mediation.

1.7 Methodology

The primary research orientation employed in this study is literature-based. Analysis of different ways of reflecting corporate responsibility in the IIA-based dispute settlement mechanism is largely based on a qualitative review of primary sources (e.g. reported cases, arbitral awards, reports and other documents issued by intergovernmental and non-governmental organisations) and scholarly works as secondary sources. It engages in a review of jurisprudence of investment law as well as international hard and soft law instruments concerning corporate environmental and human rights responsibility, which are the main focus of this study. This study also draws on research and jurisprudence in other areas of international law, bearing in mind the possible different applications and interpretations of similar rules and concepts deriving from differences in practices and objectives between these areas of law.[97] Jurisprudence and works on domestic law in certain countries are also employed.

This study also employs a quantitative data analysis based on a set of 1,000 IIAs and model IIAs (collectively, 'IIAs')[98] which were randomly selected from the UNCTAD International Investment Agreements Navigator.[99] The sample of data covers IIAs signed from 1965 to 2019 (see Appendix). The collected IIAs are classified according to the date of signature into the following periods: (a) –1999 (370 IIAs), (b) 2000–2009 (335 IIAs), (c) 2010–2019 (295 IIAs), with the aim of investigating the changes in the practice of IIA-making. The results of the data analysis are primarily employed to: confirm the general trend in the practice towards greater deference to the host states' rights to regulate, since the first decade of the twenty-first century (Chapter 2, Section 2.3); corroborate the remaining paucity of recognition of investor responsibility in IIAs and the emerging trend towards such recognition (Chapter 2, Section 2.3); discuss the jurisdiction of counterclaims under the current IIA regime (Chapter 4, Section 4.3). The IIA dataset includes one IIA and one model IIA that were terminated and replaced respectively (see Appendix); however, this does not materially affect the findings of the data analysis.

1.8 Conclusion

The current IIA regime is asymmetric. Pursuing investors' responsibility in an international dispute settlement forum, which requires *both* concluding a multilateral agreement of universal membership that provides business obligations *and* establishing an international court or tribunal

[97] *MOX Plant Case (Ireland v. the United Kingdom)*, Request for Provisional Measures Order, 3 December 2001, ITLOS Reports 2001, para. 51.

[98] According to UNCTAD World Investment Report 2021, as of the end of 2020, there are 3,360 IIAs, amongst of which at least 2,646 IIAs are in force. UNCTAD, World Investment Report 2021, 21 June 2021, UNCTAD/WIR/2021, at 122.

[99] Available at: https://investmentpolicy.unctad.org/international-investment-agreements.

that enjoys mandatory jurisdiction over investors, is a distant possibility. The story of resistance to efforts to place human rights obligations on business since the 1970s (see Chapter 2, Section 2.2.2.1) alone would suffice to indicate that this will be (to say the least) a difficult and lengthy process. Meanwhile, current IIA-based dispute settlement mechanisms are heavily utilised,[100] despite growing concerns over the 'one-sidedness' of the IIA regime.

The current IIA-based dispute settlement mechanisms have the potential to correct asymmetry by reflecting investor responsibility, which has not been fully exhausted. What is needed is the reassessment of the unexhausted potential to realise these possibilities. At the same time, when investors' environmental responsibility is at issue, the asymmetry is not just an issue of inequity between the host state and the investor, but an issue of loss and injury suffered by the victims. The analysis should therefore seek to reconceptualise the asymmetry issue to reflect the interests and perceptions of the victims.

[100] According to the UNCTAD World Investment Report 2021, '[m]ost of the 68 publicly known ISDS cases initiated in 2020 were brought under IIAs signed before the turn of the century' (xii).

2

Corporate Environmental and Human Rights Obligations in International Law

Outside and Inside the IIA Regime

2.1 Introduction: Limitations in Domestic Legal Systems

Chapter 1 demonstrated that there is growing dissatisfaction over the imbalance between the protection of foreign investors, many of whom are transnational corporations (TNCs), in the international investment agreement (IIA) regime, on the one hand, and the lack of mechanisms to hold them accountable for their conduct, on the other hand. This chapter examines the latter issue in the context of both outside (Section 2.2) and inside (Section 2.3) the IIA regime. This section first demonstrates the limitations and difficulties involved in regulating TNCs' conduct and pursuing their responsibilities in *domestic* legal systems, the fact of which makes the general lack of international mechanisms on TNCs' responsibility a particularly serious concern.

In many cases, control over TNCs through domestic legal orders has proved ineffective,[1] which has resulted in a 'large governance gap'[2] in business and human rights (Section 2.1.1). Moreover, for those who have allegedly incurred damages due to a TNC's conduct (the victims), pursuing TNCs' responsibility in host states (Section 2.1.1), TNCs' home states (countries to which the nationality of parent companies belong) (Section 2.1.2), and through the US Alien Tort Statute (ATS) (Section 2.1.3) face a number of difficulties.

[1] Lowe, 'Corporations as International Actors', 32. See also Hedley, 'Transnational Corporations and Their Regulation', 217.

[2] Ruggie, *Just Business*, 47.

2.1.1 *Regulating TNCs and Pursuing Their Responsibility in the Host State*

TNCs are capable of avoiding rigid domestic laws and regulations by adapting their global corporate structure so as to choose jurisdictions that provide the most favourable conditions to their operations.[3] This in turn has impacted on economically weaker developing countries' policies towards TNCs, causing a shift from regulation to competition to attract foreign direct investment (FDI).[4] Countries that compete for access to investments[5] are less incentivised to introduce new regulations for fear of losing foreign capital that seeks locational advantages for its operation.[6] Moreover, the limitation of administrative resources hampers some countries to effectively implement domestic laws and regulations,[7] leading them to rely on 'business regulating itself'.[8] Furthermore, in resource-dependent countries, implementation of progressive legislation is 'often undermined by a de facto policy thrust that favours' the interests of national elites who partner-up with TNCs to 'advance their own development vision'.[9]

In terms of seeking judicial redress in the host state, there are a variety of practical barriers to effective judicial remedies. Victims often lack resources to access information, legal services and 'opportunities for legal aid' in their home countries[10] to fight complex and long-duration litigation against TNCs.[11]

[3] Ratner, 'Corporations and Human Rights', 462–463; Dubin, 'Entreprise multinationale', 20; Iten, 'Les rattachements de l'entreprise multinationale', 101; Stephens, 'Corporate Liability', 402; Jamali, 'The CSR of MNC Subsidiaries', 183.

[4] Jenkins, 'Globalization, Corporate Social Responsibility and Poverty', 527. See also De Schutter, 'Responsabilité des Etats dans le contrôle des sociétés transnationales', 27–29; Anderson, 'Transnational Corporations and Environmental Damage', 409.

[5] Ruggie, 'Business and Human Rights', 838.

[6] Kamminga and Zia-Zarifi, 'Liability of Multinational Corporations', 2; Rodrik, *Has Globalization Gone Too Far?*, 79–80; Skinner, 'Beyond Kiobel', 169–173.

[7] Hilson, 'Corporate Social Responsibility', 132; Ruggie, *Obstacles to Justice and Redress for Victims*, 4.

[8] Corkin, 'Misappropriating Citizenship', 45.

[9] Cotula, '(Dis)integration in Global Resource Governance', 438.

[10] van Dam, 'Tort Law and Human Rights', 228. This was one of the reasons why the UK Supreme Court upheld the lower courts' decision to allow the claim brought by Zambian villagers against a UK parent company and its Zambian subsidiary seeking compensation for pollution to proceed to a trial of substantive issues on the ground of 'substantial justice'. *Vedanta Resources Plc and Another v. Lungowe and Others* [2019] UKSC 20 (*Vedanta* judgment), para. 89. See also *AAA v. Unilever Plc* [2017] EWHC 371, para. 170.

[11] Skinner, 'Parent Company Accountability', 10–11; Seck and Ogunranti, 'Accountability: Legal Risks and Remedies', 607.

As discussed further in Chapter 3, Section 3.2.1, certain jurisdictions also have the issue of lack of institutional capacity and independence of domestic judicial authorities, which is considered to be 'one of the worst "ailments" of the rule of law'.[12] Moreover, the host state may become partly or jointly responsible for the damage caused by a TNC if it was involved in the TNC's project or failed to fulfil its 'duty to protect' (Chapter 3, Section 3.3.2).[13] In the worst cases, collusion between the government and the TNC, whose interests are often aligned,[14] may cause damage. It is observed that collusion between regimes and investors most likely occurs in the extractive industries, because the investor 'needs to forge relations with the state' who owns natural resources, and once the project is put into operation the government also has an interest in maintaining the asset, with physical protection therefore being provided by the state.[15] In such cases, and where faith in the political independence of the judiciary is unwarranted, pursuing the TNC's responsibility in the host state's courts would be unrealistic.

2.1.2 *Pursuing TNCs' Responsibility in the Home State*

In light of the difficulties in obtaining effective remedies in certain host countries, there have been attempts to pursue legal responsibility of TNCs in their home states, through transterritorial tort claims under a theory of direct liability of parent companies. Examination of foreign direct liability cases in different jurisdictions is beyond the scope of this study.[16] Here it suffices to note that success of transterritorial tort claims primarily depends on the legal systems as well as the presence or absence

[12] UN Human Rights Council, 'Report of the Special Rapporteur on the Independence of Judges and Lawyers: Classifications of the Situations Addressed by the Special Rapporteur 1994–2006, Leandro Despouy', 18 January 2007, UN Doc. A/HRC/4/25, para. 22. See also Rose-Ackerman, 'Judicial Independence and Corruption', 15–24.

[13] Márquez, 'Legal Avenues for Holding Multinational Corporations', 65.

[14] Foster, 'Investors, States, and Stakeholders', 382.

[15] Spar, 'Foreign Investment and Human Rights', 60. For the factors existing in resource-seeking FDI that are conducive to repression of human rights, see Blanton and Blanton, 'Sectoral Analysis of Human Rights and FDI', 483. For different types of direct and indirect corporate complicity and cases, see Wettstein, *Multinational Corporations and Global Justice*, 295–305. See also Zarsky, 'Global Reach', 44–45; McCorquodale, 'Corporate Social Responsibility', 388–389.

[16] On transnational tort cases and home states' duty to regulate TNCs, see e.g. Zerk, *Multinationals and Corporate Social Responsibility*, chapters 4 and 5; Goldhaber, 'Corporate Human Rights Litigation'.

of willingness and initiative to advance such cases in the home state concerned;[17] and that, while there are cases in which jurisdiction over civil liability claims against parent companies was admitted in home states' courts,[18] there are a number of barriers and limitations to trans-territorial tort claims.[19] The principle of limited liability, which is 'recognized in most, if not all, jurisdictions',[20] may shield a parent company from liability for the torts committed by its subsidiaries, although there have been important developments concerning parent companies' due diligence obligation in certain jurisdictions (see Chapter 4, Section 4.4.2).

In addition, the *forum non conveniens* doctrine, which has been actively employed by TNCs as a litigation avoidance technique,[21] may be an obstacle to transnational tort claims in certain jurisdictions.[22] However, the doctrine does not apply to the EU, Switzerland, Norway, and Iceland, where Article 4 of the Brussels I Regulation Recast[23] and Article 2 of the 2007 Lugano Convention[24] respectively preclude the application of this doctrine for cases brought against a company domiciled in a member state and the parties to the Convention.[25] Webb also

[17] Enneking, 'Crossing the Atlantic?', 912–913.

[18] For example, *Okpabi and Others v. Royal Dutch Shell Plc and Another* [2021] UKSC 3; *Vedanta* judgment; Court of Appeal The Hague, 17 December 2015, ECLI:NL:GHDHA:2015:3586 (*Dooh/Shell*); ECLI:NL:GHDHA:2015:3587 (*Shell/Akpan*); ECLI:NL:GHDHA:2015:3588 (*Oguru-Efanga/Shell*). See Ong, 'Regulating Environmental Responsibility', 161–167; Spears, 'Corporate Responsibility', 575–584.

[19] See Skinner, McCorquodale and De Shutter, 'The Third Pillar'; Steinitz, *Case for an International Court of Civil Justice*, 84–98.

[20] UN Human Rights Council, 'Improving Accountability and Access to Remedy for Victims of Business-Related Human Rights Abuse', 10 May 2016, UN Doc. A/HRC/32/19, at 9. See also Kotuby Jr. and Sobota, *General Principles of Law*, 140.

[21] Webb, '*Forum non conveniens*', 87–88.

[22] For example, *In re Union Carbide Corporation Gas Plant Disaster at Bhopal in India*, 634 F. Supp. 842 (SDNY 1986) and *In re Union Carbide Corporation Gas Plant Disaster at Bhopal in India*, 809 F.2nd 195 (2d Cir. 1987); *Aguinda v. Texaco, Inc.*, 142 F. Supp 2d 534 (SDNY 2001); *Aguinda v. Texaco, Inc.*, 303 F.3d 470 (2d Cir. 2002) (the US courts dismissed the case on the ground of this doctrine). See also Janis, 'Doctrine of Forum Non Conveniens'; Salas-Fouksmann, 'Corporate Liability of Energy/Natural Resources Companies', 222.

[23] Regulation (EU) No. 1215/2012 of the European Parliament and of the Council of 12 December 2012 on jurisdiction and the recognition and enforcement of judgments in civil and commercial matters, OJ 2012 No. L351, 20 December 2012, 1–32. Article 4 has a mandatory effect.

[24] Convention on Jurisdiction and the Recognition and Enforcement of Judgments in Civil and Commercial Matters, OJ 2007 No. L339.

[25] Case C-281/02, *Owusu v. Jackson* [2005] ECR I-1383, para. 37. See also Augenstein, 'Torture as Tort?', 596; Aristova, 'Tort Litigation against Transnational Corporations', 10.

observes that *forum non conveniens* has gradually lost its effectiveness as an avoidance technique in the recent practices in the Netherlands, Canada, and the UK.[26]

Moreover, if the home state's court decides to apply the law of the host state,[27] this may well mean a shorter statutory limitation period,[28] significantly lower amount of damages and other limitations in the pursuit of remedy.[29] With this regard, within the EU, Article 4(1) of the Rome II Regulation[30] designates *lex loci damni* (i.e. the law of the host state in which damage occurred) as applicable law for tort liability claims with certain exceptions. However, it should be noted that in cases of extraterritorial environmental damage, Article 7 allows the person seeking compensation to choose *lex loci delicti* as applicable law,[31] and therefore when the parent company's relevant decision is found to have generated the damage (*delit*), the home state law may be selected as applicable law.[32] Further, on 10 March 2021, the European Parliament adopted a resolution with recommendations to the Commission on Corporate Due Diligence and Corporate Accountability with an annexed draft text of the new directive on mandatory human rights and

[26] Webb, '*Forum non conveniens*', 88–91.

[27] Anderson observes that, as to the choice between the *locus actus* and the *locus damni*, 'few countries provide clear statutory guidance, leaving the decision to the court'. Anderson, 'Transnational Corporations and Environmental Damage', 416–417.

[28] For example, the claims brought by the victims of the Rana Plaza incident (as discussed in Section 2.2.2.4) were dismissed by the US Delaware Superior Court on the grounds that: Under Delaware's choice of law rules, the Bangladesh's Limitation Act 1908 was the applicable law to the case; the claims were time-barred by the application of the one-year limitation period under this Act. *Abdur Rahaman et al. v. J.C. Penney Co. Inc., The Children's Place and Wal-Mart Stores Inc.*, CA. No. N15C-07-174 MMJ.

[29] Skinner, McCorquodale and De Shutter, 'The Third Pillar', 41–43; Goldhaber, 'Corporate Human Rights Litigation', 132.

[30] Regulation (EC) No 864/2007 of the European Parliament and of the Council of 11 July 2007 on the law applicable to non-contractual obligations (Rome II), OJ L 199, 31.7.2007, pp. 40–49.

[31] Article 7 provides that:

> The law applicable to a non-contractual obligation arising out of environmental damage or damage sustained by persons or property as a result of such damage shall be the law determined pursuant to Article 4(1), unless the person seeking compensation for damage chooses to base his or her claim on the law of the country in which the event giving rise to the damage occurred.

[32] Parance, 'Influence du droit international', 284.

environmental due diligence.[33] Article 20 of the draft directive provides the member states' obligation to 'ensure that relevant provisions of this Directive are considered overriding mandatory provisions in line with Article 16' of the Rome II Regulation, which enables the application of such mandatory provisions of the forum state in spite of the otherwise applicable tort law.

Likewise, some recent IIAs provide that when an investor's conduct results in certain significant damage in the host state, such conduct is subject to civil actions for liability in the investor's home state, or the rules concerning jurisdiction of the home state.[34] Article 17.2 of the 2012 Southern African Development Community (SADC) Model Investment Treaty further provides the duty of the home state to 'ensure that their legal systems and rules allow for, or do not prevent or unduly restrict, the bringing of' such civil actions on the merits. Even without such an explicit requirement, it is observed that these provisions imply that the contracting parties to these IIAs 'will amend their domestic laws accordingly'.[35]

2.1.3 Pursuing TNCs' Responsibility in the United States under the Alien Tort Statute (ATS)

The US ATS provides that '[t]he district courts shall have original jurisdiction of any civil action by an alien for a tort only, committed in violation of the law of nations or a treaty of the United States'.[36] Since *Filártiga v. Peña-Irala*,[37] the ATS has been employed by foreign plaintiffs to sue non-US (foreign) nationals and TNCs for alleged international law

[33] European Parliament, European Parliament Resolution of 10 March 2021 with Recommendations to the Commission on Corporate Due Diligence and Corporate Accountability, 2020/2129(INL), available at: www.europarl.europa.eu/doceo/document/TA-9-2021-0073_EN.html (accessed 15 December 2021).

[34] For example, Article 20 of the 2016 Morocco-Nigeria BIT; Article 17.1 of the 2012 Southern African Development Community (SADC) Model Investment Treaty; Article 18(6) of the Supplementary Act A/SA.3/12/08 Adopting Community Rules on Investment and the Modalities for their Implementation with ECOWAS (2008) (ECOWAS SIA); Article 7(4) of the 2019 Netherlands Model BIT.

[35] Seif, 'Business and Human Rights', 1769.

[36] 28 US Code § 1350.

[37] *Filártiga v. Peña-Irala*, 630 F.2d 876, 885–886 (2d Cir. 1980). This case is discussed in Chapter 5, Section 5.3.3.2.

violations committed in other nations.[38] Cases under the ATS include claims based on environmental damage.[39]

However, the US Supreme Court has limited the scope of international law that can serve as the basis for jurisdiction under the ATS (*Sosa v. Alvarez*),[40] as well as the territorial scope of permissible claims (*Kiobel v. Royal Dutch Petroleum*).[41] In *Jesner v. Arab Bank*, the Supreme Court put significant limitations on the scope of the ATS as a cause of action, by concluding (by a majority of 5–4) that '*foreign* corporations may not be defendants in suits brought under the ATS'.[42] Whether future suits against US corporations remain intact by this conclusion remains unanswered.[43] In *Doe v. Nestle*, former Malian child slaves who were forced to harvest cocoa in the Ivory Coast sued companies in the cocoa industry, including US corporations, alleging that

38 For example, *Kadic v. Karadzic*, 70 F.3d 232 (2d Cir. 1995); *Doe v. Unocal*, 395 F.3d 932 (9th Cir. 2002).

39 For example, *Amlon Metals, Inc. v. FMC Corp*, 775 F. Supp. 668 (SDNY 1991); *Beanal v. Freeport-McMoran, Inc.* (Beanal 1), 969 F. Supp. 362 (E.D. La. 1997), affd, 197 F.3d. 161 (5th Cir. 1999); *Aguinda v. Texaco, Inc.* (Aguinda I), 1994 WL 142006 (SDNY) (11 April 1994); *Flores v. S. Peru Copper, Corp.* (Flores 11) 414 F.3d 233 (2d Cir. 2003); *Sarei v. Rio Tinto*, Plc, 671 F.3d 736 (9th Cir. 2011). In all of such cases the claims based on the ATS were dismissed. See e.g. Jaeger, 'Environmental Claims'; Abadie, 'A New Story of David and Goliath'; Mowery, 'Earth Rights, Human Rights'; McBarnet and Schmidt, 'Corporate Accountability through Creative Enforcement'.

40 *Sosa v. Alvarez-Machain et al.*, 542 US 692 (2004). The Supreme Court, while assuming that 'the First Congress understood that the district courts would recognize private causes of action for certain torts in violation of the law of nations', limited the scope of international law norms to those 'accepted by the civilized world and defined with a specificity comparable to the features of the 18th-century paradigms we have recognised', that is, violation of safe conducts, infringement of the rights of ambassadors, and piracy (at 724–725).

41 *Kiobel v. Royal Dutch Petroleum*, 569 US 108 (2013) (*Kiobel*). In this case, the Supreme Court applied the presumption against extraterritoriality to the case and held that plaintiffs' 'case seeking relief for violations of the law of nations occurring outside the United States is barred' (at 14). See Davis and Whytock, 'State Remedies for Human Rights'; Alford, 'Human Rights after *Kiobel*'.

42 *Jesner v. Arab Bank*, 584 US ___ (2018), 27 (emphasis added). See Sanger, 'Transnational Corporate Responsibility in Domestic Courts'; Roorda and Ku, 'Applying International Law to Corporations', 217–218.

43 See Dodge, '*Jesner v. Arab Bank*' (supporting the position that suits against US corporations remain intact). Indeed, Bella and Clark argue that in light of the historical context of its adoption, the ATS is 'best understood as a self-executing, fail-safe measure that enabled the United States to avoid responsibility for law of nations violations by permitting aliens to sue *US citizens* for intentional torts in federal court' (emphasis added). Bellia and Clark, 'The Alien Tort Statute', 454.

they aided and abetted child slavery by providing assistance to Ivorian farmers.[44] The Ninth Circuit (the majority) concluded that the Supreme Court opinion in *Jesner* 'did not eliminate all corporate liability under the ATS', and the ATS still applies to domestic corporations.[45] It also held that *Kiobel*'s territorial limitation did not apply to the present case, because 'aiding and abetting comes within the ATS's focus', and major operational decisions including 'financing arrangements', originated in the United States.[46]

The Supreme Court (by a majority of 8–1, delivered by Justice Thomas) reversed the Ninth Circuit, on the grounds that: (a) courts should not create an aiding-and-abetting cause of action under the ATS; (b) while the ATS does not apply extraterritorially, 'allegations of general corporate activity – like decision-making – cannot establish domestic application of the ATS',[47] and (c) federal courts cannot create a cause of action under the ATS.[48] Nevertheless, Justice Thomas's opinion was silent on the question of whether domestic corporations can be sued under ATS. Several Justices explicitly stated, in their concurring and dissenting opinions, that corporations are not immune from suit under the ATS.[49]

In conclusion, although there have been developments towards greater recognition of a parent company's direct liability in certain home countries of TNCs, there remain many limitations in domestic legal systems in regulating the conduct of TNCs and in pursuing their responsibility. This underscores the role of international laws and standards with regard to these ends.

2.2 International Obligations and Responsibilities of TNCs Outside the IIA Regime

2.2.1 TNCs' Capacity as Bearers of International Obligations

A preliminary question is whether or not TNCs as juridical persons can bear obligations in international law. The legal status of corporations in

[44] *Doe v. Nestle*, S.A. 906 F.3d 1120 (9th Cir. 2018), 1120, 1122; *Doe v. Nestle*, 929 F.3d 623 (9th Cir. 2019) (Amended 5 July 2019).
[45] Ibid., at 1124.
[46] Ibid., at 1125–1126.
[47] *Nestlé USA Inc. v. John Doe*, No. 19–416, 17 June 2021 (*Nestlé v. Doe*), 2 (citing *Kiobel*). Chief Justice Roberts, Justices Breyer, Sotomayor, Kagan, Gorsuch, Kavanaugh, and Barrett joined (Justice Alito dissented).
[48] This issue is further discussed in Chapter 5, Section 5.3.3.2.
[49] *Nestlé v. Doe*, Concurring opinion of Justice Gorsuch, joined by Justice Alito; concurring opinion of Justice Sotomayor, joined by Justices Breyer and Kagan; dissenting opinion of Justice Alito.

international law, in particular whether they have become 'subjects' of international law, remains unsettled.[50] However, TNCs' *capacity of bearing international obligations* is distinguished from their *subjectivity*, with the latter also including the capacity for international law-making.[51] For the purposes of this study, it suffices to demonstrate the capacity of TNCs as bearers of international obligations, and the following considerations indeed confirm its existence.

In *Jurisdiction of the Courts of Danzig*[52] and *Reparation for Injuries Suffered in the Service of the United Nations*[53] cases, the Permanent Court of International Justice and International Court of Justice recognised that states were not the sole holders of international rights and duties.[54] Sir Waldock, in his third report on the law of treaties, having identified 'treaties which have provided special international tribunals or procedures for applying to individuals rights or obligations arising under treaties', acknowledged that: '[T]he treaty operates upon the individual not only through his national system of law but also through the international procedures prescribed in the treaty, and in that sense there seems to be an application of the treaty directly to him.'[55] While this statement concerns individuals, states do have the competence to conclude, and have concluded, international agreements that provide rights and obligations of corporations.[56] As discussed in Chapter 1, Section 1.3, juridical persons have indeed been conferred rights and the 'capacity to

[50] The 'subject/object dichotomy' has been increasingly challenged, and a functional approach to recognise individuals', international organisations' and TNCs' status as 'participants' and limited (or a degree of) international personality has been gradually accepted. See in particular Higgins, *Problems and Process*, 49–50 (on individuals); Klabbers, *Introduction to International Institutional Law*, 51–52 (on international organisations); Pentikäinen, 'Changing International "Subjectivity" and Rights', 153 (on TNCs).

[51] Karavias, *Corporate Obligations under International Law*, 7; Clapham, *Human Rights Obligations of Non-State Actors*, 28.

[52] *Jurisdiction of the Courts of Danzig* (Advisory Opinion) [1928] PCIJ Rep. Series B, No. 15 (*Danzig* (Advisory Opinion)).

[53] *Reparation for Injuries Suffered in the Service of the United Nations* (Advisory Opinion) [1949] ICJ Rep 174 (*Reparation* (Advisory Opinion)).

[54] *Danzig* (Advisory Opinion), 17–18; *Reparation* (Advisory Opinion), 178–179.

[55] International Law Commission, 'Third Report on the Law of Treaties by Sir Humphrey Waldock, Special Rapporteur', UN Doc. A/CN.4/167 and Add.1-3 (1964), YbILC, vol. II, 5, at 46.

[56] Dumberry, 'Entreprise, sujet de droit international?', 116; UN Commission on Human Rights, 'Interim Report of the Special Representative of the Secretary-General on the Issue of Human Rights and Transnational Corporations and Other Business Enterprises, John Ruggie', 22 February 2006, UN Doc. E/CN.4/2006/97 (Ruggie 2006 Report), para. 65.

enforce them'[57] by bringing claims to an international dispute settlement forum under a number of IIAs as well as under the European Convention on Human Rights. Conversely, there are a small number of international agreements as well as IIAs that provide the obligations of juridical persons (Sections 2.2.2 and 2.3.2).

In light of these developments in international law, it is safely concluded that juridical persons including TNCs bear international obligations to the extent that such obligations are conferred by states.[58] The following sections examine the two ways in which international obligations can be conferred on TNCs: through international agreements (Section 2.2.2) and customary international law (Section 2.2.3).

2.2.2 *International Agreements on Responsibilities of TNCs*

2.2.2.1 Attempts to Develop Binding Norms and TNCs' Human Rights Responsibility

There have been multiple attempts to develop legally binding international norms concerning TNCs' activities, yet none of them has borne fruit to date. The first such attempt was made following the two UN General Assembly resolutions that embody the Declaration and the Programme of Action on the Establishment of a New International Economic Order, adopted during its sixth special session in 1974.[59] In the same year, the Charter of Economic Rights and Duties of States was adopted by UN General Assembly resolution 3281 (XXIX).[60] In this context, the United Nations Commission on Transnational Corporations and United Nations Centre on Transnational Corporations (UNCTC) were established.[61] The Commission on Transnational Corporations undertook the formation of the United Nations (UN) Code of Conduct by intergovernmental Working

[57] Kinley and Tadaki, 'From Talk to Walk', 946.

[58] See in particular Nowak and Januszewski, 'Non-State Actors and Human Rights', 113–161; Lopez, 'Human Rights Legal Liability'; Alvarez, 'Are Corporations "Subjects" of International Law?'; Clapham, *Human Rights Obligations of Non-State Actors*, chapter 2.

[59] UN General Assembly, 'Declaration on the Establishment of a New International Economic Order', 1 May 1974, UN Doc. A/RES/S-6/3201, and 'Programme of Action on the Establishment of a New International Economic Order', 1 May 1974, UN Doc. A/RES/S-6/3202.

[60] UN General Assembly, 'Charter of Economic Rights and Duties of States', 12 December 1974, UN Doc. A/RES/29/3281. Chapter II, Article 2(2)(b) explicitly recognises the state's right to 'regulate and supervise the activities of transnational corporations'.

[61] Sauvant, 'Negotiations of the United Nations Code of Conduct', 16.

Group. The product of its work, a draft Code of Conduct on Transnational Corporations,[62] however, was never adopted,[63] and the UNCTC was absorbed into UNCTAD by 1994.[64] The failure of the draft Code can be attributed to various reasons, including a lack of agreement regarding the legal effect (i.e. binding or not) of the Code[65] and the regulatory, economic, and political circumstances in the 1980s and the early 1990s, such as the emergence of new market economies after the dissolution of the Soviet Union,[66] as well as the global policy shift towards greater openness and encouragement of FDI caused by the debt crisis.[67]

The second instrument concerning TNC's international obligations prepared under the UN initiative was draft norms on the responsibilities of transnational corporations and other business enterprises with regard to human rights (draft norms).[68] The draft norms employed wording that imposes obligations in relation to human rights on corporations, and were 'meant to become the basis for a later binding instrument or to become a restatement of customary international law in the making'.[69] Yet the draft norms met severe opposition from business interests,[70] and they were eventually rejected by the UN Commission on Human Rights (now the Human Rights Council) in 2004.

Then, in 2005, based on the Commission on Human Rights' resolution,[71] Professor John Ruggie was appointed as the Special Representative of the

[62] UN Commission on Transnational Corporations, 'Draft United Nations Code of Conduct on Transnational Corporations', 28 May 1983, UN Doc. E/RES/1987/57.

[63] UN General Assembly, Report by the President of the Forty-Sixth Session of the General Assembly, 15 September 1992, UN Doc. A/47/446, at 2.

[64] See MacLeod, 'United Nations, Human Rights and Transnational Corporations', 68: 'this effectively ended any possibility of using the Code as a mechanism to control human rights abuses by TNCs'.

[65] Hedley, 'Transnational Corporations and Their Regulation', 221; Moran, 'United Nations and Transnational Corporations', 96.

[66] Sornarajah, *Resistance and Change in the International Law*, 18.

[67] Sauvant, 'Negotiations of the United Nations Code of Conduct', 56–62. See also Baez, Dearing, Delatour and Dixon, 'Multinational Enterprises and Human Rights', 213; Tully, *International Documents on Corporate Responsibility*, 5–6.

[68] UN Commission on Human Rights, 'Draft Norms on the Responsibilities of Transnational Corporations and Other Business Enterprises with Regard to Human Rights', 30 May 2003, UN Doc. E/CN.4/Sub.2/2003/12/Rev.2. For the development of draft norms, see Weissbrodt and Kruger, 'Norms on the Responsibilities of Transnational Corporations', 903–905.

[69] Ramasastry, 'Corporate Social Responsibility', 244. See also Backer, 'On the Evolution', 46.

[70] Decaux, 'Présentation', 12–13.

[71] Office of the High Commissioner for Human Rights, Human Rights and Transnational Corporations and Other Business Enterprises, Human Rights Resolution 2005/69, 20 April 2005, UN Doc. E/CN.4/RES/2005/69.

Secretary-General on human rights and transnational corporations and other business enterprises. He presented in his 2008 report a 'protect, respect and remedy' framework that consists of the following principles: the state duty to protect against human rights abuses by third parties, including business; the corporate responsibility to respect human rights; and the need for more effective access to remedies.[72] Based on this approach which distinguishes states' *duties* and corporations' *responsibilities*,[73] the UN Guiding Principles on Business and Human Rights (UNGPs)[74] were developed and unanimously endorsed by the Human Rights Council in June 2011.[75] The UNGPs were quickly endorsed in the update of the OECD Guidelines for Multinational Enterprises in 2011,[76] the International Finance Corporation's (IFC) 2012 Performance Standards (IFC Performance Standards) and Environmental and Social Sustainability Policy (IFC Sustainability Policy),[77] and the revision of the International Labor Organization

[72] UN Human Rights Council, 'Protect, Respect and Remedy: A Framework for Business and Human Rights: Report of the Special Representative of the Secretary-General on the Issue of Human Rights and Transnational Corporations and Other Business Enterprises by John Ruggie, Special Rapporteur', 7 April 2008, UN Doc. A/HRC/8/5.

[73] UN Human Rights Council, 'Report of the Special Representative of the Secretary-General on the Issue of Human Rights and Transnational Corporations and Other Business Enterprises: Business and Human Rights: Further Steps toward the Operationalisation of the "Protect, Respect and Remedy" Framework' (by John Ruggie), 9 April 2010, UN Doc. A/HRC/14/27, para. 55: 'The term "responsibility" to respect, rather than "duty", is meant to indicate that respecting rights is not an obligation that current international human rights law generally imposes directly on companies'.

[74] UN Guiding Principles on Business and Human Rights (endorsed by the Human Rights Council in June 2011), available at: www.ohchr.org/Documents/Publications/GuidingPrinciplesBusinessHR_EN.pdf (accessed 15 December 2021).

[75] For critical assessments of the Guiding Principles, see e.g. Simons, 'Value-Added of a Treaty'; Augenstein and Kinley, 'Beyond the 100 Acre Wood'; Sullivan and Hachez, 'Human Rights Norms for Business'. For positive accounts on the Guiding Principles, see Sherman III, 'Beyond CSR'; Zerk, 'Corporate Social Responsibility and International Law'.

[76] OECD, OECD Guidelines for Multinational Enterprises (2011) OECD Publishing, at 73, available at: www.oecd.org/corporate/mne/48004323.pdf (accessed 15 December 2021) Chapter IV (Human Rights).

[77] Para. 1 of Performance Standards (available at: www.ifc.org/wps/wcm/connect/24e6bfc3-5de3-444d-be9b-226188c95454/PS_English_2012_Full-Document.pdf?MOD=AJPERES&CVID=jkV-X6h (accessed 15 December 2021)) and para. 12 of the 2012 version of Environmental and Social Sustainability Policy (available at: www.ifc.org/wps/wcm/connect/topics_ext_content/ifc_external_corporate_site/sustainability-at-ifc/policies-standards/sustainability-policy (accessed 15 December 2021)).

(ILO) Tripartite Declaration of Principles concerning Multinational Enterprises and Social Policy in 2017.[78]

The ongoing project towards establishing international obligations of business is the work to draft a legally binding instrument to regulate the activities of transnational corporations and other business enterprises. This process was initiated in 2014 by the Human Rights Council resolution for the establishment of an open-ended intergovernmental working group on transnational corporations and other business enterprises with respect to human rights (Working Group).[79] The Working Group published the 'zero draft' in July 2018 and issued revised drafts in July 2019, August 2020 and August 2021.[80] It should be noted that the draft adopts an 'indirect' approach by providing states', rather than private persons', obligations concerning human rights protection, including the obligation to regulate business activities, to provide access to remedy and legal liability.[81] However, it provides that a legal or natural person conducting business activities, once found responsible for reparation arising from human rights abuse, 'shall provide reparation'.[82] Although several states, including certain major economies, have

[78] International Labour Office, Tripartite Declaration of Principles concerning Multinational Enterprises and Social Policy, International Labour Office, 5th ed., March 2017, available at: www.ilo.org/empent/areas/mne-declaration/lang–en/index.htm (accessed 15 December 2021). Partiti identifies certain discrepancies in the interpretation of the human rights due diligence under the UNGP adopted by these standards, and argues for the need of centralised interpretive guidance. Partiti, 'Polycentricity and Polyphony in International Law', 147–153.

[79] UN Human Rights Council, 'Elaboration of an International Legally Binding Instrument on Transnational Corporations and Other Business Enterprises with Respect to Human Rights', 14 July 2014, UN Doc. A/HRC Res. 26/9. The draft resolution was jointly presented by Ecuador and South Africa, and co-sponsored by Algeria, Bolivia, Cuba, El Salvador, Nicaragua, Senegal and Venezuela. Russia, India, China, and South Africa supported Resolution 26/9, fourteen members of the Human Rights Council including the United States, Japan, South Korea, and the member states of the European Union opposed, and Argentina, Botswana, Brazil, Chile, Costa Rica, Gabon, Kuwait, Maldives, Mexico, Peru, Saudi Arabia, Sierra Leone, United Arab Emirates abstained. For a summary of controversies among states on the resolution, see Narine, 'Disclosing Disclosure's Defects', 104–108.

[80] The text of the third revised draft is available at: www.ohchr.org/EN/HRBodies/HRC/WGTransCorp/Session7/Pages/Session7.aspx (accessed 15 December 2021).

[81] Deva, 'International Investment Agreements and Human Rights', 1749–1756; Svoboda, 'Investors' Responsibilities beyond Investment Treaties', 467.

[82] Article 8.4 of the third revised draft.

supported this project,[83] as of the date of writing, it still lacks support from the international business community.[84]

2.2.2.2 TNCs' Obligations in International Environmental Law

In the field of environmental law, international agreements that prescribe obligations of juridical persons do exist, but they remain rare.[85] Certainly, there are a sizable number of international environmental agreements (IEAs) concerning the 'civil liability' of juridical persons, under which juridical persons such as an operator of a nuclear installation 'shall be liable' for certain environmental damage.[86] However, these treaties do not provide private entities' obligations on specific behaviour concerning environmental protection, but provide contracting states' obligations to regulate the private entities' activities or to establish the necessary mechanisms to materialise the responsibility of

[83] See footnote 79. See also Bilchitz, 'Introduction: Putting Flesh on the Bone', 20.

[84] See e.g. International Chamber of Commerce, International Organisation of Employers, Business at OECD, and Business Europe, 'Business Response to the Zero Draft Legally Binding Instrument to Regulate, in International Human Rights Law, the Activities of Transnational Corporations and Other Business Enterprises ("Zero Draft Treaty") and the Draft Optional Protocol to the Legally Binding Instrument ("Draft Optional Protocol") Annex', October 2018, available at: https://iccwbo.org/content/uploads/sites/3/2018/10/icc-joint-business-response-zero-draft-2018.pdf (accessed 15 December 2021).

[85] Chetail, 'Legal Personality of Multinational Corporations', 115. Exceptions include Article 137(1) and (3) of the United Nations Convention on the Law of the Sea (United Nations Convention on the Law of the Sea, Jamaica, 10 December 1982, in force 16 November 1994, 1833 UNTS 397 (UNCLOS)) and International Seabed Authority's exploration regulations (e.g. International Seabed Authority, 'Regulations on Prospecting and Exploration for Polymetallic Sulphides in the Area', 7 May 2010, Doc. No ISBA/16/A/12/Rev.1, Regulations 3, 4, 5, 6, 8; International Seabed Authority Council, 'Regulations on Prospecting and Exploration for Cobalt-Rich Ferromanganese Crusts in the Area', 22 October 2012, Doc. ISBA/18/A/11, Regulations 3, 4, 5, 7, 8. The Council of the International Seabed Authority may adopt binding rules, regulations, and procedures under Article 162(o)(ii) of UNCLOS).

[86] For example, Paris Convention on Third Party Liability in the Field of Nuclear Energy, as amended by the Additional Protocol of 28 January 1964 and by the Protocol of 16 November 1982, 29 July 1960, 956 UNTS 251; International Convention on Civil Liability for Oil Pollution Damage, adopted on 29 November 1969, entered into force 19 June 1975, 26 UST 765, 973 UNTS 3 (replaced by 1992 Protocol, entered into force 30 May 1996. The 2000 amendment entered into force on 1 November 2003); Vienna Convention on Civil Liability for Nuclear Damage, as amended by a 1997 Protocol, IAEA Doc. INFCIRC/566 (1998), 21 May 1963, 1063 UNTS 265. See also Directive 2004/35/CE of the European Parliament and of the Council of 21 April 2004, OJ L 143, 30 April 2004, pp. 56–75.

corporations.[87] Moreover, these IEAs on civil liability are limited to specific types of activities such as the peaceful use of nuclear energy, transport of oil, and transport of hazardous substances;[88] therefore, they only offer 'a piecemeal solution to environmental harm caused by the private sector'.[89]

An effort to establish a Global Pact for the Environment,[90] drafted by the Environment Commission of the *Club des Juristes*, was launched in 2017. The Global Pact was drafted as a legally binding instrument that incorporates the environmental principles embodied in existing international soft law instruments. Article 2 of the draft Pact provides the 'duty to take care of the environment' of 'every person, natural or legal, public or private'. It does not provide an enforcement mechanism applicable to private entities, but provides the parties' obligation to ensure access to environmental justice (Article 11).[91] The UN General Assembly Resolution of 10 May 2018[92] established an *ad hoc* open-ended working group tasked with considering the issues identified in the Secretary-General report[93] and discussing options to address them, including the conclusion of an international instrument.[94] To date, this process is ongoing.

[87] For example, Article IX(2) of the International Convention on Civil Liability for Oil Pollution Damage; Article 4 of the Basel Convention on the Control of Transboundary Movements of Hazardous Wastes and Their Disposal, Basel, 22 March 1989, in force 5 May 1992, 1673 UNTS 126; Article V B of the Vienna Convention on Civil Liability for Nuclear Damage.

[88] The Convention on Civil Liability for Damage Resulting from Activities Dangerous to the Environment provides the cross-sectoral environmental liability regime applicable to private persons, yet it has not obtained the ratifications necessary for its entry into force. Convention on Civil Liability for Damage Resulting from Activities Dangerous to the Environment, Lugano, 21 June 1993, 32 ILM 1228. See Sands, Peel, Fabra and MacKenzie, *Principles of International Environmental Law*, 149.

[89] Morgera, *Corporate Accountability in International Environmental Law*, 41. See also Sachs, 'Beyond the Liability Wall', 839: 'not a single major civil liability treaty outside the contexts of oil spills and nuclear accidents has entered into force'.

[90] Global Pact for the Environment, Draft Global Pact for the Environment, available at: https://globalpactenvironment.org/uploads/EN.pdf (accessed 15 December 2021).

[91] See Pereira de Andrade and Monebhurrun, 'Mapping Investor's Environmental Commitments and Obligations', 270.

[92] UN General Assembly, 'Towards a Global Pact for the Environment, Resolution/Adopted by the General Assembly', 10 May 2018, UN Doc. A/RES/72/277.

[93] UN General Assembly, 'Gaps in International Environmental Law and Environment-Related Instruments: Towards a Global Pact for the Environment', Report of the Secretary-General, 30 November 2018, UN Doc. A/73/419.

[94] IUCN World Commission on Environmental Law, 'Global Pact for the Environment', IUCN, available at: www.iucn.org/commissions/world-commission-environmental-law/resources/wcel-important-documentation/global-pact-environment (accessed 15 December 2021).

2.2.2.3 TNCs' Obligations under Customary International Law

Whether or not there is customary international law that applies to TNCs is a moot question. On the question of whether corporations are bound by *jus cogens* norms, different views have been presented. The 2006 Ruggie report supports the position that 'corporations may be held liable for committing, or for complicity in, the most heinous human rights violations amounting to international crimes'.[95] In the ATS jurisprudence, district Judge Schwartz in *Presbyterian Church of Sudan v. Talisman Energy Inc.*, after rejecting the position taken in declarations of Professors Crawford and Greenwood that 'there is no basis in existing international law for the liability of corporations',[96] concluded that 'corporations may also be held liable under international law, at least for gross human rights violations'.[97] Recently, in *Nevsun Resources Ltd. v. Araya*,[98] a case in which Eritrean workers sued a Canadian mining company for breaches of customary international law prohibitions against forced labour; slavery; cruel, inhuman, or degrading treatment; and crimes against humanity, the Supreme Court of Canada (the majority, Wagner CJ and Abella, Karakatsanis, Gascon, and Martin JJ) also stated, *inter alia*, that 'the breaches of customary international law, or *jus cogens*, relied on by the Eritrean workers may well apply to Nevsun'.[99]

By contrast, in another ATS case *Kiobel v. Royal Dutch Petroleum I*, the Second Circuit concluded that '[n]o corporation has ever been subject to any form of liability (whether civil, criminal, or otherwise) under the customary international law of human rights',[100] relying on Professors Crawford and Greenwood's conclusion that 'customary international law does not recognize liability for corporations that violate its norms'.[101] Therefore, even with respect to *jus cogens* norms, which cover

95 Ruggie 2006 Report, para. 61.

96 *Presbyterian Church of Sudan v. Talisman Energy, Inc.*, 244 F. Supp. 2d 289 (SDNY 2003).

97 Ibid., 318–319. See also Court of Appeals for the 2nd circuit in *Presbyterian Church of Sudan v. Talisman Energy*, 582 F.3d 244 (2d Cir. 2009) fn. 12 (citing *Sosa*, 542 US at 732 n. 20, 124 S. Ct. 2739).

98 *Nevsun Resources Ltd. v. Araya*, 2020 SCC 5 (Judgement 28 February 2020).

99 Ibid., para. 114. Justices Brown and Rowe dissented. For an analysis of this case, see Haynes, 'The Shifting Pendulum'. This case is further discussed in Chapter 5, Section 5.3.4.

100 *Kiobel v. Royal Dutch Petroleum*, 621 F.3d 111 (2d Cir. 2010), 48. See also Karavias, *Corporate Obligations under International Law*, 52–57 (analysis of the Inter-American Court of Human Rights case law).

101 Ibid., 41.

only a very limited type of conduct (excluding most environmental and human rights obligations),[102] whether corporations bear these obligations remains unsettled.

Nevertheless, it is entirely possible that adjudicators in IIA-based dispute settlement mechanisms find the claimant investors' environmental and human rights obligations under general international law. The recent *Urbaser* and *Aven* awards suggest this possibility. As discussed in Chapter 5, Section 5.3.2, in both cases, the respondent raised counterclaims on grounds that include the investors' failure to comply with international law (on human rights[103] and environmental protection[104]).

The *Urbaser* tribunal addressed the question of 'whether Claimants [sic] as investors were bound by an obligation based on international law to provide the population living on the territory of the Concession with drinking water and sanitation services'.[105] The tribunal, while stating that 'an obligation to *perform* applicable to a particular investor . . . does not find its legal ground in general international law',[106] proceeded to state that 'an obligation to *abstain*, like a prohibition to commit acts violating human rights . . . can be of immediate application . . . to individuals and other private parties'.[107]

The *Aven* tribunal first stated that Articles 10.9.3.c and 10.11 (no lowering standard clause, see Section 2.3.1) of the CAFTA-DR could be interpreted to impose the investors' obligation to 'abide and comply the environmental domestic laws and regulations'.[108] The tribunal agreed with the *Urbaser* tribunal's affirmation that investors operating internationally cannot be immune from becoming subjects of international law,[109] without even making the performance–abstention distinction.[110] It further stated that this conclusion is 'particularly convincing' for the

102 Adeola, 'Environmental Injustice and Human Rights Abuse', 54.
103 *Urbaser S.A. and Consorcio de Aguas Bilbao Bizkaia, Bilbao Biskaia Ur Partzuergoa v. The Argentine Republic*, ICSID Case No. ARB/07/26, Award, 8 December 2016 (*Urbaser* Award), para. 1156.
104 *David R. Aven and Others v. Republic of Costa Rica*, ICSID Case No. UNCT/15/3, Award, 18 September 2018 (*Aven* Award), para. 699.
105 *Urbaser* Award, para. 1206.
106 Ibid., para. 1210 (emphasis added).
107 Ibid., para. 1210 (emphasis added).
108 *Aven* Award, para. 735.
109 Ibid., para. 738.
110 Bose, '*David R Aven v Costa Rica*', 24.

obligations concerning the protection of the environment, which were recognised as obligations *erga omnes* by the ICJ.[111]

Although the counterclaims were dismissed on their merits in both cases (Chapter 5, Section 5.3.3), these cases suggest that in future cases, investment arbitration tribunals or the investment court may find the existence of certain general international law norms on environmental and human rights protection, which are broader than *jus cogens* norms, that bind foreign investors.[112]

2.2.2.4 Lack of an Enforcement Mechanism for TNCs' International Obligations

On top of the general lack of substantive international obligations binding TNCs, few mechanisms exist in international law to enforce such obligations. International courts and tribunals do not generally have jurisdiction to enforce the obligations of TNCs.[113] The IFC/Multilateral Investment Guarantee Agency (MIGA) Compliance Advisory Ombudsman (CAO)[114] and by the National Contact Points for Responsible Business Conduct (NCPs) under the OECD Guidelines for Multinational Enterprises[115] do have mandates to assess complaints from investment-affected communities and individuals against TNCs.

[111] *Aven* Award, para. 738.

[112] Scherer, Bruce and Reschke, 'Environmental Counterclaims in Investment Treaty Arbitration', 432.

[113] An exception (albeit of a limited scope) is the compulsory jurisdiction of the Seabed Disputes Chamber over certain 'disputes between parties to a contract, being States Parties, the Authority or the Enterprise, state enterprises and natural or juridical persons' (Article 187(c)–(e) of the UNCLOS).

[114] Although its mandate is limited to address complaints from people affected by IFC/MIGA projects, CAO may use different approaches to resolve issues raised about the environmental and/or social impacts of the projects. IFC/MIGA Independent Accountability Mechanism (CAO) Policy (2021), 28 July 2021 (CAO Policy), available at: www.ifc.org/wps/wcm/connect/d3e7f1c4-fd6b-40fd-ae76-fb0289166l1d/IFC-MIGA-Independent-Accountability-Mechanism-CAO-Policy.pdf?MOD=AJPERES&CVID=nFDGwP2 (accessed 15 December 2021).

[115] When a case is submitted to an NCP, it has the mandate to provide 'good offices' on issues related to the implementation of the Guidelines through different approaches including mediation. OECD, 'National Contact Points for Responsible Business Conduct: Providing Access to Remedy: 20 Years and the Road Ahead', 2020, at 13, available at: http://mneguidelines.oecd.org/NCPs-for-RBC-providing-access-to-remedy-20-years-and-the-road-ahead.pdf (accessed 15 December 2021).

However, they do not have a mechanism for enforcement.[116] Also note that the Economic Community of West African States (ECOWAS) Court of Justice has concluded that neither individuals (*Peter David v. Ambassador Ralph Uwechue*[117] and *Tandja v. Djibo and Another*[118]) nor corporations (*SERAP v. President of the Federal Republic of Nigeria and Others*[119]) can be defendants in human rights cases, despite the broadly worded provisions of the 1991 ECOWAS Community Court of Justice Protocol (as amended by the 2005 Supplementary Protocol) (ECOWAS CCJ Protocol) which establish the jurisdiction of the Court.[120]

That said, enforcing a TNC's obligations in the international sphere becomes possible when legal instruments such as contracts to which it is a party include an international arbitration agreement.[121] With this regard, an important development in the context of human rights is the adoption of the Accord on Fire and Building Safety in Bangladesh in 2013 in the aftermath of the Rana Plaza building collapse that killed over 1,100 workers.[122] The Accord, whose signatories include corporations, trade unions, and NGOs, provided binding arbitration for the final dispute settlement mechanism.[123] Two arbitration proceedings based

[116] CAO Policy; Bhatt and Türkelli, 'OECD National Contact Points', 426; Khoury and Whyte, 'Sidelining Corporate Human Rights Violations', 371; Svoboda, 'Coming of Age', 40–41.

[117] ECW/CCJ/RUL/03/10, Judgment, 11 June 2010, paras. 37–43.

[118] ECW/CCJ/05/10, Judgment, 8 November 2010.

[119] ECW/CCJ/APP/07/10, Judgment, 10 December 2010, para. 71. See also *Molmon et 114 autres c Guinée*, ECW/CCJ/JUD/16/16, Judgment, 17 May 2016, at 6.

[120] Article 9(4) ('The Court has jurisdiction to determine cases of violations of human rights that occur in any member state'). For critical analyses of these cases, see Nwauche, 'ECOWAS Community Court of Justice'; Ho, 'International Law's Opportunities for Investor Accountability', 39–41.

[121] Márquez, 'Legal Avenues for Holding Multinational Corporations', 60–61. Article 9(6) of the ECOWAS CCJ Protocol provides that the Court has jurisdiction over disputes between private parties if there is an agreement that the dispute shall be settled by the ECOWAS CCJ. Happold and Radović, 'ECOWAS Court of Justice', 104.

[122] After the expiration of the 2018 Accord, which replaced the 2013 Accord, the International Accord for Health and Safety in the Textile and Garment Industry entered into force on 1 September 2021. Available at: https://bangladesh.wpengine.com/wp-content/uploads/2021/08/1-September-International-Accord-on-Health-and-Safety-in-the-Textile-and-Garment-Industry-public-version.pdf (accessed 15 December 2021).

[123] Clause 5 of the 2013 Accord. The International Accord for Health and Safety in the Textile and Garment Industry also provides an arbitration process (Clause 50).

on the 2013 Bangladesh Accord commenced before the Permanent Court of Arbitration.[124]

Another significant development is the launch of the Hague Rules on Business and Human Rights Arbitration in December 2019 (The Hague Rules).[125] The Hague Rules, drafted by the team chaired by Professor Bruno Simma, aim to 'help to fill the access to remedy gap under Pillar III of the UNGPs'[126] and incorporate needs and issues that arrive in the context of business and human rights disputes. While the Hague Rules are employed on an *ad hoc* basis, based on the disputing parties' agreement either before (e.g. in contracts) or after a dispute arises,[127] the disputing parties may request the tribunal and the Secretary General of the Permanent Court of Arbitration to act as Secretariat and serve as registry.

Other than these developments, implementation and enforcement of international obligations of juridical persons relies on domestic legal frameworks concerning the liability of private persons.[128] The level of enforcement varies widely between countries, depending on the willingness and capacity of each state to establish and maintain the necessary enforcement mechanisms.[129] It should be recalled that the ability, capacity, and willingness of capital-importing states to do so are often hindered for the reasons discussed in Section 2.1.1.

2.2.3 Soft Law Instruments on Corporate Social Responsibility (CSR)

2.2.3.1 Development of the Concept of CSR

While attempts to establish international obligations that directly apply to TNCs have been unsuccessful, 'soft law' instruments to advance the

124 PCA Case No. 2016-36 and PCA Case No. 2016-37. See Press Release, Bangladesh Accord Arbitrations, etc. (2017), Permanent Court of Arbitration (October 2017), available at: https://pcacases.com/web/sendAttach/2238 (accessed 15 December 2021). Both cases were settled. Press Release, Settlement of Bangladesh Accord Arbitration, Permanent Court of Arbitration (July 2018), https://docs.pca-cpa.org/2018/07/20180717-Press-Release-No.-2-ENG.pdf (accessed 15 December 2021).

125 The Hague Rules are available at: www.cilc.nl/cms/wp-content/uploads/2019/06/Draft-BHR-Rules-Final-version-for-Public-consultation.pdf (accessed 15 December 2021).

126 Sherman III, 'Beyond CSR', 499.

127 The Hague Rules provide model clauses, including model arbitration clauses for contracts and other agreements and instruments in Annexes.

128 Uff, 'La réparation du dommage', 489; Stephens, 'Translating Filártiga', 34 (in the context of human rights law).

129 Stephens, 'Translating Filártiga', 34.

concept of CSR have proliferated in the same period.[130] Evolving out of philanthropy, this concept has developed to include many different dimensions, reflecting social and market pressures, as well as concerns about solely profit-driven business conduct.[131] It has been developed most actively in the field of business economics studies[132] primarily as a business strategy to handle market and reputational issues, 'even if it is genuinely aimed for a positive social end'.[133] CSR has also been developed as a form of self-regulation in efforts to avoid and/or resist external regulation,[134] and therefore its non-binding nature has been emphasised.[135] However, in today's context, this understanding of CSR as the action beyond legal requirements is no longer tenable. The distinction between voluntary CSR and binding legal standards has faded, as these two are increasingly interwoven in a number of ways.

First, it is now widely recognised that regulatory compliance is a baseline requirement of CSR. The European Commission, while in its 2001 Green Paper on CSR defined CSR as a voluntary concept,[136] in its 2011 policy on CSR, defined the concept more generally as 'the responsibility of enterprises for their impacts on society',[137] thus 'implicitly opened opportunities for public regulation on CSR'.[138] It also clearly stated that compliance with domestic laws and regulations is a

[130] Kolk and van Tulder, 'Setting New Global Rules?', 2.

[131] For history and development of CSR, see e.g. Blowfield and Murray, *Corporate Social Responsibility*, chapter 2; Carroll, 'History of Corporate Social Responsibility', 19–45; De Castro, 'Corporate Social Responsibility and Restructuring'; Vurro, 'Evolutionary Path'.

[132] Mushkat, 'Corporate Social Responsibility', 55.

[133] McCorquodale, 'Corporate Social Responsibility', 391. See also Dahlsrud, 'How Corporate Social Responsibility Is Defined'; Lim and Tsutsui, 'Globalization and Commitment', 87; Buhmann, 'Corporate Social Responsibility', 189; McBarnet, 'Corporate Social Responsibility', 21.

[134] Ratner, 'Corporations and Human Rights', 531; Shamir, 'Between Self-Regulation', 644; Hamdani and Ruffing, 'Lessons from the UN Centre', 38; Motte-Baumvol, 'Le comportement de l'investisseur', 197.

[135] Zerk, *Multinationals and Corporate Social Responsibility*, 29–30; Mushkat, 'Corporate Social Responsibility', 74.

[136] European Commission, 'Green Paper: Promoting a European Framework for Corporate Social Responsibility', 18 July 2001 (COM (2001) 366).

[137] European Commission, 'Communication from the Commission to the European Parliament, the Council, the European Economic and Social Committee and the Committee of the Regions: A Renewed EU Strategy 2011–14 for Corporate Social Responsibility', 2011, COM/2011/0681 (European Commission 2011 Strategy on CSR) at 6 (para. 3.1).

[138] Buhmann, 'Public Regulators and CSR', 702.

'prerequisite' for meeting CSR.[139] OECD, by employing the concept of responsible business conduct,[140] identifies obeying domestic laws and regulations as 'the first obligation of business'.[141]

In this regard, fundamental elements of corporate responsibility such as those recognised in the UN Ten Principles (the protection of human rights, the environment, labour rights, and abstention from corrupt practices) as well as issues relating to taxation, misleading advertisement and competition policy, are already closely regulated in many countries by domestic law.[142]

Secondly, actions to advance societal interests, which have been otherwise considered as voluntary elements of CSR, are also increasingly regulated. The EU[143] as well as specific countries such as France[144] and

139 European Commission 2011 Strategy on CSR, para. 3.1. See also Mosca and Civera, 'The Evolution of CSR', 20; Javillier, 'Corporate Social Responsibility and Law', 47.

140 Responsible business conduct is defined as: 'businesses a) should make a positive contribution to economic, environmental and social progress with a view to achieving sustainable development and b) should avoid and address adverse impacts through their own activities and prevent or mitigate adverse impacts directly linked to their operations, products or services by a business relationship'. OECD, 'Policy Framework for Investment 2015 Edition', available at: www.oecd.org/investment/investment-policy/Policy-Framework-for-Investment-2015-CMIN2015-5.pdf (accessed 15 December 2021).

141 OECD Guidelines for Multinational Enterprises, Commentary, Part I. para. 2; OECD, 'Annual Report on the OECD Guidelines for Multinational Enterprises', 2008, 237, available at: www.oecd.org/daf/inv/mne/employmentandindustrialrelations-2008annualreportontheoecdguidelinesformultinationalenterprises.htm (accessed 15 December 2021). See also Javillier, 'Corporate Social Responsibility and Law', 47; Ward, 'Legal Issues in Corporate Citizenship', 35.

142 Matten and Moon, '"Implicit" and "Explicit" CSR', 410; Ward, 'Corporate Social Responsibility', 18–19; Zerk, *Multinationals and Corporate Social Responsibility*, 34–35.

143 Directive 2014/95/EU of the European Parliament and of the Council of 22 October 2014 amending Directive 2013/34/EU as regards disclosure of non-financial and diversity information by certain large undertakings and groups Text with EEA relevance, OJ 2014 No. L330, 15 November 2014, 1–9 (Non-Financial Reporting Directive). On 21 April 2021, the European Commission adopted a proposal for a Corporate Sustainability Reporting Directive, which revises Non-Financial Reporting Directive to extend the scope of companies subject to the reporting requirement and the scope of sustainability information to be disclosed. The first set of EU sustainability reporting standards would be adopted by October 2022. European Commission, 'Proposal for a Directive of the European Parliament and of the Council Amending Directive 2013/34/EU, Directive 2004/109/EC, Directive 2006/43/EC and Regulation (EU) No 537/2014, as Regards Corporate Sustainability Reporting' COM/2021/189, 24 April 2021.

144 La loi du 15 mai 2001 relative aux nouvelles régulations économiques (NRE) and décret du 20 février 2002; l'article R. 225-105 du Code de commerce; la loi Grenelle 2 de juillet 2010; Ordonnance du 19 juillet 2017 relative à la publication d'informations non financières par certaines grandes entreprises et certains groupes d'enterprises, available at: www.legifrance.gouv.fr (accessed 15 December 2021).

the UK[145] have introduced laws and regulations that make social and environmental reporting a mandatory requirement.[146] Several stock exchanges require CSR reporting as a listing requirement.[147] More drastically, countries such as India, Mauritius, and Indonesia have enacted laws that make corporate contribution to societal development a mandatory requirement.[148]

Moreover, CSR commitments that go beyond legal requirements are sometimes incorporated into contracts such as government procurement contracts,[149] private contracts with suppliers and contractors,[150] or required as a condition for the operation of businesses.[151] In such cases, CSR commitments become legally binding through private (e.g. contract law) or public (e.g. environmental, mining, and other administrative)

145 UK Companies Act 2006 (Strategic Report and Directors' Report) Regulations 2013, Chapter 4A (Strategic Report), 414C (Contents of Strategic Report) para. 7.

146 For developments in this regard, see Ascensio, 'Les activités normatives', 272; Renneboog, Ter Horst and Zhang, 'Socially Responsible Investment Funds', 399–401; Buhmann, 'Corporate Social Responsibility', 194. For a list of domestic laws on non-financial reporting of different countries, see Initiative for Responsible Investment, 'Global CSR Disclosure', Initiative for Responsible Investment, available at: https://iri.hks.harvard.edu/csr (accessed 15 December 2021).

147 For a list of stock exchanges that require some form of CSR reporting, see Peloso and Hunt, 'Corporate Social Responsibility Reporting', 167.

148 Section 135 and Schedule VII of the Companies Act 2013 (India); Income Tax Act 1995, article 50L (Mauritius); Article 15(b) of the Law No. 25 of 2007 on Investment, Chapter V of the Law No. 40 of 2007 Concerning Limited Liability Company, Government Regulation No. 47 of 2012 on Corporate Social and Environmental Responsibility (Indonesia).

149 For example, Directive 2014/24/EU of the European Parliament and of the Council of 26 February 2014 on public procurement and repealing Directive 2004/18/EC (1), OJ 2014 No. L94, 28 March 2014, 65-242, para. 97. ('contracting authorities should be allowed to use award criteria or contract performance conditions [relating to social and environmental considerations]'). Including CSR obligations in government procurement contracts is a method to encourage CSR. European Commission, 'Communication from the Commission concerning Corporate Social Responsibility: A Business Contribution to Sustainable Development', COM (2002) 347, 2 July 2007, para. 7.6; McCrudden, 'Corporate Social Responsibility and Public Procurement', 94; Gaukrodger, 'Business Responsibilities and Investment Treaties', 58–59.

150 Bantekas, 'Corporate Social Responsibility in International Law', 322; Ward, 'Corporate Social Responsibility', 19; Schepel, *The Constitution of Private Governance*, 33.

151 For example, Loi N° 0362015/CNT portant code minier du burkina faso. JO N°44 du 29 octobre 2015, Articles 25–30; Loi N° 2014-138 du 24 mars 2014 portant code minier du Côte d'Ivoire. Articles 121–126. See also Oshionebo, *Mineral Mining in Africa*, 11; Loutit, Mandelbaum and Szoke-Burke, 'Emerging Practices in Community Development Agreements', 64–96.

laws,[152] and the consequences of contradicting such commitments are determined by these laws.[153] Furthermore, as discussed in Chapter 5, Section 5.4, when such commitments are incorporated and published in a corporation's code of conduct, CSR reports and other declarations, failure to respect these commitments may give rise to legal responsibility. All of these demonstrate an increasing interaction and gradual integration between mandatory requirements and voluntary commitments concerning corporate behaviour.

2.2.3.2 International 'Soft Law' Instruments to Advance CSR

The initiatives for the creation of soft law instruments on CSR came from both public and private sectors. Instruments from public initiatives include: the UNGPs, the OECD Guidelines for Multinational Enterprises,[154] the International Labor Organization (ILO)'s Tripartite Declaration of Principles concerning Multinational Enterprises and Social Policy, the Ten Principles of the UN Global Compact (1999),[155] the UN Environment Programme's (UNEP's) Finance Initiative (UNEP FI),[156] the IFC's Performance Standards and Environmental and Social Sustainability Policy, and the Multilateral Investment Guarantee Agency (MIGA)'s Performance Standards on Social and Environmental Sustainability.[157]

[152] Deumier, 'Les codes de conduite des entreprises', 692–694; Viñuales, *Foreign Investment and the Environment*, 94.

[153] Beckers, *Enforcing Corporate Social Responsibility Codes*, 150–156. For example, *Doe v. Wal-Mart Stores*, 572 F.3d 677 (9th Cir. 2009) 681–682. For a limitation of the contractual approach, see Beckers, 'Regulating Corporate Regulators through Contract Law?'.

[154] The Guidelines have been updated five times since its first adoption in 1976. They are supplemented by the OECD Due Diligence Guidance for Responsible Business Conduct, which provides practical support to enterprises on the implementation of the 2011 Guidelines. OECD, 'Due Diligence Guidance for Responsible Business Conduct', 2018, available at: www.oecd.org/investment/due-diligence-guidance-for-responsible-business-conduct.htm (accessed 15 December 2021).

[155] Available at: www.unglobalcompact.org/what-is-gc/mission/principles (accessed 15 December 2021).

[156] Available at: www.unepfi.org/ (accessed 15 December 2021).

[157] The 2007 Standard was revised in 2013. The 2013 version is available at: www.miga.org/sites/default/files/archive/Documents/MIGA_Performance_Standards_October_2013.pdf (accessed 15 December 2021).

Private initiatives include: the Equator Principles,[158] the ISO 26000 Guidance Standard on Social Responsibility,[159] the Global Reporting Initiative (GRI),[160] the Sustainable Accounting Standards Board (SASB),[161] the International <IR> [Integrated Reporting] Framework (2013) by the International Integrated Reporting Council (IIRC),[162] the 1999 Global Sullivan Principles of Corporate Social Responsibility,[163] and the six Principles for Responsible Investment (PRI).[164]

Some of these instruments provide mechanisms for disclosure of information on relevant CSR commitments. Participating companies to the UN Global Compact are subject to a requirement of non-financial reporting in an annual Communication on Progress.[165] As private frameworks, the GRI and ISO 26000 provide standards and guidance for sustainability reporting which are 'considerably more detailed, rigorous, and standardized compared to a simple endorsement of the Global Compact',[166] and are relied on globally. Likewise, PRI signatories are

[158] Equator Principles, The Equator Principles – EP 4, July 2020, available at: https://equator-principles.com/app/uploads/The-Equator-Principles_EP4_July2020.pdf (accessed 15 December 2021). The EP4 are 'intended to serve as a common baseline and framework for financial institutions [EPFIs] to identify, assess and manage environmental and social risks when financing Projects' (EP4 at 3), and provide different forms of EPFI's environmental and social due diligence.

[159] ISO is an independent, non-governmental international organisation with a membership of 164 national standards bodies. ISO 26000 and the International Integrated Reporting (IR) Framework are available at: www.iso.org/publication/PUB100402.html (accessed 15 December 2021).

[160] GRI is an independent international organisation which provides both universal and topic-specific (economic, environmental, and social) standards. GRI standards, available at: www.globalreporting.org/standards/gri-standards-download-center/?g=dbe18ac8-f86b-490f-a1e3-87c664665eca (accessed 15 December 2021).

[161] SASB provides industry-specific standards that are designed to assist companies in disclosing non-financial information to investors. Available at: www.sasb.org/standards-overview/download-current-standards/ (accessed 15 December 2021).

[162] Available at: https://integratedreporting.org/wp-content/uploads/2015/03/13-12-08-THE-INTERNATIONAL-IR-FRAMEWORK-2-1.pdf (accessed 15 December 2021).

[163] See Alexis, 'Global Sullivan Principles'; Frey, 'Legal and Ethical Responsibilities', 174–175.

[164] PRI was launched in 2006 as a network of financial institutions with support from the UN. Information on the principles is available at: www.unpri.org/ (accessed 15 December 2021).

[165] UN Global Compact, 'The Communication on Progress (CoP) in Brief', available at: www.unglobalcompact.org/participation/report/cop (accessed 15 December 2021).

[166] Lim and Tsutsui, 'Globalization and Commitment', 73 (on GRI). See also Fatoux, 'La différenciation normative selon les activités', 158.

required to report on their responsible investment activities annually.[167] As discussed in Chapter 5, Section 5.4, these disclosure requirements, however soft, may have significant legal implications.

2.3 International Obligations and Responsibilities of Investors in IIAs

This section examines whether, and to what extent, investor obligations and responsibilities are reflected in IIAs, with reference to the IIA dataset. It first confirms the observation that the IIA-making practice in the twenty-first century has exhibited a trend towards greater deference to the host state's rights to regulate (Section 2.3.1).[168] It then demonstrates that this development is contrasted with the remaining paucity of provisions on investor obligations in existing IIAs, although an emerging trend towards the latter's recognition can be observed in some of recent IIAs (Section 2.3.2).

The attempts towards respecting the host state's regulatory prerogative and constraining arbitrators' interpretative discretion[169] take different forms. This includes: (a) the provisions on the parties' reaffirmation of 'their right to regulate' to achieve legitimate policy objectives,[170] (b) fully elaborated investment protection standards with more caveats and limitations than those in older treaties,[171] and (c) including sustainable

[167] Principles for Responsible Investment, 'Reporting for Signatories', available at: www.unpri.org/reporting (accessed 15 December 2021). For an overview of different frameworks for voluntary CSR reporting, see Peloso and Hunt, 'Corporate Social Responsibility Reporting', 128–159.

[168] Sharma, 'What's Past Is Prologue', 169; Gordon and Pohl, 'Environmental Concerns in International Investment Agreements'; Wagner, 'Regulatory Space in International Trade Law', 36–54.

[169] Simma, 'Foreign Investment Arbitration', 581; Henckels, 'Protecting Regulatory Autonomy', 28.

[170] For example, EU-China Comprehensive Agreement on Investment (agreement in principle, 2021) Section IV, Sub-section 2, Article 1 and Sub-section 3, Article 1; the EU-Canada Comprehensive Economic and Trade Agreement (2016) Article 8.9.

[171] For example, Comprehensive and Progressive Agreement for Trans-Pacific Partnership (2018) Annex 9-B (Expropriation). For a comprehensive analysis of the trend in the IIAs (2000–2020) towards including provisions that delimit and specify the scope of the FET and expropriation obligations, see OECD Directorate for Financial and Enterprise Affairs Investment Committee, Freedom of Investment Roundtable 33: Summary of Discussion: Note by the Secretariat, 8 September 2021, DAF/INV/WD(2021)13/FINAL, Figures 1–3.

development goals in treaty preambles.[172] Among these 'more protective provisions',[173] this section selects the incorporation of 'no lowering of standards' clauses and general exception clauses as examples.

2.3.1 Towards Greater Recognition of the Host State's Regulatory Power: 'No Lowering of Standards' Clauses and General Exception Clauses

'No lowering of standards' clauses typically provide the parties' recognition that it is inappropriate to encourage investment by relaxing domestic health, safety, or environmental measures. Among the 1,000 IIAs and model IIAs (collectively 'IIAs') in the IIA dataset, 203 out of 1,000 IIAs (189 IIAs, 14 model IIAs) provide this type of clauses (Figure 2.1).

General exception clauses typically (but not necessarily) incorporate or are modelled on GATT Article XX and GATS Article XIV.[174] In the IIA dataset, 207 out of 1,000 IIAs (193 IIAs, 14 model IIAs) provide general exception clauses (Figure 2.2).

These IIAs have been classified according to the year of signature (for IIAs) and adoption (for model IIAs). Among the 203 IIAs that have 'no lowering of standard' clauses, 6 were signed before 1999, 58 were signed or adopted between 2000 and 2009, and 139 were signed between 2010 and 2019 (Figure 2.3). Among the 207 IIAs that include general exception clauses, 25 were signed before 1999, 52 were signed or adopted between 2000 and 2009, and 130 were signed between 2010 and 2019 (Figure 2.4). Thus, this confirms that the trend towards respecting the host state's rights to regulate became evident in the first decade of the twenty-first century. The IIAs that demonstrate deference to the host state's regulatory powers are hereinafter referred to as the 'second-generation IIAs'.

[172] Kethireddy identifies such preambles as an effort 'to "treatify" the right to regulate'. Kethireddy, 'Still the Law of Nations', 343–344.

[173] Alschner and Skougarevskiy, 'Convergence and Divergence', 164.

[174] It should be noted that, while the states' intention is clear, whether the incorporation of such exception clauses actually brings a greater balance in IIAs remains contested. See Legum and Petculescu, 'GATT Article XX and International Investment Law', 355–356; Lévesque, 'Inclusion of GATT Article XX Exceptions', 370. Cf. Newcombe, 'General Exceptions in International Investment Agreements', 370.

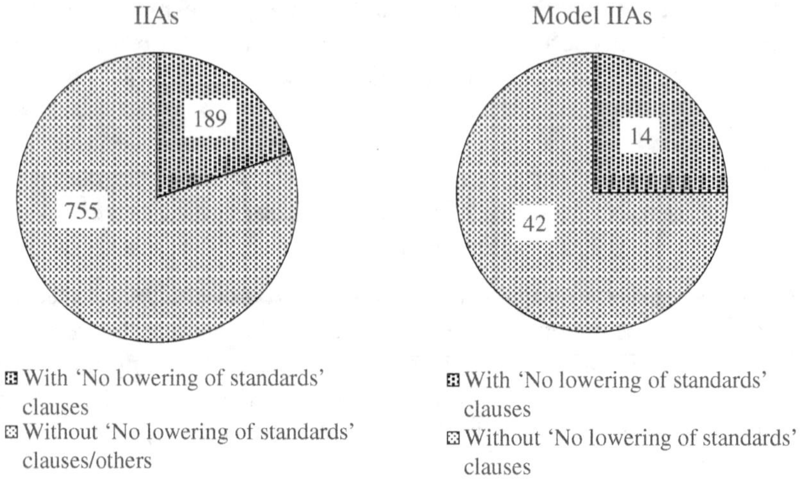

Figure 2.1 'No lowering of standards' clauses

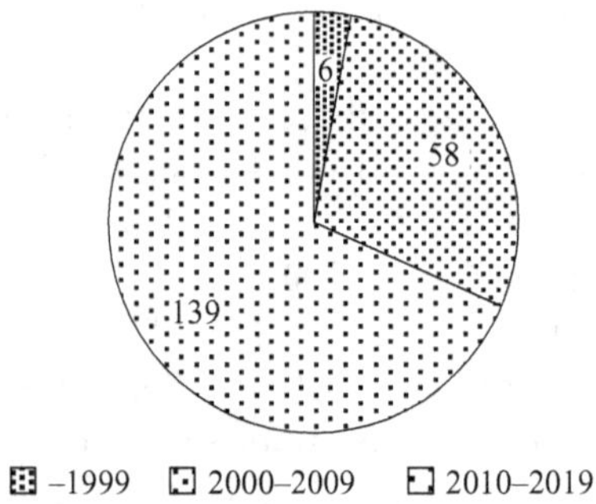

Figure 2.2 Year of signature/adoption of IIAs that have 'no lowering of standards' clauses

2.3.2 *Investors' Binding Obligations: 'Third-Generation' IIAs*

In contrast to the increasing recognition of the host state's regulatory power, the number of IIAs that recognise investor obligations is still limited; however, an emerging trend towards the latter's recognition can be observed in most recent IIAs. In the IIA dataset, 21 IIAs out of 1,000 IIAs (15 IIAs, 6 model IIAs) provide investor obligations in binding terms (Figure 2.5). The contents of investor obligations differ between these IIAs. Article 9 of the 1981 Agreement on Promotion, Protection and Guarantee of Investments amongst the Member States of the Organization of the Islamic Conference (OIC Investment Agreement)

Figure 2.3 General exception clauses

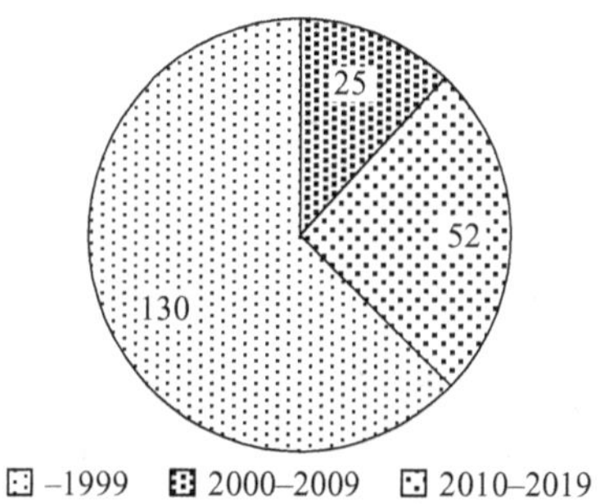

Figure 2.4 Year of signature/adoption of IIAs that have general exception clauses

primarily provides the obligations to abide by the host state's laws and regulations and to refrain from acts 'that may disturb public order or morals or that may be prejudicial to the public interest'. Article 19 of the 2016 Morocco-Nigeria BIT[175] is more progressive than Article 9 of the 1981 OIC Investment Agreement in the sense that it requires adoption of '*internationally* accepted standards in corporate governance' (emphasis added) and establishment and maintenance of 'local community liaison processes'. The 2008 ECOWAS SIA and the 2018 ECOWAS Common Investment Code (ECOWIC) also provide investor obligations with

[175] For an overview of the 2016 Morocco-Nigeria BIT, see Mbengue and Schacherer, 'Evolution of International Investment Agreements', 2605–2607.

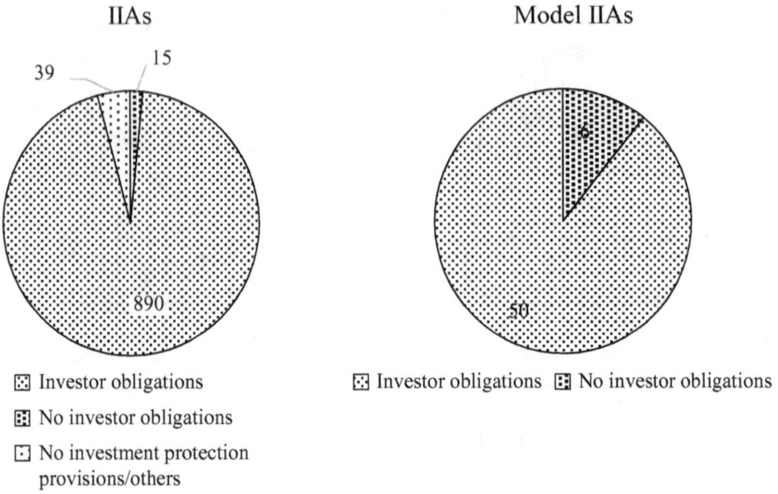

Figure 2.5 Reference to investor obligations

reference to international standards in corporate governance and social responsibility. Notably, Article 29(1)(iii) of the ECOWIC specifically requires investors to 'arrange for environmentally sound technologies to be available to affiliates of parent companies in Member States on fair terms'.

Investor obligations with reference to international standards have also been found in recent model IIAs. Article 14 of the 2012 SADC model investment treaty provides, *inter alia*, the obligation to 'maintain an environmental management system consistent with recognized international environmental management standards and good business practice standards'.[176] Article 12 of the 2016 India model BIT[177] provides the 'endeavour' obligation of the investor 'to voluntarily incorporate internationally recognized standards of corporate social responsibility in their practices and internal policies'.

Inclusion of investor obligations is a recent phenomenon. Among the twenty-one IIAs that provide investor obligations, two were signed or adopted before 1999,[178] and nineteen were signed or adopted between

[176] See also Article 18 of the 2019 Belgium-Luxembourg Economic Union model BIT.

[177] For an analysis of the 2016 India's Model BIT, see e.g. Ranjan and Anand, '2016 Model Indian Bilateral Investment Treaty'.

[178] The 1981 OIC Investment Agreement (Article 9) and the 1980 Unified Agreement for the Investment of Arab Capital in the Arab States (Article 14).

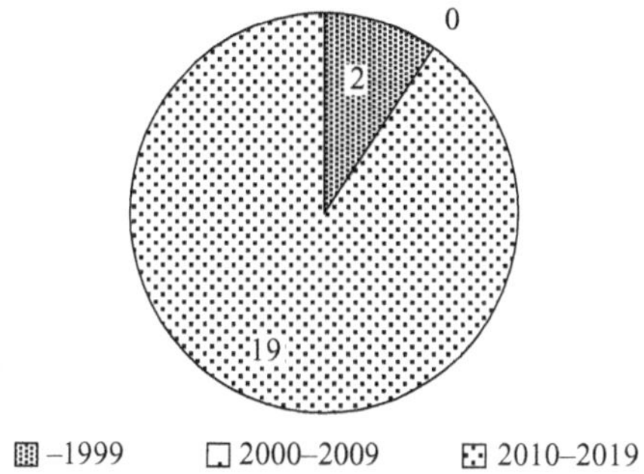

Figure 2.6 Year of signature/adoption of IIAs that provide investor obligations

2010 and 2019 (Figure 2.6). Given that the IIA dataset includes 295 IIAs that were signed or adopted between 2010 and 2019, 6.5 per cent of these IIAs in the dataset include investor obligations. Therefore, it can be concluded that there is an observable trend towards the inclusion of investor obligations in the most recent IIAs. The IIAs that incorporate international standards concerning business conduct either as a mandatory requirement or as an endeavour obligation may be considered 'third-generation IIAs'.[179] These IIAs not only address the issue of one-sidedness in the IIA regime, but also advance responsible investment, that is, investment which incorporates environmental, social, and governance (ESG) factors[180] in the regime.

2.3.3 Reference to CSR

Although the third-generation IIAs have the potential to pave the way towards more responsible forms of investment, they are still limited in number. There are a larger number of IIAs that include provisions on CSR. Among the 1,000 IIAs, 64 refer to CSR (16 in the preamble and

[179] For example, Article 10(3) of the 2016 Iran-Slovakia BIT; Article 7(1) of the 2019 Netherlands Model BIT; Chapter III of the 2018 Belarus-India BIT; Chapter III of the 2019 India-Kyrgyzstan BIT; Section III of the 2019 Morocco Model BIT; Article 13 of the 2007 Investment Agreement for the COMESA Common Investment Area; Chapter 4 of the Draft Pan-African Investment Code. PAIC is considered to be the manifestation of shared understanding of the shaping of African IIAs. Mbengue and Schacherer, 'Africa and the Rethinking', 547–569. For other IIAs that provide investor's direct obligations of conduct, see Nowrot, 'Obligation of Investors', 1161; Ranjan, 'Investor Obligations in Investment Treaties'.

[180] See Chapter 1, Section 1.4.

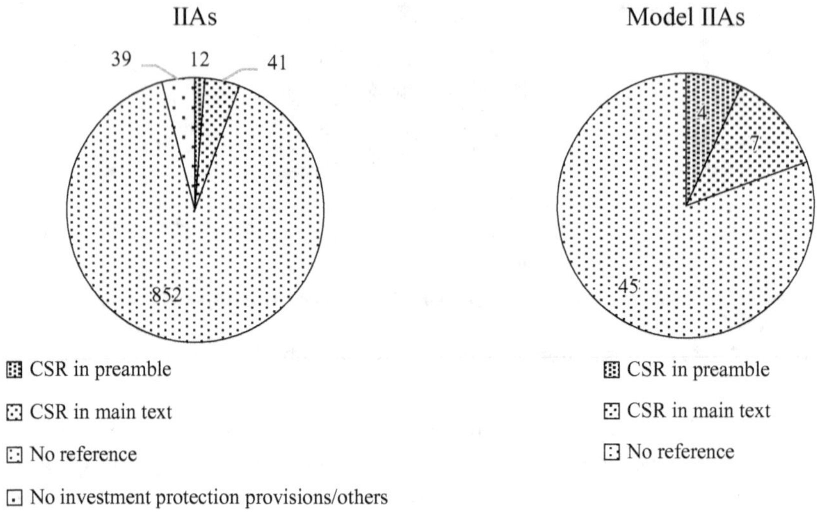

Figure 2.7 Reference to CSR

48 in the main text) (Figure 2.7). With respect to the contents of CSR provisions, in the IIA dataset, the Cooperation and Investment Facilitation Agreements (CIFAs) Brazil has concluded since 2015 (which do not provide an IIA-based dispute settlement mechanism), the 2016 Argentina-Qatar BIT, the 2018 Belarus-India BIT, the 2017 Colombia Model BIT, the 2019 India-Kyrgyzstan BIT include CSR provisions that are addressed to investors. They provide investors' endeavour obligations to contribute to the host state's sustainable development through practices based on CSR principles and standards.[181]

Apart from these IIAs, CSR provisions are typically addressed to contracting states. They provide that the contracting parties: 'should encourage',[182] or 'reaffirm the importance of each Party encouraging',[183] enterprises to voluntarily incorporate international CSR standards.[184] However, their non-obligatory language does not mean that CSR

[181] For example, Article 9.1 of the 2015 Brazil-Malawi CIFA. For IIAs that include CSR provisions addressed to investors, see also Choudhury, 'Investor Obligations for Human Rights', 88–89.

[182] For example, Article 16 of the 2014 Canada-Nigeria BIT.

[183] For example, Article 10.26 of the 2018 Singapore-Sri Lanka FTA.

[184] References to these principles and guidelines are also found in Article 31 of the 2015 Norwegian Model BIT and Article 16 of the 2021 Canadian Model Foreign Investment Promotion and Protection Agreement.

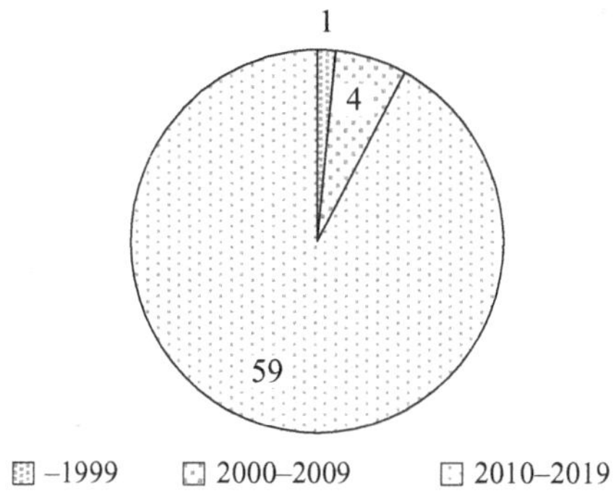

Figure 2.8 Year of signature/adoption of IIAs that refer to CSR

provisions have no practical impact.[185] In this regard, Article 23 of the 2019 Netherlands Model BIT[186] provides that a tribunal, 'in deciding on the amount of compensation, is expected to take into account noncompliance by the investor with its commitments under the UN Guiding Principles on Business and Human Rights, and the OECD Guidelines for Multinational Enterprises'. This is a significant development that directs tribunals towards the incorporation of investors' international behaviour into consideration at the quantum phase.

Reference to CSR is a fairly recent phenomenon in IIA-making. Among the sixty-four IIAs that refer to CSR, one was signed or adopted before 1999, four were signed or adopted between 2000 and 2009, and fifty-nine were signed or adopted between 2010 and 2019 (Figure 2.8), the last of which amounts to 20 per cent of the IIAs that were signed or adopted between 2010 and 2019 in the dataset.

2.4 Conclusion

Various limitations of domestic legal systems in regulating and pursuing the responsibility of TNCs' conduct underscore the role of international standards with respect to business conduct. Nevertheless, international agreements that provide obligations binding TNCs remain rare, and whether there exist customary international norms that directly bind TNCs remains controversial. Instead, various soft law instruments

[185] See Choudhury, 'Role of Soft Law Corporate Responsibilities', 166.

[186] For an analysis of the 2019 Netherlands Model BIT, see Duggal and van de Ven, 'The 2019 Netherlands Model BIT'.

concerning CSR have been developed in both the public and private sectors. Although there are situations in which these instruments give rise to the legal responsibility of TNCs, such legal effects are produced by domestic, not international, law.

Turning to the IIA regime, analysis of the IIA dataset confirms this study's assumption that while there is a clear tendency in the second-generation IIAs towards a greater recognition of the sovereign right to regulate, the incorporation of the concept of investor responsibility in IIAs remains exceptional. However, there are signs of change in this respect. A sizable number of recent IIAs refer to the concept of CSR, and there is an emerging trend towards the inclusion of investor obligations in the third-generation IIAs. As discussed in Chapter 1, Section 1.4, there have been calls for a greater recognition of investor obligation which may, together with the provisions on investor responsibility in the third-generation IIAs, have the potential to incorporate the notion of responsible investment in future IIA-making.

3

Counterclaims

Benefits, Normative Grounds, and Limits

3.1 Introduction: Rise of the Notion of Counterclaims

Chapter 2 demonstrated that the international investment agreements (IIAs) regime is 'one-sided' in the sense that most IIAs provide obligations of investment promotion and protection with respect to host states without providing investor obligations. In the IIA-based dispute settlement mechanism, the one-sidedness manifests itself more comprehensively. For investment arbitration, despite the fact that neither the ICSID Convention nor the UNCITRAL arbitration rules restrict states' access to investment arbitration,[1] access to arbitration is almost entirely limited to investors, even when the relevant IIA provides investor obligations. The few cases registered with ICSID initiated by host states are all based on contracts.[2] This one-sidedness is attributed to the manner in which an arbitration agreement is concluded through an IIA, the practice that has been followed since *AAPL v. Sri Lanka*.[3] The host state expresses its consent to arbitrate investment disputes in the IIA. This constitutes an offer to arbitrate addressed to (potential) investors of the other contracting party(ies) to the IIA, and an arbitration agreement is concluded when the investor

[1] The drafters of the ICSID Convention did consider that both investors and the states should have access to arbitration under the Convention. See Report of the Executive Directors, in ICSID, 'History of the ICSID Convention: Documents concerning the Origin and the Formulation of the Convention on the Settlement of Investment Disputes between States and Nationals of Other States', 1970, Vol. II-2 at 1074 (para. 13).

[2] *Gabon v. Société Serete S.A.*, ICSID Case No. ARB/76/1; *Tanzania Electric Supply Company Limited v. Independent Power Tanzania Limited*, ICSID Case No. ARB/98/8 (*Tanesco v. IPTL*); *Government of the Province of East Kalimantan v. PT Kaltim Prima Coal and Others*, ICSID Case No. ARB/07/3; *Republic of Peru v. Caravelí Cotaruse Transmisora de Energía S.A.C.*, ICSID Case No. ARB/13/24.

[3] *Asian Agricultural Products Ltd. v. Republic of Sri Lanka*, ICSID Case No. ARB/87/3, Final Award, 27 June 1990. This is the first investment arbitration case which is 'exclusively based on a treaty provision' (para. 18).

accepts the offer by submitting its request for arbitration.[4] Conversely, the submission of a request for arbitration by the host state needs a separate consent on the part of the investor. Therefore, an arbitration agreement cannot be concluded insofar as the investor withholds its consent to the specific request for arbitration made by the host state.[5] Provisions on investment courts in existing IIAs do not address this asymmetry.[6] As discussed in Chapter 1, Section 1.4, this procedural inequality has been criticised – indeed, providing investor obligations in IIAs lacks teeth if they are not accompanied by a means to enforce them.[7]

In this background, scholars have discussed the notion of counterclaims as a way to address the existing inequality between disputing parties in investment arbitration.[8] A counterclaim is an autonomous claim by which the host state seeks a remedy on grounds that are separate from, but closely related to, those for principal claims (Chapter 4, Section 4.1), and, in this sense, are distinguished from a pleading to set-off.[9] This difference is illustrated in *Desert Line v. Yemen*, in which the claimant challenged the validity of a settlement agreement concluded after an Yemeni arbitration (based on contract) had awarded the claimant compensation. The respondent state raised, '[u]nder the heading of set-off and counterclaim', claims for 'the amounts that the Claimant has already received under the Settlement Agreement', and for 'damages and/or set off for DLP [the

[4] *Generation Ukraine, Inc. v. Ukraine*, ICSID Case No. ARB/00/9, Award, 16 September 2003, para. 12.2; Douglas, *The International Law of Investment Claims*, 258; Hoffmann, 'Counterclaims in Investment Arbitration', 446.

[5] Laborde, 'The Case for Host State Claims', 109.

[6] For example, Article 8.23 of the EU-Canada Comprehensive Economic and Trade Agreement (CETA) (providing only the investor's right to submit a claim to the Tribunal).

[7] See Nowrot, 'Obligation of Investors', 1164.

[8] For example, Burda, 'Consentement aux demandes reconventionnelles', 29–30; Ben Hamida, 'L'arbitrage Etat-investisseur cherche son équilibre perdu', 262–263; Kryvoi, 'Counterclaims in Investor-State Arbitration'; Sornarajah, *Resistance and Change in the International Law*, 64; Dudas, 'Treaty Counterclaims under the ICSID Convention', 405; Popova and Poon, 'From Perpetual Respondent to Aspiring Counterclaimant?', 225; Bjorklund, 'The Role of Counterclaims', 463–464; Nedumpara and Laddha, 'Human Rights and Environmental Counterclaims'; Guntrip, 'Host State Human Rights Counterclaim'; Scherer, Bruce and Reschke, 'Environmental Counterclaims in Investment Treaty Arbitration'.

[9] Sharpe and Jacob, 'Counterclaims and State Claims', 349; Sabahi, Duggal and Birch, 'Principles Limiting the Amount of Compensation', 333. See e.g. *Perenco Ecuador Ltd. v. Republic of Ecuador and Empresa Estatal Petroeleos del Ecuador (Petroecuador)*, ICSID Case No. ARB/08/6, Decision on Annulment, 28 May 2021, paras. 731–733 (the annulment committee reduced the amount of compensation the tribunal awarded to Perenco, while upholding the amount of compensation for counterclaims).

Claimant]'s unfulfilled obligations decided in the [Yemeni] Arbitral Award, including damages for DLP's unfulfilled construction obligations and its obligation to maintain the bank guarantees'.[10] The former was a set-off claim because it did not require an independent ground for claim.[11] While the tribunal upheld the set-off claim (to which the Claimant did not object), it rejected the counterclaims on their merits.[12]

The concept of counterclaims has received increasing attention and support from states.[13] In the ISDS reform discussions at the UNCITRAL Working Group III (UNCITRAL ISDS reform discussions), several countries have advanced counterclaims as a reform option.[14] It should be noted, however, while the Secretariat acknowledged the possibility of devising a framework for counterclaims in ISDS,[15] as of the date of writing, in light of the opposition to formulating provisions on investor obligations as a legal basis for counterclaims, the topic of counterclaims is to be discussed 'with a focus on the procedural aspects'.[16]

[10] *Desert Line Projects LLC v. Republic of Yemen*, ICSID Case No. ARB/05/17, Award, 6 February 2008, para. 216.

[11] Sharpe and Jacob, 'Counterclaims and State Claims', 350.

[12] *Desert Line* Award, paras. 216–225.

[13] For example, European Commission, 'Towards a New Way to Settle Disputes between States and Investors', Ministère de L'Europe et des Affaires étrangères, May 2015, available at: www.diplomatie.gouv.fr/IMG/pdf/20150530_isds_papier_eng_vf_cle09912d.pdf (accessed 15 December 2021).

[14] For example, UNCITRAL, 'Possible Reform of Investor-State Dispute Settlement (ISDS) Submission from the Government of Morocco, Note by the Secretariat', 4 March 2019, UN Doc. A/CN.9/WG.III/WP.161, Annex II; UNCITRAL, 'Possible Reform of Investor-State Dispute Settlement (ISDS) Submission from the Government of South Africa, Note by the Secretariat', 17 July 2019, UN Doc. A/CN.9/WG.III/WP.176, para. 64; UNCITRAL, 'Possible Reform of Investor-State Dispute Settlement (ISDS) Submission from the Government of Costa Rica', 22 March 2019, UN Doc. A/CN.9/WG.III/WP.164, Annex I; UNCITRAL, 'Possible Reform of Investor-State Dispute Settlement (ISDS) Submission from the Government of Colombia, Note by the Secretariat', 14 June 2019, UN Doc. A/CN.9/WG.III/WP.173, at 8; UNCITRAL, 'Possible Reform of Investor-State Dispute Settlement (ISDS) Submission from the Government of Mali', 17 September 2019, UN Doc. A/CN.9/WG.III/WP.181, Annex 3.E.

[15] UNCITRAL, 'Possible Reform of Investor-State Dispute Settlement (ISDS) Multiple Proceedings and Counterclaims', Note by the Secretariat, 22 January 2020, A/CN.9/WG.III/WP.193, para. 38.

[16] UNCITRAL, 'Possible Reform of Investor-State Dispute Settlement (ISDS) Procedural Rules with Regard to Early Dismissal, Abuse of Process, Security for Costs, Allocation of Costs, and Counterclaims', 2 September 2021, paras. 59 and 61, available at: https://uncitral.un.org/sites/uncitral.un.org/files/media-documents/uncitral/en/draft_procedural_rules_for_intersessional_final_pdf.pdf (accessed 15 December 2021). See De Luca and Baltag, 'Counterclaims in Investment Arbitration'.

Despite the increasing support for the use of counterclaims in investor–state dispute settlement, there are certain issues concerning its normative grounds. First, the host state already has 'avenues of relief'[17] to pursue the investor's responsibility other than raising counterclaims in investment arbitration, particularly through its own courts. Thus, the comparative benefits of counterclaims must be weighed against those of recourse to domestic adjudicatory bodies. Secondly, counterclaims based on alleged environmental damage caused by an investor's activities would, in most cases, involve the interests of third persons to the dispute, that is, those who were actually affected (the victims). The existence of the victims' interest gives rise to the questions of whether the host state is the right recipient of the claim, and whether there are situations where the host states' counterclaims should be limited in the light of the existence of the victims' interest. This chapter addresses these issues.

3.2 Benefits of Counterclaims in Comparison with Domestic Remedies

3.2.1 Rule of Law Questions

In the context of investment arbitration in general, there is an argument that investment arbitration weakens the rule of law in the host state with a less developed judiciary, because it deprives the domestic adjudicatory bodies of both the opportunity to 'clarify relevant domestic legal standards'[18] and the incentives to improve institutional quality to compete with international tribunals.[19] These concerns have been raised also in the context of host states' counterclaims.[20] Issues of expertise and democratic accountability in dealing with disputes arising from internal regulatory matters, which have been discussed in the context of the standard of review of the decisions of domestic adjudicatory bodies by international courts and tribunals,[21] also apply to the host state's environmental counterclaims. The idea of according a greater role to domestic

[17] Dudas, 'Treaty Counterclaims under the ICSID Convention', 386.
[18] Porterfield, 'Exhaustion of Local Remedies', 4.
[19] Ginsburg, 'International Substitutes for Domestic Institutions', 119–121.
[20] See Baltag, 'Reforming the ISDS System', 478–479.
[21] The standard of review is beyond the scope of this study. For discussions on this issue, see e.g. von Staden, 'Democratic Legitimacy of Judicial Review', 1028–1030; von Bogdandy and Venzke, *In Whose Name?: A Public Law Theory*, 198–201; Paine, 'Standard of Review', para. 2; Schill, 'Deference in Investment Treaty Arbitration', 600–602.

courts for investment disputes has been supported by states and scholars.[22] In the UNCITRAL ISDS reform discussions, some states have supported the inclusion of the rule of exhaustion of local remedies in ISDS.[23] Scholars have also sought to relegate international tribunals to only a complementary, or 'backdrop' (i.e. reviewing), role to domestic adjudication.[24]

Therefore, states' felt need to defend the power and capacity of domestic adjudicatory bodies to determine issues of domestic law in contradistinction to the use of IIA-based dispute settlement mechanisms may constitute an obstacle to the use of counterclaims. Indeed, the legally restrictive approach for counterclaims found in some of the recent IIAs may reflect the state's preference for relying on its own domestic judiciary to handle claims against foreign investors.[25]

These are valid concerns. However, the choice between domestic adjudication and IIA-based dispute settlement mechanisms should consider the level of attainment of the rule of law in the host state's judiciary. In environmental counterclaims, the critical question is whether the host states' adjudicatory system can provide a remedy to redress the harm

[22] For example, Sornarajah, *The International Law on Foreign Investment*, 182; Viñuales, 'International Investment Law', 12; Dani and Akhtar-Khavari, 'Rethinking the Use of Deference', 66–67.

[23] For example, UNCITRAL, 'Possible Reform of Investor-State Dispute Settlement (ISDS) Submission from the Government of Morocco, Note by the Secretariat', 4 March 2019, UN Doc. A/CN.9/WG.III/WP.161; UNCITRAL, 'Possible Reform of Investor-State Dispute Settlement (ISDS) Comments by the Government of Indonesia, Note by the Secretariat', 9 November 2018, UN Doc. A/CN.9/WG.III/WP.156; UNCITRAL, 'Possible Reform of Investor-State Dispute Settlement (ISDS) Submission from the Government of South Africa, Note by the Secretariat', 17 July 2019, UN Doc. A/CN.9/WG.III/WP.176; UNCITRAL, 'Possible Reform of Investor-State Dispute Settlement (ISDS) Submission from the Government of Mali', 17 September 2019, UN Doc. A/CN.9/WG.III/WP.181; UNCITRAL, 'Possible Reform of Investor-State Dispute Ssettlement (ISDS) Submission from the Government of Colombia, Note by the Secretariat', 14 June 2019, UN Doc. A/CN.9/WG.III/WP.173.

[24] Van Harten, Kelsey and Schneiderman, 'Phase 2 of the UNCITRAL ISDS Review', 7; Puig and Shaffer, 'Imperfect Alternatives', 401–408. Shan and Feng argue that politically and socially sensitive cases should be left to local remedies or state-to-state mechanisms. Shan and Feng, 'Trinity Analytical Framework for ISDS Reform', 246.

[25] For example, while the first draft of India's 2015 Model BIT provided the state's right to initiate a counterclaim, the revised 2016 final draft eliminates the possibility of counterclaims (Article 13.2. This point is discussed in Chapter 4, Section 4.3.4.5). See Leikin, Gadodia and Loudon, 'State Doesn't Strike Back After All'. See also Shao, 'Environmental and Human Rights Counterclaims', 167 (on 2019 India-Kyrgyzstan BIT and 2018 Belarus-India BIT).

caused by business activities. The answer depends on whether the judiciary and other dispute settlement organs of the host state satisfy rule of law requirements, including independence, impartiality, effectiveness, and accessibility.[26] As noted in Chapter 2, Section 2.1.1, the reality in many jurisdictions is that domestic judicial institutions fail to meet these requirements, and the vindication of substantive rights are prevented by procedural injustice.[27] The Ecuadorian *Lago Agrio* judgments,[28] the Nicaraguan DBCP cases against Dole Food,[29] and the Mining case in the Democratic Republic of the Congo[30] are only a few examples that demonstrate judicial corruption remains a reality.[31] There are even cases where the host state itself avoids its own judiciary.[32] It is observed that in one contract-based ICSID arbitration initiated by a Tanzanian

[26] For a comparative institutional analysis between investment law and other adjudicatory and non-adjudicatory mechanisms including domestic dispute settlement mechanisms, see Puig and Shaffer, 'Imperfect Alternatives'; Kaufmann-Kohler and Potestà, *Investor-State Dispute Settlement and National Courts.*

[27] Douglas, 'International Responsibility for Domestic Adjudication', 884; Schill, 'Reforming Investor-State Dispute Settlement', 663.

[28] *Aguinda v. ChevronTexaco Corp.*, No. 2011-0106, Sucumbios Provincial Court of Justice, Nueva Loja Appellate Division, 3 January 2012, Ecuador; *Aguinda v. ChevronTexaco Corp.*, No. 002003, Judgment, Provincial Court of Justice, Nueva Loja in Lago Agrio, 14 February 2011, Ecuador. For the misconduct of the Eduadorian courts in this case, see *Chevron Corp. v. Donziger*, 974 F. Supp. 2d 362, 386–546 (SDNY 2014); *Chevron Corp. v. Donziger*, ___ F.3d ___, 2016 WL 4173988 (2d Cir., 8 August 2016); *Chevron Corporation and Texaco Petroleum Corporation v. Republic of Ecuador*, UNCITRAL, PCA Case No. 2009-23, Second Partial Award on Track II, 30 August 2018, parts V–VIII.

[29] In *Mejia v. Dole Food Co.*, Judge Chaney at Los Angeles Superior Court held that the court finds highly credible that the plaintiffs' Nicaraguan counsel 'conspired and colluded with ... corrupt Nicaraguan judges in a position to influence the outcome of DBCP cases' (*Mejia v. Dole Food Co.*, No. BC340049 (Cal. Super. Ct. L.A. Cnty. 15 June 2009), para. 79). See also Percival, 'Liability for Environmental Harm', 60–61.

[30] In the criminal proceedings against the employees of Anvil concerning gross human rights abuses conducted by Congolese troops, the Congolese military courts acquitted all the defendants. In *Institute for Human Rights and Development in Africa and Others v. Democratic Republic of Congo* 10), 18 June 2016, the African /10), 18 June 2016, the African Commission on Human and Peoples' Rights found a violation of Article 26 (Duty to Guarantee Independence of Courts) on the part of the DRC (paras. 132–135). See McBeth, 'Crushed by an Anvil', 143–147.

[31] Relying on Polity IV Project, Political Regime Characteristics and Transitions, 1800–2014, Sloss and Van Alstine conclude that 'Roughly one-third of the countries in the world lack an independent judiciary'. Sloss and Van Alstine, 'International Law in Domestic Courts', 80. Polity5 Project, Political Regime Characteristics and Transitions, 1800–2018, available at: www.systemicpeace.org/inscrdata.html.

[32] Anning, 'Counterclaims Admissibility in Investment Arbitration', 1285.

state-owned enterprise,[33] the claimant's choice of ICSID arbitration as 'an impartial and independent tribunal' was based on its mistrust and fear of corruption in its own domestic institutions.[34]

It is therefore acknowledged that the effectiveness of the approach to accord domestic courts a primary role depends on 'the existence of some level of judicial independence and impartiality in the domestic jurisdiction'.[35] When the host state's judiciary does not meet this standard, assessing the investor's responsibility at an international tribunal will enhance the rule of law.[36]

The issue of the lack of expertise of tribunals in domestic regulatory matters remains. However, as discussed in Chapter 5, Section 5.2.4, this issue should be addressed through the *process* of interpretation and application of domestic law. Specifically, tribunals should make a just appreciation of domestic jurisprudence, and carefully examine the sufficient and balanced sources of the domestic law at issue. To conclude, the disparities between domestic jurisdictions within the judicial capacity and the level of protection of victims justify the need for counterclaims in IIA-based dispute settlement mechanisms.

3.2.2 Enforcement Questions

Another concern over the use of domestic remedies is that in many cases domestic court judgments are difficult to enforce outside the state territory, and therefore in situations where the investor has already withdrawn from the state, the relief against a foreign investor obtained through its national courts is 'at risk never to be executed in full',[37] would have little practical benefit. The lack of enforceability of domestic court judgments against transnational corporations is attributed to the absence of a widely accepted international mechanism concerning the recognition and enforcement of domestic court judgments by other states.[38] Although the Convention on the Recognition and Enforcement

[33] *Tanesco v. IPTL.*

[34] Toral and Schultz, 'State, a Perpetual Respondent in Investment Arbitration?', 590–591.

[35] Puig and Shaffer, 'Imperfect Alternatives', 407.

[36] Bjorklund, 'The Role of Counterclaims', 477; Ishikawa, 'Counterclaims and the Rule of Law', 36–37.

[37] Amado, Kern and Rodriguez, *Arbitrating the Conduct of International Investors*, 7.

[38] Weiler, 'Balancing Human Rights and Investor Protection', 437.

of Foreign Judgments in Civil or Commercial Matters[39] was adopted in July 2019 by the Hague Conference on Private International Law, as of the date of writing (15 December 2021), Uruguay, Ukraine, Israel, Costa Rica, and Russia are the only signatories to the Convention, and the Convention has not yet entered into force.[40]

This is in contrast to the strong enforcement mechanism in place for investment arbitral awards, through which awards issuing monetary compensation are enforceable under the ICSID Convention or the New York Convention (see Chapter 1, Section 1.1). Therefore, in certain circumstances, counterclaims in IIA-based dispute settlement mechanisms are the only effective way of seeking pecuniary damages against a claimant investor.

3.2.3 *Other Benefits of Counterclaims*

The benefits of counterclaims generally applicable to any dispute settlement forum are procedural economy and consistency between claims.[41] Deciding the principal claim and a counterclaim in one set of proceedings would help the adjudicator have an overview of the dispute to fully solve disputes in a single proceeding. This enhances judicial economy,[42] finality and consistency,[43] and thereby protects the integrity of the dispute settlement system.[44]

The benefits particular to IIA-based dispute settlement mechanisms include the following. Counterclaims may incorporate external norms to the IIA, such as environmental and human rights obligations into the

[39] Convention on the Recognition and Enforcement of Foreign Judgments in Civil or Commercial Matters, The Hague, 2 July 2019.

[40] See 'Status Table', available at: www.hcch.net/en/instruments/conventions/status-table/?cid=137 (accessed 15 December 2021). Also, the scope of its application is limited to 'the recognition and enforcement of judgments in civil or commercial matters' (Article 1). See Amado, Kern and Rodriguez, *Arbitrating the Conduct of International Investors*, 7–8.

[41] *Application of the Convention on the Prevention and Punishment of the Crime of Genocide (Bosnia and Herzegovina v. Yugoslavia)* (Order) (Counter-Claims) [1997] ICJ Rep. 243, para. 30.

[42] *David R. Aven and Others v. Republic of Costa Rica*, ICSID Case No. UNCT/15/3, Award, 18 September 2018 (*Aven* Award), para. 741.

[43] Sharpe and Jacob, 'Counterclaims and State Claims', 366.

[44] Ben Hamida, 'L'arbitrage Etat-investisseur cherche son équilibre perdu', 270; Schreuer, Malintoppi, Reinisch and Sinclair, *The ICSID Convention: A Commentary*, 732; Kjos, *Applicable Law in Investor-State Arbitration*, 128; Antonopoulos, *Counterclaims before the International Court of Justice*, 57–59.

resolution of the dispute.[45] Admission of counterclaims might well discourage frivolous claims (by the claimant investor) and frivolous objections (by the defendant state), because the consideration of the possibility of counterclaims will shift the claimant's cost–benefit analysis towards more prudency, and that of the defendant towards processing the case.[46] Counterclaims may serve as a means to enhance procedural equality in IIA-based dispute settlement mechanisms,[47] and thus reduce 'pressure on the regime's legitimacy'.[48]

3.3 Is the Host State the Right (Counter) Claimant?

3.3.1 *Counterclaims Based on Harm Done to Victims*

Despite the benefits of counterclaims described in the previous section, for counterclaims based on environmental and human rights damage allegedly caused by the investor, there arises a question of appropriateness. That is, given the existence of the victims' interest, is it appropriate to allow the host state to become the recipient of compensation for such damage?

In this regard, in *Chevron v. Ecuador (II)*, the respondent presented a '"cross-claim" ... by way of an "offset" (or set-off), unjust enrichment, causation and contributory fault' alleging that Chevron's claims, if successful, would 'gravely prejudice these Lago Agrio Plaintiffs' who suffered environmental damage.[49] The tribunal dismissed these claims, stating, *inter alia*, that: 'the Respondent cannot assert against Chevron (or TexPet) personal rights possessed only by these Aguinda or Lago Agrio Plaintiffs as individuals'.[50] However, this case is distinguished in that the tribunal had concluded, in its First Partial Award, that the respondent state was barred from 'invoking the diffuse constitutional right under

[45] Boisson de Chazournes, 'Environmental Protection and Investment Arbitration', 392; Arcuri and Violi, 'Human Rights and Investor-State Dispute Settlement', 592.

[46] Bjorklund, 'The Role of Counterclaims', 476. See also Vohryzek-Griest, 'State Counterclaims in Investor-State Disputes', 87.

[47] Ben Hamida, 'L'arbitrage Etat-investisseur cherche son équilibre perdu', 271; Sornarajah, *Resistance and Change in the International Law*, 64.

[48] Sharpe and Jacob, 'Counterclaims and State Claims', 366. See also Bubrowski, 'Balancing IIA Arbitration', 215.

[49] *Chevron Corporation and Texaco Petroleum Corporation v. Ecuador (II)*, PCA Case No. 2009-23 (*Chevron v. Ecuador II*), Second Partial Award on Track II, 30 August 2018 (*Chevron II* Second Partial Award), paras. 7.30–7.45.

[50] Ibid., para. 7.40.

Article 19-2 of the [Ecuadorian] Constitution'[51] as well as from raising counterclaims in its own right, due to the effect of the 1995 Settlement Agreement and Article IV of the Final Release between TexPet and the respondent.[52] When such circumstances do not exist, the host state does generally have the legal standing to put forth environmental counterclaims.[53]

The requirement of standing is defined as 'the requirement that a State seeking to enforce the law establishes *a sufficient link* between itself and the legal rule that forms the subject matter of the enforcement action',[54] and the existence of legally protected interests is required to establish the link.[55] Applying this to environmental counterclaims by the host state, it is clear that any sovereign state has a legally protected interest in the harm done to the environment in its territory. The tribunal in *Perenco v. Ecuador* clearly recognised the existence of the host state's right to claim full reparation for environmental damage caused by an investor.[56]

Instead, the question is whether admitting the host states' counterclaims in such circumstances has sufficient normative grounds when it also affects the interest of the victims, which, as discussed in Section 3.4, may impact their admissibility. Based on these considerations, this section demonstrates the existence of such grounds for counterclaims raised both in the host state's interests and on behalf of the victims.

3.3.2 The Host State's Own Interest

In international human rights law, it is now widely recognised that 'the state duty to protect', that is, the state's obligations to protect

[51] *Chevron v. Ecuador II*, First Partial Award on Track I, 17 September 2013, para. 107. The tribunal relied on the definition of 'diffuse rights' agreed by experts that 'indivisible entitlements that pertain to the community as a whole, such as the community's collective right to live in a healthy and uncontaminated environment' (para. 97).

[52] *Chevron II* Second Partial Award, para. 7.41.

[53] Anning, 'Counterclaims Admissibility in Investment Arbitration', 1295; Pauker, 'Admissibility of Claims', 51.

[54] Tams, *Enforcing Obligations Erga Omnes*, 26 (emphasis in original).

[55] Ibid., 29.

[56] *Perenco v. Ecuador*, Interim Decision on the Environmental Counterclaim, 11 August 2015, para. 34. See also Sornarajah, *The International Law on Foreign Investment*, 135. Contra: Scherer, Bruce and Reschke, 'Environmental Counterclaims in Investment Treaty Arbitration', 427.

individuals[57] against human rights abuses committed by private persons and entities in its territory[58] applies to situations where human rights violations, including environmental harm that affects human rights,[59] are committed by business entities.[60] This is the obligation under the customary international law as well as binding human rights agreements.[61] It is also undisputed that in the case of failure to fulfil the obligation to protect, the state has an obligation to provide effective remedies.[62]

The obligation to protect arises from the fact that the state is capable of, and responsible for, taking 'appropriate steps to prevent, investigate, punish and redress private actors' abuse'[63] by exercising its control over the activities of local companies, subsidiaries, and branches of foreign

57 For the purposes of this study, 'individuals' are defined as 'all individuals within its [the host state's] territory and subject to its jurisdiction' (Article 2(1) of the International Covenant on Civil and Political Rights).

58 Human Rights Committee, General Comment No. 31 'The Nature of the General Legal Obligation Imposed on States Parties to the Covenant', 26 May 2004, UN Doc. CCPR/C/21/Rev.1/Add.13 (Human Rights Committee, General Comment No. 31), para. 8. The questions of the existence and scope of an 'extraterritorial' duty of the home states of TNCs to protect against human rights violations through the regulation of transnational business activities is beyond the scope of this study. For analysis of this issue, see e.g. O'Brien, 'Home State Duty'; Krajewski, 'The State Duty'.

59 UNHRC, 'Report of the Special Rapporteur on the Issue of Human Rights Obligations Relating to the Enjoyment of a Safe, Clean, Healthy and Sustainable Environment, Submitted to the 37th Session of the Council', 24 January 2018, UN Doc. A/HRC/37/59, para. 34.

60 See e.g. UN Human Rights Council, 'Report of the Special Representative of the Secretary-General on the Issue of Human Rights and Transnational Corporations and Other Business Enterprises: Business and Human Rights: Mapping International Standards of Responsibility and Accountability for Corporate Acts by John Ruggie, Special Rapporteur', 19 February 2007, UN Doc. A/HRC/4/35; Clapham, *Human Rights in the Private Sphere*, 118–126; Baade, 'Due Diligence and the Duty', 94; Ratner, 'Corporations and Human Rights', 470; Ruggie, 'Business and Human Rights', 828–830; McCorquodale, 'Corporate Social Responsibility', 387–390.

61 Jägers, *Corporate Human Rights Obligations*, 145–146.

62 UN Committee on Economic, Social, and Cultural Rights, 'Statement on the Obligations of States Parties Regarding the Corporate Sector and Economic, Social and Cultural Rights', 12 July 2011, E/C.12/2011/1 (UNCESCR 2011 Statement), para. 3; Article 2(3) of the International Covenant on Civil and Political Rights (ICCPR); Human Rights Committee, General Comment No. 31 (ICCPR), para. 8; Fredman, *Human Rights Transformed*, 87; Shue, *Basic Rights*, 52; Hakimi, 'State Bystander Responsibility', 346–347.

63 Principle 1 of the UN Guiding Principles on Business and Human Rights, available at: www.ohchr.org/Documents/Publications/GuidingPrinciplesBusinessHR_EN.pdf (accessed 15 December 2021). Naturally, these obligations are addressed to legislative, executive, and judiciary branches of government. Peters, 'Corruption as a Violation', 1259.

companies operating within its territory.[64] As a standard of conduct required for states, the due diligence test has been presented as a standard of conduct rather than an obligation of result.[65] The due diligence test requires the consideration of various factors, including the degree of risk, knowledge of potential risk, capacity of the state and control over private actors.[66] The assessment of the circumstances under which the state fails to meet this standard requires a context-specific analysis,[67] and in the context of business and human rights associated with environmental degradation, jurisprudence of the African Commission on Human and Peoples' Rights (see below), the Economic Community of West African States (ECOWAS) Court of Justice,[68] the Inter-American Court of Human Rights,[69] and the European Court of Human Rights[70] provide suggestions.

[64] Besson, *La due diligence en droit international*, 290–291; Krajewski, 'The State Duty', 19.

[65] *Velásquez-Rodríguez v. Honduras*, Judgment of 29 July 1988 (Merits), IACHR Series C No. 4, para. 172; International Commission of Jurists, 'Maastricht Guidelines on Violations of Economic, Social and Cultural Rights', 26 January 1997, guideline 18; Tim Stephen and Duncan French, 'International Law Association Study Group on Due Diligence in International Law: Second Report', 12 July 2016, International Law Association, at 2–5, available at: https://ila.vettoreweb.com/Storage/Download.aspx?DbStorageId=1427&StorageFileGuid=ed229726-4796-47f2-b891-8cafa221685f (accessed 15 December 2021); Baade, 'Due Diligence and the Duty', 92; Nowak and Januszewski, 'Non-State Actors and Human Rights', 142.

[66] ILA Second Report on Due Diligence. See also Baade, 'Due Diligence and the Duty', 100–104.

[67] Baade, 'Due Diligence and the Duty', 100; Besson, *La due diligence en droit international*, 302–306.

[68] *SERAP v. Federal Republic of Nigeria*, ECW/CCJ/JUD/18/12, Judgment, 14 December 2012. In this case, while the Court confirmed the Nigerian government's violation of the African Charter on Human and Peoples' Rights (Articles 1 and 24) resulting from the oil spill in the country (paras. 104–112), it declined to order the Nigerian government the pecuniary compensation for the reason of the 'impractibility' of identifying 'the victims that deserve compensation' (paras. 113–117).

[69] For example, *Kichwa Indigenous People of Sarayaku v. Ecuador*, IACHR, Judgment of 27 June 2012 (Merits and Reparations), IACHR Series C No. 245 (*Kichwa* Judgment); *Community of La Oroya v. Peru*, Petition 1473/06, Report No. 76/09, OEA/Ser.L/V/II., Doc. 51, corr. 1, 5 August 2009; *Yanomami v. Brazil*, Report of 5 March 1985, Case No. 7615, Resolution No. 12/85, March 5, 1985; *Maya Indigenous Community of the Toledo District v. Belize*, Report No. 40/04, Case 12.05, 3, OEA/Ser.L/V/II.122, Doc. 5, rev. 1, 12 October 2004, at 727; *Case of the Mayagna (Sumo) Awas Tigni Community v. Nicaragua*, Judgment of 31 August 2001, IACHR Series C No. 79; *Saramaka People v. Suriname*, Judgment of 28 November 2007 (Preliminary Objections, Merits, Reparations, and Costs), IACHR Series C No. 172.

[70] For example, *Fadeyeva v. Russia*, Application No. 55723/00, Judgment, Merits, and Just Satisfaction of 9 June 2005 (*Fadeyeva v. Russia*); *Öneryidiz v. Turkey*, Judgment,

An example is *Social and Economic Rights Action Center for Economic and Social Rights v. Nigeria*,[71] a case that arose out of environmental degradation, health problems, and human rights violations in the operations of oil production. In this case, the undisputed fact was that the military government of Nigeria was directly involved in oil production through the state oil company as the majority shareholder in a consortium with Shell Petroleum Development Corporation. The African Commission on Human and Peoples' Rights, in its decision, also confirmed that 'the security forces of the government engaged in conduct in violation of the rights of the Ogonis'.[72] On these facts, the Commission concluded that Nigeria, by giving 'the green light to private actors, and the oil Companies in particular, to devastatingly affect the wellbeing of the Ogonis', breached its obligation to protect persons against interferences in the enjoyment of their rights,[73] and thus violated various obligations of the African Charter on Human and Peoples' Rights.[74] The Commission thus appealed to the government of Nigeria 'to ensure protection of the environment, health and livelihood of the people of Ogoniland' by, *inter alia*, '[e]nsuring adequate compensation to victims of the human rights violations, including relief and resettlement assistance to victims of government sponsored raids, and undertaking a comprehensive cleanup of lands and rivers damaged by oil operations'.[75]

In other cases, violations of the state's duty to protect were found by, for example, giving 'acquiescence and protection' to an oil company's operation that planted explosives in indigenous people's territory,[76] and failing to introduce effective measures to reduce air pollution even though the state was aware of the quantifiable environmental damage.[77]

Application No. 48939/99, Judgment of 30 November 2004. See also Jägers, *Corporate Human Rights Obligations*, 157–160; Karavias, *Corporate Obligations under International Law*, 35–38, 177; Scott, 'Multinational Enterprises and Emergent Jurisprudence'; Francioni, 'International Human Rights'; McCorquodale, 'Corporate Social Responsibility', 396; Peterson and Gray, 'International Human Rights in Bilateral Investment Treaties'.

71 *Social and Economic Rights Action Center and the Center for Economic and Social Rights v. Nigeria*, AfComHPR Communication No. 155/96, 27 May 2002.

72 Ibid., para. 54.

73 Ibid., para. 58.

74 Ibid., Holding.

75 Ibid., Holding. See also Adeyeye, 'Corporate Responsibility in International Law', 144–145.

76 *Kichwa* Judgment, paras. 248–249. See also Binder and Hofbauer, 'Case Study: *Burlington Resources Inc. v Ecuador*'.

77 *Fadeyeva v. Russia*, paras. 89–92.

In the context of the International Covenant on Economic, Social and Cultural Rights (ICESCR),[78] the Committee on Economic, Social and Cultural Rights lists how a state party could violate its obligation to protect under the ICESCR in relation to corporate activities. They include, *inter alia*, 'by granting exploration and exploitation permits for natural resources without giving due consideration to the potential adverse impacts of such activities on the individual and on communities' enjoyment of Covenant rights'.[79]

In addition, when the state is found to have been negligent in authorising or monitoring the operation of private business, and this results in environmental and human rights damage, the state may be held responsible for the harm done through its own administrative, civil, criminal, or 'environmental courts, if they exist'.[80] The Supreme Court of Norway recently declared that the Norwegian government had violated the right to enjoy their own culture of the Sámi people, who are reindeer herders, under Article 27 of the ICCPR, by allowing the construction of wind farms that affected winter pastures and thereby the Sámi people's ability to practice their culture.[81]

Given that the state has the obligation to effect payment in the satisfaction of a claim of the victims, it then has the right to seek compensation against the investor accountable to the extent appropriate.[82] The following statement in the Basic Principles and Guidelines on the Right to a Remedy and Reparation for Victims of Gross Violations of International Human Rights Law and Serious Violations of International Humanitarian Law is suggestive on this account:

[78] United Nations, Treaty Series, vol. 993, p. 3.

[79] UN Committee on Economic, Social, and Cultural Rights, 'General Comment No. 24 on State Obligations under the International Covenant on Economic, Social and Cultural Rights in the Context of Business Activities', 10 August 2017, UN Doc. E/C.12/GC/24, para. 18. See also UNCESCR, 2011 Statement, paras. 3–5. See also UN Committee on Economic, Social and Cultural Rights, 'General Comment on State Obligations under the International Covenant on Economic, Social and Cultural Rights in the Context of Business Activities: Draft Prepared by Olivier De Schutter and Zdzislaw Kedzia, Rapporteurs', 17 October 2016, UN Doc. E/C.12/60/R.1, para. 7.

[80] Pigrau, Borràs, Manzano and Cardesa-Salzmann, 'Legal Avenues for EJOs', 39. See also Abramchayev, 'Social Contract Argument', 849–874.

[81] Supreme Court Judgment, 11 October 2021, HR-2021-1975-S (Case No. 20-143891SIV-HRET, Case No. 20-143892-SIV-HRET, and Case No. 20-143893SIV-HRET). Official English translation is available at: www.domstol.no/en/enkelt-domstol/supremecourt/rulings/2021/supreme-court-civil-cases/hr-2021-1975-s/ (accessed 15 December 2021).

[82] See also the discussions by Amado, Kern, and Rodriguez on 'the Espousal Model' (Amado, Kern and Rodriguez, *Arbitrating the Conduct of International Investors*, 52–55).

> ... In accordance with its domestic laws and international legal obligations, a State shall provide reparation to victims for acts or omissions which can be attributed to the State and constitute gross violations of international human rights law or serious violations of international humanitarian law. In cases where a person, a legal person, or other entity is found liable for reparation to a victim, such party should provide reparation to the victim or compensate the State if the State has already provided reparation to the victim.[83]

This forms the basis of the state's right to pursue counterclaims against investors to seek redress in its own right, even when the claims involve the interests of victims.

3.3.3 *Counterclaims 'on behalf of' the Victims: Suggestions from the Parens Patriae Doctrine*

Should, then, the host state be allowed to raise counterclaims on behalf of the victims? In the field of diplomatic protection, a normative justification of the state's claim is given by the 'fiction'[84] of treating the injury done to the citizens of a nation as if the injury was done to the state itself.[85] Although increasingly challenged,[86] this position is still widely accepted.[87] However, host states' environmental counterclaims on behalf of victims differ from the exercise of diplomatic protection in significant aspects. Whereas the latter requires the existence of the alleged breach of *international law by other states*, the former is not subject to such a requirement. Exhaustion of local remedies as a condition for exercising

[83] UN General Assembly, 'Basic Principles and Guidelines on the Right to a Remedy and Reparation for Victims of Gross Violations of International Human Rights Law and Serious Violations of International Humanitarian Law', 21 March 2006, UN Doc. A/RES/60/147.

[84] Dugard, 'Diplomatic Protection and Human Rights', 76.

[85] *Mavrommatis Palestine Concessions (Greece v. U.K.)* (Objection to the Jurisdiction of the Court) (1924) PCIJ Series A, No. 2, at 12.

[86] For example, Pellet argues that this fiction lost its place in the early twenty-first century when private persons were accorded legal personality in international law. Pellet, 'Projet d'Articles de la C.D.I.', 1135–1136.

[87] Article 1 of the Draft Articles on Diplomatic Protection is observed to be 'a faithful copy of the dictum in the Mavrommatis Palestine Concessions case' (Vermeer-Künzli, 'As If: The Legal Fiction', 38). *Ahmadou Sadio Diallo (Republic of Guinea v. Democratic Republic of the Congo)*, (Judgment) (Preliminary Objections) [2007] ICJ Rep. 582, para. 39 (endorsed Article 1 as a reflection of customary international law).

the right of diplomatic protection[88] does not apply. Therefore, normative justifications for such counterclaims should be sought elsewhere, and this section proposes that the rationale for the *parens patriae* doctrine may provide them.

3.3.3.1 History and Development of the *Parens Patriae* Doctrine

An example of the government's claims against a TNC for damages caused by an environmental disaster filed on behalf of its citizens is that of the cases arising out of the Bhopal disaster. Three months after the Bhopal gas leak incident, the Indian government adopted the Bhopal Gas Leak Disaster (Processing of Claims) Act[89] to empower itself as the exclusive legal representative for all claimants, within or outside India, under the doctrine of *parens patriae*. One month after the adoption of the Act, the Indian government filed a case against the Union Carbide Corp in the United States, acting in a *parens patriae* capacity for the victims of the incident. However, the US courts dismissed this claim under the *forum non conveniens* doctrine.[90] In 1986, the Indian government brought the case to its national courts. In 1989, the Supreme Court of India ordered the Union Carbide Corporation to pay USD 470 million to the Indian government in 'full settlement of all claims, rights and liabilities related to and arising out of the Bhopal Gas disaster'.[91]

The *parens patriae* doctrine has its origin in English law and is traced back to the time of King Edward I (1272–1307). The doctrine was first founded on the concept of 'royal prerogative', that is, the king's power of wardship derives from his duty 'to take care of his subjects as are legally unable' to care for themselves on account of mental incapacity proceeding from non-age (children), idiocy, or lunacy. The power of wardship

[88] UN General Assembly, 'Draft Articles on Diplomatic Protection with Commentaries', 1 May–9 June and 3 July–11 August 2006, 61st Session, Supplement No. 10, 2006, UN Doc. A/61/10, Article 14.

[89] Bhopal Gas Leak Disaster (Processing of Claims) Act 1985, adopted on 29 March 1985.

[90] *In re Union Carbide Corp. Gas Plant Disaster at Bhopal in India*, 634 F. Supp. 842 (SDNY 1986) 867. This order was affirmed by the Court of Appeals (Second Circuit) (*In re Union Carbide Corp. Gas Plant Disaster at Bhopal in India*, 809 F 2d. 195 (2d Cir. 1987)). See Baxi, 'Geographies of Injustice'; Butler, '*Parens Patriae* Representation in Transnational Crisis'; Koh, 'Transnational Public Law Litigation', 2370–2371.

[91] *Union Carbide Corporation v. Union of India and Others*, Order of 14 February 1989, [1989] JT (1) 296; [1989] SCALE (1) 380; *Union Carbide Corporation v. Union of India and Others*, Order of 15 February 1989, [1989] 1 SCC 654.

later extended to cover minor heirs in the feudal tenurial system, and this power became a source of profit for the crown.[92]

However, subsequently in the United States, the doctrine of *parens patriae* developed in a very different context. In the beginning of the twentieth century, this doctrine started being used by states as a basis for exercising police power to protect their 'quasi-sovereign' interests such as 'the general comfort, health, or property rights of its inhabitants',[93] before it further evolved into an alternative to class actions for antitrust and other economic claims.[94] In early cases such as *Georgia v. Tennessee Copper Co*,[95] *Missouri v. Illinois*[96] and *Kansas v. Colorado*,[97] environmental and public health concerns were behind the *parens patriae* causes of action for both injunctive relief and damages. Notably, in *New Jersey, Department of Environmental Protection v. Jersey Central Power and Light Co.* in which the State sued a power plant operator for allegedly killing fish in tidal waters by polluting the water and also causing a sharp reduction in water temperature, the New Jersey Superior Court agreed with the trial judge's conclusion that '[t]he State has not only the right but also the affirmative fiduciary obligation to ... seek compensation for any diminution in that trust corpus'.[98]

In Canada, in *British Columbia v. Canadian Forest Products Ltd*, the Attorney General sought compensation for environmental damage caused by a forest fire for which Canadian Forest Products (Canfor) was partially responsible. The majority of the Supreme Court of Canada (opinion delivered by Binnie J.), after citing US cases that acknowledged 'a common law *parens patriae* jurisdiction to represent the collective interests of the public', affirmed the right of the Crown to sue 'for compensation as well as injunctive relief in a proper case on account of public nuisance, or negligence causing environmental damage

92 For the historical origin of the *parens patriae* doctrine, see Custer, 'Origins of the Doctrine of *Parens Patriae*'; Thomas, '*Parens Patriae*'.

93 *North Dakota v. Minnesota*, 263 US 365, 375 (1923). Later, the Supreme Court defined quasi-sovereign interests as including 'its interest in the health and wellbeing – both physical and economic – of its residents in general' (*Alfred L. Snapp & Son, Inc. v. Puerto Rico*, 458 U.S. 592 (1982), 607). See also MacKay, 'Parens Patriae as Basis for Provincial Standing', 977–979.

94 Butler, '*Parens Patriae* Representation in Transnational Crisis', 179.

95 *Georgia v. Tennessee Copper Co.*, 206 US 230 (1907).

96 *Missouri v. Illinois*, 180 US 208 (1901).

97 *Kansas v. Colorado*, 206 US 46 (1907).

98 *State v. Jersey Central Power & Light Co.*, 336 A.2d 750, N.J. Super. Ct. App. Div. 1975, 392.

to public lands'.[99] In these cases, the states were allowed in a *parens patriae* capacity to litigate on behalf of their citizens without proving specific injury to the affected states.[100] In addition to the common law *parens patriae* jurisdictions, there are statutes that explicitly authorise *parens patriae* action.[101]

3.3.3.2 The *Parens Patriae* Doctrine in International Law: Rationale for the Doctrine

Recourse to *parens patriae* doctrine by states to seek reparations on behalf of its citizens for damages to persons, property, economy, and the environment, is also found in several cases heard by international courts and tribunals.[102] Borchard identifies the *parens patriae* doctrine as one of the normative bases that justify the exercise of the right of diplomatic protection.[103] Orrego Vicuña observes that the reliance on the *parens patriae* doctrine in the *Genocide Convention Case (Croatia v. Serbia)* demonstrates a shift away from the 'traditional' interpretation of diplomatic protection (as discussed above).[104] That is, with changes in

[99] *British Columbia v. Canadian Forest Products Ltd.*, [2004] SCC 38; [2004] 2 SCR 74, Judgment of McLachlin C.J. and Iacobucci, Major, Binnie, Arbour and Deschamps JJ (*British Columbia v. Canadian Forest* judgment), para. 81.

[100] Merrill, 'Golden Rules for Transboundary Pollution', 937.

[101] For example, The Comprehensive Environmental Response, Compensation, and Liability Act (CERCLA), 42 USC §9601 et seq. (1980) (US).

[102] *Military and Paramilitary Activities (Nicaragua v. U.S.)* (Merits) [1986] ICJ Rep. 14, at 19; *Case Concerning Application of the Convention on the Prevention and Punishment of the Crime of Genocide (Bosnia & Herzegovina v. Yugoslavia (Serbia & Montenegro)* (Provisional Measures) [1993] ICJ Rep. 3, at 7; *Application of the Convention on the Prevention and Punishment of the Crime of Genocide (Croatia v. Serbia)* (Preliminary Objections) [2008] ICJ Rep. 412, paras. 20–21; *Application of the Convention on the Prevention and Punishment of the Crime of Genocide (Croatia v. Serbia)* (Merits) [2015] ICJ Rep. 3, paras. 49–51; *Application of the International Convention on the Elimination of All Forms of Racial Discrimination (Qatar v. United Arab Emirates)* (Judgment of 4 February 2021) para. 21; Case 86 of the Iran-US Claims Tribunal (in which the US presented the statement of claim 'in continuance of the exercise of diplomatic protection of its nationals, acting as parens patriae, trustee, guardian, and representative on their behalf'). See also Caron, 'Nature of the Iran-United States Claims Tribunal', 133–134.

[103] Borchard, 'Protection of Citizens Abroad', 371. Lee describes the doctrine of *parens patriae* in the domestic context as 'a weaker, domestic cousin' of the international law doctrine of espousal. Lee, 'Supreme Court of the United States', 1855.

[104] International Law Association, Committee on Diplomatic Protection of Persons and Property, 2000, London Conference, available at: www.ila-hq.org/index.php/committees (accessed 15 December 2021). Croatia's claim was rejected on the merits. *Application of the Convention on the Prevention and Punishment of the Crime of Genocide (Croatia v. Serbia)* (Judgment) (Merits) 154.

the international law sphere – in particular given the increasing importance of non-state actors – it may be argued that:

> While the transition from a legal fiction to a different reality takes place, the interesting thought that a claim may actually have a 'dual nature' and represent the interest of both the individual and the state has been advanced.[105]

Certainly, as the US Court of Appeal (1st Circuit) in *Estados Unidos Mexicanos v. Decoster* stated, the *parens patriae* doctrine, in itself, has not acquired the status of customary international law.[106] The US Courts of Appeal, including in the *Bhopal* case, have consistently denied *parens patriae* jurisdiction in the US courts to foreign governments.[107] It would also be difficult to qualify it as 'the general principles of law recognized by civilized nations' within the meaning of Article 38(1)(c) of the International Court of Justice (ICJ) Statute[108] because, as a doctrine that has been developed and practised only in certain common-law countries, it lacks the recognition in 'the principal legal systems of the world'.[109] Likewise, it cannot be considered to constitute universal international law that has been 'consistently found in investment treaties, frequently recognised and applied by tribunals',[110] and therefore may not qualify as a general principle of law that emerges from existing international law.[111]

However, the question of normative justifications for allowing the defendant state to file counterclaims on behalf of the victims concerns neither the jurisdiction of counterclaims, which is determined by reference to the relevant IIAs (this point is discussed in Chapter 4, Section 4.3), nor the legal standing of the host state (see above). Therefore, there is no need to apply the *parens patriae* doctrine to

[105] Orrego Vicuña, 'Interim Report', 468.

[106] *Estados Unidos Mexicanos v. Decoster*, 229 F.3d 332 (1st Cir. 2000), 399.

[107] *Pfizer, Inc. v. Lord.*, 522 F.2d 612 (8th Cir. 1975); *Estados Unidos Mexicanos v. Decoster*.

[108] Cf. Sloss acknowledges the possibility that the *parens patriae* doctrine is a general principle of law recognised by civilised nations. Sloss, 'Using International Court of Justice Advisory Opinions', 375.

[109] International Law Association Study Group, 'Draft Report on the Use of Domestic Law Principles for the Development of International Law', 10 August 2016, para. 213, available at: www.ila-hq.org/images/ILA/DraftReports/DraftReportSG_DomesticLawPrinciples.pdf (accessed 15 December 2021). See also Dumberry, *Guide to General Principles of Law*, 109–121; Yotova, 'Challenges in the Identification'; Bassiouni, 'Functional Approach', 772–775.

[110] Dumberry, *Guide to General Principles of Law*, 40.

[111] Ibid., 35–36.

establish jurisdiction. As discussed in the following section, this is the question of 'propriety' that determines whether such counterclaims should be inadmissible due to the existence of the victims' interest. For this purpose, it suffices that the rationale of the *parens patriae* actions, that they may protect the victims' collective interest in an effective manner provides normative support to the host state's counterclaims on behalf of the victims.

An additional question arises in a situation where the defendant state is also involved in the activities that have caused environmental and human rights damage. Would it be appropriate to allow the state's counterclaim against the investor in cases where the damage is attributable not only to the investor but also to the state? It is submitted here that, even in such circumstances, the state should be allowed to pursue the investor's responsibility to the extent that the liability is apportioned to the investor in order to fulfil its obligation to protect against harms done by private persons. There is no reason to exempt the investor from the obligation to compensate the victims in such circumstances. In this regard, the case of *British Columbia v. Canadian Forest Products Ltd*, in which *parens patriae* jurisdiction was granted by the Supreme Court of Canada (see above), is suggestive. In this case, the trial judge found that the Crown's inadequate firefighting efforts also contributed to the loss resulting from the fire caused by Canfor's negligence, and then divided the responsibility evenly between them. The Court of Appeal varied this decision and allocated 70 per cent of the responsibility to Canfor and 30 per cent to the Crown. The Supreme Court upheld the Court of Appeal's order awarding compensation.[112]

3.4 Limits on the Use of Counterclaims

Inasmuch as the *parens patriae* doctrine has developed as a tool to protect the collective interest of persons who have suffered damages, concerns have also been raised over its use. This section identifies these concerns to conclude that they also apply to the host state's environmental counterclaims filed on behalf of the victims. It then proceeds to examine whether there are grounds on which a tribunal may deny the *admissibility* of the host state's counterclaim.

[112] *British Columbia v. Canadian Forest* judgment, para. 2.

3.4.1 *Concerns over Counterclaims in the Light of the Victims' Interests*

A major concern with *parens patrie* actions is that they may preclude subsequent private litigation brought by the victims, even though there is no mechanism to check in advance the adequacy of the representation of their interests by state attorneys.[113] The affected citizens may wish to file private claims subsequent to *parens patriae* and other public suits, seeking to relitigate the same issues presented in the previous actions. In the subsequent suits brought by the citizens, it is observed that courts tend to presume the adequacy of public representation.[114] There are cases in which all or part of the subsequent individual claims were precluded by preceding *parens patriae* actions.[115] In addition to the issue of representation, concerns are raised over the fact that the affected individuals do not have 'any effective means to monitor and control the attorney general's conduct in the litigation',[116] as well as the absence of the court's duty to assess whether a proposed settlement is 'fair, reasonable and adequate'.[117] Moreover, it is observed that states rarely distribute settlement funds from *parens patriae* in whole to the affected individuals, and often injured citizens do not receive compensation at all.[118]

The *Bhopal* case illustrates some of these concerns: After the orders by the Supreme Court of India instructing Union Carbide Corp. to pay USD 470 million, various groups challenged the settlement for a higher amount of compensation, but the Court confirmed the 1989 orders as 'fair, reasonable and adequate'.[119] The settlement was criticised as

[113] Lemos, 'Aggregate Litigation Goes Public', 503; Hanna, 'The Helicopter State', 1977.

[114] Hanna, 'The Helicopter State', 1983 (citing *Sam Fox Publ'g Co. v. United States*, 366 US 683, 689 (1961) and *Friends of Milwaukee's Rivers v. Milwaukee Metro. Sewerage Dist.*, 382 F.3d 743, 760 (7th Cir. 2004)). Contra: *Richards v. Jefferson County*, 517 US 793 (1996). In this case, the question was whether a previous suit by Birmingham's acting finance director and the city itself challenging a county tax precluded a later taxpayer action, and the Court concluded that the later action was not barred because taxpayers were not adequately represented in the former action.

[115] For example, *Brown and Williamson Tobacco Corp. v. Gault*, 627 S.E.2d 549, 553–554 (Ga. 2006); *Alaska Sport Fishing Ass'n v. Exxon Corp.*, 34 F.3d 769, 773 (9th Cir. 1994); *United States v. Olin Corp.*, 606 F. Supp. 1301, 1303, 1307-08 (N.D. Ala. 1985).

[116] Lemos, 'Aggregate Litigation Goes Public', 511.

[117] This is the requirement prescribed for private class actions under Rule 23(e) of Federal Rules of Civil Procedure.

[118] Lemos, 'Aggregate Litigation Goes Public', 547; Hanna, 'The Helicopter State', 1985.

[119] *Union Carbide Corporation v. Union of India and Others*, [1991] 4 SCC 584. For the disburse of compensation to the *Bhopal* victims, see Shrivastava, 'Category-wise Analysis of Awarded Cases'.

'grossly inadequate',[120] and attempts to challenge the settlement were made in various jurisdictions in India, all of which, however, were rejected.[121]

These concerns squarely apply to the host state's environmental counterclaims filed on behalf of the victims. That is, the host state, which has full control over counterclaims, may compromise the case in a way that undermines the interests of the victims.[122] The victims do not have any rights in the proceedings: The best they can hope for is to influence the tribunal's determination of the issue through *amicus curiae* submissions.[123] There might be conflicts between the victims and the defendant state over 'issues of settlement, appropriate relief, and the like'.[124] Concerns over distribution of compensation also exist, in the absence of an international mechanism to ensure that the victims will actually receive satisfaction from the state action.[125] Scholars identify the issues of representation and a lack of safeguards to ensure the disbursement of compensation and to prevent a compromise of cases inherent in the host state's counterclaims.[126]

In addition, as in the case of *parens patriae* actions, the victims may be barred from subsequently bringing claims in different forums.[127]

[120] The International Council on Human Rights and Policy, 'Beyond Voluntarism: Human Rights and the Developing International Legal Obligations of Companies', International Council on Human Rights and Policy, February 2002, available at: https://papers.ssrn.com/sol3/papers.cfm?abstract_id=1551200 at 80.

[121] See e.g. Steinitz, *Case for an International Court of Civil Justice*, 56–57; Uff, 'La réparation du dommage', 496; Seck and Ogunranti, 'Accountability: Legal Risks and Remedies', 604–605.

[122] Borchard, 'Protection of Citizens Abroad', 363–366 (on *parens patriae* actions). On this risk in the context of principal claims, see Galindo and Elsisi, 'Non-Disputing Parties' Rights in Investor-State Dispute Settlement', 177; Grossman, 'Normative Legitimacy of International Courts', 72–73.

[123] *Amicus curiae* in IIA-based dispute settlement mechanisms is outside the scope of this study. Recent works on this topic include, Baltag, 'The Role of *Amici Curiae*'; Born and Forrest, 'Amicus Curiae Participation in Investment Arbitration'; Dimsey, 'Article 4: Submission by a Third Person'; Malintoppi and Haeri, 'Non-Disputing State Party in Investment Arbitration'; Lamb, Harrison and Hew, 'Recent Developments in the Law and Practice'; Ishikawa, 'Intervention: Investment Arbitration'.

[124] *Estados Unidos Mexicanos v. Decoster*, 399 (on the *parens patriae* doctrine in the United States). See also Orrego Vicuña, 'Interim Report', 632 (on diplomatic protection).

[125] Butler, '*Parens Patriae* Representation in Transnational Crisis', 193. See Chapter 1, Section 1.1.

[126] Cotula and Schröder, 'Community Perspectives in Investor-State Arbitration', 29; Francioni, 'Access to Justice', 738.

[127] Francioni, 'Access to Justice', 738.

Determination on the admissibility of subsequent individual claims will vary depending on the law applicable to the forums to which the claims are brought and the circumstances of each case, but the courts may well deny jurisdiction over these claims on various grounds, such as preclusion by representation or prevention of double payments.[128] On the last point, it should be noted that the New York Convention does not include the possible adverse effect on third parties as one of the grounds for refusal of recognition and enforcement of arbitral awards.[129] When the victims do not receive satisfaction from the state's action, the preclusion of private suits results in a situation where the victims are left without any remedy.

3.4.2 *The Victims' Interests and the Admissibility of Counterclaims*

3.4.2.1 The Concept of Admissibility in the IIA-Based Dispute Settlement Mechanism

These concerns lead to the question of whether there are circumstances in which tribunals should deny the admissibility of the host state's environmental counterclaim. As a prerequisite to answering this question, the applicability of the admissibility concept in the IIA-based dispute settlement mechanism needs to be examined. According to a classic distinction between jurisdiction and admissibility, when a claim is objected to on a ground which does not affect the tribunal's competence to hear and decide the claim but 'affects the possibility or propriety of its deciding the particular case at the particular time', then it is a question of admissibility.[130] Admissibility presupposes jurisdiction, and is to be examined only after the court or tribunal's competence to exercise jurisdiction is established.[131]

128 Sabahi, Duggal and Birch, 'Principles Limiting the Amount of Compensation', 343 (in the context of principal claims); Lemos, 'Aggregate Litigation Goes Public', 547; Hanna, 'The Helicopter State', 1986.

129 Zamir, 'Applicability of the Monetary Gold Principle', 533.

130 Crawford, *Brownlie's Principles of Public International Law*, 667. See also *Certain Questions of Mutual Assistance in Criminal Matters (Djibouti v. France)* (Judgment of 4 June 2008) [2008] ICJ Rep. 177, para. 48; Gouiffès and Ordonez, 'Jurisdiction and Admissibility', 109–110; Heiskanen, 'Ménage à trois?', 237.

131 *Achmea BV v. Slovak Republic [II]*, PCA Case No. 2013-12, Award on Jurisdiction and Admissibility, 20 May 2014, paras. 114–119. See also Boisson de Chazournes, 'Principle of Compétence de la Compétence', 1043; Wehland, 'Jurisdiction and Admissibility in Proceedings', 232; Fontanelli, *Jurisdiction and Admissibility in Investment Arbitration*, 106.

The term 'admissibility' is absent from the ICSID Convention, as well as ICSID and other arbitration rules.[132] This contrasts Article 79 of the ICJ Statute, which explicitly provides the admissibility requirement as separate from jurisdiction. On this basis, the *Methanex* tribunal concluded that under UNCITRAL Arbitration Rules (1976) tribunals have no express power to rule on objections relating to admissibility, and 'it is not possible to infer any implied power' to do so.[133] The tribunal in *Enron v. Argentina* also stated that, as the ICSID Convention 'deals only with jurisdiction and competence', the distinction is not necessary.[134] However, the absence of a reference to admissibility does not automatically mean rejection of the concept,[135] and investment arbitration tribunals[136] and scholars[137] have recognised the function of admissibility that is distinguished from jurisdiction in investment arbitration.

[132] For example, Articles 25 and 41 of the ICSID Convention, Article 21(1) of the UNCITRAL Arbitration Rules.

[133] *Methanex Corporation v. United States of America*, UNCITRAL, Partial Award, 7 August 2002, para. 123.

[134] *Enron Corporation and Ponderosa Assets, L.P. v. Argentine Republic*, ICSID Case No. ARB/01/3, Decision on Jurisdiction, 14 January 2004, para. 33. See also *CMS Gas Transmission Company v. Republic of Argentina*, ICSID Case No. ARB/01/8, Decision of the Tribunal on Objections to Jurisdiction, 17 July 2003, para. 41; *L.E.S.I. S.p.A. and ASTALDI S.p.A. v. République Algérienne Démocratique et Populaire*, ICSID Case No. ARB/05/3, Decision, 12 July 2006, para. 58; *Consortium Groupement L.E.S.I.- DIPENTA v. République algérienne démocratique et populaire*, ICSID Case No. ARB/03/08, Award, 10 January 2005, part II, para. 2; *Supervision y Control S.A. v. Republic of Costa Rica*, ICSID Case No. ARB/12/4, Dissenting Opinion of Joseph P. Klock, 18 January 2017, 6–7. See also Söderlund and Burova, 'Is There Such a Thing as Admissibility?', 527.

[135] Paulsson, 'Jurisdiction and Admissibility', 607–608; Pauker, 'Admissibility of Claims', 69.

[136] For example, *Supervision y Control S.A. v. Republic of Costa Rica*, ICSID Case No. ARB/12/4, Award, 18 January 2017, para. 269 (the majority, arbitrator Klock dissented (Dissenting Opinion of Joseph P. Klock, 18 January 2017, 6–7)); *The Rompetrol Group N.V. v. Romania*, ICSID Case No. ARB/06/3, Decision on Respondent's Preliminary Objections on Jurisdiction and Admissibility, 18 April 2008, para. 112; *Hochtief AG v. Argentine Republic*, ICSID Case No. ARB/07/31, Decision on Jurisdiction, 24 October 2011 (*Hochtief* Decision on Jurisdiction), para. 90 (the majority, arbitrator Thomas disagreed with the majority on whether the non-compliance with a certain provision in the BIT affects jurisdiction or admissibility (Separate and Dissenting Opinion of J. Christopher Thomas, Q.C., 7 October 2011, paras. 31–42)).

[137] For example, Earnest, 'Duty of Arbitrators to Delimitate', 143; Douglas, *The International Law of Investment Claims*, 148; Waibel, 'Investment Arbitration: Jurisdiction and Admissibility', 1214; Reinisch, 'Jurisdiction and Admissibility', 23.

Rather, the question to be asked is the source of the authority of the IIA-based dispute settlement forums to dismiss a case for lack of admissibility: something which has to be found outside the ICSID Convention and arbitration rules.[138] Some argue that such power can be grounded upon the inherent powers of tribunals to preserve the integrity of the proceedings,[139] but this concept is too vague to give any guidance on the scope of the tribunal's discretion in determining the admissibility of the claim. Shany, after identifying the theory of inherent powers as 'a more controversial' ground for international courts to decide admissibility issues, identifies another ground on which the admissibility of a claim can be denied in the following terms:

> [S]ome international courts have upheld their right to decline jurisdiction where the exercise of jurisdiction would have run contrary to a *general international law principle, which binds the parties to the dispute or binds the court itself.*[140]

This applies to IIA-based dispute settlement mechanisms. General principles of law have played an important role in investment case law,[141] including in the determination of the effect of investors' misconduct on the admissibility of investment claims.[142] It is therefore concluded that tribunals do have implied power to determine the admissibility of claims, but the determination needs to be supported by general principles of international law.

138 Steingruber, 'Some Remarks on Veijo Heiskanen's Note', 688.

139 *Waste Management, Inc. v. United Mexican States ('Number 2')*, ICSID Case No. ARB (AF)/00/3, Decision of the Tribunal on Mexico's Preliminary Objection concerning the Previous Proceedings, 26 June 2002, para. 49; Rosenfeld, 'Arbitral Praeliminaria', 149; Newcombe, 'Investor Misconduct', 194 (for abuses of process or other serious forms of misconduct); Paparinskis, 'Inherent Powers of ICSID Tribunals'; Fontanelli, *Jurisdiction and Admissibility in Investment Arbitration*, 142.

140 Shany, 'Jurisdiction and Admissibility', 797 (emphasis added).

141 Dumberry, *Guide to General Principles of Law*, chapter 4; Schill, 'General Principles of Law', 141–145; Gazzini, 'General Principles of Law', 109–113; Kryvoi, 'Counterclaims in Investor-State Arbitration', 248–250; Sornarajah, *The International Law on Foreign Investment*, 105–107.

142 For example, *Vladislav Kim and Others v. Republic of Uzbekistan*, ICSID Case No. ARB/13/6, Decision on Jurisdiction, 8 March 2017, para. 593; *Churchill Mining Plc and Planet Mining Pty Ltd. v. Republic of Indonesia*, ICSID Case No. ARB/12/14 and 12/40, Award, 6 December 2016, paras. 488 and 507; *David Minnotte and Robert Lewis v. Republic of Poland*, ICSID Case No. ARB(AF)/10/1, Award, 16 May 2014, para. 131; *Metal-Tech Ltd. v. Republic of Uzbekistan*, ICSID Case No. ARB/10/3, Award, 4 October 2013, paras. 290–292.

3.4.2.2 The Effect of Third Persons' Interest on the Determination of Admissibility

The next question is whether admissibility of the host state's environmental counterclaim may be denied due to the existence of the victims' interests. In ICJ practice, 'the necessity to join a third party' has been considered to be one of the grounds of the respondent's objections to admissibility.[143] In *Monetary Gold Removed from Rome in 1943*, the Court held that it should decline to exercise its jurisdiction when a third person's legal interests would not only be affected but also 'form the very subject-matter of the decision'.[144] The Monetary Gold principle has received recognition in subsequent cases, and was applied at least in one international arbitration case.[145]

In investment arbitration, the Monetary Gold principle has been relied on in some cases as a means to challenge the admissibility of the investor's principal claims,[146] yet in none of these cases, the principle was applied.[147]

143 Ogbodo, 'Overview of the Challenges', 98; Okowa, 'Issues of Admissibility'.

144 *Monetary Gold Removed from Rome in 1943 (Italy v. France, United Kingdom of Great Britain and Northern Ireland and United States of America)* (Judgment) (Preliminary Question) [1954] ICJ Rep. 19 at 32. See also Thirlway, 'The International Court of Justice', 593; Crawford, *Brownlie's Principles of Public International Law*, 672.

145 *Larsen v. Hawaiian Kingdom*, PCA Case No. 1999-01, Award, 5 February 2001, ILR 119, paras. 11.9–11.24. Other cases that recognised this principle included: *East Timor (Portugal v. Australia)* (Judgment of 30 June 1995) [1995] ICJ Rep. 90, paras. 26–33 (applied the principle); *Military and Paramilitary Activities in and against Nicaragua (Nicaragua v. United States of America)* (Judgment) (Jurisdiction of the Court and Admissibility of the Application) [1984] ICJ Rep. 431, para. 88 (limited the scope of the principle); *Certain Phosphate Lands in Nauru Case (Nauru v. Australia)* (Judgment) (Preliminary Objections) [1992] ICJ Rep. 240, para. 55 (limited the scope of the principle); *Application of the Interim Accord of 13 September 1995 (FYRM v. Greece)* (Judgment of 5 December 2011) [2011] ICJ Rep. 644, paras. 42–43 (distinguished the principle); The South China Sea Arbitration (*The Republic of Philippines v. The People's Republic of China*), Award on Jurisdiction and Admissibility, 29 October 2015, para. 181 and Award, 12 July 2016, para. 640 (distinguished the principle). For other cases that discussed the principle, see Pomson, 'Does the Monetary Gold Principle Apply?'.

146 See also Baetens, 'Procedural Issues Relating to Shared Responsibility', 336–337 (supporting the application of the principle in investment arbitration).

147 *Raiffeisen Bank International AG and Raiffeisenbank Austria d.d. v. Republic of Croatia*, ICSID Case No. ARB/17/34, Decision on Respondent Jurisdictional Objections, 30 September 2020, paras. 288–297; *Addiko Bank AG and Addiko Bank d.d. v. Republic of Croatia*, ICSID Case No. ARB/17/37, Decision on Respondent Jurisdictional Objection Related to the Alleged Incompatibility of the BIT with the EU Acquis, 12 June 2020, paras. 306–307; *SolEs Badajoz GmbH v. Kingdom of Spain*, ICSID Case No. ARB/15/38, Award, 31 July 2019, para. 522; *Ping An Life Insurance Company of China, Limited and Ping An Insurance (Group) Company of China, Limited*

Indeed, in the current framework of IIA-based dispute settlement mechanisms, invoking the Monetary Gold principle as a ground to deny the admissibility of (counter)claims that impact legal interests of third persons would be misplaced, for the following reasons.

The prevailing understanding of the principle is that it gives effect to the principle of consensual jurisdiction, according to which a party's legal interests should not be determined without its consent to the court's jurisdiction.[148] Article 62 of the ICJ Statute provides a third state's right to 'submit a request to the Court to be permitted to intervene' in the proceedings. By contrast, in IIA-based dispute settlement mechanisms, there is no such right for non-parties to the arbitration agreement,[149] and there is no basis for considering the necessity of consent by the third party who can be a party to the court's jurisdiction. This consideration appeared to be behind the *Chevron v. Ecuador (II)* tribunal's rejection of Ecuador's reliance on the Monetary Gold principle as a ground of inadmissibility. Ecuador invoked the principle to argue that 'if Claimants' requested relief were granted, the rights of the third parties to relief in the *Lago Agrio* litigation will arguably be resolved and terminated'.[150] The tribunal, while identifying the due process principle as one of the 'aspects' of the Monetary Gold principle,[151] denied the relevance of the *Logo Agrio* plaintiff's due process rights to the determination of admissibility, on the ground that they did not possess any such rights *in the present investment arbitration proceedings.*

v. Kingdom of Belgium, ICSID Case No. ARB/12/29, Award, 30 April 2015, paras. 127–128; *Niko Resources (Bangladesh) Ltd. v. Bangladesh Petroleum Exploration & Production Company Limited and Bangladesh Oil Gas and Mineral Corporation*, ICSID Case No. ARB/10/18, Decision on Jurisdiction, 19 August 2013, para. 520 (contract-based arbitration).

148 Galindo and Elsisi, 'Non-Disputing Parties' Rights in Investor-State Dispute Settlement', 183; Sparks, 'Reassessing State Consent to Jurisdiction', 29; Jouannet, 'Impossible protection des droits du tiers', 321; Palchetti, 'Litigating Member State Responsibility', 480; Thienel, 'Third States and the Jurisdiction', 344. See also *Daimler Financial Services AG v. Argentine Republic*, ICSID Case No. ARB/05/1, Award, 22 August 2012, para. 175.

149 Zamir, 'Applicability of the Monetary Gold Principle', 534. Reform options that seek to address this issue are discussed in Chapter 7.

150 *Chevron v. Ecuador (II)*, Memorial on Jurisdictional Objections of The Republic of Ecuador, 26 July 2010, para. 168. See also Submission of Amici, 5 November 2010, paras. 6.10–6.14.

151 *Chevron v. Ecuador (II)*, Third Interim Award on Jurisdiction and Admissibility, 27 February 2012 (*Chevron II* Third Interim Award) paras. 4.64–4.68. The other two aspects identified by the tribunal are the 'consent' principle and the 'indispensible third party' principle.

Therefore, the Monetary Gold principle does not directly provide grounds for inadmissibility in IIA-based dispute settlement mechanisms. It is also true that due regard should be paid to the right to due process for disputing parties, whose choice of dispute settlement forum would become unavailable if the admissibility was denied.[152]

Nevertheless, as the *Chevron II* tribunal recognised, due process and procedural fairness requirement is one element that supports the Monetary Gold principle.[153] Scholars observe that it provides one of the 'policy-oriented justifications' for principle,[154] and that it is 'an indirect and ancillary consequence'[155] of the principle. The *Chevron II* tribunal did not rule out the 'theoretical possibility that due process rights of a third party . . . might in some extraordinary case be argued to operate' so as to deny the admissibility of the claim.[156] It is well established that due process is a general principle of international law which, as discussed above, may form the basis of inadmissibility determination.[157] Based on these considerations, it is submitted that, without needing to invoke the Monetary Gold principle, due process may directly form the basis of inadmissibility of an environmental counterclaim, in circumstances when allowing such a counterclaim would result in effective deprivation of remedy for the victims.

Factors to be considered in determining the existence or absence of such circumstances will include the following: The first factor is the state's representation of the interests of its people. Insofar as the relevant host state has representative democracy, legitimacy of the state's representation is presumed.[158] Nonetheless, where there are particular circumstances

152 *Chevron II* Third Interim Award, para. 4.69. See also Mollengarden and Zamir, 'Monetary Gold Principle'.

153 Grossman, 'Normative Legitimacy of International Courts', 82.

154 Mollengarden and Zamir, 'Monetary Gold Principle', 44. See also Grossman, 'Normative Legitimacy of International Courts', 82.

155 Jouannet, 'Impossible protection des droits du tiers', 321 (translation by author). Jouannet admits that 'l'impossibilité de statuer sur les droits d'un tiers au procès peut apparaître comme un principe général de droit partagé par les juridictions de droit interne' (at 339–340).

156 *Chevron II* Third Interim Award, para. 4.69.

157 Cheng, *General Principles of Law as Applied by International Courts and Tribunals*, 291; Schlesinger, 'Research on the General Principles of Law', 743–744; Kotuby Jr. and Sobota, *General Principles of Law*, 86.

158 See e.g. Garsten, 'Representative Government and Popular Sovereignty', 90 ('most of the political science literature simply presumes that the purpose of representative government is to be an instrument of the popular will.'); Galind and Elsisi, 'Non-Disputing Parties' Rights in Investor-State Dispute Settlement', 188.

that raise serious doubts over adequate representation, this presumption is lost. Arguably, one example of such circumstances is when the host state itself was in collusion with the investor in causing damages (as opposed to being merely jointly liable), which strongly indicates the existence of a conflict of interest between the host state and the victims. In such cases, there is a high risk of the case being compromised to the detriment of the victims' interest, with this risk being exacerbated when the state is guided by national elites with 'unique interests far removed from those of much of the population'.[159] The second factor concerns the distribution of the compensation. If there are circumstances that suggest a real possibility that the actual distribution of compensation to the injured people would not follow a successful counterclaim, it can be argued that, in light of the risk that subsequent individual cases are precluded, third persons' legal interests are crucially and negatively affected. The existence or absence of a domestic mechanism for distribution of the funds,[160] as well as the history of public compensation in the host state, will be considered in examining such a risk.

Defects in admissibility (as opposed to defects in jurisdiction) can be cured by acquiescence,[161] and therefore these factors would have to be demonstrated by the investor who contests the admissibility of the counterclaims on the grounds of third persons' legal interests. Admittedly, this would be a difficult task. After all, there is a strong presumption that the host state acts on some public purpose,[162] and tribunals would be very reluctant to interfere with internal political affairs by second-guessing the issues of representation and fair distribution. Despite these practical hurdles, it is important to leave the possibility that the admissibility of counterclaims can be denied in some extraordinary cases, given that the ultimate aim of pursuing the investor's responsibility through environmental counterclaims should be to help to redress the injury and harm done to the victims.

159 Grossman, 'Normative Legitimacy of International Courts', 82.

160 For distribution mechanisms for *parens patriae* actions in the United States, see e.g. Comprehensive Environmental Response, Compensation and Liability Act (CERCLA) or Superfund, section 128(a); Notice of Grant Funding Guidance for State and Tribal Response Programs for Fiscal Year 2021. See also Farmer, 'More Lessons from the Laboratories', 391–405.

161 *Hochtief* Decision on Jurisdiction, paras. 93–95; *Supervision y Control S.A. v. Republic of Costa Rica*, ICSID Case No. ARB/12/4, Final Award, 18 January 2017, para. 273.

162 American Law Institute, *Restatement (Third) of the Foreign Relations Law of the United States*, vol. 2 (American Law Institute) 200 (§712, Comment (e)).

3.5 Conclusion

Raising counterclaims in IIA-based dispute settlement mechanisms has, as demonstrated in this chapter, certain benefits as a way to pursue the investor's responsibility for the harm caused by its operations. The existence of the interests of victims in environmental counterclaims does not affect their admissibility, except for in certain limited circumstances where the admissibility should be denied on the basis of the due process rights of the victims.

Admittedly, counterclaims, even if successful, offer only partial remedies to the issue of asymmetry in the IIA regime. Counterclaims are only reactive and always have to wait for the investor's filing of its principal claim. Moreover, counterclaims remain an indirect means to redress the injury and harm done to victims who have neither the right to initiate nor intervene in proceedings under the current mechanism. These are limitations in the current mechanisms, and Chapter 7 discusses reform options that seek to address these limitations.

Nevertheless, as discussed in Chapter 1, Section 1.5.1, IIA-based dispute settlement mechanisms will continue to receive investors' principal claims. As discussed in Chapter 1, Section 1.4, amid the growing criticisms of various stakeholders of the regime regarding the latter's one-sidedness, the regime must address the issue of investor responsibility to continue receiving the trust and acceptance from its stakeholders. This indicates the persisting value of counterclaims as a tool not only for rebalancing the procedural inequality in IIA-based dispute settlement mechanisms but also to advance the concept of responsible investment in the IIA regime.

4

Counterclaims

Jurisdiction and Admissibility

4.1 Introduction: The Unsettled Questions

Chapter 3 demonstrated the benefits and value of counterclaims in international investment agreement (IIA)-based dispute settlement mechanisms. However, in the current practice, the question of under which circumstances jurisdiction and admissibility of counterclaims can be established remains unsettled. This uncertainty has led to a pessimistic appraisal of the possibility of raising counterclaims as an option that is not readily available to the host state.[1] Therefore, clarification of this subject is necessary for consistent practice on counterclaims, which will help to promote its use by defendant states.[2]

For this purpose, Section 4.2 identifies the requirements of jurisdiction and the admissibility of counterclaims. Section 4.3 argues that jurisdiction is determined by the language of the applicable IIA, in particular the dispute settlement provisions. While the applicable IIA can be an insurmountable jurisdictional barrier over counterclaims, the statistical analysis of the IIA dataset reveals that consent to the host state's counterclaim can be found in a majority of existing IIAs. Section 4.4 examines selected questions concerning the admissibility of counterclaims other than the issue of the third person's interest, which was the issue discussed in the previous chapter. Among the different grounds on which the admissibility of the host state's counterclaims may be denied,[3] it addresses the

[1] Francioni, 'Access to Justice', 72.

[2] Harrison, 'Environmental Counterclaims', 486.

[3] Investment case law reveals the following as other such grounds covered by the notion of admissibility: exhaustion of local remedies, negotiation periods, waiver, contractual exclusive jurisdiction clauses, absence of standing, issues relating to the judicial/arbitral function, mootness of the claim, 'Fork-in-the-Road' clauses, abuse of rights/process, illegality and corruption. See Pauker, 'Admissibility of Claims', 8–64; Anning, 'Counterclaims Admissibility in Investment Arbitration', 1295.

following concerns: the requirement of a 'close connection' between principal claims and counterclaims, and a parent company's liability under a counterclaim based on an alleged damage caused by its local subsidiary.

4.2 Conditions for Filing Counterclaims

In *Application of the Genocide Convention (Bosnia and Herzegovina v. Yugoslavia)*, the International Court of Justice (ICJ) defined a counterclaim as 'an autonomous legal act', as it is 'independent of the principal claim in so far as it constitutes a separate "claim"'.[4] As an autonomous claim by which the host state seeks a remedy on separate grounds,[5] counterclaims must meet the requirements of jurisdiction and admissibility 'in the same way the main claim does'[6] in order to be admitted.

Article 46 of the ICSID Convention and Rule 40(1) of the ICSID Arbitration Rules[7] provide the following three conditions for filing counterclaims in the absence of the parties' agreement: (a) they arise directly out of the subject matter of the dispute; (b) they are within the scope of the consent of the parties; and (c) they are otherwise within the jurisdiction of the Centre. Article 19(3) of the 1976 UNCITRAL Arbitration Rules provides that a 'respondent may make a counter-claim arising out of the same contract'. This 'limitation to contracts' was criticised as being too narrow in the context of the rise in arbitrations based on IIA.[8] Article 21(3) of the 2010 UNCITRAL Arbitration Rules thus removed the reference to a contract to state that: 'the respondent may make a counterclaim ... provided that the arbitral tribunal has jurisdiction over it'.[9] The International Chamber of Commerce (ICC)

[4] *Application of the Convention on the Prevention and Punishment of the Crime of Genocide (Bosnia and Herzegovina v. Serbia and Montenegro)* (Order) (Counter-Claims) 1997, [1997] ICJ Rep. 243, 256, para. 27. See also Antonopoulos, *Counterclaims before the International Court of Justice*, 53, 57.

[5] Murphy, 'Counter-Claims Article 80 of the Rules', para. 1; Anzilotti, 'Demande reconventionnelle en procédure internationale', 875–876 (in the context of proceedings of Permanent Court of International Justice (PCIJ)).

[6] *David R. Aven and Others v. Republic of Costa Rica*, ICSID Case No. UNCT/15/3, Award, 18 September 2018 (*Aven* Award), para. 745.

[7] ICSID Rules of Procedure for Arbitration Proceedings, April 2006.

[8] Paulsson and Petrochilos, 'Revision of the UNCITRAL Arbitration Rules'.

[9] See Atanasova, Martínez Benoit and Ostřanský, 'Counterclaims in Investor–State Dispute Settlement', 9–10.

and Stockholm Chamber of Commerce (SCC) Rules of Arbitration also provide certain procedural requirements on counterclaims.[10]

These non-ICSID arbitration rules, except for Article 19(3) of the 1976 UNCITRAL Rules are silent on the requirement of the connection between the principal claim and the counterclaim. However, this should be a generally applicable requirement, given the fundamental rationale for admitting counterclaims of enhancing procedural economy and consistency.[11] Therefore, the three elements for filing counterclaims under Article 46, as identified above, are applied analogously to cases under non-ICSID arbitration rules.[12] The ICSID Convention, ICSID Arbitration Rules, and non-ICSID arbitration rules are clear in that they do not establish jurisdiction over counterclaims.[13] In IIA-based dispute settlement mechanisms, in the absence of the parties' agreement, jurisdiction must be established by examining whether these requirements are met under the relevant IIA[14] and other circumstances of the case.

The next question is whether each of these requirements is jurisdictional or conditions for the admissibility of the claim. As discussed in Chapter 3, Section 3.4.2.1, jurisdiction concerns the competence of the tribunal to hear and decide the claim, while admissibility concerns the question of whether the presented claim should be dismissed on grounds other than merits. Applying this distinction, it is clear that the consent and the 'otherwise within the jurisdiction of the Centre' requirements[15] are jurisdictional. Conversely, the wording of Article 46 of the ICSID

[10] Article 5 of the 2021 ICC Arbitration Rules; Article 9 of the 2017 SCC Arbitration Rules. See also Article 9 of the 2021 Vienna International Arbitral Centre Rules of Investment Arbitration.

[11] See *Limited Liability Company Amto v. Ukraine*, SCC Case No. 080/2005, Final Award, 26 March 2008 (*AMTO* Award), para. 118.

[12] See Bjorklund, 'The Role of Counterclaims', 473.

[13] *Oxus Gold plc v. Republic of Uzbekistan, the State Committee of Uzbekistan for Geology & Mineral Resources, and Navoi Mining & Metallurgical Kombinat*, UNCITRAL, Award, 17 December 2015 (*Oxus* Award), para. 944; See also *Saluka Investments B.V. v. Czech Republic*, UNCITRAL, Decision on Jurisdiction over the Czech Republic's Counterclaim, 7 May 2004 (*Saluka* Decision on Counterclaim), para. 39; *Sergei Paushok, CJSC Golden East Company and CJSC Vostokneftegaz Company v. Government of Mongolia (Paushok v. Mongolia)*, UNCITRAL, Award on Jurisdiction and Liability, 28 April 2011 (*Paushok* Award), para. 689.

[14] *AMTO* Award, para. 118; *Oxus* Award, paras. 944–945.

[15] The tribunal in *Teinver v. Argentina* acknowledged that, for ICSID arbitration, this includes the requirement that a counterclaim must involve 'a legal dispute'. *Teinver S.A., Transportes de Cercanías S.A. and Autobuses Urbanos del Sur S.A. v. Argentine Republic*, ICSID Case No. ARB/09/1, Award, 21 July 2017, paras. 1065–1066.

Convention clearly suggests that the connection ('arising directly') requirement is distinguished from jurisdictional requirements.[16]

The distinction between the connection requirement and jurisdictional requirements is recognised in the rules and practice of the ICJ. Article 80 of the 1978 Rules of the International Court of Justice (amended in 2001) provides that:

> The Court may entertain a counter-claim only if it comes within the jurisdiction of the Court and is directly connected with the subject-matter of the claim of the other party.

In *Jurisdictional Immunities of the State (Germany v. Italy)*, the ICJ recognised this distinction by stating that admissibility of counterclaims 'must be understood broadly to encompass both the jurisdictional requirement and the direct-connection requirement'.[17]

It is therefore concluded that the connection requirement must be satisfied separately from the establishment of jurisdiction, as a matter of admissibility.[18] Section 4.3 examines jurisdictional requirements for counterclaims, before discussing issues of admissibility in Section 4.4.

4.3 Jurisdictional Requirements

4.3.1 Consent as the Key Element in Determining Jurisdiction over Counterclaims

The first draft of the ICSID Convention (Article 49)[19] provided only the 'arising directly' requirement and the 'otherwise within the jurisdiction of the Centre' requirement, in a manner similar to paragraph 1 of Article 63 of the 1946 Rules of the International Court of Justice (now Article 80 of the 1978 Rules, cited above).[20] The consent requirement was then singled

[16] Atanasova, Martínez Benoit and Ostřanský, 'Counterclaims in Investor–State Dispute Settlement', 37.

[17] *Jurisdictional Immunities of the State (Germany v. Italy)* (Order) (Counter-Claims) [2010] ICJ Rep. 310, para. 14.

[18] *Metal-Tech Ltd. v. Republic of Uzbekistan*, ICSID Case No. ARB/10/3, Award, 4 October 2013 (*Metal-Tech* Award), para. 407.

[19] ICSID, 'History of the ICSID Convention: Documents concerning the Origin and the Formulation of the Convention on the Settlement of Investment Disputes between States and Nationals of Other States', 1970 (History of the ICSID Convention), Vol. I, at 206.

[20] Rules of Court, entered into force in 1978, available at: www.icj-cij.org/en/rules (accessed 15 December 2021). It required that a counterclaim comes within the jurisdiction of the Court and is directly connected with the subject-matter of the claim of the other party for the Court to entertain a counterclaim. A reference to Article 63 of the Rules of the

out from other jurisdictional requirements in the final text of Article 46 of the Convention.[21] Given that consent is already one of the jurisdictional conditions of the tribunal,[22] this change indicates that the wording of Article 46 reflects the emphasis placed by the drafters on this element.

In *Roussalis v. Romania*, the majority of the tribunal brought the issue of 'the consent of the parties' in Article 46 of the ICSID Convention to the forefront in the assessment of jurisdiction over counterclaims by identifying it as 'the first issue' the tribunal must determine 'irrespective of the particular counterclaims advanced in these proceedings'.[23] Subsequent ICSID tribunals have generally treated the requirement of consent as the first hurdle to overcome to establish jurisdiction.[24]

4.3.2 *Scope of the Consent to Arbitration*

As noted in Chapter 3, Section 3.1, in IIA-based arbitration, consent to arbitration given by the host state in the IIA is to be perfected by the investor's submission of a request for arbitration which meets the conditions and procedural requirements provided in the relevant IIA. Some scholars argue that mutual consent of the parties to arbitration exists only to the extent of the investor's particular consent, for '[t]here would normally be no reason for the consent of the investor to be broader than is necessary' to establish jurisdiction over its own specific claim.[25]

International Court of Justice is found in *travaux préparatoires* of the Convention (History of the ICSID Convention Vol. II-1, 422). See also *Antoine Goetz and Others and S.A. Affinage des Metaux v. Republic of Burundi* (*Goetz v. Burundi II*), ICSID Case No. ARB/01/2, Award, 21 June 2012 (*Goetz v. Burundi II* Award), para. 273.

21 See also History of the ICSID Convention, Vol. II-1, 422 (statement by Alan Broches).

22 See *Goetz v. Burundi II* Award, para. 274.

23 *Spyridon Roussalis v. Romania (Roussalis v. Romania)*, ICSID Case No. ARB/06/1, Award, 7 December 2011 (*Roussalis* Award), para. 864 (the majority).

24 See *Inmaris Perestroika Sailing Maritime Services GmbH and Others v. Ukraine*, ICSID Case No. ARB/08/8, Award, 1 March 2012 (*Inmaris* Award), para. 432; *Goetz v. Burundi II* Award, para. 278; *Metal-Tech* Award, para. 408; *Vestey Group Ltd. v. Bolivarian Republic of Venezuela*, ICSID Case No. ARB/06/4, Award, 15 April 2016 (*Vestey* Award), para. 333; *Urbaser S.A. and Consorcio de Aguas Bilbao Bizkaia, Bilbao Biskaia Ur Partzuergoa v. The Argentine Republic* (*Urbaser v. Argentina*), ICSID Case No. ARB/07/26, Award, 8 December 2016 (*Urbaser* Award), para. 1147; *Karkey Karadeniz Elektrik Uretim A.S. v. Islamic Republic of Pakistan*, ICSID Case No. ARB/13/1, Award, 22 August 2017 (*Karkey* Award), para. 1011. Cf: *Tethyan Copper Company Pty Limited v. Islamic Republic of Pakistan*, ICSID Case No. ARB/12/1, Decision on Jurisdiction and Liability, 10 November 2017 (*Tethyan Copper* Decision on Jurisdiction and Liability).

25 Shihata and Parra, 'Experience of the International Centre for Settlement', 320. See also Schreuer, Malintoppi, Reinisch and Sinclair, *The ICSID Convention: A Commentary*, 756.

This approach effectively eliminates the possibility of the host state's submission to raise a counterclaim. However, such a restrictive position is inconsistent with Article 46 of the ICSID Convention, which requires the tribunal to determine ancillary claims upon fulfilling the three conditions, unless otherwise agreed upon by the disputing parties.[26] As Douglas points out, restrictive reading also leads to unreasonable consequences, such as precluding the possibility of amending or supplementing the investor's principal claims during the course of arbitration, 'as this would be a derogation from the meeting of the minds of the parties upon the perfection of the arbitration agreement'.[27] Another point is that limiting the scope of consent would amount to a modification of the terms of the offer by the offeree.[28] This constitutes a counter-offer, which requires an acceptance on the part of the counter-offeree in order to conclude the agreement.[29]

Therefore, to conclude an arbitration agreement by simply filing a request for arbitration, the claimant investor must accept the 'offer as set out in that treaty, nothing more and nothing less'.[30] Thus, whether or not the host state's offer to arbitration extends to them, is crucial to determine the presence or absence of consent to jurisdiction over counterclaims.

4.3.3 *Different Approaches to Finding Consent to Counterclaims*

With regard to the question of how consent to ancillary claims must be given, investment arbitration tribunals have adopted different approaches. The first approach is to scrutinise the language of the dispute resolution clause of the relevant IIA in which the host state's consent is expressed,[31] an approach adopted by the majority of the *Roussalis* tribunal. The second approach, which was advanced by Professor

[26] Burda, 'Consentement aux demandes reconventionnelles', 47. See also Bravin and Kaplan, 'Arbitrating Closely Related Counterclaims at ICSID', 6–7; Schreuer, Malintoppi, Reinisch and Sinclair, *The ICSID Convention: A Commentary*, 33.

[27] Douglas, 'Enforcement of Environmental Norms', 429.

[28] Ben Hamida, 'L'arbitrage Etat-investisseur cherche son équilibre perdu', 269.

[29] For example, Andrews, *Contract Law*, 58; Code civil (France), Article 1118, al. 3; Civil Code (Japan), Article 528.

[30] Kjos, *Applicable Law in Investor-State Arbitration*, 35. See also *Urbaser* Award, para. 1147; *Wintershall Aktiengesellschaft v. Argentine Republic*, ICSID Case No. ARB/04/14, Award, 8 December 2008 (*Wintershall* Award), para. 160; Douglas, *The International Law of Investment Claims*, 258.

[31] Lalive and Halonen, 'On the Availability of Counterclaims', 146.

Reisman in his dissent to the *Roussalis* majority decision,[32] considers that where the host state's consent to ICSID jurisdiction over the dispute exists, the consent to ancillary claims is '*ipso facto* imported into any ICSID arbitration'.[33] This approach is based on the consideration that rejecting jurisdiction over counterclaims would force the defendant state to 'pursue its claims in its own courts', thereby constraining the investor as the defendant at a forum it avoided when filing its principal claims.[34] The tribunal in *Goetz v. Burundi II* appears to have endorsed the 'importing consent' approach.[35]

However, a fundamental issue with this approach is that it would amount to presuming the existence of the consent without assessing the applicable IIA. This is not consistent with the principle that in international adjudication 'non-consent is the default rule; consent is the exception'.[36] Even though the 'importing consent' approach may better achieve procedural efficiency and consistency, this cannot justify introducing a relaxed standard for the consent requirement for counterclaims.[37] Moreover, this approach is not consistent with Article 46 of the ICSID Convention, primarily because it would make the consent requirement 'entirely circular and extraneous'.[38] Nor is this approach supported by the *travaux preparatoires* of the ICSID Convention,[39] which demonstrate the drafters' intention that Article 46 was 'in no way intended to

[32] *Roussalis v. Romania*, Declaration by W. Michael Reisman, 28 November 2011.

[33] Ibid.

[34] Ibid.

[35] *Goetz v. Burundi II* Award, paras. 279–280.

[36] *Daimler Financial Services AG v. Argentine Republic*, ICSID Case No. ARB/05/1, Award, 22 August 2012 (*Daimler* Award), para. 175 (the majority, Arbitrator Brower disagreed with the majority opinion that 'consent to international arbitration via an MFN [most favoured nation] clause "requires affirmative evidence"' (Dissenting Opinion of Judge Charles N. Brower, 15 August 2012, para. 2)); *Wintershall* Award, para. 160. See also *Factory at Chorzów (Germany v. Poland)* (Jurisdiction) (1927) PCIJ, Series A, No. 9, at 32.

[37] Pathak, 'Consenting to Counterclaims', 112.

[38] Kalicki, 'Counterclaims by States in Investment Arbitration'. See also Kjos, 'Counterclaims by Host States', 25; Popova and Poon, 'From Perpetual Respondent to Aspiring Counterclaimant?', 230; De Nanteuil, 'Counterclaims in Investment Arbitration', 379.

[39] Recourse to *travaux preparatoires* as 'supplementary means of interpretation' is permitted under Article 32 of the Vienna Convention on the Law of Treaties (Vienna Convention on the Law of Treaties, 23 May 1969, in force 27 January 1980, 1155 UNTS 331). See in particular Dörr, 'Article 32', 574–578; Gardiner, *Treaty Interpretation*, 327; Mortenson, '*Travaux* of *Travaux*', 820–822.

extend the jurisdiction of the arbitral tribunal'.[40] Lastly, it should be noted that in *Goetz v. Burundi II*, the tribunal did also confirm that the wording of the dispute resolution clause in the Belgium-Luxembourg-Burundi BIT (Article 8) was broad enough to cover the grounds for counterclaim advanced by the respondent.[41] The approaches by the *Roussalis* majority and *Goetz v. Burundi II* tribunal are therefore reconcilable, both reflecting 'a careful analysis . . . of the wording of the dispute resolution provisions'.[42]

For these reasons, it is concluded that consent to jurisdiction over counterclaims must be established through the interpretation of the relevant IIA. In assessing the question of whether the host state's offer to arbitration extends to counterclaims, of particular importance are the dispute resolution clauses in the IIAs.

4.3.4 *Dispute Resolution Clause: Different Wording between IIAs and Interpretative Options*

4.3.4.1 Provisions on Counterclaims in IIAs

Dispute settlement clauses of some IIAs provide an indication that counterclaims are excluded from the scope of the tribunal's jurisdiction. For example, Article 8(3) of the UK-Venezuela BIT provides that:

> The jurisdiction of the arbitral tribunal shall be limited to determining whether there has been a breach by the Contracting Party concerned of any of its obligations under this Agreement, whether such breach of its obligations has caused damage to the national or company concerned, and, if such is the case, the amount of compensation.

In *Anglo American Plc v. Venezuela*, a case based on this BIT, the tribunal dismissed jurisdiction on counterclaims, stating that the restrictive wording of the arbitration offer in Article 8(3) excludes 'the possibility that the Counter-claim is "within the scope of the arbitration

[40] 'Summary Record of Proceedings, Geneva Consultative Meeting of Legal Experts, February 17–22 1964', in History of the ICSID Convention Vol. II-1, 367, 422.

[41] *Goetz v. Burundi II* Award, paras. 276–277. See also Steingruber, '*Antoine Goetz and others v Republic of Burundi*', 296 (stating that Article 8 includes disputes concerning 'the interpretation or application of any investment authorisation granted by the authorities of the host state governing foreign investments' (translation by author)). Cf. De Nanteuil, 'Counterclaims in Investment Arbitration', 379 (presenting a different reading of Article 8).

[42] Steingruber, '*Antoine Goetz and others v Republic of Burundi*', 296. Contra: Kendra, 'State Counterclaims in Investment Arbitration', 594.

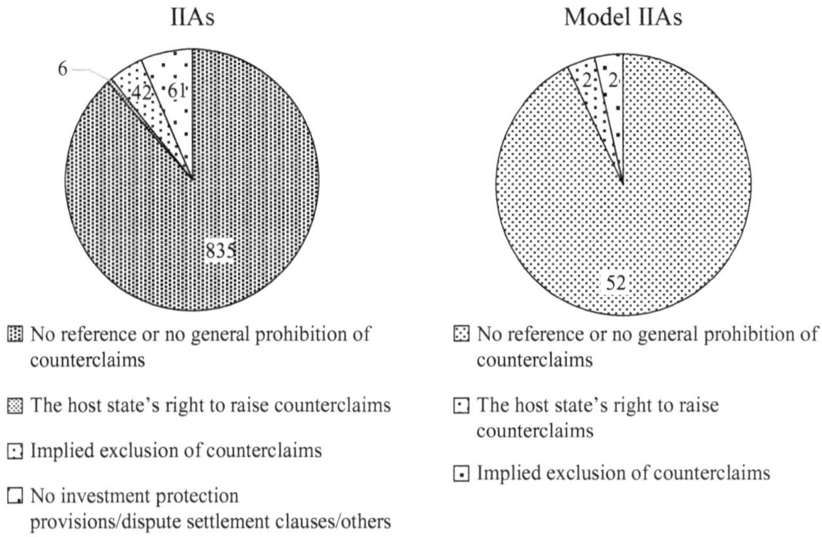

Figure 4.1 Provisions on counterclaims

agreement of the parties"'.[43] Among the IIA dataset, forty-four (forty-two IIAs, two model IIAs) indicate general exclusion of counterclaims, by limiting the scope of the tribunal's jurisdiction or the award of the tribunal to a determination of the defendant state's breach of the IIA obligations, in a similar manner to Article 8(3) of the UK-Venezuela BIT (Figure 4.1). It should be noted that, among these IIAs, only five provide a broad scope of investment disputes (see Section 4.3.4.5).

Conversely, Article 14(3) of the 2016 Iran-Slovakia BIT explicitly provides that the host state may assert as a counterclaim that 'the claimant has not fulfilled its obligations under this Agreement to comply with the Host State law'. Article 19.2 of the 2012 Southern African Development Community (SADC) model investment treaty, which provides investor obligations (Chapter 2, Section 2.3.2), also provides the host state's right to initiate a counterclaim 'for damages or other relief resulting from an alleged breach of the Agreement'. Article 9.19 (suspended by Article 2) of the Comprehensive and Progressive Agreement for Trans-Pacific

[43] *Anglo American Plc v. Bolivarian Republic of Venezuela*, ICSID Case No. ARB(AF)/14/1, Award, 18 January 2019, paras. 527–528. See also *Vestey* award, para. 333 (the tribunal however relied not on Article 8(3) but the narrow definition of the investment dispute in Article 8(1)).

Partnership (CPTPP) provides the state's right to file counterclaims, albeit in a limited situation where the principal claim is based on an investment authorisation or investment agreement. However, provisions on the host state's right to raise counterclaims remain highly exceptional. According to the IIA dataset, among the 1,000 IIAs and model IIAs (collectively 'IIAs'), only eight (six IIAs, two model IIAs) provide the respondent state's right to raise counterclaims (four IIAs, including CPTPP, with a limited scope) (Figure 4.1).

Notably, 104 IIAs (93 IIAs, 11 model IIAs) explicitly exclude counterclaims but in a very limited context, by prohibiting those based on the claim that the investor 'has received or will receive, pursuant to an insurance or guarantee contract, indemnification or other compensation for all or part of its alleged damages'. In *Aven v. Costa Rica*, the tribunal discussed this type of limited exclusion of counterclaims (Article 10.20.7 of the CAFTA-DR). After confirming the broad definition of an 'investment dispute' in CAFTA-DR, it stated that, except for the cases stipulated in Article 10.20.7, the host state's right to counterclaim under the CAFTA-DR 'is contemplated and falls within the scope of jurisdiction'.[44] These partial counterclaim exclusions are therefore not considered as prohibitive in general, and categorised in Figure 4.1 as IIAs that provide 'no general prohibition of counterclaims'.

4.3.4.2 Relevant Factors in Assessing the Scope of Consent to Counterclaims

Where the relevant IIAs are silent on counterclaims, tribunals have taken into account the following elements in assessing whether the host state's offer to arbitration extends to counterclaims: (a) the scope of arbitrable disputes as expressed in the dispute resolution clause; (b) the presence or absence of a reference to the host state's *locus standi*;[45] and (c) the applicable law clause in the relevant IIA, if any. The next sections examine these elements to demonstrate that the decisive factor is the scope of arbitrable disputes and arbitrable claims as expressed in the dispute resolution clause.

4.3.4.3 Locus Standi

Dispute settlement provisions of many IIAs provide that the investor may submit its claim to arbitration without a reference to the host state's

[44] *Aven* Award, para. 693.

[45] Kjos, *Applicable Law in Investor-State Arbitration*, 133.

locus standi. In *Karkey v. Pakistan*, the dispute resolution clause (Article VII) of the applicable 1995 Turkey-Pakistan BIT provided a broad definition of disputes (see Section 4.3.4.5). Nevertheless, the tribunal rejected its jurisdiction over Pakistan's counterclaim on the following two grounds: (a) absence of provisions on counterclaims in the BIT and (b) Article VII referred only to the investor's right to file claims to arbitration.[46] The same approach was adopted by the tribunal in *Iberdola Energía, S.A. (Spain) v. The Republic of Guatemala (II)*.[47] Bubrowski also argues that offers to arbitrate counterclaims can be given in IIA dispute resolution clauses only when they 'accord to host states the right to bring an action against an investor'.[48]

However, in dispute settlement clauses of IIAs, the investor's *locus standi* is defined in the context of the filing of a *principal claim*. Accordingly, it can be argued that the absence of reference to the host state's right to file a counterclaim, which is always responsive to the principal claim, is a logical choice and does not necessarily indicate the parties' intention to exclude counterclaims.[49] Indeed, to establish jurisdiction over principal claims, a reference to the host state's *locus standi* in IIAs is practically speaking of little significance, as the investor's separate written consent to arbitration would always be necessary. This suggests another reading of the unilateral reference to the investor's *locus standi*, that it is 'to underline the host State's willingness and unequivocal consent to arbitrate'.[50]

In *Inmaris v. Ukraine*, the relevant dispute settlement clause (Article 11 of the Germany-Ukraine BIT) provided a narrow *locus standi*, whereas broadly defining investment disputes as those 'with regard to investments'. The tribunal concluded that the broad definition of investment disputes was decisive in establishing its jurisdiction over the

[46] *Karkey* Award, paras. 1012–1014. See also *Iberdola Energía, S.A. (Spain) v. Republic of Guatemala (II)*, PCA Case No. 2017-41, Final Award, 24 August 2020, paras. 386–390.

[47] *Iberdola Energía, S.A. (Spain) v. Republic of Guatemala (II)*, PCA Case No. 2017-41, Final Award, 24 August 2020 (*Iberdola* Award) paras. 386–390. See also *Marco Gavazzi and Stefano Gavazzi v. Romania*, ICSID Case No. ARB/12/25, Decision on Jurisdiction, Admissibility and Liability, 21 April 2015 (*Gavazzi* Decision on Jurisdiction) paras. 151, 153 (the majority, see Dissenting Opinion by Arbitrator Mauro Rubino-Sammartano, 14 April 2015).

[48] Bubrowski, 'Balancing IIA Arbitration', 221. See also Hoffmann, 'Counterclaims in Investment Arbitration', 450.

[49] Atanasova, Martínez Benoit and Ostřanský, 'Counterclaims in Investor–State Dispute Settlement', 16.

[50] Kjos, 'Counterclaims by Host States', 21–22.

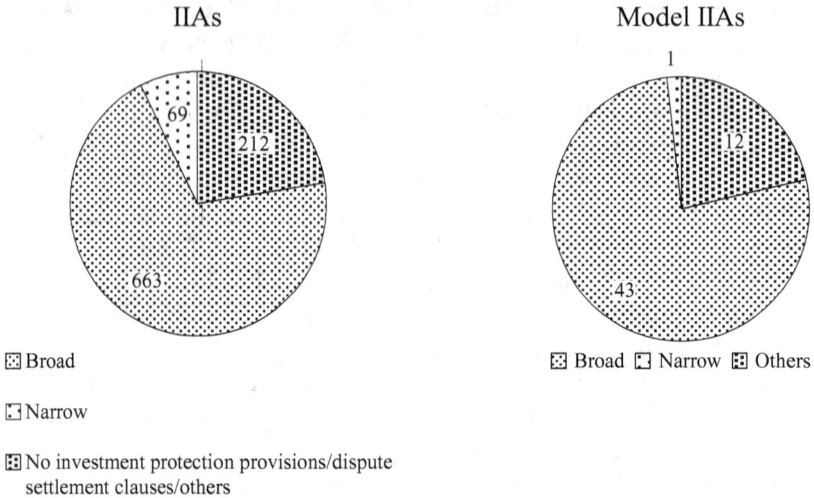

Figure 4.2 Scope of *locus standi*

counterclaim, stating that: 'Respondent's counterclaim is a dispute between it and Claimants "with regard to [Claimants'] investments"; further, it is a component of the larger dispute that Claimants have consented to submit to this arbitration'.[51]

Lastly, the IIA dataset shows that there is little correlation between definitions of investment disputes and investment claims and *locus standi* provisions. That is, among the 1,000 IIAs, 667 IIAs (634 IIAs and 33 model IIAs) do not limit the scope of investment disputes and investment claims to those relating to the host states' obligations (Figure 4.3, see Section 4.3.4.5). By contrast, 224 (212 IIAs and 12 model IIAs) provide broad *locus standi* (Figure 4.2). Conversely, while 706 (663 IIAs and 43 model IIAs) provide narrow *locus standi* (Figure 4.2), 263 IIAs (242 IIAs and 21 model IIAs) provide narrow definitions of investment disputes and investment claims (Figure 4.3). This also suggests that narrow *locus standi* provisions are chosen as a matter of logic, not as an expression of the contracting parties' intent to exclude counterclaims by the respondent state. Therefore, the absence of a reference to the host state's *locus standi*, in itself, does not have exclusionary effect with respect to counterclaims.

[51] *Inmaris* Award, para. 432.

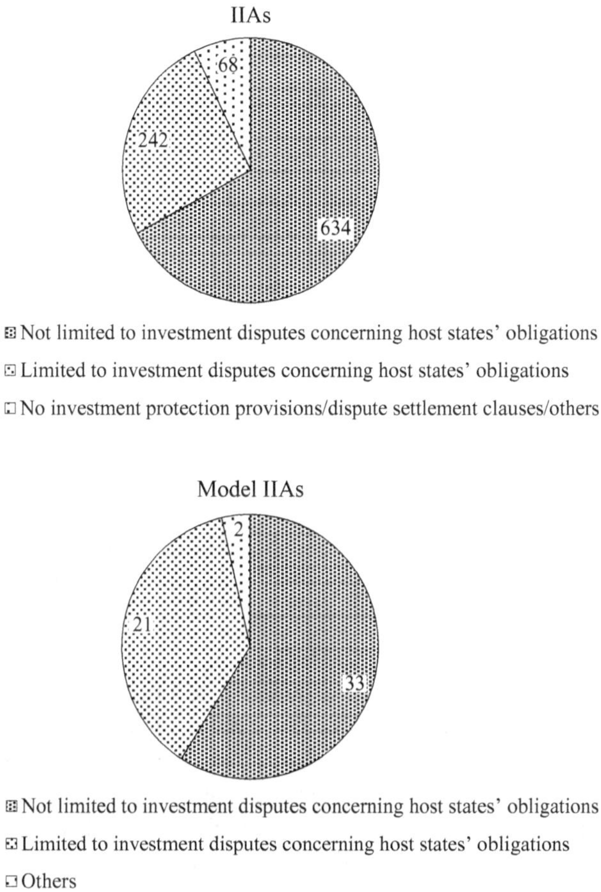

Figure 4.3 Scope of investment dispute or investment claim

4.3.4.4 Applicable Law

Given the paucity of provisions on the investors' obligations in IIAs and other international instruments (Chapter 2, Sections 2.2.2 and 2.3.2), in most cases, the host state's counterclaims are based on a contract with the claimant investor and/or its own domestic law.[52] However, there are IIAs that provide applicable law clauses that only mention the IIA and international law, without a reference to domestic law (hereinafter 'narrow applicable law clauses'). According to the IIA dataset, 152 (140

[52] See also Viñuales, *Foreign Investment and the Environment*, 228.

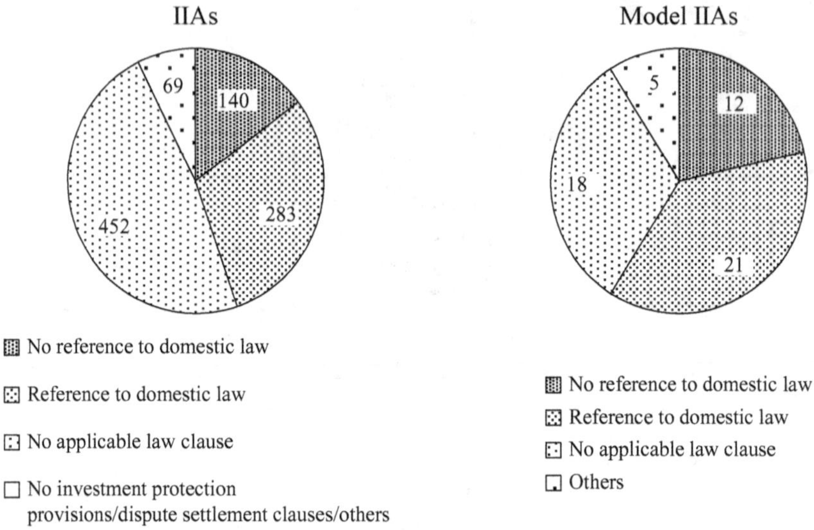

Figure 4.4 Applicable law clause

IIAs and 12 model IIAs) out of 1,000 IIAs provide narrow applicable law clauses, 304 (283 IIAs and 21 model IIAs) provide applicable law clauses with express reference to domestic law, and 470 (452 IIAs and 18 model IIAs) do not provide an applicable law clause (Figure 4.4).

If narrow applicable law clauses are interpreted as excluding the host state's domestic law from the laws applicable to the dispute, it effectively forecloses the possibility of raising counterclaims based on the domestic laws of the host state. This approach was adopted by the majority in *Roussalis v. Romania*. The applicable law clause (Article 9(4)) of the 1997 Greece-Romania BIT provides that:

> The arbitral tribunal shall decide the dispute in accordance with the provisions of this Agreement and the applicable rules and principles of international law.

On this clause, the majority stated that:

> [T]he BIT imposes no obligations on investors, only on contracting States. Therefore, where the BIT does specify that the applicable law is the BIT itself, counterclaims fall outside the tribunal's jurisdiction.[53]

[53] *Roussalis* Award, para. 871. Dudas's criticism of this conclusion is that 'the tribunal overlooked the fact that the parties explicitly agreed at the beginning of the proceedings that the domestic Romanian law would govern the merits of the dispute and that the BIT

In reaching this conclusion, the majority relied on Lalive and Halonen's argument that: '[T]he arbitration agreement should refer to disputes that can also be brought under domestic law for counterclaims to be within the tribunal's jurisdiction'.[54] The tribunal in *AMTO v. Ukraine* also rejected jurisdiction over counterclaims on the basis that Ukraine did not present any basis in the applicable law under Article 26(6) of the Energy Charter Treaty (ECT), which refers only to the ECT and 'the applicable rules and principles of international law', for its counterclaim.[55]

However, in these cases, the relevant IIAs also provided the dispute resolution clauses which limit the scope of disputes to those arising out of claims alleging a violation of the investment protection obligations by the host state (see Section 4.3.4.5).[56] As discussed further in Chapter 5, Section 5.2.2, fundamentally, the existence of a narrow applicable law clause in the relevant IIA should not be read as an implication of exclusion of the application of the host state's domestic law in the IIA-based dispute settlement mechanism: Tribunals always possess the incidental jurisdiction to apply domestic law to questions that cannot be answered by international law. For these reasons, narrow applicable law clauses are not decisive for the determination of whether the consent to arbitrate extends to counterclaims.

4.3.4.5 Scope of Investment Disputes or Claims

It is submitted that the scope of arbitrable disputes or claims as expressed in the dispute resolution clause is a decisive indicator of the contracting parties' intention with respect to the scope of consent to arbitration.[57] If it is limited to those relating to the host state's IIA

would be considered as part of the domestic law' (*Roussalis* Award, para. 306) (Dudas, 'Treaty Counterclaims under the ICSID Convention', 400). However, the majority made it clear that determination of the scope of consent under the IIA is made 'irrespective of the particular counterclaims advanced in these proceedings by the Respondent' (para. 864), and therefore the agreement on applicable law by the disputing parties of a particular dispute would not affect the majority's finding.

54 Lalive and Halonen, 'On the Availability of Counterclaims', 146.

55 *AMTO* Award, para. 118.

56 Article 9 of the Greece-Romania BIT (*Roussalis v. Romania*); Article 26(1) of the ECT (*AMTO v. Ukraine*).

57 Lalive and Halonen, 'On the Availability of Counterclaims', 147; Bubrowski, 'Balancing IIA Arbitration', 219.

obligations, this demonstrates the contracting parties' intention to limit the scope of consent to the tribunal's jurisdiction to the extent necessary to decide the claims that arise from the host state's breach of such obligations, excluding counterclaims. Conversely, if there is no such limitation in the scope of investment disputes or claims, it suggests the contracting parties' intention to confer consent to the tribunal jurisdiction to decide not only disputes based on principal claims but also those over counterclaims.[58]

Bravin and Kaplan present a different view, arguing that the definition of disputes 'could be understood simply to define or limit the types of claims that an investor may assert at ICSID', rather than indicating any assertion of counterclaims.[59] Certainly, we have already argued that a limited *locus standi* in the dispute settlement provision does not constitute a bar to consent to the host state's counterclaims as it is no more than a reflection of the fact that dispute settlement provisions primarily concern the filing of a principal claim. However, for the following reasons, the same logic does not apply to the narrow definition of arbitrable disputes. *Locus standi* in a dispute settlement provision is a question of *who may commence arbitral proceedings* on the basis of *consent* given in the IIA and, logically, it is only the investor who is the addressee of the offer to arbitrate. In contrast, the definition of arbitrable disputes determines the subject matter scope of dispute settlement proceedings, and it is not logically limited to those arising from a breach of IIA obligations.

Indeed, states may decide to exclude disputes concerning counterclaims from the scope of arbitrable disputes for different reasons, including: to avoid a 'chilling effect' on their own investors, that is, they may refrain from invoking international arbitration fearing counterclaims,[60]

[58] *Urbaser* Award, para. 1187; *Hesham Talaat M. Al-Warraq v. Republic of Indonesia*, UNCITRAL, Final Award, 15 December 2014; *Inmaris* Award; *Goetz v. Burundi II* Award; *Saluka* Decision on Counterclaim; *Paushok* Award; *Tethyan Copper* Decision on Jurisdiction and Liability; *Aven* Award. In *Saluka v. Czech Republic*, *Paushok v. Mongolia* and *Tethyan Copper v. Pakistan* (for counterclaims based on domestic law of the host state), jurisdiction over counterclaims were rejected for reasons other than the absence of consent. See Scherer, Bruce and Reschke, 'Environmental Counterclaims in Investment Treaty Arbitration', 419; Lahlou, Willard and Craven, 'Rise of Environmental Counterclaims', 56.

[59] Bravin and Kaplan, 'Arbitrating Closely Related Counterclaims at ICSID', 8.

[60] See Kalicki, 'Counterclaims by States in Investment Arbitration', 3.

or to let their own national courts handle claims against foreign investors (Chapter 3, Section 3.2.1). The states' selection of a forum for claims against the investor that is expressed in the relevant IIA must be respected.[61] Limiting the scope of arbitrable disputes or claims of the host state's breach of IIA obligations clearly expresses this intention, in the same manner as the express provisions that generally prohibit counterclaims do.

Investment arbitration case law supports this position. For IIAs that have a narrow definition of arbitrable disputes, there is no case that has found consent to counterclaims,[62] even where it is accompanied by a neutral *locus standi* provision,[63] or in the absence of a narrow applicable clause in the relevant IIA.[64]

It is therefore concluded that the decisive factor in determining the contracting states' intention as to whether the scope of their consent to arbitration extends to counterclaims is the scope of investment disputes and investment claims. This admittedly sets limits on the availability of counterclaims. However, as shown in Figure 4.3, in the IIA dataset, 667 out of 1,000 IIAs do not limit the scope of investment disputes to those concerning the host states' obligations. Amongst these, only five IIAs have provisions that can be interpreted to generally exclude counterclaims (as discussed above). It means that in a majority of IIAs of the IIA dataset, consent as the first hurdle for jurisdiction over counterclaims is likely to be found.

[61] The host state may also exclude counterclaims by designating its own courts as a dispute settlement forum with exclusive jurisdiction for the issue concerned. Douglas points out that this is often the case with environmental legislations. Douglas, 'Enforcement of Environmental Norms', 434 (citing the 1980 Comprehensive Environmental Response, Compensation and Liability Act (US) as an example).

[62] *Rusoro Mining Ltd. v. Bolivarian Republic of Venezuela*, ICSID Case No. ARB(AF)/12/5, Award, 22 August 2016; *Roussalis* Award; *Vestey* Award; *Oxus* Award.

[63] *Gustav F W Hamester GmbH & Co KG v. Republic of Ghana* (*Hamester v. Ghana*), ICSID Case No. ARB/07/24, Award, 10 June 2010 (*Hamester* Award). In this case, the tribunal noted the mismatch of the narrow scope of investment disputes and neutral *locus standi* (para. 354), but dismissed its jurisdiction over counterclaims on the ground, *inter alia*, of 'the absence of any submissions on the nature of the Respondent's counterclaim under the BIT' (para. 355).

[64] *Vestey* Award, paras. 117, 333. In this case, Venezuela contested the full reparation for the claimant's expropriated business. Alternatively, Venezuela claimed that, if the fair market value was to be paid, it would have the right to claim transfer of the title of certain assets from the investor to Venezuela (ibid., para. 332). The tribunal discussed this alternative claim, assuming that 'this argument is characterized as a counterclaim'.

4.4 Admissibility Requirements

4.4.1 A Factual Nexus Theory as the Connection between Principal Claims and Counterclaims

A controversial question regarding the requirement of the connection between the counterclaim and the principal claim is whether it entails not only a factual connection but also a legal one,[65] that is, a connection between the grounds of the counterclaim and the principal claims based on *IIA obligations*. When the investor's principal claim is based on IIA obligations, requiring legal connection between principal claims and counterclaims will exclude counterclaims based on the domestic laws of the host states.[66] This would severely limit the situations in which the host state could raise counterclaims because under this approach counterclaims would become available only where: the relevant IIA provides investors' obligations; or the investor invoked the so-called umbrella clause based on a contractual breach.[67]

In *Saluka v. Czech Republic*, the tribunal noted that certain heads of counterclaim had their legal basis in the general law of the Czech Republic, and rejected its jurisdiction over these counterclaims on the ground that they lacked sufficient connection with the principal claim.[68] Citing the language used in *Klöckner v. Cameroon*, the tribunal concluded that the counterclaim cannot be regarded as constituting 'an indivisible whole' with the principal claim, or 'invoking obligations which share with the principal claim "a common origin, identical sources, and an operational unity"', or 'which were assumed for "the accomplishment of a single goal, [so as to be] interdependent"'.[69] The *Saluka* tribunal also relied on *Amco v. Indonesia II*,[70] in which the tribunal distinguished rights and obligations 'that are applicable to legal or natural persons … as a matter of general law' from those under an investment agreement

[65] Kjos, *Applicable Law in Investor-State Arbitration*, 148–154.

[66] Friedman and Popova, 'Can State Counterclaims Salvage Investment Arbitration?', 165.

[67] Hoffmann, 'Counterclaims: *Spyridon Roussalis v. Romania*', 514; Viñuales, *Foreign Investment and the Environment*, 93–94; Douglas, *The International Law of Investment Claims*, 260; Douglas, 'Enforcement of Environmental Norms', 431; Popova and Poon, 'From Perpetual Respondent to Aspiring Counterclaimant?', 233–235.

[68] *Saluka* Decision on Counterclaim, paras. 78–79.

[69] Ibid., para. 79, citing *Klöckner Industrie-Anlagen GmbH and Others v. United Republic of Cameroon and Société Camerounaise des Engrais*, ICSID Case No. ARB/81/2, Award, 21 October 1983 (*Klöckner* Award), para. 65. It must be noted that the *Klöckner* Award was annulled in full (Ad hoc Committee Decision on Annulment, 3 May 1985).

[70] *Saluka* Decision on Counterclaim, para. 82.

(contract) between the investor and the host state[71] and found that the counterclaim of tax fraud, which concerns the former, did not meet the connection requirement under Article 46 of the ICSID Convention.[72] The *Saluka* tribunal's approach to requiring a legal nexus was adopted in certain decisions, including *Paushok v. Mongolia*, in which the tribunal rejected jurisdiction over the public law-based counterclaims on the ground, *inter alia*, that they 'cannot be considered as constituting an indivisible part of the Claimants' claims based on the BIT and international law or as creating a reasonable nexus between the Claimants' claims'.[73]

It should be noted that, in the *Saluka* and *Paushok* cases, the tribunal emphasised the restrictive wording of Article 19(3) of the 1976 UNCITRAL Arbitration Rules ('arising out of the same contract', see Section 4.2), and this is not the place to second-guess whether these heads of counterclaims should have been admitted. Nevertheless, the tribunals' reliance on *Klöckner v. Cameroon* and *Amco v. Indonesia II* is misplaced for the following reasons.

First, both of these cases are based on contracts between the investor and the host state, not an IIA.[74] As Lalive and Halonen argue, where the principal claims do not arise out of a contract but are based on IIA obligations, there is no basis to require that the counterclaim was 'assumed for the accomplishment of a single goal' with the principal claim, or has 'a common origin, identical sources, and an operational unity'.[75] Secondly, the *Amco* decision was on a resubmitted claim, and the tribunal stated that a procedure for resubmission of an existing dispute is different from a new arbitration, the latter of which is restricted only by the requirements of Article 25 of the ICSID Convention.[76] The tribunal then interpreted 'existing dispute' as including only the causes of

[71] *Amco Asia Corporation and Others v. Republic of Indonesia*, ICSID Case No. ARB/81/1, Decision on Jurisdiction in Resubmitted Proceeding, 10 May 1988 (*Amco* Decision on Jurisdiction in Resubmitted Proceeding), para. 125.

[72] Ibid., para. 126; *Saluka* Decision on Counterclaim, para. 75.

[73] *Paushok* Award, paras. 693–699. See also *Oxus* Award, para. 954.

[74] Vohryzek-Griest, 'State Counterclaims in Investor-State Disputes', 96–104.

[75] Lalive and Halonen, 'On the Availability of Counterclaims', 153. See also Friedman and Popova, 'Can State Counterclaims Salvage Investment Arbitration?', 165: '[S]ome of the language in Klöckner on which the Saluka tribunal relied formed no part of the tribunal's analysis of counterclaims jurisdiction – it instead related to whether a party's obligations were excused due to non-performance by the other party (*exceptio non adimpleti contractus*)'.

[76] *Amco* Decision on Jurisdiction in Resubmitted Proceeding, para. 133.

action in the original claim, and thereby rejected the counterclaim based on tax fraud.[77] The tribunal therefore imposed 'heightened limitations on counterclaims' for a resubmitted claim.[78]

There are views that the distinction between legal and factual connection is 'misleading'[79] and 'highly theoretical, as in practice both aspects will be closely inter-related'.[80] However, what should be emphasised is the uniqueness of the IIA regime that investors' obligations are neither provided in the vast majority of IIAs nor in international law. Insofar as a legal connection requires the existence of a legal relationship between the grounds of the counterclaims and the invoked investment protection obligations in the IIA, counterclaims are effectively excluded, as it would be impossible to find such a relationship between claims that belong to different legal orders (i.e. domestic law of one jurisdiction and international law).[81]

The Explanatory Notes to Rule 40 of the ICSID Arbitration Rules explicitly state that the connection requirement is factual:

> [W]hether the factual connection between the original and the ancillary claim is so close as to require the adjudication of the latter in order to achieve the final settlement of the dispute, the object being to dispose of all grounds of dispute arising out of the same subject matter.[82]

The approach requiring only a factual connection is also in line with a broad scope of arbitrable disputes that forms the basis of consent to counterclaims (Section 4.3.4.5).[83] Indeed, the rationale of counterclaims, that is, judicial economy, consistency, and finality requires all aspects of a dispute to be heard and decided in a single set of proceedings, is attained only by admitting counterclaims that have the same factual basis as the principal claims.[84] Several investment arbitration tribunals have supported this approach. For example, in *Inmaris v. Ukraine*, the tribunal

[77] Ibid.

[78] Vohryzek-Griest, 'State Counterclaims in Investor-State Disputes', 103–104.

[79] Anning, 'Counterclaims Admissibility in Investment Arbitration', 1313.

[80] De Nanteuil, 'Counterclaims in Investment Arbitration', 388.

[81] De Nanteuil argues that the legal connection requirement 'is established when both parties pursue the "same legal aim" – that is, in most cases, the recognition of the other party's responsibility – on the basis of the same rules of international law' (De Nanteuil, 'Counterclaims in Investment Arbitration', 388).

[82] Note B.(a) to Arbitration Rule 40 of 1968, 1 ICSID Rep. 100.

[83] Douglas, *The International Law of Investment Claims*, 260; Waibel, 'Investment Arbitration: Jurisdiction and Admissibility', 1240.

[84] Sharpe and Jacob, 'Counterclaims and State Claims', 358.

found that a close connection on a factual basis would suffice by stating that the respondent's counterclaim was 'a component of the larger dispute that Claimants have consented to submit to this arbitration'.[85]

A question that follows is how to determine the closeness of the factual connection that justifies the adjudication of the counterclaim. In the context of an environmental counterclaim, a narrow understanding of the closeness would be to require causality between the state's measure in question and the alleged misconduct on the part of the investor, that is, that the challenged measure of the host state was prompted by the investor's environmental misconduct.[86] However, while this causality is indeed a requirement for asserting a contributory fault (Chapter 6, Section 6.4.3), there is no reason to apply this requirement to determine whether the connection is close enough to allow the counterclaim for the purpose of final settlement of the dispute. The rationale underlying counterclaims requires that the factual connection be established with reference to the relation to the investment that is the subject of the principal claim – specifically, 'the rights comprising the investment and the disagreement between the investor and the host state on questions of law and fact relating to those rights'.[87]

4.4.2 A Parent Company's Liability for Damage Caused by Its Subsidiary: Control-Based Approach

An issue that relates to the connection requirement is whether a counterclaim against a parent company, based on the alleged damage caused by its local subsidiary, becomes inadmissible under the principle of limited liability.[88] This becomes an issue where a subsidiary company brings a principal claim on behalf of the parent company, and where a parent company brings claims for damages incurred on their investment in its subsidiaries, which, as discussed below, is often possible in investment arbitration.

Under the principle of limited liability, a parent company is exempted from liability for the torts committed by its subsidiary companies, unless

[85] *Inmaris* Award, para. 432. See also *Tethyan Copper* Decision on Jurisdiction and Liability, para. 1414; *Urbaser* Award, para. 1153; *Goetz v. Burundi II* Award, para. 285.

[86] Shao, 'Environmental and Human Rights Counterclaims', 171.

[87] Douglas, 'Enforcement of Environmental Norms', 430.

[88] See Chapter 2, Section 2.1.2.

the 'corporate veil' is pierced by the courts and tribunals.[89] Criteria on when to pierce the corporate veil vary depending on jurisdictions as well as the context and facts of the case, yet it has been observed that 'in domestic legal practice in some jurisdictions, it [the doctrine of piercing the corporate veil] is rarely and always cautiously applied'.[90]

In investment arbitration, corporate veil-piercing have been discussed in situations where the defendant state seeks to pierce the corporate veil with the view to asserting that the 'real' nationality of the claimant investor is not that of another contracting state to the relevant IIA, and therefore it lacks *locus standi*. In this context, tribunals have indeed set a high threshold for piercing the corporate veil by generally requiring the existence of situations where corporate formalities are misused to perpetrate fraud, engage in malfeasance and disguise a true identity to avoid liability.[91] However, it should be noted that the context of determining the nationality of the investor as the purpose of seeking to pierce the veil between a parent company and its subsidiary is very different from the context of pursuing the liability of the parent company for tortious conduct of its subsidiary, and therefore investment arbitration case law on veil-piercing is less relevant in the latter context.

There is a view that the admissibility of counterclaims is denied where domestic laws applicable to the counterclaim do not allow piercing of the corporate veil, as 'the problem of legal personality can only be addressed under domestic laws'.[92] However, even though domestic courts treat this question as a jurisdictional requirement, for instance, as the existence of 'a real issue which it is reasonable for the

[89] Vastardis and Chambers, 'Overcoming the Corporate Veil Challenge', 395.

[90] *ADC Affiliate Limited and ADC & ADMC Management Limited v. Republic of Hungary*, ICSID Case No. ARB/03/16, Award, 2 October 2006 (*ADC* Award), para. 358. See also, Ruggie, 'Multinationals as Global Institution', 320 (citing Easterbrook and Fischel, 'Limited Liability and the Corporation', 89); Grušić, 'Responsibility in Groups of Companies'; Muchlinski, 'Limited Liability and Multinational Enterprises', 919–922 (on Anglo-American corporate law); Eroglu, *Multinational Enterprises and Tort Liabilities*, 146–147.

[91] For example, *Tokios Tokelés v. Ukraine*, ICSID Case No. ARB/02/18, Decision on Jurisdiction, 29 April 2004, para. 55 (the majority's decision. Chairman Prosper Weil dissented and resigned from the tribunal); *ADC* Award, para. 358; *Rumeli Telekom A.S. and Telsim Mobil Telekomunikasyon Hizmetleri A.S. v. Republic of Kazakhstan*, ICSID Case No. ARB/05/16, Award, 29 July 2008, para. 328. For a comprehensive empirical study of 'corporate restructuring' cases in which jurisdiction was challenged, see Poulton, Kryvoi, Finkel and Bednarz, 'Empirical Study: Corporate Restructuring'.

[92] Shao, 'Environmental and Human Rights Counterclaims', 175.

court to try' between the parties,[93] whether investment arbitration tribunals treat this as a matter of admissibility is a separate issue. Mares argues that the principle of 'separate corporate personality' under company law is 'not the end of discussions on a parent company's liability', because other bodies of law including the duty of care doctrine 'either make the separation principle inapplicable or push against it for policy reasons specific to that body of law',[94] and the determination of a parent company's liability involves questions such as whether the totality of evidence is sufficient to justify the imposition of a duty of care on it.[95] As discussed below, there have been developments on the parent companies' *direct* duty of care owed to tort victims in certain jurisdictions, without invoking the principle of corporate veil-piercing. Whether the tribunal should treat such complex questions of domestic laws as admissibility requirements or as elements that determine the merits of the case may be decided independently of whether the jurisdiction of the local courts would have been granted or denied.[96]

With these considerations, it is argued here that, insofar as a parent company is allowed access to claims in the IIA-based dispute settlement mechanism, the admissibility of counterclaims involving the parent company's liability should be granted. That is, in the current IIA-based dispute settlement mechanism, the corporate veil between a parent company and its local subsidiary is disregarded in favour of investors so as to allow the investor to have access to investment arbitration in the following ways. First, under Article 25(2)(b) of the ICSID Convention, a local subsidiary which has the nationality of the host state but is 'controlled' by a national of the other contracting party to the relevant IIA may bring a claim against the host state on behalf of its parent company.

[93] UK, Paragraph 3.1(3) of Practice Direction 6B–Service out of the Jurisdiction.

[94] Mares, 'Liability within Corporate Groups', 454.

[95] Ibid., 455–458.

[96] In *Saluka* Decision on Counterclaim, the respondent raised counterclaims against the claimant (Saluka)'s parent company (Nomura), and the claimant investor argued that the tribunal 'had no jurisdiction *rationae personae* over Nomura' (para. 25). However, the tribunal showed a flexibility on this account by stating that 'the question of the relationship between Saluka and Nomura is assumed to be determined on the basis most favourable to the Respondent. Accordingly the Tribunal will initially proceed on the assumption, but without deciding, that the relationship between Saluka and Nomura Europe is sufficiently close to enable the Tribunal's jurisdiction in proceedings instituted by Saluka to extend to claims against Nomura' (para. 44). As noted, however, the counterclaim was found inadmissible due to the lack of a close connection.

Secondly, under many IIAs, a parent company may 'bring claims for harms to their investments in locally incorporated companies'.[97]

The extent of control as a requirement to establish jurisdiction for a parent company's principal claims in investment arbitration differs between cases, depending on the text of the relevant IIA and all other circumstances of the case.[98] Once the threshold is met, a parent company benefits from the disregard of the corporate veil on account of having access to an IIA-based dispute settlement forum, even when it can successfully challenge jurisdiction of domestic courts by invoking corporate separation and limited liability.[99] In such cases, consideration of procedural equity supports a disregard of the corporate veil for the purpose of admitting counterclaims against a parent company, *to the extent that* a parent company, or a local subsidiary acting on behalf of its parent company, benefits from the 'control' test to have access to investment arbitration.[100] It is rightly observed that this does not contradict with the consent requirement because 'the counterclaims are still directed against the claimant investor'.[101]

As discussed above, whether a parent company can escape from liability under the principle of limited liability is a question that must be assessed consistent with the relevant domestic laws. Which domestic law would apply to this question is determined by reference to the choice of law rules of the host state's law (which is always applicable, as discussed in Chapter 5, Section 5.2) and relevant jurisdictions,[102] the

[97] *Daimler* Award, para. 91. See also Kryvoi, 'Piercing the Corporate Veil', 181–186.

[98] Some tribunals required the parent company's actual ability to exercise control, whereas others required only the potential to exercise control via ownership. Vastardis and Chambers, 'Overcoming the Corporate Veil Challenge', 401–402.

[99] Gaukrodger, 'Business Responsibilities and Investment Treaties', 64. For a critical assessment of this point, see Dubin, 'Entreprise multinationale', 24, 29.

[100] Vastardis and Chambers cite the *Chevron* cases as an example where the investor relied on corporate separation in US (*Aguinda v. Texaco*, 142 F. Supp. 2d 534 (SDNY 2001)) and Canadian courts (*Yaiguaje v. Chevron Corp*, 2013 ONCA 758; *Chevron Corp v. Yaiguaje*, 2015 SCC 42, [2015] 3 SCR 69), while suing Ecuador in investment arbitration as TexPet's parent company (*Chevron Corporation and Texaco Petroleum Corporation v. Republic of Ecuador*, UNCITRAL, PCA Case No. 2009-23). Vastardis and Chambers, 'Overcoming the Corporate Veil Challenge', 407–411.

[101] Pathak, 'Consenting to Counterclaims', 120.

[102] Regarding the determination of applicable laws to extraterritorial tort cases, see e.g. Article 7 of the Rome II Regulation (environmental damage) and Article 20 of the European Parliament's draft directive on mandatory human rights and environmental due diligence (human rights violations) (as discussed in Chapter 2, Section 2.1.2). See also Palombo, 'Duty of Care of the Parent Company'.

facts of the case (e.g. the determination of the place of the wrong), and the relevant IIA. It is beyond the scope of this study to discuss the choice of law rules of different jurisdictions for 'multistate' non-contractual civil liability.[103] However, it should be noted that certain third-generation IIAs (see Chapter 2, Section 2.3.2)[104] provide that investors' conduct that has resulted in certain significant damage is subject to civil actions for liability in the investor's home state, or the rules concerning jurisdiction of the home state (see Chapter 2, Section 2.1.2).

Significantly, there have been important developments in certain jurisdictions that demonstrate a shift towards recognising direct liability of a parent company for a breach of its duty of care owed to tort victims. For example, Article L.225-102-4 of the French commercial code, modified in 2017, provides a due diligence obligation for certain parent companies to identify and prevent adverse human rights and environmental impacts with respect to the activities of (in particular) their affiliates and the subsidiaries they control.[105] Under this approach, the victims need not demonstrate the parent company's fraudulent purpose or that 'the subsidiary was the *alter ego* or agent of the parent'.[106] Instead, the new law establishes the parent company's responsibility under the following three conditions: (a) negligence in the application of preventive measures listed in the requested due diligence plan; (b) serious damage to human rights, fundamental freedom, health, and the environment; and (c) the causation between them.[107]

On 11 June 2021 the German government adopted the Act on Corporate Due Diligence in Supply Chains (LkSG),[108] which will come into effect on 1 January 2023. Under the LkSG, certain companies owe due diligence obligations to human rights and a limited scope of

[103] For discussions of this issue, see e.g. Symeonides, *Codifying Choice of Law Around the World*, chapter 2; Vázquez, 'Jurisdiction and Choice of Law'.

[104] For example, Article 20 of the 2016 Morocco-Nigeria BIT; Article 17.1 of the 2012 Southern African Development Community Model Investment Treaty; Article 18 (6) of the Supplementary Act A/SA.3/12/08 Adopting Community Rules on Investment and the Modalities for Their Implementation with ECOWAS (2008); Article 7(4) of the 2019 Netherlands Model BIT.

[105] Code de commerce, article L225–102-4 Modifié par Ordonnance n°2017-1162 du 12 juillet 2017, article 11.

[106] Vastardis and Chambers, 'Overcoming the Corporate Veil Challenge', 395.

[107] Danis-Fatôme and Viney, 'Responsabilité civile dans la loi relative', 1612–1616. See also Palombo, 'Duty of Care of the Parent Company', 276.

[108] Act on Corporate Due Diligence Obligations in Supply Chains, BGBl I 2021, 2959.

environmental protection in their supply chains.[109] It should be noted that failure to comply with the due diligence obligations under the LkSG does not give rise to civil law liability; therefore, victims will still have obstacles to bring claims against these companies in German civil courts. Nevertheless, Krajewski, Tonstad, and Wohltmann observe that 'this does not exclude liability claims on general tort law which would most likely be adjudicated based on the law in the jurisdiction where the damages occurred (*lex loci damni*)'.[110]

As noted in Chapter 2, Section 2.1.2, in March 2021, the European Parliament adopted a resolution with recommendations to the Commission on Corporate Due Diligence and Corporate Accountability, with an annexed draft text of the new directive on mandatory human rights and environmental due diligence.[111] This requires certain European corporations[112] to fulfil the due diligence requirements to 'identify, assess, prevent, cease, mitigate, monitor, communicate, account for, address and remediate the potential and/or actual adverse impacts on human rights, the environment and good governance that their own activities and those of their value chains and business relationships may pose'.[113] Certain countries, including the UK,[114] Norway,[115] Netherlands,[116]

[109] White & Case, 'The German Parliament passed the "Act on Corporate Due Diligence in Supply Chains" on 11 June 2021', White & Case, 21 June 2021, available at: www.whitecase.com/publications/alert/german-parliament-passed-act-corporate-due-diligence-supply-chains-11-june-2021 (accessed 15 December 2021).

[110] Krajewski, Tonstad and Wohltmann, 'Mandatory Human Rights Due Diligence', 9.

[111] European Parliament, European Parliament Resolution of 10 March 2021 with Recommendations to the Commission on Corporate Due Diligence and Corporate Accountability, 2020/2129(INL), available at: www.europarl.europa.eu/doceo/document/TA-9-2021-0073_EN.html (accessed 15 December 2021).

[112] Ibid., Article 2(1)(2).

[113] Ibid., Article 1(2). See also Regulation (EU) 2017/821 of the European Parliament and of the Council of 17 May 2017 laying down supply chain due diligence obligations for Union importers of tin, tantalum and tungsten, their ores, and gold originating from conflict-affected and high-risk areas, OJ 2017 No. L130, 19 May 2017, 1–20.

[114] In August 2020, the UK government announced its decision to introduce a new law that requires companies to perform due diligence on their supply chains to ensure that key commodities were produced consistent with local laws protecting forests and other natural ecosystems (www.gov.uk/government/news/world-leading-new-law-to-protect-rainforests-and-clean-up-supply-chains).

[115] Act relating to enterprises' transparency and work on fundamental human rights and decent working conditions, LOV-2021-06-18-99 (2021).

[116] The Child Labor Due Diligence Act (2019, Netherlands). As of December 2021, the Dutch Parliament is debating a bill on Responsible and Sustainable International Business Conduct.

Switzerland,[117] and Canada,[118] have either adopted or are considering draft laws and regulations on (general or subject-focused) corporate due diligence.[119] Article 6.3 of the third revised draft of the legally binding instrument (see Chapter 2, Section 2.2.2.1) provides the state parties 'require business enterprises to undertake human rights due diligence, proportionate to their size, risk of human rights abuse or the nature and context of their business activities and relationships'.[120]

Likewise, recent decisions by domestic courts have enabled victims to circumvent the principle of limited liability and bring direct claims against parent companies. In *Vedanta Resources Plc and Another v. Lungowe and Others*,[121] a case concerning the jurisdiction of the English courts in relation to a group tort claim arising out of toxic emissions from a copper mine in Zambia, the UK Supreme Court (lead judgment by Lord Briggs, with which all members of the Court agreed) stated that:

> It is difficult to see why the parent's responsibility would have been diminished if the unsafe system of work ... had formed part of a group-wide policy...[122]

and that:

> Even where group-wide policies do not of themselves give rise to such a duty of care to third parties, they may do so if the parent does not merely

[117] After the rejection of the proposal to amend the Constitution to create control-based environmental and human rights due diligence obligations for parent companies on 19 November 2020, the Swiss government has begun working on a counter-proposal for a due diligence law. The Swiss Federal Council, 'Popular Initiative 'For responsible businesses – protecting human rights and the environment" available at: www.admin.ch/gov/en/start/documentation/votes/20201129/iniziativa-popolare-per-imprese-responsabili-a-tutela-dell-essere-umano-e-dell-ambiente.html (accessed 15 December 2021); Palombo, 'Duty of Care of the Parent Company', 276–278.

[118] Bill S-216, An Act to enact the Modern Slavery Act and to amend the Customs Tariff passed its second reading in the Senate in March 2021, but 'died on the Order Paper with the recent election call' in August 2021. It is expected that a new bill on the same issue, or even more ambitious bill that addresses supply chain due diligence, will be introduced. Boscariol, Taborda and Zaccaria, 'Mitigating Risk Exposure to Forced Labour'.

[119] For developments on due diligence (both general and subject-focused) legislation in European countries, see Gaukrodger, 'Business Responsibilities and Investment Treaties', 46–55; Svoboda, 'Investors' Responsibilities beyond Investment Treaties', 469–473; Spears, 'Corporate Responsibility', 570–571.

[120] Available at: www.ohchr.org/EN/HRBodies/HRC/WGTransCorp/Session7/Pages/Session7.aspx (accessed 15 December 2021).

[121] *Vedanta Resources Plc and Another v. Lungowe and Others* [2019] UKSC 20 (April 2019) (*Vedanta* judgment).

[122] Ibid., para. 52.

> proclaim them, but takes active steps, by training, supervision and enforcement, to see that they are implemented by relevant subsidiaries. Similarly, it seems to me that the parent may incur the relevant responsibility to third parties if, in published materials, it holds itself out as exercising that degree of supervision and control of its subsidiaries, even if it does not in fact do so. In such circumstances its very omission may constitute the abdication of a responsibility which it has publicly undertaken.[123]

In *Okpabi v. Royal Dutch Shell*,[124] a case brought by the affected citizens in Niger Delta against Royal Dutch Shell and one of its Nigerian subsidiaries for environmental damage, the UK Supreme Court reversed the Court of Appeal's ruling in 2018 (i.e. preceding the Supreme Court's judgment on *Vedanta*) which declined jurisdiction. The Supreme Court rejected the Court of Appeal's indication that 'the promulgation by a parent company of group wide policies or standards can never in itself give rise to a duty of care', as being inconsistent with *Vedanta*.[125] The Court then endorsed the statement of Lord Briggs in *Vedanta*, cited above, as an example of 'a case in which a duty of care may arise regardless of the exercise of control'.[126] It is observed that this approach 'significantly broadens the spectrum of situations where a parent company could incur a duty of care'.[127]

While, at the date of writing, the *Vedanta* and *Okpabi* cases are still pending on the merits, in *Four Nigerian Farmers and Milieudefensie v. Shell*,[128] a case brought by Nigerian citizens for damage resulting from an oil spill against Royal Dutch Shell and its Nigerian subsidiary, the Hague Court of Appeals found Royal Dutch Shell liable under its duty of care. It concluded that, under the circumstances of the case, Royal Dutch Shell not only owned a duty of care 'to ensure that an LDS [Leak

[123] Ibid., para. 53. van Dam argues that codes of conduct are 'a strong indication of control by the parent over its subsidiaries', because they are 'usually company-wide, applying to all group entities and internally enforced accordingly'. van Dam, 'Tort Law and Human Rights', 249. Cf. *Kadie Kalma & Others v. African Minerals Ltd. & Others* [2020] EWCA Civ 144, paras. 110–135 (rejecting the parent company's duty of care in a 'pure omissions case').

[124] *Okpabi and Others v. Royal Dutch Shell Plc and Another* [2021] UKSC 3.

[125] Ibid., para. 145.

[126] Ibid., para. 148 (citing *Vedanta* judgment, para. 53).

[127] Roorda and Leader, 'Okpabi v Shell and Four Nigerian Farmers v Shell', 372.

[128] *Four Nigerian Farmers and Milieudefensie v. Shell*, Court of Appeal The Hague, 28 January 2021, ECLI:NL: GHDHA:2021:132.

Detection System] is installed on the Oruma pipeline', but also failed to comply with this.[129] The Court ordered Royal Dutch Shell to equip the relevant pipelines with an LDS within one year.[130] This case is further discussed in Chapter 5, Section 5.4.1.

In addition to such changes in practice, scholars have also presented theories for corporate veil-piercing and direct liability of parent companies that may guide future development of law in jurisdictions that still adopt a restrictive approach with respect to a parent company's liability in transterritorial tort claims. Many argue that in light of the rights and remedies of the victims, justice supports a control-based, or enterprise-based, approach.[131] Mendelson also considers veil-piercing as a question of whether a parent company or tort victims would be better bearers of risk arising from the tortious acts of the former's subsidiary, and argues that the former 'almost certainly will be a better bearer of risk' than individual tort victims.[132] Skinner proposes enacting a legislation to pierce the corporate veil 'for claims of customary international human rights violations and serious environmental torts' in situations where a parent company 'takes a majority interest or creates a subsidiary as part of a unified economic enterprise that operates in a "high-risk host country," i.e., one that has a weak, ineffective, or corrupt judicial system'.[133]

To conclude, in IIA-based dispute settlement mechanisms, the principle of limited liability should not make a claim against a parent company inadmissible. The question of whether the parent company directly owes a duty of care or is shielded from liability in a particular case must be considered at the merits stage, in accordance with a careful interpretation and application of the relevant domestic law (see Chapter 5, Section 5.2.4).[134]

[129] Ibid., para. 7.26.

[130] Ibid., para. 7.27 and operative part. As of the date of writing, damage assessment procedure is still pending. See also *Angelica Choc et al. v. Hudbay Minerals Inc. et al.*, [2013] ONSC 1414 (Ontario Superior Court of Justice, Canada).

[131] See e.g. Ratner, 'Corporations and Human Rights', 519; Mendelson, 'Control-Based Approach to Shareholder Liability'; Rühmkorf, *Corporate Social Responsibility*, 179–183; Knight, 'International Human Rights Litigation after *Bauman*', 246; van Dam, 'Tort Law and Human Rights', 247–251.

[132] Mendelson, 'Control-Based Approach to Shareholder Liability', 1282.

[133] Skinner, 'Parent Company Accountability', 28.

[134] Issues of application of domestic law in IIA-based dispute settlement mechanisms are discussed in Chapter 5, Section 5.2.

4.5 Conclusion

Beginning with the assumption that the significant uncertainty regarding questions of jurisdiction and admissibility of counterclaims in IIA-based dispute settlement mechanisms has led to pessimistic appraisals of the possibility of counterclaims on the part of host states, this chapter aims to clarify these questions. Importantly, the parties' consent to counterclaims, which is a crucial element in establishing jurisdiction, is actually given under a majority of IIAs. This chapter has also demonstrated that admissibility requires a factual rather than legal connection and, under an approach treating the principle of limited liability as a question for the merits stage, the circumstances in which a counterclaim's admissibility must be denied on these grounds are actually limited.

5

Counterclaims

Merits

5.1 Introduction: Rare Success at the Merits Stage

Although limited in number, there are cases, as identified in Chapter 4, in which jurisdiction and admissibility of counterclaims were established in *international investment agreement (IIA)-based* arbitration. However, among these, only in two cases, that is, *Burlington v. Ecuador* and *Perenco v. Ecuador*, the host states' counterclaims succeeded on their merits.[1] These two cases were exceptional because the tribunals found the jurisdiction of the counterclaims to be based on the explicit (*Burlington*)[2] or tacit (*Perenco*)[3] consent by the claimant investor. In the remaining

[1] *Burlington Resources Inc. v. Republic of Ecuador*, ICSID Case No. ARB/08/5, Decision on Ecuador's Counterclaims, 7 February 2017 (*Burlington* Decision on Counterclaims); *Perenco Ecuador Ltd. v. Republic of Ecuador and Empresa Estatal Petroeleos del Ecuador*, ICSID Case No. ARB/08/6 (*Perenco v. Ecuador*), Award, 27 September 2019 (*Perenco* Award), paras. 423–966. Examples of a (partially) successful counterclaim in *contract-based* investment arbitration are: *Zeevi Holdings v. Republic of Bulgaria and the Privatisation Agency of Bulgaria*, UNCITRAL Case No. UNC39/DK, Award, 25 October 2006; *Gardabani Holdings B.V. v. Government of Georgia, Ministry of Economy and State Service Bureau LLC*, ICSID Case No. ADM/18/1 and SCC Case No. V2018/039, Partial Award, 19 April 2021, para. 676.

[2] *Burlington* Decision on Counterclaims, paras. 61–62. The investor also consented to the applicability of Ecuadorian law to such counterclaims (para. 72). In this case, the respondent state 'waived its right to file the counterclaims against Burlington, its subsidiaries or any other corporation in the ConocoPhillips Group before "any jurisdiction whatsoever whether arbitral or judicial, national or international except for this Arbitration"' (para. 72).

[3] In *Perenco v. Ecuador*, after the *Burlington* decision on counterclaims was issued (five years after the arbitral proceedings commenced), Perenco raised an objection to the admissibility of Ecuador's counterclaims on the ground of *res judicata*. The tribunal dismissed this objection, noting that: '[a]t no previous stage of the proceedings relating to Ecuador's counterclaims has Perenco raised objections, either to the Tribunal's jurisdiction or to the admissibility of the counterclaims' (*Perenco v. Ecuador*, Decision on Claimant's Application for Dismissal of Respondent's Counter-Claims, 18 August 2017,

cases, counterclaims have faced a significant obstacle at the merits stage, that is, which laws should be applied to determine the merits and the remedy of the claim?

In the general absence of provisions on investor obligations in IIAs (Chapter 2, Section 2.3.2), in most cases, respondent states have relied on their domestic laws when pursuing counterclaims. However, as discussed below, tribunals have been reluctant to apply domestic laws to the merits of a counterclaim, and this has formed an obstacle to its success. Against this background, this chapter first challenges the stated obstacles to the application of the host state's domestic law as a basis for counterclaims in the IIA-based dispute settlement mechanism (Section 5.2). It examines the following controversies: whether a narrow applicable law clause, that is, an applicable law clause which refers only to the IIA and international law, excludes the application of the host state's domestic law; and whether awarding counterclaims based on environmental regulations of the host state is inconsistent with the principle of 'non-extraterritorial enforceability of national public laws', or with principles informing the so-called public law taboo.[4]

Having concluded that none of these controversies constitute an obstacle to the application of domestic law in the context of counterclaims, this chapter proceeds to the question of legitimacy concerning the application of domestic law by tribunals in the IIA-based dispute settlement mechanism. The concerns of legitimacy arise from the fact that, in many cases, tribunal members have to interpret and apply the domestic law that is unfamiliar to them. It is argued that this concern should be addressed by the consistent application by tribunals of the approach of carefully examining sufficient sources of domestic law, with the help of, whenever necessary, legal experts.

The chapter then examines counterclaims based on international law (Section 5.3). It first observes that, while counterclaims based on investor obligations under IIAs (such as those in *Al-Warraq v. Indonesia*[5]) remain

para. 44). Therefore, the tribunal arguably found its jurisdiction on the basis of tacit consent. See also Interim Decision on the Environmental Counterclaim, 11 August 2015 (*Perenco* Interim Decision on Counterclaims), paras. 43–54. For an examination of the cases in which explicit and tacit consent by the investor was considered to have been given, see Kjos, *Applicable Law in Investor-State Arbitration*, 142–145.

4 See e.g. Lowenfeld, 'Public Law in the International Arena', 322–326; McConnaughay, 'Reviving the "Public Law Taboo"', 283.

5 *Hesham Talaat M. Al-Warraq v. Republic of Indonesia*, UNCITRAL, Final Award, 15 December 2014 (*Al-Warraq* Award).

highly exceptional in the current IIA regime, international norms external to the IIA regime (external international norms) may also constitute grounds for counterclaims. This is the possibility presented by *Urbaser v. Argentina*[6] and *Aven v. Costa Rica.*[7] Nevertheless, in both cases, the counterclaims were dismissed at the merits stage. It observes that one of the main reasons why the host states' counterclaims did not succeed on merits in these cases is the respondent states' failure to identify secondary rules that determine the consequences of a breach of such norms. It then examines the role of domestic law as a provider of secondary rules for the investor's violation of international norms.

Lastly, this chapter examines the possibility that the investor's breach of its own voluntary standards and non-binding corporate social responsibility (CSR) commitments may provide a basis for counterclaims by the respondent state (Section 5.4). CSR-based counterclaims have significant implications in situations where domestic regulatory standards fall below international standards on business conduct, and do not provide obligations that cover the investor's relevant conduct. It is argued that, in certain circumstances, investor's conduct which technically meets the former standards yet fails to satisfy the latter may give rise to legal responsibility under the relevant domestic laws, and thereby provide legal grounds for counterclaims.

5.2 Counterclaims Based on Domestic Law

5.2.1 Applicability of Domestic Law of the Host State in IIA-Based Dispute Settlement

While major international arbitration rules that apply generally to international arbitration do not specifically mention domestic law in their applicable law provisions,[8] rules that are designed for investment

[6] *Urbaser S.A. and Consorcio de Aguas Bilbao Bizkaia, Bilbao Biskaia Ur Partzuergoa v. The Argentine Republic*, ICSID Case No. ARB/07/26, Award, 8 December 2016 (*Urbaser* Award).

[7] *David R. Aven and Others v. Republic of Costa Rica*, ICSID Case No. UNCT/15/3, Award, 18 September 2018 (*Aven* Award).

[8] For example, Article 35.1 of UNCITRAL Arbitration Rules (2010); Article 27.1 of the Arbitration Institute of the Stockholm Chamber of Commerce (SCC) Arbitration Rules (2017), Article 21.1 of the International Chamber of Commerce (ICC) Arbitration Rules (2021), Article 22.3 of the London Court of International Arbitration (LCIA) Arbitration Rules (2020), Article 31.1 of the Singapore International Arbitration Centre (SIAC) Arbitration Rules (2016).

arbitration do include reference to domestic law. Article 42(1) of the ICSID Convention explicitly acknowledges the applicability of the domestic law of the host state by providing that, in the absence of the parties' agreement on applicable law, the tribunal shall apply 'the law of the Contracting State party to the dispute (including its rules on the conflict of laws) and such rules of international law as may be applicable'. Rule 28.1 of the 2017 Singapore International Arbitration Centre Investment Arbitration Rules and Article 27(2) of the 2021 Vienna International Arbitral Centre Rules of Investment Arbitration also include 'relevant national law(s) of any state' in the law or rules the tribunal shall apply in the absence of a designation of applicable law by the parties.

This is appropriate, because in investor–state dispute settlements, international law unavoidably interacts with the domestic law of the host state. It is observed that the states, when concluding IIAs, 'envisage a relationship of coordination between international and municipal laws'.[9] Nevertheless, a restrictive view that requires the 'explicit reference to domestic law' in the relevant IIA for the application of domestic law has sometimes been presented. For example, in the ICSID case *Capital Financial Holdings Luxembourg SA v. Republic of Cameroon*, the tribunal stated that:

> [I]t is the international law which applied in the interpretation of the notions of investor and investment which determines the scope of protection offered by the investment treaties . . . However, an exception to this rule is when the investment treaty itself makes explicit reference to domestic law.[10]

The restrictive view has been presented also in the context of counterclaims.[11]

However, it should be noted that the domestic law of the host state (including its rules on the conflict of laws) is a default choice under

[9] Douglas, *The International Law of Investment Claims*, 23.

[10] *Capital Financial Holdings Luxembourg S.A. v. Republic of Cameroon*, ICSID Case No. ARB/15/18, Award, 22 June 2017, para. 203 (the majority). In this case, the majority examined Luxembourg law to determine the concept of siège social on the finding that Article 1(2)(a) of the relevant IIA (1980 BLEU (Belgium-Luxembourg Economic Union)-Cameroon BIT) allows the application of Luxembourg law (paras. 204–211. Arbitrator Mourre disagreed with the majority's reliance on the Luxembourg law. Dissenting Opinion by Arbitrator Alexis Mourre, 22 June 2017, paras. 28–29).

[11] For example, Lalive and Halonen, 'On the Availability of Counterclaims', 150; Viñuales, *Foreign Investment and the Environment*, 104.

Article 42(1), without requiring a *renvoi*.[12] Tribunals have 'inherent jurisdiction' in '[d]eciding "preliminary" or "incidental" questions of national law', which is necessary to give effect to 'the object and purpose of most, if not all, investment treaties'.[13] In this sense, the IIA-based dispute settlement mechanism is distinguished from other forms of public international adjudication[14] in which it is traditionally considered that 'municipal laws are merely facts which express the will and constitute the activities of States, in the same manner as do legal decisions or administrative measures'.[15] It is also argued that the use of 'and' to connect domestic law of the host state and international law in Article 42(1) suggests that there is no hierarchy between the two bodies of law.[16] Rather, both domestic law and international law play 'simultaneous roles',[17] supplementing each other. As Schreuer, Malintoppi, Reinisch, and Sinclair observe, tribunals must first identify the legal issues relevant to the case, and then 'apply international law to some of these issues and domestic law to other issues'.[18] To conclude, in the IIA-based dispute settlement mechanism, the applicability of domestic law is, 'to the extent justified',[19] a rule.

5.2.2 A Narrow Applicable Law Clause Does Not Exclude the Application of Domestic Laws

Although the applicability of the host state's domestic law in IIA-based dispute settlement mechanisms is thus confirmed, a question arises when

12 See *MTD Equity Sdn. Bhd. and MTD Chile S.A. v. Republic of Chile*, ICSID Case No. ARB/01/7, Decision on Annulment, 21 March 2007, para. 72; *Enron Corporation and Ponderosa Assets, L.P. v. Argentine Republic*, ICSID Case No. ARB/01/3, Award, 22 May 2007, para. 207 (citing *Wena Hotels Limited v. Arab Republic of Egypt*, ICSID Case No. ARB/98/4, Ad Hoc Committee Decision on Application for Annulment, 5 February 2002, para. 941).

13 Spiermann, 'Applicable Law', 112.

14 Grisel, 'The Sources of Foreign Investment Law', 222; Hepburn, *Domestic Law in International Investment Arbitration*, 108.

15 *Certain German Interests in Polish Upper Silesia (Germany v. Poland)* (Merits) (1926) PCIJ, Series A, No. 7, 25 May 1926, at 19. See also Jennings and Watts, *Oppenheim's International Law*, 83.

16 Gaillard and Banifatemi, 'The Meaning of "and" in Article 42(1)', 408–409 (rejecting the proposition that international law only has a supplementary role to domestic law of the host state).

17 *Sempra Energy International v. Argentine Republic*, ICSID Case No. ARB/02/16, Award, 28 September 2007, para. 235.

18 Schreuer, Malintoppi, Reinisch and Sinclair, *The ICSID Convention: A Commentary*, 630. See also Bjorklund and Vanhonnaeker, 'Article 42', 360–365.

19 *CMS Gas Transmission Company v. Republic of Argentina*, ICSID Case No. ARB/01/8, Award, 12 May 2005, para. 117.

the relevant IIA provides a narrow applicable law clause (Chapter 4, Section 4.3.4.4 and Figure 4.4 (152 out of 1,000 IIAs in the IIA dataset). If a narrow applicable law clause is read to exclude domestic laws from the scope of laws applicable to the dispute, it would effectively foreclose the possibility of raising counterclaims based on, for example, the host state's environmental regulations or tort law. Indeed, as discussed in Chapter 4, Section 4.3.4.4, several tribunals relied on a narrow applicable law clause in the relevant IIA as one of the grounds to dismiss counterclaims for lack of jurisdiction.[20]

However, different interpretations of a narrow applicable law clause are entirely possible. Some scholars argue that rules and principles of international law include international 'conflict of laws' rules, which require the tribunal to select the appropriate law to solve the issue.[21] A narrow applicable law clause may reflect the contracting parties' intention to confirm that the host state's conduct is to be judged by the international law standards, rather than excluding the application of domestic laws to questions that are necessary to solve the dispute. Other scholars point out that party autonomy with respect to the choice of law is not absolute, and cannot override the mandatory laws and public policy considerations of the host state.[22]

Indeed, as international law 'may not provide answers to all the questions put to the arbitral tribunal',[23] for certain questions, the international conflict of law rules will point to the selection of the domestic law of the host state.[24] For example, determining whether the alleged right falls within the definition of an investment under the relevant IIA requires an examination of its characterisation as rights in the host state, a matter to be determined by the host state's domestic law.[25] Specifically,

[20] *Spyridon Roussalis v. Romania*, ICSID Case No. ARB/06/1, Award, 7 December 2011 (*Roussalis* Award), para. 871; *Limited Liability Company Amto v. Ukraine*, SCC Case No. 080/2005, Final Award, 26 March 2008, para. 118.

[21] Roe and Happold, *Settlement of Investment Disputes*, 51.

[22] Dalhuisen and Guzman, 'The Applicable Law', 240–241. See also Cordero-Moss, 'International Arbitration and the Quest', 28.

[23] Igbokwe, 'Determination, Interpretation and Application', 285.

[24] Sasson, *Substantive Law in Investment Treaty Arbitration*, 12–13; Grisel, 'The Sources of Foreign Investment Law', 223.

[25] Douglas, *The International Law of Investment Claims*, 170–189 (Rule 22); Schreuer, 'Jurisdiction and Applicable Law', 17–18; Montt, *State Liability in Investment Treaty Arbitration*, 248; Sasson, *Substantive Law in Investment Treaty Arbitration*, 103; Roe and Happold, *Settlement of Investment Disputes*, 37–38, 49; Kjos, *Applicable Law in Investor-State Arbitration*, 242; Banifatemi, 'Law Applicable in Investment Treaty Arbitration',

the determination of the concept of property rights makes the application of domestic law inevitable, because international law 'does not define or regulate contractual or property rights related to an investment'.[26] An example of this is the Energy Charter Treaty (ECT)-based *Libananko v. Turkey*. In spite of the fact that the ECT provides a narrow applicable law clause (Article 26(6)), the tribunal confirmed the applicability of domestic law of the host state for the 'issue of whether (and when) Libananco acquired the shares in question and thus had an "Investment" under Article 26(1) of the ECT and Article 25(1) of the ICSID Convention'.[27] The tribunal then applied the Turkish Commercial Code and the Civil Code to determine whether the claimant's alleged acts had the effect of transferring ownership of the shares.[28]

Likewise, *Bayview v. Mexico* is based on North American Free Trade Agreement (NAFTA), within which Article 1131 provides a narrow applicable law clause.[29] Nevertheless, the tribunal did apply Mexican law in assessing the question of whether the claimants had the relevant property rights in the territory of Mexico.[30] Therefore, as Hepburn observes, despite the narrow applicable law clause in the NAFTA, 'the arbitrators considered domestic law to be inescapably relevant' for the purpose of determining jurisdiction.[31]

Lastly, in *TECO v. Guatemala*, the claims were based on the Free Trade Agreement between the Dominican Republic, the United States of America, and Central America (CAFTA-DR). Article 10.22 of the CAFTA-DR is almost identical to Article 1131 of the NAFTA. This did not prevent the tribunal from acknowledging the applicability of

204–207; McLachlan, Shore and Weiniger, *International Investment Arbitration: Substantive Principles*, 246–247.

[26] Sasson, *Substantive Law in Investment Treaty Arbitration*, 10. See also *Emmis International Holding, B.V., Emmis Radio Operating, B.V., MEM Magyar Electronic Media Kereskedelmi és Szolgáltató Kft. v. Republic of Hungary*, ICSID Case No. ARB/12/2, Award, 16 April 2014, para. 169; Montt, *State Liability in Investment Treaty Arbitration*, 248.

[27] *Libananco Holdings Co. Limited v. Republic of Turkey*, ICSID Case No. ARB/06/8, Award, 2 September 2011, para. 112.

[28] Ibid., paras. 385–399. See also *Georg Gavrilovic and Gavrilovic d.o.o. v. Republic of Croatia*, ICSID Case No. ARB/12/39, Award, 26 July 2018, para. 432.

[29] Article 14.D.9 of the US-Mexico-Canada Agreement, which replaced NAFTA as of 1 July 2020, also adopts a narrow applicable law clause.

[30] *Bayview Irrigation District et al. v. United Mexican States*, ICSID Case No. ARB(AF)/05/1, Award, 19 June 2007, paras. 109–118.

[31] Hepburn, *Domestic Law in International Investment Arbitration*, 107.

Guatemalan law to the dispute. Relying on Article 42(1) of the ICSID Convention, the tribunal stated that:

> The fact that, in order to assess the Respondent's alleged responsibility in international law, the Arbitral Tribunal will have to decide certain points of interpretation of the regulatory framework by applying Guatemalan law, does not and cannot deprive the Arbitral Tribunal of its jurisdiction.[32]

Similarly, the application of domestic law is inevitable in assessing the jurisdictional objections based on the 'legality requirement' found in some IIAs that provide that an investment must be made in accordance with the law of the host state (see Chapter 6, Section 6.2.1).[33] Therefore, there are circumstances where the application of domestic law is necessary for solving the dispute. As Dodge argues, in such cases tribunals always have '"incidental" jurisdiction' to apply domestic law.[34] These considerations strongly suggest that a narrow applicable law clause does not exclude the application of domestic law whenever necessary for solving disputes that come within the jurisdiction of the tribunal.

As discussed in Chapter 4, Section 4.3.4.5, the contracting parties' intention to confer consent to the tribunal jurisdiction to decide disputes over counterclaims is established when the dispute settlement clause of the relevant IIA provides a broad scope of arbitrable investment disputes. Once consent is established, and other conditions for filing a counterclaim are met, deciding the principal claim and a counterclaim in one set of proceedings becomes necessary for the tribunal to resolve the investment dispute. When the counterclaim is based on domestic laws, their application is required for this purpose, in the same manner as it is for other domestic law questions discussed above.

In this regard, the provisions on counterclaims and applicable law in the 2016 Slovakia-United Arab Emirates BIT are suggestive. Its dispute settlement clause (Article 17(3)) explicitly provides the host state's right

[32] *TECO Guatemala Holdings, LLC v. Republic of Guatemala*, ICSID Case No. ARB/10/23, Award, 19 December 2013, paras. 468–469. This part of the award was upheld by the Annulment Committee. Decision on Annulment, 5 April 2016, paras. 235–236.

[33] Miles, 'Corruption, Jurisdiction and Admissibility', 343; Schreuer, 'Jurisdiction and Applicable Law', 5. See also Parra, 'Applicable Law in Investor-State Arbitration', 5; Bjorklund, 'The Role of Counterclaims', 469–470.

[34] Dodge, 'Local Remedies under NAFTA Chapter 11', 40–41 (on Article 1131 NAFTA). This position was endorsed in *Bilcon of Delaware et al. v. Government of Canada*, PCA Case No. 2009-04, Judgment of the Federal Court of Canada, 2 May 2018, 2018 FC 436, para. 139.

to file a counterclaim 'arising out of the investment'. The BIT does not provide general obligations of investors, except that Article 12(3) provides that investors 'should ... apply national and internationally accepted standards of corporate governance for the sector involved, in particular for transparency and accounting practices'. This implies that the substantive bases of the counterclaim 'arising out of the investment' include domestic laws. However, its applicable law clause refers to only the BIT and 'applicable rules of international law' (Article 18(1)). Article 18(2) further provides that:

> The Tribunal shall not have jurisdiction to determine the legality of a measure, alleged to constitute a breach of this Agreement, under the domestic law of the disputing Contracting Party. For greater certainty, in determining consistency of a measure with this Agreement, the tribunal may consider, as appropriate, domestic law of the disputing Contracting Party as a matter of fact.

This conforms with the understanding that the purpose of a narrow applicable law clause is to subject the host state's conduct to international law standards, as well as to avoid the consequence that the tribunals determine the legality of the host state's regulatory measures under its domestic laws.

For these reasons, a narrow applicable law clause should not result in the inadmissibility of the host state's counterclaim. Counterclaims create a situation where the application of domestic law is necessary for solving the dispute, which is not overridden by the existence of a narrow applicable law clause.

5.2.3 *The 'Public Law Taboo'*

Another controversy concerning the application of domestic law as a basis of counterclaims is whether awarding counterclaims based on a breach of regulatory laws of the host state[35] contradicts the principle of non-extraterritorial application of national public laws. In *Paushok v. Mongolia*, the tribunal rejected jurisdiction over some heads of the respondent's counterclaim based on the alleged violation of public laws (specifically national tax laws) on the grounds that admitting jurisdiction

[35] This does not apply to counterclaims that are based on tort claims for environmental damage (e.g. in *Burlington v. Ecuador* and *Perenco v. Ecuador*, Ecuador's counterclaims were based on Ecuadorian tort law. *Burlington* Decision on Counterclaims, para. 73; *Perenco* Interim Decision on Counterclaims, para. 319).

of these counterclaims would 'be acquiescing to a possible exorbitant extension of Mongolia's legislative jurisdiction' and thereby contradicting the non-extraterritorial enforceability of national public laws.[36]

The following observations can be made on this reasoning. First, the tribunal's consideration regarding the extraterritorial enforcement of tax law does not apply to counterclaims based on environmental regulations. This is because, as Dodge observes, a 'public law taboo' has been developed from the following two rules: (a) 'a rule against enforcing foreign penal laws' and (b) 'the "revenue rule" barring enforcement of foreign revenue laws'.[37] Environmental regulations fall within neither of these rules.[38]

Secondly, an explanation of the public law taboo is that the enforcement of a claim for public rights that belong to a foreign nation is contrary to independent sovereignty. Thus, it is possible to argue that enforcing an award on counterclaims that imposes pecuniary obligations on an investor on the grounds of the investor's infringement of national environmental regulations on the request of the host state does not compromise state sovereignty.[39] For these reasons, the 'public law taboo' will not bar counterclaims based on an alleged breach of the domestic environmental law of the host state.

5.2.4 Legitimacy Questions in the Application of Domestic Law: A 'Domestic Jurisprudence' Approach and Use of Legal Experts

Another explanation for the public law taboo is the difficulty for tribunals, which do not necessarily have the expertise in the domestic laws of the host state, to interpret and apply such laws.[40] As discussed in

[36] *Sergei Paushok, CJSC Golden East Company and CJSC Vostokneftegaz Company v. Government of Mongolia (Paushok v. Mongolia)*, UNCITRAL, Award on Jurisdiction and Liability, 28 April 2011, para. 695 (citing *Computer Sciences Corporation and The Government of the Islamic Republic of Iran, et al.*, Award No. 221-65-1, 16 April 1986, 10 Iran-US C.T.R. 269, 55–56).

[37] Dodge, 'Breaking the Public Law Taboo', 165. Dodge also observes that there is very little authority for the extension of the rules against enforcing penal and revenue laws to other public laws, a position presented by Mann, *Further Studies in International Law*, 355–376 (Dodge, 'Breaking the Public Law Taboo', 183). See also Strebel, 'The Enforcement of Foreign Judgements', 58.

[38] Shao, 'Environmental and Human Rights Counterclaims', 170.

[39] Bubrowski, 'Balancing IIA Arbitration', 225–226.

[40] Dodge, 'Breaking the Public Law Taboo', 209, citing *Government of India v. Taylor*, [1955] AC 491, 514 (HL) (Lord Somervell).

Chapter 3, Section 3.2.1, whether the tribunal is well equipped to handle counterclaims based on the host state's domestic law, in comparison with national courts, has indeed been a matter of concern[41] and needs to be addressed independently of the public law taboo question. Certainly, in counterclaims based on the host state's domestic law, it is the host state that requests the tribunal to apply its own laws; apparently, the state's consent for its application is always given. Nevertheless, this question involves a broader issue than the host state's consent to the application of its own laws, namely the issue of the legitimacy of investment arbitration proceedings. Franck argues that legitimacy is measured by 'the extent to which the rules are made and applied in accordance with what the participants perceive as right process'.[42] Specifically on dispute settlement proceedings, one of the measures used to assess the legitimacy of a dispute settlement forum is whether its authority is 'accepted by relevant audiences', based on reason and the efficacy of its outcomes.[43]

For IIA-based dispute settlement mechanisms which deal with regulatory disputes within the public law sphere,[44] the 'relevant audiences' encompass not only the parties to a particular dispute but also a variety of other stakeholders, including the investor's home state and the citizens of the host state. There are also an indefinite number of candidates that may have recourse to the mechanisms in the future, whose trust is essential for its sustainable operation. Thus, if the application of domestic law by tribunals comes as a surprise or is materially

[41] Kalicki, 'Counterclaims by States in Investment Arbitration'; Popova and Poon, 'From Perpetual Respondent to Aspiring Counterclaimant?', 245; Grossman, 'Normative Legitimacy of International Courts', 84.

[42] Franck, *Fairness in International Law and Institutions*, 7.

[43] Bodansky, 'Legitimacy in International Law', 327. See also Al Faruque, 'Mapping the Relationship', 544; Esty, 'The World Trade Organization's Legitimacy Crisis', 10 (on a 'systemic dimension' to legitimacy).

[44] On this point, see e.g. *Bilcon of Delaware et al. v. Government of Canada*, PCA Case No. 2009-04, Application to the Federal Court of Canada for Set Aside of the Award, 16 June 2015, para. 16; Dissenting Opinion of Roberts, C. J. and Kennedy, J., in *BG Group v. Republic of Argentina*, 572 US 25, 58 (2014); Kingsbury, Krisch and Stewart, 'The Emergence of Global Administrative Law'; Burke-White and von Staden, 'Private Litigation'; Van Harten, *Investment Treaty Arbitration and Public Law*, chapter I; Hansen, 'Parallel Proceedings in Investor-State Treaty Arbitration'. Cf. Alvarez, 'Is Investor-State Arbitration "Public"?' (emphasising the difference between the 'judicial review' effects of ISDS and the constitutional review by the US Supreme Court or other constitutional courts).

inconsistent in light of the jurisprudence of the relevant jurisdiction,[45] trust in the system on the part of these stakeholders may well be undermined.

Given that the application of domestic law is inevitable for certain questions (Section 5.2.1), the difficulty for arbitrators to apply domestic law for which they lack expertise and language capacity 'is no excuse for avoiding it'.[46] This being so, these concerns must be addressed through the *process* of interpretation and application of domestic law by tribunals in the IIA-based dispute settlement mechanism. With this regard, an approach that requests international adjudicators to 'make a just appreciation' of domestic jurisprudence was presented by the Permanent Court of International Justice (PCIJ) in the *Brazilian Loans* case. After concluding that the Court 'must seek to apply it [the municipal law of a particular country] as it would be applied in that country',[47] it stated that:

> [T]he Court will endeavour to make a just appreciation of the jurisprudence of municipal courts. If this is uncertain or divided, it will rest with the Court to select the interpretation which it considers most in conformity with the law.[48]

This approach, which is called hereafter the 'domestic jurisprudence' approach, has been confirmed in the case law of the International Court of Justice (ICJ).[49] There is no reason why it should not apply to IIA-based dispute settlement mechanisms, in which domestic laws play a significant role as applicable laws (Section 5.2.1). Although there are

45 An example of an inconsistent interpretation of domestic law as a basis of counterclaims by different investment arbitration tribunals is *Burlington v. Ecuador* and *Perenco v. Ecuador*, in which the tribunals reached different interpretation of the 2008 Ecuadorian Constitution and Ecuadorian court cases as to the question of when strict liability for environmental harm became applicable in Ecuadorian law. *Perenco* Interim Decision on Counterclaims, para. 359; *Burlington* Decision on Counterclaims, paras. 247–248.

46 Reisman, 'The Regime for *Lacunae*', 369.

47 *Payment in Gold of Brazilian Federal Loans Contracted in France (France v. Brazil)* [1929] PCIJ, Series A, No. 21 (July 12) (*Brazilian Loans* judgment), para. 80.

48 Ibid., para. 82. See also *Payment of Various Serbian Loans Issued in France (Fr. V. Yugo.)* (Judgment of 12 July 1929) [1929] PCIJ, Series A, No. 20, para. 105.

49 *Elettronica Sicula S.p.A. (ELSI) (United States of America v. Italy)* (Judgment of 20 July 1989) [1989] ICJ Rep. 15, para. 62; *Ahmadou Sadio Diallo (Republic of Guinea v. Democratic Republic of the Congo)* (Judgment) (Merits) [2010] ICJ Rep. 639, para. 70.

investment arbitration decisions that do not follow this approach,[50] endorsement of this approach is found in other cases.[51]

Under the domestic jurisprudence approach, the interpretation and application of domestic law which is unfamiliar to the tribunal must be based on the analysis of a wide range of sources of the relevant domestic law, including texts of the relevant legal instruments, relevant case law on the interpretation and application of such laws, commentaries, and treatises, in conjunction with translations of these materials.[52] These sources are provided not only by the submissions of the parties but also by legal experts appointed by the disputing parties.[53] On the latter, there are different techniques to assess the credibility of the evidence presented by party-appointed experts, including: cross-examination,[54] pre-hearing meetings of the experts,[55] 'witness conferencing'

[50] For example, in *Occidental v. Ecuador*, Arbitrator Stern, in her dissenting opinion, criticised the majority's interpretation of Ecuadorian law concerning the effectiveness of the contract in question arguing *inter alia* that the majority's interpretation ignored the *jurisprudence constante* of the Ecuadorian Supreme Court (*Occidental Petroleum Corporation and Occidental Exploration and Production Company v. Republic of Ecuador*, ICSID Case No. ARB/06/11, Dissenting Opinion of Professor Brigitte Stern, 20 September 2012, paras. 105–107). Hepburn identifies 'the common faults of tribunals when dealing with questions of domestic law', including the failure to investigate and engage with domestic law sources. Hepburn, *Domestic Law in International Investment Arbitration*, 163–182. See also Risso and Amato, 'Pleas of Illegality', 102.

[51] For example, *Fouad Alghanim & Sons Co. for General Trading & Contracting, W.L.L. and Fouad Mohammed Thunyan Alghanim v. Hashemite Kingdom of Jordan*, ICSID Case No. ARB/13/38, Award, 14 December 2017, paras. 357–359; *Fraport AG Frankfurt Airport Services Worldwide v. Republic of the Philippines I*, ICSID Case No. ARB/03/25, Decision on the Application for Annulment of Fraport AG Frankfurt Airport Services Worldwide, 23 December 2010 (*Fraport I* Annulment Decision), para. 236; *Hussein Nuaman Soufraki v. United Arab Emirates*, ICSID Case No. ARB/02/7, Decision of the ad hoc Committee on the Application for Annulment of Mr Soufraki, 5 June 2007, paras. 96–97.

[52] Kaufmann-Kohler, 'The Arbitrator and the Law', 637–638. For different ways for international arbitration tribunals to ascertain the contents of applicable domestic law, see De Ly, Friedman and di Brozolo, 'International Law Association International Commercial Arbitration '; Hepburn, *Domestic Law in International Investment Arbitration*, 112–119; Van Damme, 'The Assessment of Expert Evidence'.

[53] For example, *Pac Rim Cayman LLC v. Republic of El Salvador*, ICSID Case No. ARB/09/12, Award, 14 October 2016, paras. 8.1–8.44; *Philip Morris Brands Sàrl, Philip Morris Products S.A. and Abal Hermanos S.A. v. Oriental Republic of Uruguay*, ICSID Case No. ARB/10/7, Award, 8 July 2016, paras. 235–271.

[54] Senogles, 'Some Views from the Crucible', 362.

[55] See e.g. Article 5(4) of the International Bar Association (IBA) Rules on the Taking of Evidence in International Arbitration 2020, adopted by a resolution of the IBA Council on 17 December 2020, available at: www.ibanet.org/resources (accessed 15 December 2021) (IBA Rules on the Taking of Evidence); UNCITRAL, 'Notes on Organizing Arbitral

(simultaneous examination of experts during hearings),[56] and ordering joint reports by experts.[57]

Nevertheless, when it remains difficult to assess the relative credibility of the party-appointed experts evidence or the evidence left some confusion,[58] the adjudicators do have the duty and power to conduct research on their own motion.[59] One of the means of fulfilling this duty is to appoint *ex curia* experts.[60] The right of arbitration tribunals to appoint experts after consulting the parties is provided in arbitration rules that are often used for investment arbitration.[61] The ICSID Convention and ICSID arbitration rules are silent on tribunal-appointed experts, but it is considered to be founded on Articles 43 and 44 of the Convention.[62]

Proceedings (2016)', available at: https://uncitral.un.org/en/texts/arbitration/explanatory texts/organizing_arbitral_proceedings (accessed 15 December 2021) (UNCITRAL Notes). See also Hodgson and Stewart, 'Experts in Investor-State Arbitration', 460.

56 Boisson de Chazournes, Mbengue, Das and Gros, 'One Size Does Not Fit All', 496; Blackaby and Wilbraham, 'Practical Issues', 667.

57 See *Occidental v. Ecuador*, Award, 5 October 2012, paras. 692–694 (on the quantum of damages). See also Daly and Poon, 'Technical and Legal Experts', 371; Rosenberg, 'Practical and Innovative Use of Experts', 22.

58 Bennouna, 'Experts before the International Court of Justice', 347; Beuscher, 'Use of Experts by the Courts', 1106; Fenton, 'Civil Matter for a Common Expert', 281.

59 *Brazilian Loans* judgment, para. 79. See also Jenks, 'Interpretation and Application of Municipal Law', 100.

60 The ICJ has appointed experts only in a few cases. *Corfu Channel case (United Kingdom of Great Britain and Northern Ireland v. Albania)* (Order) (Expert Opinion) [1948] ICJ Rep. 124; *Delimitation of the Maritime Boundary in the Gulf of Maine Area (Canada/ United States of America)* (Order) (Appointment of Expert) [1984] ICJ Rep. 165; *Maritime Delimitation in the Caribbean Sea and the Pacific Ocean (Costa Rica v. Nicaragua)* (Order) (Decision to Obtain an Expert Opinion) [2016] ICJ Rep. 235; *Armed Activities on the Territory of the Congo (Democratic Republic of the Congo v. Uganda)* (Order) (Decision to Obtain an Expert Opinion) [2020] ICJ GL No 116, ICGJ 547 (ICJ 2020). See Tanaka, *Peaceful Settlement of International Disputes*, 183; Parlett, 'Parties' Engagement with Experts', 444. In the WTO dispute settlement proceedings, panel-appointed experts 'have become almost commonplace' (Hamann, 'The Use of Ex Curia Experts', 112). See also Pauwelyn, 'The Use of Experts', 325. Arbitral tribunals, constituted under Annex VII of the United Nations Convention on the Law of the Sea, have also appointed experts. *Guyana v. Suriname*, PCA Case No. 2004-04, Procedural Order No. 1 of 18 July 2005; The South China Sea Arbitration (*The Republic of Philippines v. The People's Republic of China*), PCA Case No. 2013-19, Award, 12 July 2016, para. 58.

61 Article 29 of the 2013 UNCITRAL Arbitration Rules; Article 25 of the 2021 ICC Arbitration Rules; and Article 34 of the 2017 SCC Arbitration Rules.

62 *Abaclat and Others v. Argentine Republic*, ICSID Case No. ARB/07/5, Procedural Order No. 15, 20 November 2012 (*Abaclat* Procedural Order No. 15), para. 12. However, Arbitrator Torres Bernárdez, in his dissenting opinion, argued that the issue of the tribunal's competence to appoint experts arises when the appointment lacks the parties' agreement. Dissenting Opinion of Dr. Torres Bernárdez to Procedural Order No. 15,

In the IIA dataset, fourteen IIAs explicitly refer to the tribunal's power to appoint *ex curia* experts (unless the disputing parties disapprove), though only for factual issues concerning 'environmental, health, safety or other scientific matters'.[63] Certainly, scientific, technical, and valuation questions arising out of disputes that involve claims for environmental damage are beyond the ordinary competence of tribunal members, and therefore require the assistance of scientific experts.[64] Thus, for example, the tribunal in *Perenco v. Ecuador*, in assessing Ecuador's counterclaims, decided to appoint, after consulting the parties, its own expert to examine the extent of environmental damage and costs of remediation, in the light of significant disagreements between the party-appointed experts on these points.[65]

It is also clear that tribunal members, as highly experienced experts in law themselves, have general competence in dealing with questions of law. Nevertheless, the domestic jurisprudence approach, which requires a thorough investigation of the sources of domestic law as well as an understanding of the context specific to the jurisdiction, would justify the appointment of tribunal experts when the tribunal finds it necessary.[66] Provisions on tribunal-appointed experts typically specify that the appointment of other kinds of experts authorised by the applicable arbitration rules remains unaffected.[67] Investment arbitration tribunals

20 November 2012 (*Abaclat* Torres Bernárdez dissenting opinion), para. 15. See also Schreuer, Malintoppi, Reinisch and Sinclair, *The ICSID Convention: A Commentary*, 654; De Brabandere, *Investment Treaty Arbitration*, 119–120.

63 For example, Article 34(1) of the 2014 Canada-Senegal BIT; Article 9.27 of the Comprehensive and Progressive Agreement for Trans-Pacific Partnership.

64 *Pulp Mills on the River Uruguay (Argentina v. Uruguay)* (Judgment of 20 April 2010) Joint dissenting opinion Judges Al-Khasawneh and Simma [2010] ICJ Rep. 14, para. 3 (arguing for the need for experts for the assessment of scientific questions).

65 *Perenco* Interim Decision on Counterclaims, paras. 568–610. In its award, the *Perenco* tribunal adjusted the independent expert's calculation of environmental damages upwards 'to account for certain sites identified by Ecuador which the Expert had overlooked or was unable to sample'. *Perenco* Award, para. 889. See also Harrison, 'Environmental Counterclaims in Investor-State Arbitration', 484; Yamamoto, Ramesh and Seelmann-Eggebert, '*Perenco Ecuador v Republic of Ecuador*', 465–467. See also *Peter A. Allard v. The Government of Barbados*, PCA Case No. 2012-06, Award, 27 June 2016, para. 110.

66 See UNCITRAL, 'Possible Reform of Investor-State Dispute Settlement (ISDS) Submission from the Governments of Chile, Israel, Japan, Mexico and Peru, Note by the Secretariat', 2 October 2019, UN Doc. A/CN.9/WG.III/WP.182, at 9.

67 For example, Article 34(3) of the 2014 Canada-Senegal BIT; Article 9.27 of the Comprehensive and Progressive Agreement for Trans-Pacific Partnership.

have appointed experts for different purposes, including legal experts on domestic laws.[68]

Having said this, it is the sole responsibility of tribunals, whose competence to decide a case is based on the disputing parties' consent,[69] to identify, interpret, and apply the law to the facts they have determined,[70] and they may not delegate this role to experts.[71] Otherwise, the legitimacy of the decision – and if this reoccurs, the legitimacy of the dispute settlement system – will be put in doubt.[72] Moreover, even for *ex curia* experts who are expected to be independent and neutral, there remains the risk that their professional or other (e.g. personal or political) convictions results in certain biases in their reports.[73]

There are different ways that can be employed to address these issues. Clear identification of the issues and questions in the terms of reference would be essensial to make a clear delineation between the role of tribunals and that of experts.[74] The tribunal may also use soft law guidelines for the administration of evidence, including the International Bar Association (IBA) Rules on the Taking of Evidence in International Arbitration[75] and the UNCITRAL Notes on Organizing

[68] *Abaclat* Procedural Order No. 15 (the majority) and dissenting opinion; *BSG Resources Limited, BSG Resources (Guinea) Limited and BSG Resources (Guinea) SÀRL v. Republic of Guinea*, ICSID Case No. ARB/14/22, Procedural Order No. 14, 28 August 2017 (forensic expert); *Chevron Corporation and Texaco Petroleum Corporation v. Ecuador (II)*, PCA Case No. 2009-23, Second Partial Award on Track II, 30 August 2018, para. 1.26 (forensic expert); *PJSC CB PrivatBank and Finance Company Finilon LLC v. The Russian Federation*, PCA Case No. 2015-21, Press Release, 15 August 2016; *Aeroport Belbek LLC and Mr. Igor Valerievich Kolomoisky v. Russian Federation*, PCA Case No. 2015-07, Press Release, 15 August 2016; *Limited Liability Company Lugzor and Others v. The Russian Federation*, PCA Case No. 2015-29, Press Releace, 13 December 2017 (legal experts on Ukranian and Russian law).

[69] Jacur, 'Remarks on the Role of *Ex Curia* ', 444.

[70] Foster, 'New Clothes for the Emperor?', 152–153.

[71] *Starrett Housing Corp. v. Iran*, Interlocutory Award, Award No. ITL 32-24-1, 19 December 1983, 4 Iran-US C.T.R. 122, 197, para. 266; Savadogo, 'Le recours des juridictions', 244; Marceau and Hawkins, 'Experts in WTO Dispute Settlement', 503; Flett, 'When Is an Expert Not an Expert?', 353.

[72] Nardin, 'Is there a Future?', 55 (in the context of cases on industrial and construction contracts).

[73] Hepburn, *Domestic Law in International Investment Arbitration*, 137; Boisson de Chazournes, Mbengue, Das and Gros, 'One Size Does Not Fit All', 485; Hodgson and Stewart, 'Experts in Investor-State Arbitration', 455; Foster, 'New Clothes for the Emperor?', 162 (noting that the same risk exists for judges).

[74] Marceau and Hawkins, 'Experts in WTO Dispute Settlement', 503 (on WTO panel experts).

[75] Article 6 of the IBA Rules on the Taking of Evidence (Tribunal-appointed Experts).

Arbitral Proceedings[76] in dealing with expert evidence.[77] It would be essential to guarantee parties' due process rights, including the opportunity to submit comments on a draft report and witness conferencing.[78] Another means to seek a balanced view by tribunal-appointed experts is 'expert teaming', that is, appointing two experts.[79] Ultimately, however, most important is clear recognition on the part of the tribunals of the assisting nature of experts' evidence, and that it is their responsibility to interpret and apply domestic law to the case. Indeed, insofar as the tribunals are furnished with sufficient and balanced sources of information on the relevant domestic laws,[80] discharging this role would not be difficult for the tribunal members.[81]

A final question regarding the application of domestic laws is the treatment of prior domestic court decisions that handled disputes that are based on, or related to, the same set of laws and facts as those that form the basis of the investment dispute. While it is clear that domestic court judgments do not have the *res judicata* effect on IIA-based dispute settlement forums,[82] the domestic jurisprudence approach, in principle, requires the tribunal to respect the determination of the law presented in the decision.[83]

Albeit limited to the context of the determination of the consistency of the host state's challenged measure with the Agreement, some of the

[76] UNCITRAL Notes, paras. 101–107 (Tribunal-appointed experts).

[77] von Wobeser, 'The Arbitral Tribunal-Appointed Expert', 4–5; Blackaby and Wilbraham, 'Practical Issues', 656–657.

[78] These procedural safeguards were employed by the *Perenco* tribunal (*Perenco* Award, paras. 627–630). See Rudall, 'The Tribunal with a Toolbox', 498. See also Hamann, 'The Use of Ex Curia Experts', 120; Pauwelyn, 'The Use of Experts', 350 (in the context of WTO law).

[79] Sachs and Schmidt-Ahrendts, 'Protocol on Expert Teaming', 144–146; Savadogo, 'Le recours des juridictions', 238; Blackaby and Wilbraham, 'Practical Issues', 664. In his dissenting opinion to Procedural Order No. 15 in *Abaclat v. Argentina*, Arbitrator Torres Bernárdez explained that his earlier proposal to appoint a second expert 'in order to maintain the advisable balance of confidence of the three members of the Tribunal in the projected verification undertaking' was rejected by the majority (*Abaclat* Torres Bernárdez dissenting opinion, paras. 4–5).

[80] Igbokwe, 'Determination, Interpretation and Application', 294.

[81] Hepburn, *Domestic Law in International Investment Arbitration*, 135; Risso and Amato, 'Pleas of Illegality', 115; Blackaby and Wilbraham, 'Practical Issues', 661.

[82] Hepburn, *Domestic Law in International Investment Arbitration*, 129–132.

[83] For discussions of the issue of judicial deference to domestic adjudicatory bodies by international adjudicatory bodies, see e.g. Mitra, 'Relevance of Domestic Court Decisions'; Shirlow, *Judging at the Interface*, 94–96, 120–123; Fahner, *Judicial Deference in International Adjudication*, 112–118.

recent EU IIAs actually require such deference as a rule.[84] However, the EU IIAs' approach is criticised as 'overly definitive' in situations where 'a domestic interpretation gives rise to concerns around impartiality'.[85] It should be recalled that the rule of law is not guaranteed in certain domestic legal systems (Chapter 3, Section 3.2.1). Requiring deference to domestic courts' determination in *all* such cases would, therefore, be problematic. Investment arbitration tribunals have carefully assessed the extent of deference given to domestic courts' decisions.

In the context of the plea of illegality of investment, the Annulment Committee in *Fraport v. Philippines I*, while clearly endorsing the domestic jurisprudence approach,[86] discussed the treatment of 'the Prosecutor's Resolution' which determined the relevant issue concerning the investment's legality. In doing so, the Committee noted the need to assess 'the impartiality of the relevant decision-maker, in view of the pendency of proceedings against the state of which that decision-maker is an organ'.[87] The Committee then concluded that 'the Prosecutor's Resolution was of singular significance' on several grounds, including that 'his decision, being adverse to the interests of the state, appeared to have been reached independently'.[88] In *PAO Tatneft v. Ukraine*, the tribunal stated that: '[D]eference on the part of international tribunals requires the clear perception that domestic courts are independent, competent and above all clear of suspicion of corruption'.[89] Hepburn likewise argues that 'while domestic case-law should be given considerable weight in ascertaining the contents of relevant domestic law, exceptional circumstances might call for departure from this', identifying the situation where 'there are justifiable doubts about the quality or integrity' of domestic authorities as such exceptional circumstances.[90] The approach stressing the need for carefully assessing the integrity, independence, impartiality, and procedural propriety of the local courts[91] squarely applies to the context of local courts' determination relevant to counterclaims.

[84] For example, Article 3.42 of the EU-Viet Nam Investment Protection Agreement provides that the Tribunal 'shall be bound by the interpretation given to the domestic law by the courts or authorities'.

[85] Paine, 'Standard of Review', 18.

[86] *Fraport I* Annulment Decision, para. 236.

[87] Ibid., para. 242.

[88] Ibid., para. 243.

[89] *PAO Tatneft (formerly OAO Tatneft) v. Ukraine*, PCA Case No. 2008-8, Award on the Merits, 29 July 2014, para. 476.

[90] Hepburn, *Domestic Law in International Investment Arbitration*, 128, 132.

[91] Schill, 'Deference in Investment Treaty Arbitration', 600–604.

In conclusion, given that application of domestic laws is inevitable for the determination of counterclaims, legitimacy concerns must be addressed through the process of application and interpretation of domestic laws by tribunals in the IIA-based dispute settlement mechanism. Admittedly, this case-by-case approach would not eliminate the possibility of inconsistent and controversial (e.g. from the viewpoint of highest courts of the relevant domestic jurisdictions) interpretations of domestic laws. However, consistent adoption of the domestic jurisprudence approach, in which the tribunal demonstrates its respect of such jurisprudence, by identifying, obtaining, and analysing sufficient and balanced sources of the domestic law at issue, would address the legitimacy issue concerning the application of domestic laws.

5.3 Counterclaims Based on International Law

5.3.1 Investor Obligations in IIAs

When the relevant IIA provides the investors' binding obligations, the alleged violation of these obligations by the investor would make direct grounds for the respondent state's counterclaims. *Al-Warraq v. Indonesia* is the first case where a counterclaim based on a provision on the investor's obligations in the relevant IIA (Article 9 of the OIC Investment Agreement, cited in Chapter 2, Section 2.3.2)[92] was held admissible. In this case, the claimant investor was the owner of an Indonesian bank called Bank Century, and the dispute arose out of criminal proceedings concerning the bailout of the bank. The complaints lodged by the central bank of the Republic of Indonesia about banking irregularities with regard to the bailout included the allegation that bailout funds had been used to fund the 2009 presidential election campaign. The claimant was convicted of theft, corruption, and money laundering.[93] Mr Al-Warraq's assets in Indonesia were confiscated,[94] and he filed claims to investment arbitration based on the OIC Investment Agreement. Indonesia filed a counterclaim based on the allegation that the claimant investor unjustly enriched himself by holding on to Bank Century's assets rather than either selling them or returning them, which

[92] Agreement on Promotion, Protection and Guarantee of Investments among Member States of the Organization of the Islamic Conference, adopted 1981, entered into force 1988.

[93] *Al-Warraq* Award, paras. 108–125, 141.

[94] Ibid., para. 141.

resulted in the loss for Bank Century and ultimately for the people of the Republic of Indonesia.[95]

The tribunal confirmed the admissibility of the counterclaim on the following grounds: lack of a definition of 'disputes' and neutral *locus standi* in the dispute settlement clause of the OIC Investment Agreement (Article 17),[96] and that Article 9 of the Agreement offers support for the interpretation of Article 17 so as to authorise counterclaims.[97] The tribunal then dismissed the counterclaim on its merits on the grounds that the counterclaim did not distinguish the actions of the claimant from the actions of various other entities, and that whereas the counterclaim was based on fraud committed against Bank Century, a legal basis for the respondent's rights to recover these losses was not demonstrated.[98] It is observed that, despite its dismissal, the counterclaim in the *Al-Warraq* case presents the potential for future development of the IIA regime towards a 'symmetrical regime in which foreign investors have international rights as well as obligations'.[99]

5.3.2 *Investor Obligations in International Law outside IIAs*

Unlike the OIC Investment Agreement that was applied in the *Al-Warraq* case, the vast majority of IIAs still lack provisions regarding investors' obligations (Chapter 2, Section 2.3.2). The absence of investors' obligations in IIAs has been considered as a crucial obstacle for the host state to invoke international law as a ground for counterclaims.[100]

However, *Urbaser v. Argentina* introduced a new potential in counterclaims by admitting the possibility of invoking the investor's international obligations in counterclaims, even though the relevant IIA did not contain investors' obligations. This case concerns a concession for water and sewage services to be provided in Buenos Aires granted to a company in which the claimants had shares. The claimants alleged that Argentina's measures, including the emergency measures taken after the economic crisis that began in mid-2001 rendered it difficult to operate the

[95] Ibid., paras. 459–474.
[96] Ibid., para. 661.
[97] Ibid., para. 663.
[98] Ibid., paras. 669–670.
[99] Newcombe and Marcoux, '*Hesham Talaat M. Al-Warraq*', 532.
[100] Cazala, 'Le respect des droits de l'homme', 348. See also Atanasova, Martínez Benoit and Ostřanský, 'Counterclaims in Investor-State Dispute Settlement', 4.

concession, which was eventually terminated in 2006.[101] In response, Argentina raised counterclaims on the ground that, by failing to make the investments under the water service concession, the claimants 'violated the principles of good faith and *pacta sunt servanda* that are recognized both by Argentine law and by international law'.[102] It further argued that such a failure affected 'human rights, as well as the health and the environment of thousands of persons, most of which lived in extreme poverty'.[103]

The tribunal first confirmed the host state's right to bring counterclaims under the Argentina-Spain BIT on the ground, *inter alia*, of the broad definition of 'disputes' in the dispute settlement clause.[104] Then, the tribunal proceeded to state that in light of the recognition of CSR in the international law sphere, 'it can no longer be admitted that companies operating internationally are immune from becoming subjects of international law'.[105] Referring to the 1948 Universal Declaration of Human Rights[106] and the 1966 International Covenant on Economic, Social and Cultural Rights,[107] the tribunal stated that: 'The BIT has to be construed in harmony with other rules of international law of which it forms part, including those relating to human rights'.[108] Significantly, as discussed in Chapter 2, Section 2.2.2.3, the tribunal acknowledged that 'an obligation to abstain, like a prohibition to commit acts violating human rights . . . can be of immediate application' to private parties.[109]

Also demonstrating this potential is the case of *Aven v. Costa Rica*, which arose from the claimants' investment in a tourism project. Neighbours to the project site raised concerns and complaints about the negative environmental impacts on wetlands and forest grounds, and Costa Rican authorities undertook inspections which resulted in the issuance of a judicial injunction against the continuance of works and other

[101] *Urbaser* Award, para. 34.
[102] Ibid., para. 1156.
[103] Ibid.
[104] Ibid., para. 1187.
[105] Ibid., para. 1195.
[106] Universal Declaration of Human Rights (UN General Assembly, 'Universal Declaration of Human Rights', 10 December 1948). *Urbaser* Award, paras. 1158, 1162, 1196, 1198.
[107] International Covenant on Economic, Social and Cultural Rights (UN General Assembly, International Covenant on Economic, Social and Cultural Rights, 16 December 1966, United Nations, Treaty Series, vol. 993, p. 3, G.A. Res. 22001 (XXI), UN GAOR, 21st Sess., Supp. No. 16, UN Doc. A/6316, 993 UNTS 3 (1966). *Urbaser* Award, paras. 1160, 1162, 1197, 1198.
[108] *Urbaser* Award, para. 1200.
[109] Ibid., para. 1210.

measures. Criminal proceedings against individuals including Mr Aven were raised on the ground of a violation of local laws on forestry and wildlife conservation.[110] Mr Aven and other claimants went to investment arbitration, arguing that Costa Rica's measures preventing the project amounted to a breach of the fair and equitable treatment and expropriation obligations under CAFTA-DR. In turn, Costa Rica raised counterclaims asserting that unlawful work carried out on the part of the investor caused environmental damage to a wetland, and thereby violated 'domestic provisions as well as the obligation under customary international law to respect the environment'.[111] It also claimed that the investor was obliged to make reparations according to the *Chorzów Factory* standard.[112] As discussed in Chapter 2, Section 2.2.2.3, the tribunal agreed with the *Urbaser* tribunal's affirmation that investors operating internationally cannot be immune from becoming subjects of international law.[113] On this basis, the tribunal found its *prima facie* jurisdiction over the counterclaim.[114]

The approach adopted by the *Urbaser* and *Aven* tribunals clearly suggests that where there is international law – either customary international law or treaty law – that provides binding obligations applicable to the investor, rules drawn from it can be relied on as primary rules by the host state in pursuing a counterclaim. In light of the ongoing efforts to draft legally binding instrument to regulate the activities of transnational corporations and other business enterprises (Chapter 2, Section 2.2.2.1) and the Global Pact for the Environment (Chapter 2, Section 2.2.2.2), this is not a merely theoretical possibility. Moreover, in both cases, tribunals kept the door open to the possibility that 'an obligation to abstain, like a prohibition to commit acts violating human rights'[115] and 'obligations *erga omnes*'[116] may directly bind investors.

5.3.3 *Quest for Secondary Rules for Corporate International Responsibility*

5.3.3.1 Absence of Secondary Rules in International Law

Both of the *Urbaser* and *Aven* cases, however, point that counterclaims based on external international law would face the same obstacle, that is

110 *Aven* Award, paras. 93–174.
111 Ibid., para. 699.
112 Ibid., para. 709.
113 Ibid., para. 738.
114 Ibid., para. 742.
115 *Urbaser* Award, para. 1210.
116 *Aven* Award, para. 738.

the seeming lack of *secondary* rules. For the purposes of this chapter, which discusses the investor's responsibility for the alleged breach of international obligations, the concept of 'secondary rules' is narrowly defined as those 'concerned with determining the consequences of failure to fulfil obligations established by the primary rules'.[117] The *Urbaser* tribunal pointed out the failure of the respondent state to identify secondary rules governing its counterclaims:

> Respondent does not state any legal ground for any individual's right to claim damages as a consequence of an alleged violation of the human right to water. Respondent does not demonstrate either that the alleged violation of such human right entails a duty of reparation equally based on international law, with the effect that the individuals concerned by such an alleged harm obtain an appropriate compensation.[118]

Likewise, the tribunal in *Aven* dismissed the respondent state's counterclaims due to lack of specification of the grounds for a breach of 'imperative norms of environmental protection'[119] (domestic and international) alleged by the respondent. The tribunal stated that a counterclaim, as an autonomous claim, must satisfy the requirements under Articles 20.2 and 20.4 of the 2010 UNCITRAL Arbitration Rules. It then observed that Costa Rica provided neither a 'precise statement of the facts supporting the claims' nor 'specification of the relief sought', and therefore it did not meet these requirements.[120] Indeed, albeit dismissed based on other grounds, the counterclaims based on Article 9 of the OIC Investment Agreement in *Al-Warraq v. Indonesia* would have faced the same issue, because the Agreement only provides the investor's right to monetary

[117] International Law Commission, 'Second Report on State Responsibility by Roberto Ago, Special Rapporteur', 20 April 1970, UN Doc. A/CN.4/233, 2 YbILC 177, 179. Hart perceives secondary rules broadly as those that specify the ways in which the primary rules may be conclusively ascertained, introduced, eliminated, varied, and the fact of their violation conclusively determined. Hart, *The Concept of Law*, 89–96. The narrow definition thus excludes secondary rules 'on the creation, application, revision or termination of primary rules' (Pauwelyn, 'Role of Public International Law', 536). See also UN General Assembly, First Report on State Responsibility by James Crawford, Special Rapporteur, 24 April 1999, UN Doc. A/CN.4/490, paras. 12–18; Crawford, 'ILC's Articles on Responsibility of States', 878; Pauwelyn, *Conflict of Norms*, 149; Bodansky and Crook, 'Introduction and Overview', 779; International Law Commission, 'Fragmentation of International Law: Difficulties arising from the Diversification and Expansion of International Law, Report of the Study Group of the International Law Commission, Finalized by Martti Koskenniemi', 13 April 2006, UN Doc. A/CN.4/L.682, paras. 27, 128.

[118] *Urbaser* Award, para. 1220.

[119] *Aven* Award, para. 721.

[120] Ibid., para. 745.

compensation for any damage resulting from the host state's violation of obligations.[121]

As discussed in Chapter 2, Section 2.2.2, there are no international instruments that provide the consequences of a breach of international environmental and human rights obligations by corporations.[122] Nor is there customary international law in this regard. It may be argued that Part Two of the International Law Commission (ILC) Articles on State Responsibility[123] can be applied by analogy to the investors' international responsibility because, despite the fact that Article 33 makes it clear that Part Two, which deals with the legal consequences for the responsible state of its internationally wrongful act, 'does not apply to obligations of reparation to the extent that these arise towards or are invoked by a person or entity other than a State',[124] investment arbitration tribunals have routinely referred to and applied Part Two of the Articles.[125] However, the analogous application of Part Two to the responsibility *of the host state* owed to investors as 'the best available source of guidance as to the law of remedies in international law'[126] has the following grounds, none of which applies to private persons' international responsibility.

The commentary to Article 33 explains the limitation of its scope in the following terms: In situations where 'the primary obligation is owed to a non-State entity [as "the ultimate beneficiaries and in that sense as the holders of the relevant rights"], it may be that some procedure is available whereby that entity can invoke the responsibility on its own

121 Article 13 of the OIC Investment Agreement.

122 This is contrasted to the situations where 'mechanisms to adjudicate non-state actors' international responsibilities' have been established in the context of international criminal law. Vázquez, 'Direct vs. Indirect Obligations of Corporations', 939.

123 International Law Commission, 'Draft Articles on Responsibility of States for Internationally Wrongful Acts', UN GAOR 56th Session, Supp. No. 10, at 43, UN Doc. A/56/10 (2001), YbILC 2001, vol. II. The UN General Assembly took note of the Draft Articles and annexed them to the resolution. UN General Assembly, 'Responsibility of States for Internationally Wrongful Acts: Resolution/Adopted by the General Assembly on 12 December 2001', 28 January 2002, A/RES/56/83. See Galvão Teles, 'Impact and Influence of the Articles'.

124 International Law Commission, 'Commentaries to Draft Articles on Responsibility of States for Internationally Wrongful Acts', UN GAOR 56th Session, Supp. No. 10, at 43, UN Doc. A/56/10 (2001), YbILC, vol. II, Part Two, 87–88 (commentary to Article 28).

125 For example, *Chevron Corporation (USA) and Texaco Petroleum Company (USA) v. Republic of Ecuador*, UNCITRAL, PCA Case No. 34877, Interim Award, 1 December 2008, para. 118; *Hamester* Award, Sections VIII–IX.

126 Stephens-Chu, 'Is It Always All About the Money?', 667. See also Endicott, 'Remedies in Investor-State Arbitration', 531; Hindelang, 'Restitution and Compensation', 195.

account and without the intermediation of any State', and therefore '[i]t will be a matter for the particular primary rule to determine whether and to what extent persons or entities other than States are entitled to invoke responsibility on their own account'.[127] The commentary cites human rights treaties as such rules.

This may well suggest that the limitation under Article 33 concerns 'issues of implementation, invocation, and enforcement of responsibility, rather than the substantive content of responsibility'.[128] This is confirmed by the following statement by Crawford on the function of Article 33(2):

> This provision completes the framework of the subject of the responsibility *of* states, allowing the full range of possibilities in terms of right-duty relationships and avoiding any negative inferences that might otherwise have been drawn from the decision to deal in detail only with issues of invocation of responsibility *by* states.[129]

De Brabandere argues that 'the involvement of a private actor does not alter the fundamental premise that treaty breaches by a state are governed by the principles applicable to the international responsibility of states'.[130] Therefore, Crawford and Olleson acknowledge that the frequent reference to Article 31 by investment arbitral tribunals is 'unproblematic, as it is not obvious that the content of the responsibility owed to an investor (or at least those rules relating to the manner in which compensation is to be quantified) differ from those applicable in the context of inter-State responsibility'.[131]

As noted, none of these grounds provide the basis for an analogous application of Article 31 to *investors' international responsibility* owed to the host state. Nor is this the approach adopted by investment arbitration tribunals in *Urbaser v. Argentina* and *Aven v. Costa Rica* which, as discussed above, pointed out the failure of identifying secondary rules that determine the consequences of a breach of external international law

[127] Commentaries to Draft Articles, 95.

[128] Wittich, 'Domestic Courts and the Content', 648. Therefore, for example, 'There is nothing in the Draft Articles that restricts the ability of States to conclude investment treaties that, for example, limit the ability of investors to recover moral damages, or restrict the power of tribunals to award certain remedies' (Pearsall and Heath, 'Causation and Injury', 89–90).

[129] Crawford, 'ILC's Articles on Responsibility of States', 887 (emphasis in original).

[130] De Brabandere, *Investment Treaty Arbitration*, 27–28.

[131] Crawford and Olleson, 'Application of the Rules', 418. See also Douglas, 'Other Specific Regimes of Responsibility', 820.

in the host states' claims. For these reasons, there is no basis for analogous application of the ILC Articles to investors' international responsibility. The situation, therefore, remains that 'a glass is half-full or half-empty'[132] after the *Urbaser* and *Aven* cases – secondary rules for such responsibility must be sought elsewhere than in international law.

5.3.3.2 Enforcement through Domestic Law

As discussed above (Section 5.2.1), in the IIA-based dispute settlement mechanism, domestic law and international law supplement each other. Article 42(1) of the ICSID Convention, according to Reisman's interpretation, engenders a relationship of coordination between these laws at the remedy phase: 'if the remedy [applicable to the issue in dispute at hand] is not provided by the host State's law, the [ICSID] Tribunal must then proceed to search for it in international law'.[133] Conversely, then, in situations where international law does not provide the remedy applicable to the counterclaim, the tribunal must search for it in domestic law in the same manner as set out by Reisman.

First, the domestic law of the host state may provide a mechanism for incorporating the relevant international obligations into domestic law by implementing legislation, which enables the enforcement of such obligations. Likewise, establishing the necessary mechanisms to enforce the responsibility of corporations is a requirement under international environmental agreements on the 'civil liability' of juridical persons (see Chapter 2, Section 2.2.2.2). For example, in the case of *Erika*, which is discussed in Section 5.4.1, the French Cour de Cassation held Total SA liable for civil damages under the 1992 Protocol to the International Convention on Civil Liability for Oil Pollution Damage.[134]

Second, the enforcement of international law in the domestic legal order is possible through different means. The status, applicability, and means of the enforcement of international law in the domestic legal order vary considerably between legal systems; discussions of the relationship between international and domestic law in different jurisdictions are beyond the scope of this study.[135] When a counterclaim is based on a

[132] Šturma, 'Public Goods and International Investment Law', 15.
[133] Reisman, 'The Regime for *Lacunae*', 371.
[134] Communiqué relatif à l'arrêt n° 3439 du 25 septembre 2012 (10-82.938) de la Chambre criminelle, (l'arrêt Erika), 203–210.
[135] See e.g. Sloss, 'Treaty Enforcement in Domestic Courts'; Sloss and Van Alstine, 'International Law in Domestic Courts'; Zerk, 'Corporate Liability for Gross Human Rights Abuses'.

parent company's transterritorial tort allegations, the determination of the applicable domestic law also arises, which, as discussed in Chapter 4, Section 4.4.2, will be determined by reference to different factors including the 'rules on the conflict of laws' of the host state's law (Article 42(1) of the ICSID Convention), which is always applicable (see Section 5.2), the laws of relevant jurisdictions, the facts of the case, and the relevant IIA. In this regard, case law of certain jurisdictions, in particular that under the US Alien Tort Statute (ATS)[136] (see Chapter 2, Section 2.1.3), is suggestive regarding the use of domestic law as a source of secondary rules for international responsibility owed by private entities.

In *Urbaser v. Argentina*, Argentina appears to have relied on the judgment of the US Court of Appeals (2nd Circuit) in *Filártiga v. Peña-Irala*,[137] which admitted jurisdiction for the claim based on the ATS; however, the tribunal rejected its relevance to the current case on the grounds that the case does not concern an international law obligation of immediate application to individuals and other private parties (see Section 5.3.2).[138] This is a logical conclusion, given the finding of the tribunal that there was no international obligation applicable to the investor in this case. However, what is significant with the *Filártiga* case is that the US District Court for the Eastern District of New York in *Filártiga v. Peña-Irala* (on remand)[139] employed domestic law as secondary rules for the violation of international obligations by a private person, even in the absence of implementing legislation, as explained below.

Filártiga was a suit brought against a Paraguayan police officer for the torture and murder of another Paraguayan. Following the judgment of the Court of Appeal (2nd Circuit), the case was brought to the District Court for the Eastern District of New York on remand. The court, having confirmed that the Court of Appeals decided only that Section 1350 gave jurisdiction, concluded that for the determination of the nature of the action, that is, whether or not it is a 'tort' under Section 1350, substantial principles in international law need to be applied. Facing the fact that

136 28 US Code §1350.

137 *Filártiga v. Peña-Irala*, 630 F.2d 876 (2d Cir. 1980) (*Filártiga* (2d Cir.)). This was the first ATS-based case in which the US court allowed aliens to sue other aliens for violations of international law, that is, the prohibition of torture. See Rusk, 'Comment on *Filartiga v. Pena-Irala*', 315; Hartka, 'Role of International Law in Domestic Courts', 111; George, 'Defining *Filartiga*'; Stephens, 'Translating *Filártiga*'; Bellia and Clark, 'The Alien Tort Statute'.

138 *Urbaser* Award, para. 1210 (fn 446).

139 *Filártiga v. Peña-Irala*, 577 F. Supp. 860 (EDNY 10 January 1984) (*Filártiga* (EDNY)).

customary international law does not afford a victim of torture a damage remedy against the individual offender,[140] the court then sought the source of the remedy in domestic law. It stated that:

> [P]lainly international 'law' does not consist of mere benevolent yearnings never to be given effect. ... The international law prohibiting torture established the standard and referred to the national states the task of enforcing it. By enacting Section 1350 Congress entrusted that task to the federal courts and gave them power to choose and develop federal remedies to effectuate the purposes of the international law incorporated into United States common law.[141]

The court decided to 'look first to Paraguayan law in determining the remedy for the violation of international law', by reference to the choice of law factors listed in Section 145(2) of the Restatement (Second) of Conflict of Laws (1971), on the findings, *inter alia*, that: the torture and death occurred in Paraguay, that the plaintiffs and the defendant were Paraguayan and lived in Paraguay when the torture occurred, that the pertinent formal Paraguayan law is ascertainable.[142] However, the court proceeded to note that in this case Paraguay might well not hold Peña responsible for his official acts, and concluded to award punitive damages that were not provided under Paraguayan law in order to 'give effect to the manifest objectives of the international prohibition against torture'.[143]

By contrast, in the recent case of *Nestlé USA Inc. v. John Doe*, the Supreme Court (opinion delivered by Justice Thomas, joined by Justices Gorsuch and Kavanaugh) concluded that Federal courts may not create a cause of action for ATS claims.[144] Justice Thomas stated that: 'Aliens harmed by a violation of international law must rely on legislative and executive remedies, not judicial remedies, unless provided with an

[140] The *Filártiga* case predates the enactment of the Torture Victim Protection Act of 1991, which provides that an offender committing torture or extrajudicial killing 'shall, in a civil action, be liable for damages' (Torture Victim Protection Act 1991. Pub. L. 102-256, 12 March 1992, 106 Stat. 73). The Act implemented certain aspects of the 1984 UN Torture Convention (Convention Against Torture and Other Cruel, Inhuman or Degrading Treatment or Punishment, Geneva, 10 December 1984, in force 26 June 1987, 1465 UNTS 85).

[141] *Filártiga* (EDNY), 863.

[142] Ibid., 864.

[143] Ibid., 865. The awards made against the defendant in this case were however neither paid nor enforced in Paraguayan domestic courts. See Baez, Dearing, Delatour and Dixon, 'Multinational Enterprises and Human Rights', 319.

[144] *Nestlé USA Inc. v. John Doe*, 17 June 2021 (*Nestlé v. Doe*) 5. See Chapter 2, Section 2.1.3.

independent cause of action',[145] stressing 'the Constitution's separation of legislative and judicial power'.[146] He then argued that 'creating a cause of action to enforce international law beyond three historical torts [identified in *Sosa*][147] invariably gives rise to foreign-policy concerns'.[148] However, only Justices Gorsuch and Kavanaugh joined on this point, and Justice Sotomayor, in her concurring opinion (joined by Justices Breyer and Kagan), strongly contested this argument. She first observed that 'from the moment the ATS became law, Congress expected federal courts to identify actionable torts under international law and to provide injured plaintiffs with a forum to seek redress'.[149] She then stated as follows, offering strong support for the use of domestic tort law:

> Courts must, based on their interpretation of international law, identify those norms that are so specific, universal, and obligatory that they give rise to a 'tort' for which Congress expects federal courts to entertain 'causes' – or, in modern parlance, 'civil action[s],' 28 U. S. C. §1350 – for redress.[150]

Notably, none of the concerns expressed by the Supreme Court over the use of the ATS to establish causes of action *in US courts* for claims based on violations of international norms by defendants *committed against foreign plaintiffs in other countries*, that is, their 'tenuous connections' to the US and diplomatic disruptions or foreign-policy concerns caused by their admission,[151] apply to international dispute settlement forums.

A recent judgment by the Supreme Court of Canada in *Nevsun Resources Ltd. v. Araya*[152] acknowledged the role of domestic law as a determinant of remedies for international wrongdoing by corporations.

[145] *Nestlé v. Doe*, 6.

[146] Ibid., 7 (citing Hernández, 589 U. S., at ___ (slip op., at 5)).

[147] See Chapter 2, Section 2.1.3.

[148] *Nestlé v. Doe*, 9 (citing *Jesner et al. v. Arab Bank*, PLC, No. 16-499, 584 U.S. ___ (2018) (*Jesner v. Arab Bank*), majority opinion, 18–19).

[149] Ibid. Concurring opinion of Justice Sotomayor, joined by Justices Breyer and Kagan, 6.

[150] Ibid., 7. See also *Jesner v. Arab Bank*, Dissent, Justice Sotomayor (joined by Justice Ginsburg, Justice Breyer, and Justice Kagan), 3. See also Vázquez, 'Alien Tort Claims and the Status', 532.

[151] *Jesner v. Arab Bank*, 26; *Nestlé v. Doe*, 8. It should be noted that Justice Sotomayor pointed out, in her concurring opinion in *Nestlé v. Doe*, the other side of foreign-policy concerns: 'that foreign nations may take (and, indeed, historically have taken) umbrage at the United States' refusal to provide redress to their citizens for international law torts committed by US nationals within the United States'. Concurring opinion of Justice Sotomayor, 9.

[152] *Nevsun Resources Ltd. v. Araya*, [2020] SCC 5, Judgment, 28 February 2020 (*Nevsun* judgment).

As discussed in Chapter 2, Section 2.2.2.3, in this case, the majority (Wagner CJ and Abella, Karakatsanis, Gascon, and Martin JJ) concluded that 'the breaches of customary international law, or *jus cogens*' may (potentially) apply to the Canadian corporation.[153] The court then proceeded to examine the question of whether or not 'our domestic common law [can] develop appropriate remedies for breaches of adopted customary international law norms'.[154] It noted that its case law had recognised the general principle that 'where there is a right, there must be a remedy for its violation',[155] and stated that 'it is not "plain and obvious" that Canadian courts cannot develop a civil remedy in domestic law for corporate violations of the customary international law norms adopted in Canadian law'.[156]

The court then acknowledged that the customary international law norms alleged in this case, that is, forced labour; slavery; cruel, inhuman, or degrading treatment; and crimes against humanity, 'are inherently different from existing domestic torts. Their character is of a more public nature than existing domestic private torts since the violation of these norms "shock[s] the conscience of humanity"'.[157] The court decided to leave the question of how the violation of these norms may become compensable to the trial judge, providing the following suggestions:

> The claims may well be allowed to proceed based on the recognition of new nominate torts, but this is not necessarily the only possible route to resolving the Eritrean workers' claims. A compelling argument can also be made, based on their pleadings, for a direct approach recognizing that since customary international law is part of Canadian common law, a breach by a Canadian company can theoretically be directly remedied based on a breach of customary international law.[158]

It should be noted that in civil law systems where '*every* act that is contrary to that which people in general . . . and that caused damage' potentially gives rise to compensate such damage,[159] a specific cause of action for each tortious act is not required. However, this does not

[153] Ibid., para. 114. Whether Nevsun breached these norms on the finding of the facts of the case was left to the trial judge (para. 131).
[154] Ibid., para. 117.
[155] Ibid., para. 120 (citation omitted).
[156] Ibid., para. 122.
[157] Ibid., para. 124 (citation omitted).
[158] Ibid., para. 127. Justices Brown and Rowe dissented.
[159] Enneking, 'Crossing the Atlantic?', 922 (emphasis in original).

change the fact that a legal ground to seek the remedy for damages resulting from a wrongful act needs to be identified in civil law systems.

Once again, whether a domestic law remedy becomes available for a violation of international norms by private entities depends on the applicable domestic law, which varies between cases and jurisdictions.[160] The determination will also depend on factors such as the nature of the norms (customary international law or a treaty).[161] However, it is worth noting in this regard that: (a) in the context of international environmental and human rights norms, their effects have been sought through the application of civil tort law[162] and (b) in several jurisdictions including both monist and dualist countries, there is a growing tendency of the internalisation of international law through a greater openness to the indirect effect of international law,[163] a 'transnational legal process',[164] the movement of 'fondamentalisation',[165] and the application of an 'interpretive presumption that domestic statutes should be construed in a manner consistent with international norms' by courts.[166]

Therefore, the respondent state that raises a counterclaim based on investors' international obligations, which include both those provided in IIAs and external international law, may consider the application of a domestic law remedy through the effect of international law in the domestic legal order. If it can establish that remedies for the investor's violation of such obligations are provided in this way, grounds for the counterclaim could be established.

Counterclaims based on international obligations have a particularly significant impact when they have more stringent demands than domestic

[160] For a comparative study of private law claims for international torts, see e.g. Zerk, 'Corporate Liability for Gross Human Rights Abuses', 43–53.

[161] See *Nevsun* judgment, para. 127 (cited above); Anton and Shelton, *Environmental Protection and Human Rights*, 65; Gazzini, 'General Principles of Law', 105.

[162] Knight, 'International Human Rights Litigation after *Bauman*', 222 (citing Alford, 'Future of Human Rights Litigation', 1750); Sachs, 'Beyond the Liability Wall'; Davis and Whytock, 'State Remedies for Human Rights'; Zerk, *Multinationals and Corporate Social Responsibility*, 44, 200–207.

[163] Bronckers, 'Is ISDS Superior to Litigation', 664.

[164] Koh, 'Transnational Legal Process', 183–186.

[165] Helleringer and Garcia, 'Le rayonnement des droits de l'Homme', 308.

[166] Sloss and Van Alstine, 'International Law in Domestic Courts', 109. See also International Law Association, 'Principles on the Engagement of Domestic Courts with International Law' (2011–2016), available at: www.ila-hq.org/index.php/study-groups?study-groupsID=57 (accessed 15 December 2021).

standards, in particular those of the host state as the place of injury.[167] The potential gap between international standards and domestic regulatory standards also warrants the need to examine the possibility that a breach of *non-binding* commitments undertaken by the investor may form the basis of a counterclaim in the IIA-based dispute settlement mechanism.

5.4 CSR Commitments as a Source of Counterclaims

The *Urbaser* tribunal is the first investment arbitration tribunal which acknowledged that 'international law accepts corporate social responsibility as a standard of crucial importance for companies operating in the field of international commerce'.[168] However, as the tribunal dismissed Argentina's counterclaims for lack of a source for Urbaser's 'obligation to perform' as well as the specification of secondary rules (as discussed in Section 5.3.3.1), it did not examine the question of how CSR can actually give rise to corporations' obligations.[169]

This section discusses the possibility that the investor's voluntary standards and CSR commitments may provide grounds for the host state's counterclaim in the IIA-based dispute settlement mechanism. It also demonstrates different ways through which CSR commitments can give rise to legal obligations under domestic laws.

5.4.1 Legal Obligations under CSR through Domestic Law

As discussed in Chapter 2, Section 2.2.3, CSR and law heavily interact. When the relevant CSR commitments are obligatory in the domestic law of the host state (Chapter 2, Section 2.2.3.1), the investor's failure to meet such commitments would directly constitute a violation of the host state's domestic law.

However, the real potential of CSR arises where a host country's domestic regulatory standards fall below international CSR standards or standards in the investors' home countries.[170] It is argued here that

[167] See the third-generation IIAs that subject investors to international standards of business conduct, which are higher than domestic standards (see Chapter 2, Section 2.3.2).

[168] *Urbaser* Award, para. 1195.

[169] For an analysis of the CSR commitment undertaken by the ACS group to which Urbaser belonged, see Crow and Lorenzoni Escobar, 'International Corporate Obligations', 25.

[170] Zerk identifies 'a lack of information necessary to set minimum standards at the appropriate level, regulatory standards falling behind changing needs and expectations or technology ("regulatory lag")' as difficulties associated with regulatory approach.

the liability of an investor for a breach of such commitments may be established through the application of the domestic laws in different ways. In the context of investor–state relationships, the most straightforward situation would be where CSR commitments are incorporated in contracts between them or required by the host state as a condition to receive licences or permissions for the operation of businesses.[171] In such cases, they become legally binding through private laws (e.g. contract law) or the host state's public laws (e.g. environmental, mining, and other administrative laws),[172] and these laws will determine the consequences of a breach of such commitments. Domestic law may thus form the basis for a counterclaim, if the investor's conduct has caused damages (Section 5.2).

Even in the absence of such a direct legal relationship, a transnational corporation (TNC)'s internal self-regulation concerning their environmental management and human rights issues may, in itself, give rise to legal responsibility when they are found to standardise the practice in a group operating in different jurisdictions.[173] An example where conduct that fell below the standard set out by the group's internal regulations gave rise to corporate liability is the case of *Erika*.[174] This case arose out of the sinking of an oil tanker (Erika) owned by a subsidiary of Total SA, a major French oil company, which resulted in a large oil spill affecting the French coastline in 1999. The Paris Court of Appeal found criminal responsibility with respect to Total on the basis of erroneous operation of 'vetting', a procedure of vessel control not required by law but prescribed in internal regulations of the Total group (in particular inspection), and imposed criminal fines on Total SA.[175] The Cour de Cassation confirmed the analysis of the Court of Appeal

Zerk, *Multinationals and Corporate Social Responsibility*, 37. For a comparison of environmental laws and performance between countries, see e.g. 2018 Environmental Performance Index, available at: https://epi.envirocenter.yale.edu/about-epi (accessed 15 December 2021); Environmental Democracy Index, available at: www.environmentaldemocracyindex.org/ (accessed 15 December 2021). See also Corkin, 'Misappropriating Citizenship', 45–46; Hilson, 'Corporate Social Responsibility', 132.

171 Parker, 'Meta-Regulation', 219–220.

172 Deumier, 'Les codes de conduite des entreprises', 692–694.

173 Kolk and van Tulder, 'Setting New Global Rules?', 19.

174 On this case, see Daoud and Le Corre, 'Arrêt Erika'; Neyret, 'L'affaire Erika'. See also Dubin, 'Entreprise multinationale'; Uff, 'La réparation du dommage'; Vallat, 'Les apports'; Ong, 'Regulating Environmental Responsibility'.

175 CA Paris, Pôle 4, ch. 11, 30 mars 2010, Clemente et a. c/ Conseil général de la Vendée et al., n° 08/02278.

which ordered Total to pay €375,000 as criminal fine, finding that Total 'failed to perform its normal due diligence'.[176]

Furthermore, a breach of CSR commitments by the investor may lead to its legal responsibility through the civil tort law[177] as follows. Investors or their parent companies may publish declarations and commitments,[178] such as CSR reports and codes of conduct for different reasons, including: as a way to express their affirmation that they do bear social responsibilities;[179] in response to hard and soft law reporting requirements (see Chapter 2, Sections 2.2.3.1 and 2.2.3.2); and for marketing purposes.[180] Company codes of conduct are described as 'policy statements that outline the ethical standards of conduct to which a corporation adheres'[181] and as norms that stand at the top of hierarchy of the group's internal norms.[182] Notably, McBarnet and Kurkchiyan observe that: 'Some supply codes also made it clear that where domestic law falls below international standards, it is international standards that should be observed, and on some issues, the standard is expressly set higher than in domestic law'.[183] Glinski also observes that codes of conduct and other self-regulatory instruments 'all use the language of promises'.[184]

Once such commitments in these instruments are published, they create certain expectations about the standard of investors' conduct on the part of stakeholders and the host state's society as beneficiaries.[185] Specifically, they may give rise to the expectation that when there is a gap between stated commitments and local standards, investors will apply the

[176] L'arrêt Erika, 167 (translation by author).

[177] As noted, in *Burlington v. Ecuador* and *Perenco v. Ecuador*, the host state's environmental counterclaims were based on Ecuadorian tort law as the law of the place of injury. *Burlington* Decision on Counterclaims, para. 73; *Perenco* Interim Decision on Counterclaims, para. 319.

[178] These declarations and representations include: 'mission statements', 'social auditing schemes', labelling and certification. See Shamir, 'Between Self-Regulation', 645; Eroglu, *Multinational Enterprises and Tort Liabilities*, 146–147, 226.

[179] Shamir, 'Between Self-Regulation', 645.

[180] Glinski, 'Corporate Codes of Conduct', 122.

[181] Bantekas, 'Corporate Social Responsibility in International Law', 322.

[182] Vallat, 'Les apports', 479.

[183] McBarnet and Kurkchiyan, 'Corporate Social Responsibility through Contractual Control?', 67. See also Vallat, 'Les apports', 480.

[184] Glinski, 'Corporate Codes of Conduct', 123.

[185] Buhmann, 'Corporate Social Responsibility', 199. See also Laryea, 'Legitimate Expectations in Investment Treaty Law', 118.

former.[186] It is argued that through these published commitments and initiatives corporations 'enter into social contracts'.[187]

In situations where a TNC's conduct falls below the former standard and results in damage, the generated expectations may determine the content of its duty of care (and equivalent concepts). Likewise, the investors' failure to satisfy their own 'promises' may be considered as a failure to act with a required level of environmental and social risk due diligence, which 'interweave elements of legal and regulatory compliance with good practice expectations and established norms'.[188]

In the context of common law, the assessment of due diligence[189] and duty of care (required conduct)[190] as commonly recognised elements of tort[191] is, by nature, case-specific, retroactive, and, for each case, the identified facts must be evaluated 'in light of an applicable standard, policy or expectation'.[192] Peter Ward further observes that the question of what constitutes tortious acts requires balancing where 'the interests of one must be weighed against those of another or others on scales of absolute or relative values'.[193] Similar observations have also been made for the civil law of tort in the specific context of the legal effects of CSR commitments. It is observed that: tort law assessment is *ex post* and requires adjudicators to consider 'general considerations of justice, fairness and reasonableness';[194] and that in this assessment, societal

186 Buhmann, 'Corporate Social Responsibility', 197.

187 Narine, 'Disclosing Disclosure's Defects', 90.

188 Drimmer and Torrance, 'CSR Risk Management and Due Diligence', 613–614.

189 McCorquodale and Smit, 'Human Rights, Responsibilities and Due Diligence', 222. Black's Law Dictionary defines diligence as: '2. The attention and care required from a person *in a given situation*; care; heedfulness', and due diligence as: '1. The diligence reasonably expected from, and ordinarily exercised by, a person who seeks to satisfy a legal requirement or to discharge an obligation' (Garner, *Black's Law Dictionary*, 573, emphasis added).

190 Glinski distinguishes the required criteria for the determination of the standard of due diligence and the required conduct, arguing that while the former needs to be technically or substantially correct, the latter is 'a question that has to reflect the public interest [and] social values'. Glinski, 'Corporate Codes of Conduct', 134–135. See also Stoyanova, 'Common Law Tort of Negligence', 638.

191 See American Law Institute, *Restatement of the Law, Third, Torts: Liability for Physical and Emotional Harm* (2010) Vol. 1 (on US law).

192 Drimmer and Torrance, 'CSR Risk Management and Due Diligence', 613.

193 Ward, 'Tort Cause of Action', 48.

194 Enneking, *Foreign Direct Liability and Beyond*, 544.

expectations may also affect the determination of the standard of diligence or required conduct as an element of duty.[195]

Beckers, in her comprehensive study on the legal effects of corporate social responsibility codes in 2015, examined the possible effects of corporate voluntary assumption of responsibility in the English common law tort of negligence and the German law tort concept of *Verkehrspflicht*, which (according to her) 'resembles the common law duty of care'.[196] She recognises the potential that the publicly declared code could in principle assist in establishing a duty of care/*Verkehrspflicht* in both jurisdictions, while also noting that a cautious approach which requires additional factors such as implementing practices by the corporation would be taken.[197]

Scholars provide strong support for the legal effects of CSR commitments expressed in codes of conduct through tort law. They argue that these are obtained through the determination of 'the way the standard of care in tort law is shaped',[198] 'the application of basic notions of reasonable behaviour, or the scope of duties of care',[199] and 'the criterion "just, fair and equitable" for the imposition of a duty of care in the tort of negligence'.[200] Arguably, this is even more so when the standard set out in internal regulations and other commitments is so widely practised outside the host state that it can be defined as the minimum standard in the industry.[201]

Admittedly, realisation of this proposition depends entirely on the interpretation and application of tort law in each state, and a cautious approach may be adopted in many jurisdictions for different reasons, including fear of creating unforeseeability for corporations. However, the recent decisions of domestic courts in certain jurisdictions, including both common law and civil law jurisdictions, suggest developments towards recognising the legal effects of CSR commitments through tort law.

[195] Ascensio, 'Les activités normatives', 275–276.

[196] Beckers, *Enforcing Corporate Social Responsibility Codes*, 167–175.

[197] Ibid., 175.

[198] van Dam, 'Tort Law and Human Rights', 241.

[199] Ward, 'Corporate Social Responsibility', 19. See also Kinley and Tadaki, 'From Talk to Walk', 958 (citing Johnson, 'Public-Private-Public Convergence' 291). Cf. McCorquodale, 'Corporate Social Responsibility', 393.

[200] Rühmkorf, *Corporate Social Responsibility*, 168. See also Schepel, *The Constitution of Private Governance*, 400; Seck and Ogunranti, 'Accountability: Legal Risks and Remedies', 591; Beckers, 'Regulating Corporate Regulators through Contract Law?', 16.

[201] Glinski, 'Corporate Codes of Conduct', 135–136.

Choc v. HudBay Minerals Inc.[202] was brought by indigenous people from Guatemala against a Canadian mining company, on the basis of the allegation that security personnel working for its subsidiaries, 'who were allegedly under the control and supervision of Hudbay', had committed human rights violations.[203] The claimants alleged *direct* negligence in tort by the parent company that authorised the subsidiary's security personnel.[204] The parent company sought to dismiss the claim, arguing that 'there is no recognized duty of care owed by a parent company to ensure that the commercial activities carried on by its subsidiary in a foreign country are conducted in a manner designed to protect those people with whom the subsidiary interacts'.[205] The Judgment of the Ontario Superior Court of Justice rejected this argument and found the existence of a *prima facie* duty of care owned *directly* by the parent company on the grounds that: (a) the harm was reasonably foreseeable; (b) there was sufficient proximity between the parties that it would not be unjust or unfair to impose a duty of care on the parent company; and (c) no policy reasons to negate or otherwise restrict that duty existed.[206] Significantly, in assessing the proximity question, the court held that: '[f]actors considered in defining the proximity of a relationship include . . . the "expectations, representations, reliance, and the property or other interests involved"'.[207] On the facts, the court found, *inter alia*, that:

> [Hudbay] had adopted the *Voluntary Principles on Security and Human Rights*, a detailed set of standards applicable to the use of private security forces at resource extractive projects, and it made public statements that it had extensively trained the security personnel.[208]

The court then concluded that:

> [T]here were numerous expectations and representations on the part of Hudbay/Skye and the plaintiffs. In particular, Hudbay/Skye made public representations concerning its relationship with local communities and its commitment to respecting human rights, which would have led to expectations on the part of the plaintiffs.[209]

[202] *Angelica Choc et al. v. Hudbay Minerals Inc. et al.*, 2013 ONSC 1414.
[203] Ibid., para. 4.
[204] Ibid., para. 50.
[205] Ibid., para. 18.
[206] Ibid., paras. 54–75.
[207] Ibid., para. 69 (citing *Cooper v. Hobart*, 2001 SCC 79, [2001] 3 SCR 537, para. 34).
[208] Ibid., para. 67.
[209] Ibid., para. 69.

Therefore, the expectations of local people concerning the standards of corporate conduct created by public representations made by the parent company directed the court to find 'sufficient proximity' which justifies the imposition of a duty of care on a parent company. It is observed that this reasoning 'lays the foundation for voluntary CSR standards to become legally binding under Canadian law'.[210]

Another case is *Four Nigerian Farmers and Milieudefensie v. Shell*,[211] a landmark case that arose from oil spillage in the Nigerian Oruma village in 2005 caused by the Shell group's Nigerian subsidiary oil extraction company. On 29 January 2021 the Hague Court of Appeal noted that Shell Global Solutions International BV *published* the Design and Engineering Pratice (DEP) 31.40.60.11 in September 2002, which provided requirements and recommendations for the application of Leak Detection Systems (LDS).[212] As a technology that 'enables the operator to quickly identify and correct a leak', LDS was embodied in Standard 1160 of the American Pipeline Institute (API) of November 2001.[213] The Court found that:

> Now that SPDC [Royal Dutch Shell's Nigerian subsidiary] knew before mid-2005 that a spill could occur in the Oruma pipeline, and it was foreseeable that it would be denied access to the site of the spill, it was – bearing in mind that ... SPDC must have known, under those circumstances the damage would have been prevented to a (very) large extent with an LDS – it is foreseeable for SPDC that failure to install an LDS would lead to (significant) damage to local residents.[214]

On this basis, the Court concluded that SDPC 'had a duty of care to provide the Oruma pipeline with an LDS before the 2005 spill', which violated this duty.[215] As discussed in Chapter 4, Section 4.4.2, the Court also concluded that Royal Dutch Shell also owed a duty of care 'to ensure that an LDS is installed on the Oruma pipeline', and breached this duty.[216]

210 Aftab, 'Intersection of Law', 24. For the analysis of this case, see also Peña, 'Human Rights Violations by Canadian Companies'.

211 *Four Nigerian Farmers and Milieudefensie v. Shell*, Court of Appeal The Hague, 28 January 2021, ECLI:NL:GHDHA:2021:132.

212 Ibid., para. 6.13.

213 Ibid., para. 6.11. LDC is also described as a best available technology. Steiner, 'Double Standard'.

214 *Four Nigerian Farmers and Milieudefensie v. Shell*, para. 6.22.

215 Ibid., para. 6.25.

216 Ibid., para. 7.26.

These decisions set a precedent for establishing tort liability for environmental and human rights damages based on a breach of commitments published in corporate codes of conduct and other policy statements.[217] Following this approach, certain CSR commitments may constitute measurable criteria by which the investor's standard of care is judged, and thereby influence the determination of tort liability.

5.4.2 *Towards Quality Non-Financial Reporting*

An issue with this approach is that at present, many published codes of conduct and CSR reports employ qualitative rather than quantitative, and general rather than specific, statements, from which objective standards may be difficult to find.[218] In environmental codes, it is observed that 'the specifics of the commitment vary'.[219] Similarly, qualitative indicators concerning the respect for human rights provided in the Global Reporting Initiative (GRI) standards make it difficult to compare each company's performance in an objective manner.[220] Given that a higher quality of codes leads to their higher effectiveness,[221] it may even be paradoxical that specific and comprehensive codes have a higher likelihood of incurring legal responsibility.

However, the content and quality of companies' CSR commitments are increasingly monitored and evaluated with the rise of the notion of environmental, social, and governance (ESG) investing. A recent survey (with 652 responses) revealed that 'a large majority of investors (82%) consider ESG information when making investment decisions'.[222] It has

217 These cases also demonstrate the development on the application of the law of the home state of a parent company (see Chapter 2, Section 2.1.2 and Chapter 4, Section 4.4.2), but this question is beyond the scope of this study.

218 Deumier, 'Les codes de conduite des entreprises', 681: 'moins d'un code sur cinq comporterait des objectifs précis et mesurables'; van Dam, 'Tort Law and Human Rights', 240.

219 OECD, 'Codes of Corporate Conduct: Expanded Review of Their Contents', May 2001, OECD Working Papers on International Investment 2001/06, at 2.

220 Fatoux, 'La différenciation normative selon les activités', 158. See also Gaukrodger, 'Business Responsibilities and Investment Treaties', 70.

221 Erwin, 'Corporate Codes of Conduct', 544–545.

222 Amel-Zadeh and Serafeim, 'Why and How Investors Use', 98. See also US SIF, 'Report on US Sustainable, Responsible and Impact Investing Trends 2018', US SIF, November 2018, available at: www.ussif.org/files/Trends/Trends%202018%20executive%20summary%20FINAL.pdf (accessed 15 December 2021) 1; European SRI Study 2018, available at: www.eurosif.org/wp-content/uploads/2021/10/European-SRI-2018-Study-LR.pdf (accessed 15 December 2021).

been observed that corporations are increasingly under pressure to make quality, that is, specific and comprehensive, ESG information disclosure to have access to capital,[223] and this has affected the quality of reporting. Fernandez-Feijoo, Romero, and Ruiz observe, based on the analysis of data from 1,047 companies from the GRI (in the period 2008–2010), that high pressure from investors and employees increases the levels of reporting transparency and disclosure.[224] García-Sánchez, Hussain, Martínez-Ferrero, and Ruiz-Barbadillo, including the analysis of more than 6,000 companies' CSR reporting from the GRI database, identify the existence of 'a positive effect of quantity, quality, availability, and quality of external assurance' of CSR disclosure on access to financial resources.[225] Therefore, the quality of non-financial reporting is expected to improve under market pressure.

To conclude, in certain circumstances, a violation of CSR commitments undertaken by the investor may result in legal responsibility under domestic law, in particular the civil tort law. Although this question is determined through interpretation and application of the relevant domestic laws, under which the consequences would vary widely between jurisdictions, the case law in certain jurisdictions described above does signal development of law towards a greater recognition of the legal impact of voluntary standards and CSR commitments. If it is established that these soft instruments lead to tort liability under the relevant domestic law, this may provide legal grounds for counterclaims by the respondent state in IIA-based dispute settlement mechanisms.[226]

5.5 Conclusion

This chapter has examined different ways to overcome the 'obstacles' that are allegedly behind the paucity of cases where counterclaims succeeded on their merits. While the availability of some of these measures depends on the relevant domestic laws, there have been developments in certain

[223] Eccles and Klimenko, 'The Investor Revolution'.

[224] Fernandez-Feijoo, Romero and Ruiz, 'Effect of Stakeholders' Pressure', 60–61.

[225] García-Sánchez, Hussain, Martínez-Ferrero and Ruiz-Barbadillo, 'Impact of Disclosure and Assurance Quality', 833, 836, 841–845. See also S&P Global, 'Deeper ESG Transparency for Corporates – Transparency for Investors to Follow', S&P Global, 5 November 2020, available at: www.spglobal.com/esg/csa/insights/deeper-esg-transparency (accessed 15 December 2021) (identifying the growing link between ESG disclosure and corporate value).

[226] Dubin, 'Entreprise multinationale', 50.

jurisdictions that signal a shift towards a greater recognition of TNCs' responsibility. Insofar as counterclaims have persisting value as a way of advancing responsible investment in the IIA regime, it is hoped that the analysis presented in this chapter broadens the use of counterclaims in IIA-based dispute settlement mechanisms.

At the same time, counterclaims are by no means the only approach to materialise the investors' environmental and human rights responsibilities in IIA-based dispute settlement mechanisms. Chapter 6 discusses different methods by which the host state invokes these responsibilities at various stages of dispute settlement proceedings as a defence in the assessment of the investor's principal claim.

6

Corporate Environmental Responsibility and the Investor's Principal Claims

6.1 Introduction: Focus on Investors' Performance-Phase Misconduct

Previous chapters discussed the investor's environmental responsibility as a ground for the host state's counterclaims. This chapter will discuss the effects of such responsibility in the assessment of the investor's principal claims against the host state. It does so by examining different ways in which investor's responsibility may be invoked to prevent or reduce the liability of the host state, at different stages of the proceedings.

Although investors' environmental responsibility arises in the process of making an investment – a typical example is a required environmental impact study,[1] this chapter focuses on the responsibility that arises during the performance of the investment, a breach of which having caused an actual or perceived threat of environmental harm. With this focus, Section 6.2 argues that such performance-phase misconduct has only a limited impact on the determination of the tribunal's jurisdiction or the admissibility of the claim.

Section 6.3 discusses the impact of investors' performance-phase environmental responsibility on the determination of the host state's liability. Focusing on the assessment of the investor's 'legitimate expectations', it assesses the impact of the investor's performance-phase misconduct, referring to the concept of 'social licence to operate' (SLO). Lastly, Section 6.4 examines selected aspects of the application of contributory fault as a way of materialising the investor's responsibility at the quantum phase.

[1] For example, in *Cortec v. Kenya*, the investor's failure to comply with the legislature's regulatory regime and obtain an Environmental Impact Assessment Study licence barred the jurisdiction of the tribunal. *Cortec Mining Kenya Limited, Cortec (Pty) Limited and Stirling Capital Limited v. Republic of Kenya*, ICSID Case No. ARB/15/29, Award, 22 October 2018 (*Cortec* Award), paras. 343–365.

6.2 Corporate Performance-Phase Environmental Responsibility Does Not Bar Jurisdiction

6.2.1 *Jurisdiction: Temporal Element of Illegality*

It is generally uncontested that when the relevant international investment agreement (IIA) includes a legality requirement clause connected to the notion of investment,[2] pleas of certain illegality may constitute a jurisdictional bar, because the legality requirement in such clauses is considered to limit the consent of contracting parties to arbitration.[3] Investment arbitration tribunals have consistently held that jurisdiction-depriving illegality includes violations of the host state's foreign investment restrictions[4] and non-technical and non-trivial violation of the host state's legal order, such as corruption or fraud.[5]

[2] This type of legality requirement is generally provided by defining an investment as an asset that is 'made', 'acquired', 'effected', 'implemented', 'owned or controlled', or 'established' in accordance with domestic laws of the host state, or by limiting the scope of application of the relevant IIA to investments that meets the requirements above. Bottini, 'Legality of Investments under ICSID Jurisprudence', 297–298. Notably, in *Churchill Mining v. Indonesia*, the relevant IIA limited the legality requirement to a specific law (the Foreign Capital Investment Law No. 1 of 1967). The tribunal concluded that the allegation of illegality based on fraud did not affect jurisdiction, and addressed this issue as a ground of inadmissibility. *Churchill Mining Plc and Planet Mining Pty Ltd. v. Republic of Indonesia*, ICSID Case No. ARB/12/14 and 12/40 (*Churchill Mining*), Decision on Jurisdiction, 24 February 2014, paras. 286–315.

[3] For example, *Metal-Tech Ltd. v. Republic of Uzbekistan*, ICSID Case No. ARB/10/3, Award, 4 October 2013 (*Metal-Tech* Award), para. 373; *Quiborax S.A., Non-Metallic Minerals S.A. and Allan Fosk Kaplún v. Plurinational State of Bolivia*, ICSID Case No. ARB/06/2, Decision on Jurisdiction, 27 September 2012, para. 255. See also Mouawad and Beess und Chrostin, 'Illegality Objection in Investor-state Arbitration', 62; Lorz and Busch, 'Investment in Accordance with the Law', 584. Contra: Douglas, 'Plea of Illegality', 178.

[4] For example, *PAO Tatneft (formerly OAO Tatneft) v. Ukraine*, PCA Case No. 2008-8, Partial Award on Jurisdiction, 28 September 2010, para. 200; *Mamidoil Jetoil Greek Petroleum Products Societe Anonyme S.A. v. Republic of Albania* (*Mamidoil v. Albania*), ICSID Case No. ARB/11/24, Award, 30 March 2015 (*Mamidoil* Award), para. 372; *Cairn Energy Plc and Cairn UK Holdings Limited v. The Republic of India*, PCA Case No. 2016-07, Award, 21 December 2020, paras. 709–710.

[5] For example, *Desert Line Projects LLC v. Republic of Yemen*, ICSID Case No. ARB/05/17, Award, 6 February 2008, paras. 104–106; *Gustav F W Hamester GmbH & Co KG v. Republic of Ghana*, ICSID Case No. ARB/07/24, Award, 18 June 2010, paras. 131–136; *Alasdair Ross Anderson et al. v. Republic of Costa Rica*, ICSID Case No. ARB(AF)/07/3, Award, 19 May 2010, paras. 51–59; *Fraport AG Frankfurt Airport Services Worldwide v. Republic of the Philippines*, ICSID Case No. ARB/03/25, Award, 16 August 2007, paras. 396–404 (the majority, Arbitrator Cremades dissented on this point); *ECE Projektmanagement v. Czech Republic*, UNCITRAL, PCA

When the relevant IIA is silent on the legality of investment, or contains references to domestic law compliance which are not connected to the notion of investment,[6] investment arbitration tribunals have been reluctant to import a legality requirement as a condition to establish jurisdiction.[7] However, tribunals also generally agree that even in the absence of a legality clause in the relevant IIA, there are circumstances where investment made in violation of the host state's domestic law should be denied access to the substantive protection of the IIA,[8] and in this case the issue of illegality should be addressed as a ground of inadmissibility or at the merits phase.[9]

In any of these cases where the illegality of the investment is invoked as a bar to jurisdiction of the tribunal, investment arbitration tribunals

Case No. 2010-5, Award, 19 September 2013, paras. 3.169–3.171; *Energoalians SARL v. Republic of Moldova*, UNCITRAL, Award, 23 October 2013, para. 260; *Peter A. Allard v. Government of Barbados*, PCA Case No. 2012-06, Award on Jurisdiction, 13 June 2014, para. 94; *Getma International and Others v. Republic of Guinea*, ICSID Case No. ARB/11/29, Award, 16 August 2016, para. 174; *Álvarez y Marín Corporación S.A. and Others v. Republic of Panama*, ICSID Case No. ARB/15/14, Award, 12 October 2018 (*Álvarez y Marín* Award), para. 156; *Mytilineos Holdings SA v. State Union of Serbia & Montenegro and Republic of Serbia*, UNCITRAL, Partial Award on Jurisdiction, 8 September 2006, paras. 151–152; *Krederi Ltd. v. Ukraine*, ICSID Case No. ARB/14/17, Award (Excerpts), 2 July 2018, para. 386. See also Article 16(2) of the 2019 Netherlands Model BIT. For the analysis of the cases on corruption, see Llamzon, *Corruption in International Investment Arbitration*, chapter 6.

6 For example, an 'approval' clause concerning the host state's investment admission requirements for specific investments to certain business sectors. See Wongkaew, 'Specific Approval Requirement in Investment Treaties', 73; Diel-Gligor and Hennecke, 'Investment in Accordance with the Law', 567–568.

7 For example, *Metal-Tech* Award, para. 127; *Bear Creek Mining Corporation v. Republic of Peru* (*Bear Creek v. Peru*), ICSID Case No. ARB/14/21, Award, 30 November 2017 (*Bear Creek* Award), paras. 319–320; *Plama Consortium v. Republic of Bulgaria* (*Plama v. Bulgaria*), ICSID Case No. ARB/03/24, Decision on Jurisdiction, 8 February 2005, paras. 126–130; *Malicorp Limited v. Arab Republic of Egypt*, ICSID Case No. ARB/08/18, Award, 7 February 2011, para. 119; *Saba Fakes v. Republic of Turkey*, ICSID Case No. ARB/07/20, Award, 14 July 2010, para. 114. Contra: *Cortec* Award, para. 333; *South American Silver Limited v. Plurinational State of Bolivia* (*South American Silver v. Bolivia*), PCA Case No. 2013-15, Award, 22 November 2018 (*South American Silver* Award), paras. 456–462.

8 For example, *Khan Resources Inc., Khan Resources B.V., and CAUC Holding Company Ltd. v. Government of Mongolia and Monatom Co., Ltd.*, PCA Case No. 2011-09, Decision on Jurisdiction, 25 July 2012, para. 383.

9 Risso and Amato, 'Pleas of Illegality', 96; Söderlund and Burova, 'Is There Such a Thing as Admissibility?', 547; Schill, 'Illegal Investments in International Arbitration', 323; Diel-Gligor and Hennecke, 'Investment in Accordance with the Law', 571. Cf: Mouawad and Beess und Chrostin, 'Illegality Objection in Investor-state Arbitration', 66.

have consistently held that the decisive moment for the determination of such illegality is at the time of making the investment.[10] These tribunals have considered performance-phase illegality to be relevant to the determination of admissibility and merits.[11] While determining the time of investment-making may be difficult because 'investment is often a process rather than an instantaneous act',[12] what is decisive is that the allegedly illegal conduct is directed to the creation, not performance, of the investment.[13]

Sornarajah objects to the distinction between illegality at the time of making investment and performance illegality, arguing that dealing with the latter at the merits phase does nothing more than 'prolong the arbitration'.[14] However, given the risks of frequent and non-transparent changes in domestic laws, requiring compliance throughout the life of investment as a jurisdictional condition may undermine the effectiveness of the protection of investments under IIAs.[15] Moreover, the determination of the existence and the effects of the investor's performance-phase misconduct requires a comprehensive assessment of the 'whole picture'

[10] For example, *Infinito Gold Ltd. v. Costa Rica*, ICSID Case No. ARB/14/5, Award, 3 June 2021 (*Infinito Gold* Award), para. 180; *Bernhard von Pezold and Others v. Republic of Zimbabwe*, ICSID Case No. ARB/10/15, Award, 28 July 2015 (*von Pezold* Award), para. 420; *Oxus Gold plc v. Republic of Uzbekistan, the State Committee of Uzbekistan for Geology & Mineral Resources, and Navoi Mining & Metallurgical Kombinat*, UNCITRAL, Final Award, 17 December 2015, para. 707; *Copper Mesa Mining Corporation v. Republic of Ecuador*, PCA Case No. 2012-2, Award, 15 March 2016 (*Copper Mesa* Award), para. 5.54; *Vladislav Kim and Others v. Republic of Uzbekistan*, ICSID Case No. ARB/13/6, Decision on Jurisdiction, 8 March 2017 (*Vladislav Kim* Decision), para. 374; *David R. Aven and Others v. Republic of Costa Rica*, ICSID Case No. UNCT/15/3, Final Award, 18 September 2018, para. 342; *Churchill Mining Plc and Planet Mining Pty Ltd. v. Republic of Indonesia*, ICSID Case No. ARB/12/14 and 12/40, Award, 6 December 2016 (*Churchill Mining* Award), para. 488; *Yukos Universal Limited (Isle of Man) v. Russian Federation*, UNCITRAL, PCA Case No. AA 227, Award, 18 July 2014; *Hulley Enterprises Limited (Cyprus) v. Russian Federation*, UNCITRAL, PCA Case No. AA 226, Award, 18 July 2014; *Veteran Petroleum Limited (Cyprus) v. Russian Federation*, UNCITRAL, PCA Case No. AA 228, Award, 18 July 2014 (collectively, *Yukos* Awards), paras. 1354–1355; *Oko Pankki Oyj, VTB Bank (Deutschland) AG and Sampo Bank Plc v. Republic of Estonia*, ICSID Case No. ARB/04/6, Award, 19 November 2007, paras. 189–190.

[11] For example, *Copper Mesa* Award, para. 5.62.

[12] Kriebaum, 'Investment Arbitration', 330.

[13] *South American Silver* Award, paras. 463–471.

[14] Sornarajah, *The International Law on Foreign Investment*, 373.

[15] *Copper Mesa* Award, para. 5.55; Obersteiner, '"In Accordance with Domestic Law" Clauses', 280.

of the case[16] and may involve issues of public policy, for which the conduct of the host state is relevant.[17] These are valid reasons for requiring the temporal element as one of the conditions for the plea of illegality as a jurisdictional bar, and this makes the plea of performance illegality fall outside the scope of objection to jurisdiction.[18]

6.2.2 *Inadmissibility Based on Performance Illegality*

Nevertheless, performance illegality has been discussed as a ground of the inadmissibility of a claim, before constituting a defence at the merits phase.[19] In assessing objections to the admissibility of an investment claim based on a plea of illegality, tribunals and scholars find the source of authority to deny the admissibility in international public policy[20] and the general principles of international law.[21] The two concepts are considered similar in the context of investor-state disputes.[22]

In contesting the admissibility of the claim, the host state has also relied on the clean hands doctrine, which was defined by Sir Gerald Fitzmaurice as 'he who comes to equity for relief must come with clean

[16] Pauker, 'Admissibility of Claims', 62–63. See also Diel-Gligor and Hennecke, 'Investment in Accordance with the Law', 570–571; Schill, 'Illegal Investments in International Arbitration', 323.

[17] Reisman, 'Apportioning Fault for Performance Corruption', 14.

[18] Cazala, 'Le respect des droits de l'homme', 337; Mouawad and Beess und Chrostin, 'Illegality Objection in Investor-state Arbitration', 67.

[19] *Copper Mesa* Award, para. 5.62; *Yukos* Awards, paras. 1343–1374; *Hesham Talaat M. Al-Warraq v. Republic of Indonesia*, UNCITRAL, Final Award, 15 December 2014 (*Al-Warraq* Award), paras. 634–648. Reisman, 'Apportioning Fault for Performance Corruption', 3.

[20] Transnational or international public policy derives from certain fundamental principles of law that 'are supported by a widespread, if not universal consensus'. Lalive, 'Transnational (or Truly International) Public Policy', 288. Marceaux distinguishes transnational public policy from international public policy in that the former 'comprises the fundamental values and interests of the international community as a whole, without being attached to any domestic legal order in particular'. Marcoux, 'Transnational Public Policy', 861–862.

[21] For example, *Vladislav Kim* Decision, para. 593; *Churchill Mining* Award, paras. 488, 507; *David Minnotte and Robert Lewis v. Republic of Poland*, ICSID Case No. ARB(AF)/10/1, Award, 16 May 2014 (*Minnotte* Award), para. 131; *Metal-Tech* Award, paras. 290–292. Douglas, 'Plea of Illegality', 169 (international public policy); Pauker, 'Admissibility of Claims', 62; Mbengue, 'Les obligations des investisseurs etrangers', 312.

[22] Dumberry, *Guide to General Principles of Law*, 44–46; Bjorklund and Vanhonnaeker, 'Yukos', 374.

hands'.[23] In investment arbitration case law, tribunals have expressed different views on whether this doctrine is a general principle of law and, therefore, applicable in investment arbitration.[24] While an endorsement of the doctrine in investment arbitration can be found in *Al-Warraq v. Indonesia*[25] and *Litttop v. Ukraine*,[26] other investment arbitration tribunals have been cautious not to qualify this doctrine as a general principle of law.[27] In the jurisprudence of the Permanent Court of International Justice (PCIJ) and the International Court of Justice (ICJ), while support for this doctrine was offered by several judges in their opinions,[28] the Court has neither explicitly declared nor denied the status of the doctrine as a general principle of international law.[29] The status of

[23] Fitzmaurice, 'The General Principles of International Law', 119.

[24] Scholarly views that support the doctrine's status of general principle of law include: Dumberry, 'The Clean Hands Doctrine'; *Anatolie Stati, Gabriel Stati, Ascom Group SA and Terra Raf Trans Traiding Ltd. v. Republic of Kazakhstan* , SCC Case No. V 116/2010, Legal Opinion by Christoph Schreuer (submitted in the enforcement proceedings before the Svea Court of Appeal), 21 January 2020, paras. 28–51; Kreindler, 'Corruption in International Investment Arbitration', 319; Moloo and Khachaturian, 'Compliance with the Law Requirement', 1485.

[25] *Al-Warraq* Award, para. 647. Cf. *South American Silver* Award, para. 449 (noting that the *Al-Warraq* tribunal had already concluded that the investor was precluded from the IIA protection by the application of Article 9).

[26] *Littop Enterprises Limited, Bridgemont Ventures Limited and Bordo Management Limited v. Ukraine*, SCC Case No. V 2015/092, Final Award, 4 February 2021 (*Littop* Award), para. 438 ('the doctrine of clean hands, just like the concept of good faith, is now a principle of international law').

[27] *Yukos* Awards, paras. 1357–1363; *South American Silver* Award, paras. 443–453 (in this case, Arbitrator Guglielmino dissented, arguing that the tribunal lacked jurisdiction for the absence of the claimant's investment. Dissenting Opinion of Osvaldo Cesar Guglielmino, 22 November 2018 (*South American Silver* Guglielmino dissenting opinion)). See also *Copper Mesa* Award, para. 6.93; *Churchill Mining* Award, para. 493; *Infracapital F1 S.à r.l. and Infracapital Solar B.V. v. Kingdom of Spain*, ICSID Case No. ARB/16/18, Award, 13 September 2021 (*Infracapital* Award) para. 460.

[28] Judge Hudson and Judge Anzilotti in the *Case Concerning the Diversion of Water from the River Meuse*; Judge Schwebel in the *Military and Paramilitary Activities in and against Nicaragua case* (Judge Schewebel sit as an arbitrator in *Yukos* cases); *Arrest Warrant of Apr. 11, 2000 (Democratic Republic of the Congo v. Belgium)* (Judgment of 14 February 2002) [2002] ICJ Rep. 3. However, in his separate opinion on *Certain Iranian Assets*, Judge ad hoc Brower offered a cautious reading of Judge Hudson's individual opinion on the *River Meuse* case that it was not 'specifically about the clean hands doctrine, but more generally addressed principles of equity applicable by international courts and tribunals'. *Certain Iranian Assets (Islamic Republic of Iran v. United States of America)* (Judgment) (Preliminary Objections) [2019] ICJ Rep. 7, Separate Opinion of Judge ad hoc Brower, paras. 4–7.

[29] See e.g. *Guyana v. Suriname*, PCA Case No. 2004-04, Award, 17 September 2007, para. 418; *Certain Iranian Assets*, para. 122.

the doctrine of clean hands as a general principle of international law thus remains unsettled.[30] Nevertheless, the doctrine can be, and has been, manifested by alternative bases, that is, through other international law principles and treaty provisions in the IIA-based dispute settlement mechanism. Scholars view a legality clause in IIAs as a manifestation of 'the principle behind the clean hands doctrine'.[31] Investment arbitration tribunals, while cautiously avoiding the application of the doctrine of clean hands, have applied established legal principles underlying the doctrine, including good faith, *nemo auditur propriam turpitudinem allegans*, *ex injuria non oritur*, and *ex turpi causa non oritur actio* as the basis of the inadmissibility of the claim.[32] Some scholars argue that the application of the principle of contributory fault in the *Yukos* cases, in which the tribunal explicitly denied the clean hand docrine status as a general principle of international law, is one form of application of this doctrine.[33] The *Copper Mesa* tribunal equated 'causation, contributory fault (based on wilful or negligent act or omission) or unclean hands' as 'materially the same', and addressed the alleged illegal conduct of the investor by applying contributory fault.[34]

A question to follow is at which stage such an admissibility objection should be assessed. In this regard, it should be noted that although inadmissibility in principle defeats jurisdiction,[35] in certain investment arbitration cases, including *Al-Warraq v. Indonesia*,[36] *Plama*

[30] Pomson and Horowitz, 'Humanitarian Intervention and the Clean Hands', 226; Llamzon and Sinclair, 'Investor Wrongdoing in Investment Arbitration', 512–513. Cf: Amianto, 'The Role of "Unclean Hands" Defences', 15–16.

[31] Moloo, 'Comment on the Clean Hands Doctrine', 40; Dumberry, 'State of Confusion', 234–235; Kaldunski, 'Principle of Clean Hands', 81.

[32] See e.g. *Inceysa Vallisoletana S.L. v. Republic of El Salvador*, ICSID Case No. ARB/03/26, Award, 2 August 2006 (*Inceysa* Award), para. 240; *Plama v. Bulgaria*, Award, 27 August 2008 (*Plama* Award), paras. 141–146; *Álvarez y Marín* Award, para. 135 (the majority); *Littop* Award, para. 441. See also Uribe, 'Drawing the Line', 324–325; Kryvoi, 'Economic Crimes in International Investment Law', 583.

[33] Giorgetti, 'Hulley Enterprises Ltd. (Cyprus) v. Russian Federation', 392; Marquais, 'Faute contributive et calcul des dommages'.

[34] *Copper Mesa Award*, para. 6.97.

[35] *Supervision y Control S.A. v. Republic of Costa Rica*, ICSID Case No. ARB/12/4, Final Award, 18 January 2017, para. 269 (arbitrator Klock disagreed with the majority's rejection of jurisdiction based on inadmissibility. Dissenting Opinion of Joseph P. Klock, 18 January 2017).

[36] *Al-Warraq* Award, paras. 646–648.

v. Bulgaria,[37] and *Lao Holdings v. Laos*,[38] inadmissibility claims based on a plea of illegality have been examined at the merits phase, in the assessment of the host state's liability under the relevant IIAs.

There are justifications for the approach to examine admissibility objections based on a plea of illegality at the merits phase. As discussed above (Section 6.2.1), the allegation of the investor's performance-phase misconduct is closely related to the content of the investor's principal claims and requires holistic consideration of all the circumstances of the case, including the host state's conduct. This is better done at the merits stage.[39] Scholars who support the application of the clean hands doctrine in investment arbitration also argue that the doctrine should be assessed at the merits phase to enable a consideration of both parties' conduct and responsibility.[40] Certain investment arbitration tribunals have explicitly acknowledged that admissibility objections should go to merits when they do not amount to or overlap with jurisdictional objections[41] or when they target 'the substantive content of the [claimant's] complaints'.[42]

In assessing a plea of inadmissibility based on illegality, investment arbitration case law sets a high threshold, by identifying the following as conduct that is contrary to international or transnational public policy or otherwise deprives the investor of protection as a whole: corruption,[43] 'deliberate concealment amounting to fraud',[44] 'particularly serious cases

[37] *Plama* Award, para. 306.

[38] *Lao Holdings N.V. v. Lao People's Democratic Republic*, ICSID Case No. ARB(AF)/12/6, Award, 6 August 2019, para. 280.

[39] See Dumberry and Dumas-Aubin, 'When and How', 366. See also Balcerzak, *Investor-State Arbitration and Human Rights*, 133; Reisman, 'Apportioning Fault for Performance Corruption', 8.

[40] Dumberry, 'The Clean Hands Doctrine', 524; Kotuby Jr. and Sobota, *General Principles of Law*, 133–134; Llamzon, '*Yukos Universal Limited (Isle of Man)*', 324.

[41] *Chevron Corporation and Texaco Petroleum Corporation v. Ecuador (II)*, PCA Case No. 2009-23, Third Interim Award on Jurisdiction and Admissibility, 27 February 2012, para. 4.91.

[42] *The Rompetrol Group N.V. v. Romania*, ICSID Case No. ARB/06/3, Decision on Jurisdiction and Admissibility, 18 April 2008, paras. 113–114. For other investment arbitration cases in which a matter of admissibility went to merits, see Söderlund and Burova, 'Is There Such a Thing as Admissibility?', 556.

[43] *Glencore International A.G. and C.I. Prodeco S.A. v. Republic of Colombia*, ICSID Case No. ARB/16/6, Award, 27 August 2019, para. 665. See *Penwell Business Limited (by MegaCom) v. Kyrgyz Republic*, PCA Case No. 2017-31, Award, 8 October 2021, para. 317 (a case based on domestic investment law).

[44] *Plama* Award, para. 135 (stating that such conduct was contrary to Bulgarian law and international law).

of fraudulent conduct, such as corruption',[45] fraudulent investment,[46] fraudulent misrepresentation,[47] 'violation of the most fundamental rules of protection of human rights',[48] and 'an illegal wrongdoing that is so egregious'.[49] Likewise, Dumberry, while arguing that an investor's misconduct '*during the post-establishment phase* of the investment' typically constitutes the situations where the clean hands doctrine should apply to make the claim inadmissible, limits the nature of such misconduct to 'serious wrong'.[50] In addition, in cases of performance-phase misconduct, illegality must taint the overall business scheme.

It is suggested here that even though the investors' performance-phase environmental misconduct does not cross the threshold described above, it may then impact the assessment of the merits of the case, that is, whether the host state has breached its investment protection obligations. The next section examines this issue, focusing on the impact of such misconduct on the assessment of the principle of 'legitimate expectations'.

6.3 Corporate Performance-Phase Environmental Responsibility at the Merits Phase: Impact on the Principle of 'Legitimate Expectations'

6.3.1 *Relevance of Investor Conduct to the Assessment of the Fair and Equitable Treatment (FET) Standard*

As a preliminary matter, whether the investor's conduct should influence the assessment of the host state's liability remains a contested question. Many scholars support the relevance of the investor's conduct to the

[45] *Churchill Mining* Award, para. 493; *Metal-Tech* Award, para. 292 (citing *World Duty Free Company v. Republic of Kenya*, ICSID Case No. ARB/00/7, Award, 4 October 2006, para. 157 and *Niko Resources (Bangladesh) Ltd. v. Bangladesh Petroleum Exploration & Production Company Limited ('Bapex') and Bangladesh Oil Gas and Mineral Corporation ('Petrobangla')* (*Niko v. Bangladesh Petroleum*), ICSID Case No. ARB/10/18, Decision on Jurisdiction, 19 August 2013 (*Niko* Decision on Jurisdiction), paras. 431–433, both contract-based cases).

[46] *Inceysa* Award, paras. 203–207 (the tribunal declined jurisdiction as a matter of interpretation of the legality clause in the relevant IIA); *Minnotte* Award, para. 131.

[47] *Robert Azinian, Kenneth Davitian, & Ellen Baca v. The United Mexican States*, ICSID Case No. ARB(AF)/97/2, Award, 1 November 1999, paras. 121–125.

[48] *Phoenix Action, Ltd. v. Czech Republic*, ICSID Case No. ARB/06/5, Award, 15 April 2009, para. 78 (*obita dictum*). See also *Bear Creek* Award, para. 335.

[49] *Infracapital* Award, para. 468.

[50] Dumberry, 'State of Confusion', 231 (emphasis added).

assessment of the host state's liability under the FET standard. An early proponent is Muchlinski, who argues that the investor's conduct becomes a central question in the host state's defence to the claim of a breach of the standard because perceptions of investor conduct and its impact on the wider public interest are 'key to administrative effectiveness'.[51] He identifies 'three major duties' of the investor: 'a duty to refrain from unconscionable conduct, a duty to engage in the investment in the light of an adequate knowledge of its risks, and a duty to conduct business in a reasonable manner'.[52] Sornarajah argues that the investor's environmental responsibility influences the assessment of fairness of the host state's interference which is 'a concept that cuts both ways and must be assessed in light of the whole situation'.[53] He also argues that a violation of 'standards of good corporate responsibility' by a foreign investor deprives it of the ground for an FET-based claim, 'particularly in situations where the state that took measures complained of in response to the violations'.[54] Francioni argues that the principle of equity, which is affiliated to the FET standard, requires consideration of the investor's accountability to the social and environmental impacts arising from its conduct.[55]

A sharply contrasting view is presented by Tudor. In her comprehensive assessment of the FET standard, Tudor denies the relevance of the investor's conduct to the assessment of the conformity of the host state's behaviour with the standard. This position is based on the following arguments: The standard is aimed only at the host states and investors do not have an obligation to behave fairly and equitably towards the host state; '[T]he *genesis* and original aim of the FET standard is to create a positive and attractive legal environment in order to attract foreign investment'.[56] She criticises Muchlinski's approach for posing 'too many obstacles in the way' to leading to achieve a successful FET claim, which can lead to a loss of the standard's *raison d'être*.[57] She also argues that introducing such exterior elements other than the host state's behaviour

[51] Muchlinski, 'Caveat Investor?', 528.
[52] Ibid., 530.
[53] Sornarajah, *The International Law on Foreign Investment*, 182–183.
[54] Ibid., 556.
[55] Francioni, 'Access to Justice', 739. See also Kläger, *'Fair and Equitable Treatment'*, 205; Diehl, *Core Standard of International Investment Protection*, 412; Leinhardt, 'Some Thoughts on Foreign Investors' Responsibilities', 20 (on human rights responsibilities).
[56] Tudor, *The Fair and Equitable Treatment Standard*, 210.
[57] Ibid.

into the assessment of the FET would undermine the legal security of the law.[58] On these considerations, she concludes that the investor's behaviour, together with the more specific circumstances of the host state, should be considered at a later stage of determining the final quantum of compensation.[59]

However, assessing the conformity of the host state's measure with the FET standard solely by reference to the host state's behaviour disregards the fact that measures of the host state cannot be detached from the context within which they were taken. Many tribunals have acknowledged that specific circumstances within the host state, such as 'changing geopolitical priorities',[60] political and socioeconomic volatility,[61] an economic crisis,[62] the political, socioeconomic, cultural, and historical conditions,[63] are relevant to the legitimacy of the investor's expectations, primarily as a matter of the investor's 'due diligence'[64] or business risk.[65] There is no reason why the investor's alleged misconduct during the

[58] Ibid., 212.

[59] Ibid., 213.

[60] *Parkerings-Compagniet AS v. Republic of Lithuania*, ICSID Case No. ARB/05/8, Award, 11 September 2007, para. 335.

[61] *Toto Costruzioni Generali S.p.A. v. Republic of Lebanon*, ICSID Case No. ARB/07/12, Award, 7 June 2012 (*Toto Costruzioni* Award), paras. 241–245; *Genin v. Republic of Estonia*, ICSID Case No. ARB/99/2, Award, 25 June 2001, para. 348; *Mamidoil* Award, paras. 623–629 (Arbitrator Hammond dissented the majority's analysis of the FET violation claim); *Bayindir Insaat Turizm Ticaret Ve Sanayi A.S. v. Islamic Republic of Pakistan*, ICSID Case No. ARB/03/29, Award, 27 August 2009, paras. 193–194; *Generation Ukraine, Inc. v. Ukraine*, ICSID Case No. ARB/00/9, Award, 16 September 2003, para. 20.37.

[62] *Eudoro Armando Olguín v. Republic of Paraguay*, ICSID Case No. ARB/98/5, Award, 26 July 2001, para. 65(c).

[63] *Duke Energy Electroquil Partners and Electroquil S.A. v. Republic of Ecuador*, ICSID Case No. ARB/04/19, Award, 18 August 2008 (*Duke Energy* Award), para. 340.

[64] With regard to the content of due diligence required for the investor when making the investment, see e.g. *SunReserve Luxco Holdings S.À.R.L, SunReserve Luxco Holdings II S.À.R.L and SunReserve Luxco Holdings III S.À.R.L v. Italian Republic*, SCC Case No. V2016/32, Final Award, 25 March 2020, para. 714; *SolEs Badajoz GmbH v. Kingdom of Spain*, ICSID Case No. ARB/15/38, Award, 31 July 2019, para. 331; *Jurgen Wirtgen and Others v. Czech Republic*, PCA Case No. 2014-03, Dissenting Opinion of Gary Born, 11 October 2017, para. 98.

[65] Recent examples include: *Cavalum SGPS, S.A. v. Kingdom of Spain*, ICSID Case No. ARB/15/34, Decision on Jurisdiction, Liability and Directions on Quantum, 31 August 2020 (*Cavalum* Decision), paras. 471–475; *RWE Innogy GmbH and RWE Innogy Aersa S.A.U. v. Kingdom of Spain*, ICSID Case No. ARB/14/34, Decision on Jurisdiction, Liability and Certain Issues of Quantum, 30 December 2019, paras. 507–513; *Georg Gavrilovic and Gavrilovic d.o.o. v. Republic of Croatia*, ICSID Case No. ARB/12/39, Award, 26 July 2018 (*Gavrilovic* Award), paras. 986–987. See also Dani and Akhtar-Khavari, 'Rethinking the

performance of its investment should not constitute the context against which the measure and its conformity with the FET standard is assessed. Furthermore, Tudor's emphasis on the FET as 'a unilateral obligation of the State',[66] a view presented in 2008, does not reflect more recent developments in both international and domestic laws as well as private practices on the issue of corporate responsibility (Chapter 2, Section 2.2). In addition, investors owe obligations under 'a wide array of domestic norms' and 'contractual arrangements'.[67]

For these reasons, it is submitted here that the investor's conduct does influence the assessment of the host state's liability under the relevant IIA. Nevertheless, Tudor's concern that incorporating the investor's conduct in the assessment of the FET standard undermines the standard's effectiveness needs to be addressed. As a way of addressing this issue, the following sections seek to clarify the remaining ambiguity in the question of *how* the investor's alleged misconduct should impact the assessment of the host state's conformity or violation of investment obligations.

6.3.2 *Investors' Legitimate Expectations: Justifications and Status*

In claims based on the FET standard, the most often invoked ground is a violation of the legitimate expectations of the investor. In expropriation claims, many IIAs and model IIAs provide 'distinct, reasonable investment-backed expectations' as an element to consider in the assessment of indirect expropriation,[68] and such expectations have also been relied on.[69]

Use of Deference', 49; Viñuales, 'Investor Diligence in Investment Arbitration', 362–363. Contra: Dolzer, 'Fair and Equitable Treatment', 27.

66 Tudor, *The Fair and Equitable Treatment Standard*, 212–213.

67 Viñuales, 'Investor Diligence in Investment Arbitration', 367.

68 For example, Annex 9-B of the Comprehensive and Progressive Agreement for Trans-Pacific Partnership, Annex B of the 2012 US Model BIT, Annex 812.1 of the Canada-Peru FTA. See UNCTAD, 'Expropriation: A Sequel', UNCTAD Series on International Investment Agreements II, United Nations Publication, UNCTAD/DIAE/IA/2011/7 (2012), 73–76.

69 E.g., *Archer Daniels Midland Company and Tate & Lyle Ingredients Americas, Inc. v. United Mexican States*, ICSID Case No. ARB(AF)/04/5, Award, 21 November 2007, para. 250; *ADC Affiliate Limited and ADC & ADMC Management Limited v. Republic of Hungary*, ICSID Case No. ARB/03/16, Award of the Tribunal, 2 October 2006, para. 424; *Técnicas Medioambientales Tecmed, S.A. v. United Mexican States*, ICSID Case No. ARB(AF)/00/2, Award, 29 May 2003 (*Tecmed* Award), para. 122; *Azurix Corp. v. Argentine Republic*, ICSID Case No. ARB/01/12, Award, 14 July 2006, paras.

As outlined below, the assessment of the protection of an investor's legitimate expectations is based on their alleged reliance on those expectations generated by the state's conduct, and to this extent takes the subjective elements of this reliance on the part of the investor into account. Indeed, the application of the principle of legitimate expectations by arbitral tribunals has been criticised as a 'one-sided application of the reliance reasoning' in favour of foreign investors.[70] In addition, it has been aptly observed that the principle 'has transmuted into a growing sense of common obligations, accountability, and ultimately even acceptance of responsibility [for their conduct]'[71] by investors. These justify the approach of considering the investor's own fault and responsibility in the assessment of this principle.

For the FET standard, evidently, this approach cannot escape the questions of whether and how the principle of legitimate expectations should have a place in the assessment of the standard, which (with certain exceptions discussed below), unlike expropriation provisions, has no reference to this concept. Scholars have presented divergent views on this issue. Despite the wide acceptance of the principle as a 'dominant' or 'central' element constituting the FET standard by investment arbitration tribunals,[72] there are strong objections to the incorporation of legitimate expectations covering substantive expectations in the FET standard. They are based on the arguments that many domestic

316–322; *International Thunderbird Gaming Corporation v. United Mexican States*, UNCITRAL (*Thunderbird v. Mexico*), Award, 26 January 2006 (*Thunderbird* Award), paras. 145–167. See also Whitsitt and Bankes, 'The Evolution of International Investment Law', 228–230. Contra: *El Paso Energy International Company v. Argentine Republic*, ICSID Case No. ARB/03/15, Award, 31 October 2011 (*El Paso* Award), para. 227.

70 Perrone, 'International Investment Regime and Local Populations', 403.

71 Ong, 'Regulating Environmental Responsibility', 155.

72 See e.g. *Saluka Investments B.V. v. Czech Republic*, UNCITRAL, Partial Award, 17 March 2006 (*Saluka* Partial Award), para. 302; *EDF (Services) Limited v. Romania*, ICSID Case No. ARB/05/13, Award, 8 August 2009 (*EDF* Award), para. 216; *Antoine Abou Lahoud and Leila Bounafeh-Abou Lahoud v. Democratic Republic of the Congo*, ICSID Case No. ARB/10/4, Award, 7 February 2014, para. 440; *Electrabel S.A. v. Republic of Hungary*, ICSID Case No. ARB/07/19, Decision on Jurisdiction, Applicable Law and Liability, 30 November 2012, para. 7.75; *Deutsche Telekom v. India*, PCA Case No. 2014-10, Interim Award, 13 December 2017, para. 336. NAFTA and other tribunals have accepted the relevance of the principle to the FET standard connected to the minimum standard of treatment, which 'has moved on since the *Neer* case' (*von Pezold* Award, para. 546). For example, *Thunderbird* Award, para. 147; *Glamis Gold, Ltd. v. United States of America* (*Glamis Gold v. US*), UNCITRAL, Award, 8 June 2009, paras. 620–621; *Eli Lilly and Company v. Government of Canada*, ICSID Case No. UNCT/14/2, Final Award, 16 March 2017, paras. 380–385.

jurisdictions limit this principle to procedural protection;[73] this concept is 'an arbitral innovation' without any textual basis in IIAs;[74] and it 'risks giving too much weight to the investor's interests at the expense of public interests and a state's right to regulate legitimately'.[75] At the other end of the spectrum, there are views that its wide acceptance has made this principle a general principle of law.[76] Other scholars who accept the role of legitimate expectations in the assessment of the FET standard are cautious in concluding on the status of the principle as a general principle of law, emphasising the diversity in the approaches to its application between domestic jurisdictions.[77]

The status as a general principle of law would indeed be required if the frustration of legitimate expectations of the investor in itself and immediately gives rise to a breach of the FET standard. However, this is not the case. For both FET provisions that are connected to the minimum standard of treatment in international law and those that are not, tribunals have regularly described the protection of legitimate expectations as 'a (relevant) factor',[78] 'a touchstone',[79] 'relevant',[80] 'legal sources',[81]

[73] Zeyl, 'Charting the Wrong Course', 224; Sornarajah, *Resistance and Change in the International Law*, 248; Haynes, 'The Evolving Nature', 134.

[74] Campbell, 'House of Cards', 362. See also *Suez, Sociedad General de Aguas de Barcelona S.A. and Interagua Servicios Integrales de Agua S.A. v. Argentine Republic*, ICSID Case No. ARB/03/17, Separate Opinion of Arbitrator Pedro Nikken, 30 July 2010, para. 3; *Windstream Energy LLC v. Government of Canada*, PCA Case No. 2013-22, United States Article 1128 Submission, 12 January 2016, para. 16 (in the context of the minimum standard of treatment under Article 1105 of NAFTA).

[75] Campbell, 'House of Cards', 362.

[76] Schill, 'General Principles of Law', 168–169; Brown, 'The Protection of Legitimate Expectations', 10; Hamamoto, 'Protection of the Investor's Legitimate Expectations', 141.

[77] Ostřanský, 'An Exercise in Equivocation', 376–377; Wongkaew, *Protection of Legitimate Expectations*, 18–20; Roberts, 'Power and Persuation', 214; Dupuy and Dupuy, 'What to Expect from Legitimate Expectations?', 279; Potestà, 'Legitimate Expectations in Investment Treaty Law', 98.

[78] *Bilcon of Delaware et al. v. Government of Canada*, PCA Case No. 2009-04, Award on Jurisdiction and Liability, 17 March 2015 (*Bilcon* Award), para. 455; *Mobil Investments Canada Inc. and Murphy Oil Corporation v. Government of Canada*, ICSID Case No. ARB(AF)/07/4, Decision on Liability and on Principles of Quantum, 22 May 2012, para. 152.

[79] *El Paso* Award, para. 348.

[80] *Waste Management, Inc. v. United Mexican States ('Number 2')*, ICSID Case No. ARB (AF)/00/3, Award, 30 April 2004, para. 98.

[81] *Gold Reserve Inc. v. Bolivarian Republic of Venezuela*, ICSID Case No. ARB(AF)/09/1, Award, 22 September 2014 (*Gold Reserve* Award), para. 576.

'indicative',[82] or 'an operational method'[83] for determining a breach of the standard. The FET clause in the EU-Canada Comprehensive Economic and Trade Agreement confirms this understanding, as it treats the investor's legitimate expectation as a factor the tribunal 'may take into account' in the assessment of the standard.[84] The principle of legitimate expectations is not an independent treaty standard that operates outside the framework of the FET standard,[85] and should not be used as 'a supervening and overriding source of the applicable law'.[86] Therefore, even if one takes the view that the principle is a stand-alone *element* of the FET standard,[87] rather than a factor to assess a breach of other elements of the standard such as arbitrariness,[88] whether a failure to respect the investor's legitimate expectations amounts to a breach of the FET standard still requires a separate assessment.[89]

Accordingly, what matters is not its status but whether the application of the principle has normative foundations, and those have indeed been offered by scholars and tribunals. Certain tribunals have stated that the principle is based on good faith[90] and 'the converging considerations of

[82] *Philip Morris Brands Sàrl, Philip Morris Products S.A. and Abal Hermanos S.A. v. Oriental Republic of Uruguay*, ICSID Case No. ARB/10/7, Award, 8 July 2016 (*Philip Morris* Award), para. 324.

[83] *Suez, Sociedad General de Aguas de Barcelona, S.A.and Vivendi Universal, S.A. v. Argentine Republic*, ICSID Case No. ARB/03/17, Decision on Liability, 30 July 2010, para. 222.

[84] Article 8.10.4. See also Article 9.6.4 of the Comprehensive and Progressive Agreement for Trans-Pacific Partnership.

[85] McLachlan, Shore and Weiniger, *International Investment Arbitration: Substantive Principles*, 309 (para. 7.157) (citing *MTD Equity Sdn. Bhd. and MTD Chile S.A. v. Republic of Chile*, ICSID Case No. ARB/01/7, Decision on Annulment, 21 March 2007 (*MTD* Annulment Decision) paras. 67–68); Dumberry, 'Protection of Investors' Legitimate Expectations', 58–61; Laryea, 'Legitimate Expectations in Investment Treaty Law', 109–110.

[86] Crawford, 'Treaty and Contract in Investment Arbitration', 374.

[87] For example, *Merrill and Ring Forestry L.P. v. Government of Canada*, ICSID Case No. UNCT/07/1, Award, 31 March 2010, para. 155; *Thunderbird v. Mexico*, Separate Opinion of Thomas Wälde, 1 December 2005 (*Thunderbird* Wälde separate opinion), para. 37.

[88] For example, *Mesa Power Group, LLC v. Government of Canada* (*Mesa Power v. Canada*), UNCITRAL, PCA Case No. 2012-17, Award, 24 March 2016, para. 502; *Unión Fenosa Gas, S.A. v. Arab Republic of Egypt*, ICSID Case No. ARB/14/4, Award, 31 August 2018 (*Unión Fenosa* Award), para. 9.53.

[89] Dumberry observes that this is the reason why tribunals do not have to assess whether the principle has become a general principle of law. Dumberry, *Guide to General Principles of Law*, 337.

[90] *Total S.A. v. The Argentine Republic*, ICSID Case No. ARB/04/01, Decision on Liability, 27 December 2010, para. 128 (the tribunal also identifies good faith as a general principle

good faith and legal certainty'.[91] Long before investment arbitral tribunals started to introduce legitimate expectations into the FET standard,[92] Franck recognised the relevance of this principle in the context of protection of foreign investors, by linking it to the notion of stability.[93] Henckels, having observed that 'no single theory offers a complete justification for the protection of legitimate expectations',[94] identifies good faith, protection from arbitrary conduct, abuse of power or unfairness, reliance and legal certainty as an element of the rule of law as justifications for the protection of legitimate expectations.[95] Other scholars emphasise the protection of reliance on the part of the investor as a normative basis of the principle of legitimate expectations.[96] These justifications for the principle of legitimate expectations, in addition to the justification on the grounds of wide recognition in the arbitral jurisprudence and '*opinio doctoris*',[97] provide sufficient ground for the role of the principle in the assessment of the FET standard.

6.3.3 *Distinction between the Generation of Investor's Legitimate Expectations and Their Protection*

In assessing the investor's legitimate expectations as an element of the FET standard, it is important to recognise that the *generation* of the investor's legitimate expectations and their *protection* – more specifically, whether a frustration of the (once generated) legitimate expectations can be justified in certain circumstances – are distinct doctrinal questions.

within the meaning of Article 38(1)(c) of the ICJ statute); *El Paso* Award, para. 348; *Tecmed* Award, para. 154; *Gavrilovic* Award, para. 954; *CC/Devas (Mauritius) Ltd., Devas Employees Mauritius Private Limited and Telecom Devas Mauritius Limited v. Republic of India*, PCA Case No. 2013-09, Award on Jurisdiction and Merits, 25 July 2016, para. 458. See also Gazzini, 'General Principles of Law', 117–118. Conversely, Wongkaew and Diehl argue that good faith is too vague to provide a justification for legitimate expectations (Wongkaew, *Protection of Legitimate Expectations*, 37; Diehl, *Core Standard of International Investment Protection*, 358).

91 *Gold Reserve* Award, para. 576.

92 *CME Czech Republic B.V. v. Czech Republic*, UNCITRAL, Partial Award, 13 September 2001, para. 611; *Tecmed* Award, para. 154.

93 Franck, *Fairness in International Law and Institutions*, 439–440.

94 Henckels, 'Legitimate Expectations and the Rule of Law', 5.

95 Ibid., 5–9.

96 Bonnitcha, *Substantive Protection under Investment Treaties*, 211; Kingsbury and Schill, 'Investor-State Arbitration as Governance', 12; Wongkaew, *Protection of Legitimate Expectations*, 139; Đajić, 'Mapping the Good Faith Principle', 216.

97 Mach, 'Legitimate Expectations as Part of the FET Standard', 112.

Discussions on legitimate expectations have tended to focus on the former question, specifically what kind of grounds – ranging from specific and enforceable legal rights under domestic law to expectations for the stability and consistency created by the laws and regulations – may generate the investor's legitimate expectations. Most tribunals identify the time of making the investment as the time when legitimate expectations may be generated.[98]

It may be argued that the investor's subsequent performance-phase misconduct is relevant to the determination of the content of an investor's legitimate expectations in the sense that they should not reasonably expect that their investment will be protected regardless of their subsequent misconduct concerning such an investment. However, this approach will result in the investor's legitimate expectations being too vague to be practicable. A better place to consider the investor's performance-phase misconduct is the assessment of the protection of the investor's legitimate expectations, as discussed below.

Even if the investor's legitimate expectations are found to exist, the questions of their protection still remain. In the context of the protection of substantive legitimate expectations in domestic and European Community law, Craig explains the two-stage analysis as follows:

> If such an expectation were found to exist, it would then be for the public body to show that there was a countervailing public interest which required it to act in the way in which it proposed.[99]

In investment arbitration case law, many tribunals recognise the two-stage analysis by arguing that legitimate expectations should be weighed against the state's legitimate regulatory interests.[100] Many scholars

[98] Paparinskis, *International Minimum Standard*, 258. Recent cases that confirm this point include: *Infinito Gold* Award, para. 515; *Unión Fenosa* Award, para. 9.53; *Gavrilovic* Award, para. 956; *Consutel Group S.p.A. in liquidazione v. People's Democratic Republic of Algeria*, PCA Case No. 2017-33, Final Award, 3 February 2020, para. 421; *Ortiz Construcciones y Proyectos S.A. v. People's Democratic Republic of Algeria*, ICSID Case No. ARB/17/1, Award, 29 April 2020, para. 283; *Cavalum* Decision, para. 474. Contra: *Ioannis Kardassopoulos v. Republic of Georgia*, ICSID Case No. ARB/05/18, Award, 3 March 2010, para. 441; Kläger, *'Fair and Equitable Treatment'*, 187.

[99] Craig, 'Substantive Legitimate Expectations', 304.

[100] For example, *Saluka* Partial Award, para. 306; *BG Group Plc v. Republic of Argentina*, UNCITRAL, Final Award, 24 December 2007, para. 298; *Flemingo DutyFree Shop Private Limited v. Republic of Poland*, UNCITRAL, Award, 12 August 2016, para. 551; *Urbaser S.A. and Consorcio de Aguas Bilbao Biskaia, Bilbao Biskaia Ur Partzuergoa v. Argentine Republic*, ICSID Case No. ARB/07/26, Award, 8 December 2016, para. 620; *Eureko B.V. v. Republic of Poland*, Partial Award, 19 August 2005, paras. 232–233; *Eco*

acknowledge the need for this final stage of the analysis where the provisional protection of legitimate expectations is weighted against public interest considerations, which is necessary to allow for certain flexibility to the host state to react to public interest needs.[101]

Therefore, it is safely concluded that the finding of the investor's legitimate expectation and its frustration by the host state's measure is only the first step of the analysis. The generated expectations do not warrant absolute protection. There are circumstances where the public interest advanced by the measure in question on the part of the host state outweighs the investor's interest in fulfilment of its expectations, and therefore justifies the frustration of the investor's legitimate expectations.[102]

6.3.4 *Investors' Performance-Phase Conduct in the Assessment of the Protection of Legitimate Expectations*

6.3.4.1 Analysis of the Protection of Legitimate Expectations as a Balancing Exercise

As discussed above, the protection of the investor's legitimate expectations has been recognised as a matter of balancing between the investor's interest embodied in its expectations and the host state's need to introduce the measure in question, taking into consideration the specific situation in the host state. Different standards and methods[103] have been discussed as a way to balance the investor's rights or interests

Oro Minerals Corp. v. Republic of Colombia, ICSID Case No. ARB/16/41, Decision on Jurisdiction, Liability and Directions on Quantum, 9 September 2021, paras. 762, 806 (the majority, Arbitrator Sands disagreed with the tribunal's finding of the investor's legitimate expectations; however, he agreed that 'the failure to observe a claimant's legitimate expectations is just one factor a tribunal may take into account in determining whether there has been a breach of the MST [minimum standard of treatment]'. Partial Dissent of Professor Philippe Sands, para. 13). See also *Thunderbird* Wälde separate opinion, para. 30.

101 Diehl, *Core Standard of International Investment Protection*, 429; Schill, 'Fair and Equitable Treatment', 48; Radi, 'The "Human Nature"', 11; Wongkaew, *Protection of Legitimate Expectations*, 137.

102 Ahmed and Perry, 'The Coherence of the Doctrine', 63; Snodgrass, 'Protecting Investors' Legitimate Expectations', 57.

103 This chapter follows Paine's use of terms that particular methods of review such as the proportionality analysis 'can be incorporated within a broader understanding of the term "standard of review"'. Paine, 'Standard of Review', para. 1 (citation omitted).

and the host state's regulatory power in the IIA-based dispute settlement mechanism, including the proportionality principle (specifically, proportionality *stricto sensu* as a prong of the proportionality principle),[104] other public law standards of review such as margin of appreciation,[105] reasonableness and deference,[106] and a 'contractual approach'.[107] There is a controversy over these standards, including over the application of the proportionality principle in investor–state disputes.[108] However, the comparison and discussion of these standards and methods is beyond the scope of this study. It has been argued that a determination of the standard of review depends on the text of the applicable IIA and the relevant issue areas.[109] Based on this recognition, the following sections demonstrate that the investor's performance-phase misconduct may crucially impact the balancing exercise through the application of a chosen standard, because there are circumstances where such misconduct results in a lesser ground for protection of the investor's legitimate expectations.

104 While the proportionality principle *per se* concerns a proportion between means and ends (Vaypan, 'Choosing among the Shades of Nuance', 250), proportionality *stricto sensu* requires an weighing the investor's and host state's competing interests to decide 'whether the measure's impact is proportionate to or too severe relative to the gain that the measure seeks to achieve'. Henckels, *Proportionality and Deference in Investor-State Arbitration*, 25; Kethireddy, 'Still the Law of Nations', 335.

105 See e.g. *Philip Morris* Award, para. 399 (Arbitrator Born dissented. Concurring and Dissenting Opinion Co-Arbitrator Gary Born, 8 July 2016, para. 87).

106 See e.g. Schill, 'Deference in Investment Treaty Arbitration'; Ghouri, 'On Genealogy of Proposals', 10–11; Burke-White and von Staden, 'Need for Public Law Standards'.

107 Chen, 'Contractual Approach to Investor-State Regulatory Disputes'.

108 Major concern over the use of the proportionality principle is that its fundamental indeterminacy allows the tribunal, which may not sufficiently understand the socio-political and cultural situation of the host state, to engage in value- and policy-judgments (Chen, 'Contractual Approach to Investor-State Regulatory Disputes', 297; Gourgourinis, 'Fair and Equitable Treatment', 358; Kethireddy, 'Still the Law of Nations', 337; Vadi, 'Migration of Constitutional Ideas', 560; Sornarajah, *Resistance and Change in the International Law*, 368). Conversely, scholars who support the applicability of the principle argue that it provides a more robust and predictable method than 'the lack of any intelligible standard of weighing and balancing', or 'relatively transparent and coherent analytical structure'. Kingsbury and Schill, 'Investor-State Arbitration as Governance', 22–23; Schill and Djanic, 'International Investment Law and Community Interests', 237–239; Henckels, *Proportionality and Deference in Investor-State Arbitration*, 43; Stone Sweet, 'Investor-State Arbitration'; Cottier et al., 'Principle of Proportionality in International Law'.

109 Paine, 'Standard of Review', para. 3; von Staden, 'Deference or No Deference'.

6.3.4.2 The Context for the Assessment of the Protection of Legitimate Expectations

The weighing between the investor's interest and the regulatory need of the host state in the analysis of the protection of legitimate expectations is 'a highly context-sensitive determination',[110] which requires consideration of all the circumstances of the case including the degree of reliance and other public policy issues.

When assessing the legitimacy of the investor's expectations by reference to its due diligence and business risk, investment arbitration tribunals have regularly considered the economic, regulatory, and socio-political conditions prevailing in the host state at the time of making the investment.[111] This is a logical consequence of these tribunals' approach to limit the time of generation of legitimate expectations to the time of making the investment, as noted above (Section 6.3.3).

In contrast, the assessment of whether the frustration of legitimate expectations could be justified for public purposes is based on the circumstances that existed at the time when the measure that allegedly frustrated the legitimate expectations was taken, including those arising after the generation of the investor's legitimate expectations. Radi thus provides an example of changes in socio-political circumstances that may justify the infringement of the legitimate expectations of investors, where 'a state enacts measures for protecting human rights from a situation threatening their enjoyment by local societies in an unpredictable context'.[112] As noted, the investor's performance-phase conduct forms part of the circumstances that existed at the time of the adoption of the measures in question.

6.3.4.3 Investors' Performance-Phase Conduct as Part of the Context

Therefore, it is concluded that the investor's performance-phase conduct should be considered in the assessment of the protection of legitimate expectations.[113] The host state's ability to defend measures taken in

[110] Ahmed and Perry, 'The Coherence of the Doctrine', 63–64 (on the application of the principle of legitimate expectations in domestic law) (citations omitted).

[111] *EDF* Award, para. 219; *Toto Costruzioni* Award, para. 165. See also *Mamidoil* Award, para. 731; *Philip Morris* Award, para. 427; *Duke Energy* Award, para. 340; *Gavrilovic* Award, para. 987. See Montt, *State Liability in Investment Treaty Arbitration*, 365; Levashova, 'Fair and Equitable Treatment', 253.

[112] Radi, 'The "Human Nature"', 15.

[113] Leinhardt, 'Some Thoughts on Foreign Investors' Responsibilities', 23.

response to the environmental harm or threat created by the investor's performance-phase misconduct may impact the assessment of the protection of legitimate expectations in the following two ways. First, the regulatory nature of the measure to address the environmental and human rights concerns is *prima facie* established in such situations.[114] Unless, for example, the alleged environmental harm was proven as a pretext for the host state's measures whose real purposes were to destroy the investment,[115] the public interest nature of the measures is satisfied. This provides a basis for the existence of the *public* interest of the host state that is to be weighed against the investor's interest in the analysis of the protection of legitimate expectations. Second, in this weighing process, the investor's environmental responsibility may lead to a loss or diminishment of the grounds for protecting its legitimate expectations in the ways discussed below.

It should be recalled here that environmental degradation almost always affects the local people (the victims), and their interests and perceptions should be reflected in any attempt to materialise environmental responsibility on investors in IIA-based dispute settlement mechanisms (as discussed in Chapter 1, Section 1.5.1). For this reason, this section examines the role the concept of social licence to operate (SLO) may play in the assessment of the protection of the investor's legitimate expectations as a way to reflect the perceptions of the victims. This is because an SLO, as discussed further below, is based on the acceptance (at a minimum) of an investment project by local stakeholders affected by it.

6.3.4.4 Social Licence to Operate (SLO) and Legitimate Expectations

6.3.4.4.1 SLO: Definition, Recognition, and Nature This section demonstrates that, when the investor's environmental misconduct

[114] Sornarajah, *Resistance and Change in the International Law*, 321.

[115] For example, in the *Yukos* cases, the accusation of the investor's violation of tax law was found to be a pretext for the State apparatus to 'crush Mr. Khodorkovsky and expropriate Yukos'. *Yukos* Awards, paras. 515–516. It should be however noted that this finding contrasts the findings of the European Court of Human Rights (ECtHR) in *Khodorkovsky and Lebedev v. Russia* that 'none of the accusations against them concerned their political activities *stricto sensu*, even remotely'. *Khodorkovsky and Lebedev v. Russia*, Application Nos. 11082/06 and 13772/05, Judgment of 25 July 2013, para. 906. See also *OAO Neftyanaya Kompaniya Yukos v. Russia*, Application No. 14902/04, Judgment of 31 July 2014, para. 665. For criticism of the Yukos tribunal's finding of a political motive, see Nappert, 'Mammoth Arbitrations'.

contributes to a loss of the SLO for its project, it may impact the protection of its legitimate expectations in certain circumstances. The concept of SLO has been defined in different ways.[116] It includes different levels of perceptions of local stakeholders, ranging from 'a minimum and broad-based level of legitimacy, trust, acceptance and support'[117] from local stakeholders to 'institutionalized trust' which implies a partnership based on common interests between industry and these stakeholders.[118] For the purposes of this study, the focus is on the minimum acceptance or approval of an investment project by local communities,[119] a loss of which may necessitate a government intervention.[120] Although the concept of SLO emerged and was discussed primarily in the context of extractive industries,[121] the recognition of this concept has extended to other types of industrial activities which potentially have negative impacts on the local population.[122]

With the increasing adoption of the concept of SLO,[123] the indeterminacy of the concept has also come under scrutiny. Unlike regulatory licences (i.e. formal authorisations and regulatory requirements) that can

116 For different definitions of this concept, see Baba and Raufflet, 'L'acceptabilité sociale', 101.

117 Cosbey et al., 'Mining a Mirage?', iv. See also Owen and Kemp, 'Social Licence and Mining', 31; Yates and Horvath, 'Social License to Operate', 2; Van Putten et al., 'Emergence of Social Licence Necessitates Reforms', 1.

118 Jijelava and Vanclay, 'Legitimacy, Credibility and Trust', 1079. In *Gabriel Resources v. Romania*, the claimant asserted that the level of RMGC's [the titleholder's] social license was materially higher (referred to as 'approval') than 'acceptance'. *Gabriel Resources Ltd. and Gabriel Resources (Jersey) v. Romania*, ICSID Case No. ARB/15/31, Claimants Reply and Counter-Memorial on Jurisdiction, 2 November 2018, para. 15.

119 Baba and Raufflet define local communities as 'all the stakeholders located near the places of operation of a company and who are exposed to the nuisance caused by the operation'. Baba and Raufflet, 'L'acceptabilité sociale', 99 (citation omitted. Translation by author).

120 Peralta, 'Judicialisation of the Social License', 115.

121 Baba and Raufflet, 'L'acceptabilité sociale', 100 (citation omitted).

122 UN Human Rights Council, 'Report of the Special Representative of the Secretary-General on the Issue of Human Rights and Transnational Corporations and Other Business Enterprises', 22 April 2009, UN Doc. A/HRC/11/13, para. 46; Boutilier, 'Frequently Asked Questions about the Social Licence', 264.

123 Consultation, engagement, or 'community development agreements' with stakeholders have been increasingly made mandatory for mining operations in certain jurisdictions. See Columbia Center on Sustainable Development, 'Requirements for Community Development in Mining Laws', February 2017, available at: https://justice-project.org/wp-content/uploads/2017/08/mining-community-development-requirements-summary-table-ccsi-2017_february.pdf (accessed 15 December 2021); Mines and Minerals Act, Act No. 8 of 2019 (Malawi).

be defined in contents and time of receipt, SLO is fundamentally indeterminate, intangible and informal, depending on the perception of stakeholders.[124] SLO is also dynamic in the sense that it is subject to changes of interests, perceptions, values, and objectives of the relevant communities and therefore requires continuous efforts and sustained attention to maintain.[125] Required conduct for a company to earn and maintain an SLO is difficult to determine for several reasons. It includes a variety of activities and behaviours, including timely provision of sufficient information (transparency), providing fair (inclusive, responsive, consistent, impartial, and correctable) processes,[126] community engagement in a respectful manner, benefit-sharing with local communities,[127] and community building.[128] However, as their evaluation depends on the perceptions held by local stakeholders, the precise demands of the stakeholders as 'social licensors' and the ways to respond to them remain indeterminate.[129]

An exacerbating factor is that local communities are 'never homogenous',[130] consisting of 'many groups and individuals with different interests and abilities to influence events'.[131] Some may welcome the benefits brought about by, and others may be more concerned about adverse effects of, a proposed investment.[132] This diversity, together with the dynamic nature of an SLO, make its attainment and maintenance an extremely complex and multi-dimensional task. This gives rise to the risk of abuse and manipulation of the concept, as discussed in Section 6.3.4.4.3.

6.3.4.4.2 Loss of SLO and Regulatory Reactions As discussed in the previous section, the baseline element of an SLO is the *acceptance* of the

[124] Baba and Raufflet, 'L'acceptabilité sociale', 99 (citation omitted); Moffat, Lacey, Zhang and Leipold, 'The Social Licence to Operate', 481.

[125] Yates and Horvath, 'Social License to Operate', 3, 21; Owen and Kemp, 'Social Licence and Mining', 30; Lehtonen et al., 'Roles of the State and Social Licence?', 2.

[126] Stern, 'Coercion, Voluntary Compliance and Protest', 201 (citation omitted).

[127] Sattorova, 'Foreign Investor as a Good Citizen', 67–68.

[128] Yates and Horvath, 'Social License to Operate', 8.

[129] Gunningham, Kagan and Thornton, 'Social License and Environmental Protection', 309.

[130] Jijelava and Vanclay, 'Legitimacy, Credibility and Trust', 1084 (citation omitted).

[131] Buur, Nystrand and Pedersen, 'Political Economy of Land', 12.

[132] *Bear Creek* Award, para. 172. See also Cotula and Schröder, 'Community Perspectives in Investor-State Arbitration', 11; Stern, 'Coercion, Voluntary Compliance and Protest', 201 (citation omitted); Van Putten et al., 'Emergence of Social Licence Necessitates Reforms', 1 (citation omitted).

project and the presence of a company by local stakeholders, which Boutilier, Black, and Thomson define as 'a tentative willingness to let the project proceed'.[133] Acceptance is provisional, and therefore an SLO 'can be lost or degraded in response to events and behaviors exhibited by a company or its agents'.[134] Loss of an SLO may lead to social unrest, which may necessitate regulatory interventions to address community dissatisfactions. Such interventions (ranging from monitoring to taking over the project)[135] may indeed be required as an exercise of the government's duty to protect against human rights abuses caused by business activities (Chapter 3, Section 3.3.2).

An example of the host state's regulatory reaction to loss of an SLO is the case of the Groningen gas project by Nederlandse Aardolie Maatschappij (NAM) in the Netherlands. Several incidents of earthquakes associated with gas production caused property damage in the area, and the local people perceived the strategy of NAM for responding to these incidents as 'insincere' and 'singularly unsuccessful'.[136] These resulted in strong social opposition to the project in the local community and NGOs, and thereby the loss of the project's SLO.[137] This led to the Dutch government's decision to order NAM to reduce yearly production gradually, culminating in the decision in March 2018 to order a complete reduction to zero by 2030 at the latest.[138] It is observed that the 2018 decision was 'the logical outcome of the loss of a social licence to operate and the resulting political and legal measures'.[139] This case illustrates how loss of an SLO may necessitate a strong regulatory reaction leading to the termination of the project.

This example reveals the existence of the following circumstances: (a) the investor's *certain* conduct that resulted in an actual or perceived threat of harm contributed to a loss of an SLO and (b) loss of the SLO

[133] Boutilier, Black and Thomson, 'From Metaphor to Management Tool', 230.

[134] Yates and Horvath, 'Social License to Operate', 3.

[135] Gunningham, Kagan and Thornton, 'Social License and Environmental Protection', 322; Cotula and Schröder, 'Community Perspectives in Investor-State Arbitration', 15.

[136] van den Beukel and Geuns, 'Groningen Gas', 15.

[137] Ibid., 21.

[138] Ibid., 3; Van Loo, 'Rise and Fall'.

[139] van den Beukel and Geuns, 'Groningen Gas', 21. Boutilier also identifies the 2009 and 2012 withdrawal of legal licenses of mineral exploration projects with reimbursement to two Canadian companies by the Ontario government in response to strong oppositions and protests from an indigenous community group as 'cases of a government admitting that the social licence has at least as much force as the legal licence'. Boutilier, 'Frequently Asked Questions about the Social Licence', 267.

necessitated the host state's intervention. It is argued that, when these circumstances exist, then the ground for protecting the investor's interest in fulfilling its legitimate expectations is lessened, tilting the balance towards the host state's interest in protecting the public interest.

Having said this, not all conduct of the investor that results in a loss of the project's SLO should be subject to this consequence. The following sections demonstrate that there is a risk of abuse and manipulation of an SLO which necessitates a certain threshold standard for the investor's conduct.

6.3.4.4.3 Risk of the Manipulation of the Concept of SLO As discussed in Section 6.3.4.4.1, the concept of SLO has a fundamentally indeterminate and dynamic nature. This gives rise to a risk of abuse and manipulation of the concept in different circumstances, including when the host state intervenes in the investment on the ground of a lack of an SLO. The tribunal's finding in *Tethyan Copper v. Pakistan* illustrates this risk. In this case, the respondent state invoked the absence of an SLO to justify its rejection of the investor's mining application. It argued that the investor failed to obtain an SLO on the ground, *inter alia*, that the investor's investment plan 'to export all of the concentrate via a pipeline to the sea' did not meet the 'value addition' requirement, specifically the requirement to establish a smelter and refinery facility in the region, and would not bring any local benefits such as technology and skill transfer and job creation.[140] However, the tribunal rejected this argument by stating that if the value addition requirement was part of the relevant regulation, it was presumably introduced to specifically to 'target Claimant's project and to prevail with the GOB's [municipal government's] request for a local smelter and refinery'. Therefore, such conduct, in the view of the tribunal, would amount to 'an abuse of sovereign power to achieve a concession that the Governments had failed to achieve through negotiations with Claimant'.[141]

The SLO can also be used as a tool for political campaigning at the municipal or central governmental level.[142] Further, there lies the risk, perceived by professionals in the extractive industries, that the concept

[140] *Tethyan Copper Company Pty Limited v. Islamic Republic of Pakistan*, ICSID Case No. ARB/12/1, Decision on Jurisdiction and Liability, 10 November 2017 (*Tethyan Copper* Decision on Jurisdiction and Liability), para. 1065.

[141] Ibid., para. 1201.

[142] Buur, Nystrand and Pedersen, 'Political Economy of Land', 24 (citation omitted).

'masks political gamesmanship of questionable legitimacy on the part of project opponents'.[143] Scholars point out the risk of manipulation and opportunistic use 'to advance private agendas'[144] or 'to disguise or silence opposition'.[145] These also suggest the risk that this concept is abused by the relevant community.[146]

The risk of an SLO as a tool for political campaigning is illustrated by *Abengoa v. Mexico*. In this case, the respondent state alleged that the investor's failure to implement social communication with the local community in an effective manner contributed to the revocation of the operating licence for the investor's waste management facility. However, the tribunal found on the facts that local opposition against the investor's facility, which became a key issue in municipal elections, was for electoral purposes, and that the facility posed no threat to the environment or public health. Accordingly, the tribunal concluded that the deficiencies of the communication programme cannot exonerate the host state from its responsibility for expropriating the investment.[147]

Therefore, invocation of the concept of SLO as a way to counterbalance the investor's interest in the assessment of the protection of legitimate expectations needs to be handled with caution, taking into account the risk of its abuse. It necessitates establishing a threshold standard for the investor's conduct as one of the requirements for imposing the consequences of the loss of an SLO on the investor.[148]

6.3.4.4.4 SLO and Balancing in the Protection of Legitimate Expectations: Threshold Question Defining the threshold standard for the investor's conduct in a fixed manner is impossible because its determination is highly context- and fact-sensitive. Nevertheless, certain elements that form the standard can be identified. First, compliance with the host state's laws and regulations and fulfilment of its contractual obligations would always be relevant. However, in assessing whether the investor's breach of domestic regulations and contractual obligations falls below the threshold, factors such as the degree (non-trivial or trivial) and

143 Boutilier, 'Frequently Asked Questions about the Social Licence', 269.

144 Van Putten et al., 'Emergence of Social Licence Necessitates Reforms', 1 (citation omitted).

145 Owen and Kemp, 'Social Licence and Mining', 30.

146 See also Newman, 'Be Careful What You Wish For', 3.

147 *Abengoa S.A. y COFIDES S.A. v. United Mexican States*, ICSID Case No. ARB(AF)/09/2, 18 April 2013, paras. 659–673.

148 Peralta, 'Judicialisation of the Social License', 107.

nature (intentional or inadvertent) of the claimed violation by the investor must be considered.

Secondly, the investor's conduct may fall below the threshold standard even in the absence of a violation of formal laws and regulations. Even though the relevant international standards are not addressed to private entities, this does not necessarily render these standards irrelevant for the investor's conduct.[149] As discussed in Chapter 5, Section 5.4.1, once specific commitments concerning business operations are expressed by the investor in their self-regulation, codes of conduct and other statements, these commitments create expectations on the part of local stakeholders that the investor's conduct will implement these commitments. In such cases, it is their own representations and commitments that determine the standard of required conduct. Therefore, when an investor's conduct, which contravenes its own commitments, leads to the loss of an SLO, it is a strong indicator that they have failed to meet the threshold. This is regardless of whether the breach of voluntary commitments leads to legal responsibility under the relevant domestic laws, such as tort law, because the purpose of setting the threshold is not to pursue the investor's legal responsibility through counterclaims (as discussed in Chapter 5, Section 5.4.1) but balance the investor's interests in fulfilling its legitimate expectations against the host state's public interest.

Thirdly, when the investor's management of its operations causes actual damage, or serious threat of such damage in the local community (as was the case of the Groningen gas project, as noted above), it would be justified to let the investor bear the consequences of the loss of an SLO, because such a situation would warrant the strong need for the host state's urgent intervention. This consequence also requires neither a violation of domestic regulations nor that the host state's law has a strict liability regime for environmental harm, because, again, the purpose of determining the threshold in this context is not to pursue the investor's legal responsibility.

The next section seeks to test the application of these elements of the threshold standard by reference to investment arbitration cases. The concept of SLO has been relied on by the host state and advanced by *amici* in recent investment arbitration cases as a ground to justify the

[149] This issue was discussed in *Bear Creek Mining v. Mexico*, as examined in Section 6.3.4.4.5.

measures in question of the host state.[150] Among these cases, the next section examines *Bear Creek v. Peru* and *South American Silver v. Bolivia* as cases in which SLO was discussed in the context of the investor's environmental responsibility, and the tribunals reached contrasting conclusions as to the impact of an SLO on the protection of investor's legitimate expectations.

6.3.4.4.5 Investment Arbitration Cases that Discussed SLO

Bear Creek v. Peru This case arose out of the suspension of the investor's Environmental and Social Impact Assessment (ESIA) and the subsequent revocation (by Supreme Decree 032) of the authorisation for mining concessions (by Supreme Decree 083). Specifically, the revocation took place in the context of protests against the investor's mining project and after the election of the new President who, according to the claimant, 'crucially needed votes from the [relevant] Puno region'.[151] In this case, the investor's 'distinct, reasonable investment-backed expectations' (Annex 812.1 of the Canada-Peru FTA) and legitimate expectations were discussed in the indirect expropriation and FET claims, respectively.[152] The respondent state alleged, *inter alia*, that the revocation was a legitimate exercise of its police powers to 'address the causes of violent protests that threatened the health and safety of Peru's citizens',[153] and that the claimant investor did not have legitimate expectation to assume that its authorisation 'could not be revisited under dramatically changed circumstances', that is, the social unrest incited by the investor's operations.[154]

150 *Glamis Gold v. US*, Non-Party Supplemental Submission, Submission of the Quechan Indian Nation, 16 October 2006, para. 8; *Bear Creek v. Peru*; *Pac Rim Cayman LLC v. Republic of El Salvador*, ICSID Case No. ARB/09/12 (The Republic of El Salvador's Rejoinder on the Merits, 11 July 2014, paras. 266–288; Submission of *amicus curiae* Brief by the Center for International Environmental Law of 20 May 2011, p. 10); *Gabriel Resources v. Romania*, Respondent's Comments on the Non-Disputing Parties' Submission, 18 March 2019; *Lone Pine Resources Inc. v. Government of Canada*, ICSID Case No. UNCT/15/2; *Tethyan Copper v. Pakistan*; *Mesa Power v. Canada*; *South American Silver v. Bolivia*.

151 *Bear Creek* Award, para. 195.

152 Ibid., paras. 343, 482.

153 *Bear Creek v. Peru*, Respondent's Rejoinder on the Merits and Reply on Jurisdiction, 13 April 2016 (*Bear Creek* Respondent's rejoinder), para. 463. See also Respondent's Counter-Memorial on the Merits and Memorial on Jurisdiction, 6 October 2015 (*Bear Creek* Respondent's Counter-Memorial), para. 243.

154 *Bear Creek* Respondent's rejoinder, para. 533.

In this regard, the respondent state argued that the investor's engagement with the communities, which focused solely on 'buying support with jobs', failed to sufficiently address the cultural and environmental concerns of the local communities and thereby failed to obtain an SLO,[155] and thus also caused the social unrest.[156] *Amici* also stressed a lack of an SLO for the project, arguing that the investor's project lacked legitimacy, trust, and consent due to the investor's failure to 'understand the doubts, worries and anxieties' of the communities and assess the environmental risks of the project.[157]

The claimant contested the insufficiency of its community outreach programme, but also argued that even if there was a failure of communication, lack of communication, transparency, and resulting fallout, these failings should be attributed to the respondent.[158] In particular, the claimant stressed that the respondent deprived it of a chance to continue its community outreach efforts, as '[t]he suspension of Claimant's ESIA prevented Claimant from continuing to implement its community relations program in Santa Ana'.[159] In his witness statement, the claimant's CEO claimed that 'we had never produced any silver at Santa Ana, and the exploratory work performed in the area had never resulted in environmental pollution of any sort', and therefore the suspension of the ESIA was 'not based on environmental concerns, but rather on the climate of political violence in the Puno region'.[160]

The tribunal found the existence of the investor's distinct, reasonable investment-backed expectations on the grounds of its reliance on 'the express governmental authorization by Supreme Decree 083' when making the investment.[161] On the other hand, the tribunal accepted that, at the time of the issuance of Supreme Decree 032, the government was 'under strong political pressure and was urgently looking for steps that could be hoped to improve the

155 *Bear Creek* Respondent's Counter-Memorial, paras. 69, 75, 85. See also Expert Report of Antonio Alfonso Peña Jumpa, 6 October 2015, para. 96.

156 *Bear Creek* Award, para. 253.

157 Non-Disputing Party Written Submission of DHUMA and Dr. Carlos Lopez, 9 May 2016, 5–8, 12–17; *Bear Creek* Award, paras. 218, 227.

158 *Bear Creek* Award, para. 236.

159 Ibid., para. 250.

160 Witness Statement of Andrew T. Swarthout (Bear Creek CEO), 29 May 2015, paras. 48–50. See also Witness Statement of Elsiario Antunez de Mayolo (Bear Creek's Chief Operational Officer), 29 May 2015, para. 18.

161 *Bear Creek* Award, para. 376.

situation',[162] and that the claimant could have taken further actions of outreach than it actually took.[163]

However, the tribunal concluded that such further outreach activities were not legally required and the investor did not cause the social unrest, and therefore the investor's failure to conduct these activities did not justify Supreme Decree 032. The tribunal also found, on the facts, that the respondent's authorities were aware of the community discontent yet gave approval, support, and endorsement to the claimant's outreach activities until June 2011, which made the claimant believe that it had 'complied with all legal requirements with regard to its outreach to the local communities'.[164] On this basis, the majority concluded that the respondent state cannot claim that the claimant's outreach activity was 'contrary to the ILO Convention 169 or was insufficient, and caused or contributed to the social unrest in the region'.[165] Relying on the tribunal's statement in the *Abengoa* Award made in the context of the defence of contributory fault, the tribunal concluded that absent a causal link between the claimant's activity and the social unrest, lack of an SLO would not justify Supreme Decree 032, which therefore constituted indirect expropriation.[166]

The tribunal also found that there was no legalisation element such as due process in Supreme Decree 032 and therefore the indirect expropriation was unlawful,[167] and a lack of a causal link between the claimant's conduct and Supreme Decree 032 made discussions on any police power exception and general exceptions (Article 2201.1 of the FTA) unnecessary in this case.[168] The respondent state had also claimed illegality in the process of the investor obtaining authorisation (Supreme Decree 083), but this claim was rejected by the tribunal on the facts.[169] The tribunal concluded that the finding of an unlawful indirect expropriation made the examination of the FET and other claims unnecessary.[170]

162 Ibid., para. 380.
163 Ibid., paras. 404–408.
164 Ibid., paras. 409–412.
165 Ibid., para. 412 (Arbitrator Sands dissented. Partial Dissenting Opinion of Professor Philippe Sands, 30 November 2017 (Sands dissenting opinion), para. 1).
166 Ibid., paras. 410–416.
167 Ibid., paras. 442–449.
168 Ibid., paras. 471–478.
169 Ibid., paras. 395–399.
170 Ibid., paras. 533, 553.

The tribunal was split on the question of the investor's contributory fault. Arbitrator Sands, in his partial dissenting opinion, argued that it was the investor's inability to obtain an SLO that brought about the collapse of the project, and that the investor's outreach programme failed to meet the consultation requirements under Article 15 of the ILO Convention 169, which was incorporated into Peruvian law.[171] On this basis, he argued that the investor's contribution to its own damages should be no less than 50 per cent. By contrast, the majority declined to employ ILO Convention 169 as a yardstick for the standard of the investor's conduct, on the ground that: 'a private company cannot "fail to comply" with ILO Convention 169 because it imposes no direct obligations on them'.[172]

While the tribunal's conclusion was based on a lack of a causal link between the investor's conduct and the social unrest, if we apply the elements for the threshold standard for the investor's conduct identified in the previous section to this case, the following observations can be made. The illegality in the performance of the investment was not contended by the respondent, and the allegation of illegality in the obtaining of the investment was rejected by the tribunal. Likewise, there was no finding that the investor's operations caused actual or a threat of environmental harm.

Investor's social outreach programmes are more controversial. Although there is no indication in the award or the *amicus* submission as such (and this is not the place to second-guess the majority's finding of facts), if the investor had made specific promissory representations on the standard of their conduct that created expectations on the part of local stakeholders, breach of its own commitments could have indicated the failure to meet the threshold standard. In this respect, a survey conducted in 2010 on extractive companies' global policies and other published statements concerning indigenous rights revealed that approximately half of these statements 'refer to consent; free, prior, and informed consultation; or broad community support'.[173] Nevertheless, the specificity of their language and the level of commitment vary widely between companies.[174]

171 *Bear Creek v. Peru*, Sands dissenting opinion, paras. 10–12, 33.

172 *Bear Creek* Award, para. 664. See Peralta, 'Judicialisation of the Social License', 126 (supporting the majority's conclusion on this point); Marcoux and Newcombe, '*Bear Creek Mining Corporation v Republic of Peru*', 659 (supporting Sands dissenting opinion).

173 Lehr and Smith, *Implementing a Corporate*, 51.

174 Ibid., 51–54.

South American Silver v. Bolivia A conclusion different from the *Bear Creek* case regarding the impact of an SLO on the protection of investors' expectations was reached in *South American Silver v. Bolivia*. This case arose out of a reversion of ten mining concessions held by the claimant's indirect Bolivian subsidiary, CMMK. The investor claimed Bolivia's breach of investment protection obligations including, in particular, expropriation and the FET. The respondent raised various arguments concerning a lack of an SLO for the investor's mining project. According to the respondent, in the face of the 'radical and generalized opposition' to the mining project, CMMK 'started a campaign of threats (physical and legal) and incitement to violence amongst Indigenous Communities that both supported and opposed the Project' which resulted in a situation of uncontrollable conflict.[175] The respondent state also argued that the project caused a serious environmental risk to the mountains where it was planned, together with the surrounding lagoons, upon which the survival of the indigenous communities depended, and this gave rise to the fear on the part of these communities and brought about the resulting social tension.[176] On this basis, the respondent state argued that the reversion was the only option available to restore public order by addressing the conflict directly created by CMMK's conduct.[177] In the Award, the majority of the tribunal first concluded, on the facts, that: '[D]espite having implemented a community relations program, the Company [CMMK] had serious shortcomings in its relationship with the community from the outset which were not corrected'.[178] Having confirmed the occurrence of a direct expropriation,[179] the majority then examined the lawfulness of the expropriation to conclude that the reversion decree was taken to end the social conflict and the situation of violence that had resulted in deaths, and was therefore for a public purpose[180] and that due process had been observed.[181] Nevertheless, the majority held that payment of just and effective compensation as the last element for lawfulness of the expropriation was missing in this

[175] *South American Silver v. Bolivia*, Respondent Counter-Memorial, 31 March 2015 (*South American Silver* Respondent Counter-Memorial), paras. 80–84.

[176] *South American Silver* Respondent Counter-Memorial, paras. 107, 320–324; South American Silver Award, para. 377.

[177] *South American Silver* Respondent Counter-Memorial, paras. 84, 328.

[178] *South American Silver* Award, para. 490.

[179] Ibid., para. 551.

[180] Ibid., paras. 559–561.

[181] Ibid., paras. 579–586.

case,[182] and that the police powers doctrine or state of necessity did not excuse the non-payment of compensation for the expropriation. On these bases, the majority found a breach of the expropriation provision.[183]

By contrast, the majority rejected the claimant's FET claims based on legitimate expectation, on the ground of CMMK's operational misconduct. It first concluded that, in the circumstances of the case, the investor did not have legitimate expectations in particular regarding the stability of Bolivia's legal and business framework,[184] because it 'knew, or should have known, that CMMK operated in an area inhabited by indigenous communities, under specific political, social, cultural, and economic conditions'.[185] The majority then found the existence of the circumstances identified in Section 6.3.4.4.2, by finding that: CMMK's conduct contributed to social conflict and its aggravation and thus created a 'supervening situation'; the reversion was enacted 'to end the social conflict in the Project area', which was necessary 'to restore public order and thus protect the life and integrity of the population in the area and CMMK's employees'.[186]

The nature and consequences of the investor's conduct found in this case are different from those found in *Bear Creek v. Peru* in several ways. In this case, there was some evidence that the project did cause environmental pollution and serious concerns over the environmental harm in the project site.[187] Moreover, the majority found that CMMK employed aggressive acts targeting those opposed to its project by, in particular, filing criminal complaints against community leaders without a basis for

[182] Ibid., paras. 587–610.

[183] Ibid., paras. 611–630. Arbitrator Guglielmino dissented (in addition to the majority's finding of jurisdiction) also to the majority's finding of an unlawful expropriation (*South American Silver* Guglielmino dissenting opinion, paras. 184–235). Arbitrator Orrego Vicuña, while concurring in the award, noted his different views that 'the reasons for expropriation are considerably broader than the non-payment of compensation to the expropriated investor'. *South American Silver v. Bolivia*, Separate Opinion of Prof. Francisco Orrego Vicuña, 22 November 2018 (*South American Silver* Orrego Vicuña separate opinion), 2.

[184] Ibid., para. 652.

[185] Ibid., para. 655.

[186] Ibid., para. 656. While concurring in the award, Arbitrator Orrego Vicuña noted his different views on this point by stating that: 'the Award dismisses conduct that may be considered irreconcilable with the treatment required, in particular in respect of its transparency and consistency'. *South American Silver* Orrego Vicuña separate opinion, 3.

[187] *South American Silver* Award, paras. 113–114, 481.

legal action 'as a means to scare the members of the community',[188] and by taking actions aimed at 'weakening the opposition and consolidating a majority opinion, supposedly represented by COTOA-6A [a local organisation that supported CMMK], which contributed to the aggravation of the conflict'.[189] Although the majority cautiously avoided identifying the illegality associated with these acts, these findings suggest that some of these acts were not far from being non-trivial and intentional infringements of local laws. Therefore, even if the majority (although in this case it did not) had found that the investor's expectations were legitimate, it would have been possible to conclude that the subsidiary's conduct fell below the threshold standard and the investor lost the ground for protection of its legitimate expectations.

To conclude, when the circumstances identified in Section 6.3.4.4.2 (i.e. the contribution of a certain conduct of the investor to the loss of an SLO, and the fact that it necessitated the host state's intervention) exist, and the investor's conduct falls below the threshold standard discussed in Section 6.3.4.4.4 (i.e. as per referencing legality, certain commitments by the investor, and the degree and nature of the impact of the investor's conduct), the loss of an SLO leads to a loss or lesser ground for the protection of its legitimate expectations against the host state's public interest.

Even if the host state can successfully invoke this defence, it is possible that the host state's liability is established based on other elements of the FET standard, or grounds other than the FET standard, despite the finding of the investor's performance-phase misconduct. In such cases, the claim will proceed to the remedy phase in which, in most cases, compensation is awarded.[190] The next section examines the role of the investor's performance-phase misconduct at the quantum phase, focusing on certain controversies over the application of contributory fault.

6.4 Corporate Performance-Phase Environmental Responsibility in the Quantum Phase: Selected Questions of Contributory Fault

6.4.1 Application of Contributory Fault in the IIA-Based Dispute Settlement Mechanism

There are different ways by which the investor's performance-phase misconduct may impact the determination of the amount of

[188] Ibid., paras. 494–495.

[189] Ibid., para. 507.

[190] Jana, 'Reparation in Investment Treaty Arbitration', 289.

compensation. For example, when it leads to loss of an SLO, the project may no longer qualify as a 'going concern', which excludes a Discounted Cash Flow (DCF) valuation, a forecast-based valuation method that calculates the present value of future cash flows of an investment.[191]

This impact on the determination of the methods of valuation, is indirect and (normative) value-neutral, because the choice is based on the examination of the profit-generating capacity of the property taken at the relevant time. In contrast, a way to directly reflect the investor's responsibility in determining the amount of compensation is the application of contributory fault.[192]

Contributory fault has been recognised in investment arbitration case law[193] and by scholars[194] as a concept that leads to a reduction of compensation when the claimant investor's certain conduct contributed to the creation of its own damages.[195] This concept has been widely

[191] See *Bear Creek* Award, para. 657. By contrast, in *Tethyan Copper v. Pakistan*, the tribunal refused to displace the DCF method on the basis of the finding that none of the risks claimed by the respondent, including those associated with an SLO, 'would have stopped the project or rendered it unprofitable' (*Tethyan Copper* Award, para. 333).

[192] This section follows Bederman's choice of the term 'fault' as 'a more neutral term than "negligence" which does refer to violation of a legally required standard of care'. Bederman, 'Contributory Fault and State Responsibility', 335.

[193] Investment arbitration cases in which the amount of compensation was reduced by application of contributory fault are: *MTD Equity Sdn. Bhd. and MTD Chile S.A. v. Republic of Chile* (*MTD v. Chile*), ICSID Case No. ARB/01/7, Award, 25 May 2004 (*MTD* Award), paras. 242–246; *Occidental Petroleum Corporation, Occidental Exploration and Production Company v. Republic of Ecuador* (*Occidental v. Ecuador*), ICSID Case No. ARB/06/11, Award, 5 October 2012 (*Occidental* Award), paras. 687, 825; *Yukos* Awards, paras. 1633–1637; *Copper Mesa* Award, paras. 6.97–6.102, 6.133; *UAB E energija (Lithuania) v. Republic of Latvia*, ICSID Case No. ARB/12/33, Award, 22 December 2017 (*UAB* Award), paras. 1143–1145; *STEAG GmbH v. Kingdom of Spain*, ICSID Case No. ARB/15/4, Decision on Jurisdiction, Liability and Principles of Quantum, 8 September 2020 (*STEAG* Decision), para. 760. In *UAB v. Latvia*, the tribunal did not explicitly mention the concept of contributory fault, but awarded only 50 per cent of the actual loss on the grounds that the claimant's subsidiary's 'decision to stop paying the full price for the natural gas used' led to the revocation of the licence by the host state. In the annulment decision, the Annulment Committee described the tribunal's approach as the application of contributory fault. *UAB v. Latvia*, Decision on Annulment, 8 April 2020 (*UAB* Annulment Decision), para. 195.

[194] Sabahi and Duggal, '*Occidental Petroleum v Ecuador*', 288; Kantor, 'Impact of Contributory Investor Conduct', 534; Marboe, *Calculation of Compensation and Damages*, 120–121; Sabahi, *Compensation and Restitution in Investor-State Arbitration*, 175–176; Ripinsky and Williams, *Damages in International Investment Law*, 314–319.

[195] It is observed that, in both Roman law and common law, contributory negligence (or the equivalent doctrine) as the complete defence has been 'set aside since long' to the

accepted by international courts and tribunals[196] and is recognised in Article 39 of the International Law Commission (ILC) Articles on State Responsibility. Article 39 reads that:

> In the determination of reparation, account shall be taken of the contribution to the injury by wilful or negligent action or omission of the injured State or any person or entity in relation to whom reparation is sought.

The Annulment Committee in *MTD v. Chile* confirmed the analogous applicability of Article 39 to investor–state disputes,[197] and Article 39 has been relied on by subsequent tribunals, including in *Occidental v. Ecuador*,[198] the *Yukos* cases,[199] *Copper Mesa v. Ecuador*[200] and *STEAG v. Spain*.[201]

Investment arbitration tribunals have applied contributory fault to damage determinations as a way of recognising investor contribution to its injury in the following two ways: (a) through the reckless taking of business risk (*MTD* and *STEAG*) and (b) through the performance-phase misconduct that prompted or provoked the host state's measures found to be a breach of the relevant IIA (*Occidental*, *Yukos*, *Copper Mesa* and *UAB*).[202]

approach (in common law 'comparative negligence') to apportion the damage between the parties. Magnus and Martin-Casals, 'Comparative Conclusions', 259–260; Grehan, 'Comparative Negligence', 1668–1670.

196 Sabahi, *Compensation and Restitution in Investor-State Arbitration*, 176 (citing *LaGrand (Germany v. United States of America)* (Judgment of 27 June 2001) [2001] ICJ Rep. 466, paras. 57, 116); *S.S. Wimbledon, Judgment on Intervention by Poland* (Judgment of 28 June 1923) PCIJ Series A, No.1; *Delagoa Bay & East African RR Co (US & Great Britain v. Portugal (1900))*; Bederman, 'Contributory Fault and State Responsibility', 359–360 (international arbitration cases).

197 *MTD v. Chile*, Decision on Annulment, 21 March 2007 (*MTD* Annulment Decision), para. 99; Marcoux and Bjorklund, 'Foreign Investors' Responsibilities and Contributory Fault', 883 (fn 28); Gill and Gupta, 'Principle of Contributory Fault after Yukos', 95.

198 *Occidental* Award, 665–669 (Article 39 was applied in conjunction with Article 31).

199 *Yukos* Awards, paras. 1595–1598 (Article 39 was applied in conjunction with Article 31).

200 *Copper Mesa* Award, paras. 6.91–6.92. See also *Burlington Resources v. Ecuador*, ICSID Case No. ARB/08/5, Decision on Reconsideration and Award, 7 February 2017 (*Burlington* Decision on Reconsideration), paras. 572–574 (Article 39 was applied in conjunction with Article 31).

201 *STEAG* Decision, para. 760.

202 (b) refers to the situation relevant to the investor's performance-phase environmental responsibility, which is termed by Jarrett as the 'investment reprisal' situation. Jarrett, *Contributory Fault and Investor Misconduct*, 182–183.

However, the application of contributory fault by investment arbitration tribunals has been criticised. This section focuses on the criticism that applies to all the cases identified above, that is, their adoption of the 'percentage reduction' approach in reducing the amount of compensation as a result of contributory fault. After reviewing the function of contributory fault, it is concluded that the percentage-based approach is actually defensible in this light, and the impossibility of calculating the amount to be reduced with precision should not deter the application of contributory fault.

6.4.2 *Function of Contributory Fault*

The language of Article 39 of the ILC Articles that contributory fault concerns 'the determination of reparation' may be interpreted to suggest that 'the relationship between causation and contributory fault is only relevant for the determination of reparation in the international law of State responsibility'.[203] However, the following discussions on the 'situations which in national law systems are referred to as "contributory negligence", "comparative fault", "faute de la victime", etc.', which the ILC Commentary identifies as the 'focus' of Article 39,[204] point to the conclusion that this rule actually functions to divide the liability between the claimant and the wrongdoer.

In the context of common law, Schwartz argues that the fairness idea 'calls on tort law to take some account of the plaintiff's contributory negligence in ascertaining the liability of a negligent defendant', and describes comparative negligence as 'a liability-dividing rule', which satisfies this fairness demand.[205] Based on a comparative study of contributory negligence in different European countries, Magnus and Martin-Casals conclude that 'the most common justification of contributory negligence as a defense is justice and fairness', which 'does not allow a victim to place the consequences of own conduct or risk fully on the shoulders of someone else'.[206] In the context of investor–state disputes,

[203] Marcoux and Bjorklund, 'Foreign Investors' Responsibilities and Contributory Fault', 888.

[204] International Law Commission, 'Commentaries to Draft Articles on Responsibility of States for Internationally Wrongful Acts', UN GAOR 56th Session, Supp. No. 10, at 43, UN Doc. A/56/10 (2001), YbILC, vol. II, Part Two.

[205] Schwartz, 'Contributory and Comparative Negligence', 725. See also Grehan, 'Comparative Negligence', 1670.

[206] Magnus and Martin-Casals, 'Comparative Conclusions', 262.

Jarrett argues that the finding of contributory fault 'acts as a cap on the respondent's liability, and the remedies are calculated with reference to that cap'.[207] Therefore, it is concluded that contributory fault is a rule that divides liability between the host state (as a wrongdoer) and the investor.

6.4.3 *Reduction of Compensation by Percentage*

When the requirements for the application of contributory fault specified in Article 39 ILC Articles, that is, (a) wilful or negligent action or omission by the injured party[208] (b) that contributes to the injury,[209] are met, the last stage is to determine the extent to which the amount of compensation is reduced. In practice, this is done by determining a certain percentage by which the investor's original damage, that is, the damage that would otherwise be awarded in the absence of contributory fault, is reduced. Based on a comparative study of domestic contributory fault applications in European countries, Magnus and Martin-Casals observe that:

[207] Jarrett, *Contributory Fault and Investor Misconduct*, 23. Fahner argues that in situations where 'the investor's contributory fault did not relate to the host state's breach', such as when it failed to mitigate damage, contributory fault is a matter of quantum and not of liability. Fahner, 'Conundrum of Contributory Fault', 774. However, it can be argued that even in this type of scenario, contributory fault determines the extent each party should be liable for the consequences to which its conduct has contributed.

[208] Commentary to Article 39 defines this as conduct that 'manifest[s] a lack of due care on the part of the victim of the breach for his or her own property or rights', while it does not qualify this notion by 'a requirement that the negligence should have reached the level of being "serious" or "gross"'. Jarret argues for the need to have a minimum standard for 'a lack of due care', to avoid the risk that 'provocation can too readily be used as a licence to breach'. Jarrett, *Contributory Fault and Investor Misconduct*, 125. In *Caratube v. Kazakhstan*, the tribunal concluded that the alleged 'sub-standard' performance by the investor, which, however, is not a 'material breach' of the contract did not constitute 'willful or negligent, reproachable behavior' that gives rise to contributory fault. *Caratube International Oil Company LLP and Devincci Salah Hourani v. Republic of Kazakhstan*, ICSID Case No. ARB/13/13, Award, 27 September 2017 (*Caratube* Award), paras. 1192–1193.

[209] There is a presumption that the contribution of the investor to the host state's breach would qualify as a contribution to the injury, which is alleged to have been caused by the breach. Gill and Gupta, 'Principle of Contributory Fault after Yukos', 108. Another major criticism concerning the application of contributory fault by investment arbitration tribunals is the inconsistent approaches to this requirement, but this is beyond the scope of this study. For discussions on this issue, see in particular Jarrett, *Contributory Fault and Investor Misconduct*, chapter 3; Sadowski, 'Yukos and Contributory Fault'.

> [I]n most cases a reduction within the range of 10–90% and, more often, within the range of 25–75% will be the final outcome. Smaller fractions than steps of 5 or 10% are very rarely used.[210]

MTD (50%),[211] *Occidental* (25%),[212] the *Yukos* cases (25%),[213] *Copper Mesa* (30%),[214] *UAB* (50%),[215] and *STEAG* (25%)[216] all conform to this observation.

The determination of the percentage depends exclusively on the tribunal's judicial assessment of the impact of the investor's contributory fault,[217] and 'is not based on any particular formula'.[218] Admittedly, the determination by nature 'defies any mathematical precision',[219] and it has been acknowledged that the tribunal has discretion in this apportionment.[220]

This percentage-reduction approach has been criticised for its lack of scientific rigor. Urdaneta criticises the tribunals' approach for contributory fault as an exercise of 'excessive discretion',[221] comparing it to the award in *Rurelec v. Bolivia* that treated the calculation of damages as almost 'an exact science'.[222] He then proposes the approach of imposing on the respondent state the obligation of proving the extent of the claimant's fault on the basis of the data, and the approach of resorting 'to an economic analysis to quantify the victim's fault'.[223] Jarret likewise criticises that the *Occidental* tribunal's 'apportionment based on causal

210 Magnus and Martin-Casals, 'Comparative Conclusions', 283.

211 *MTD* Award, paras. 242–246.

212 *Occidental* Award, paras. 687, 825. Arbitrator Stern dissented, arguing that 'the split 50/50 would have been even more justified'. *Occidental v. Ecuador*, Dissenting Opinion of Professor Brigitte Stern, 20 September 2012, para. 7.

213 *Yukos* Awards, para. 1637.

214 *Copper Mesa* Award, para. 6.102.

215 *UAB* Award, paras. 1144–1145.

216 *STEAG* Decision, para. 796.

217 Ancelin, 'À propos de la "théorie des mains propres"', 854.

218 Sabahi, Duggal and Birch, 'Principles Limiting the Amount of Compensation', 328.

219 Sabahi and Duggal, '*Occidental Petroleum v Ecuador*', 289.

220 *MTD* Annulment Decision, para. 101; *UAB* Annulment Decision, para. 197; *Caratube* Award, para. 1192.

221 Urdaneta, 'Proportionality, Contributory Negligence and Other Equity Considerations', 306 (citing *Guaracachi America, Inc. and Rurelec Plc v. Plurinational State of Bolivia*, UNCITRAL, PCA Case No. 2011-17, Award, 31 January 2014 and Annex to Award, 31 January 2014).

222 Urdaneta, 'Proportionality, Contributory Negligence and Other Equity Considerations', 320. See also Simmons, 'Valuation in Investor-State Arbitration', 196–197.

223 Urdaneta, 'Proportionality, Contributory Negligence and Other Equity Considerations', 323.

potency' approach as nonsensical, because 'causality is a binary concept – either an event is a cause or it is not'.[224]

Certainly, when the damage caused by the investor's misconduct is calculable in monetary terms, reflecting the amount in the percentage reduction would be desirable to address the issue of arbitrariness in apportionment. Jarret proposes the following approach: When the investor's damage is of 3,000,000 ducats, and 'the investor's misconduct causes environmental damage that will cost 2,200,000 ducats to repair, then the investor should be apportioned 73.3 per cent of the international responsibility'.[225] Likewise, on the *Yukos* awards, Kantor argues that 'quantified measurements of the contributory fault events' could have been taken, specifically the approach that 'the contributory fault reduction could have been calculated as the amount of re-assessed Russian Taxes, charges and penalties remaining unpaid after the YNG auction and by the time of the Yukos bankruptcy, together with interest accruing thereon up to discharge in bankruptcy at the applicable Russian statutory rate'.[226]

Nevertheless, this does not mean that the precise calculation of the damage attributable to the investor's conduct is a necessary condition for the application of contributory fault. Indeed, not all investor's contributory faults are as measurable in monetary terms as environmental clean-up costs or a failure to pay tax.[227] For example, when the investor's conduct causes actual or perceived threats to the environment that require governmental intervention before the harm materialises, the investor's contributory fault may still be established.[228] Although it is impossible to calculate the monetary value of the investor's fault in measurable terms in such cases, this should not deter the application of contributory fault. As discussed in Section 6.4.2, reduction of compensation is a *consequence* of the division of liability between the parties. In other words, unlike set-off claims and counterclaims, contributory fault is not to pursue the financial responsibility of the investor for its conduct. Gill and Gulpa, after confirming that the estimation approach is also adopted in many common law and civil law jurisdictions, support the percentage-reduction approach as 'a more flexible tool with which to

224 Jarrett, 'Responding to Investor Misconduct', 190.
225 Ibid., 191.
226 Kantor, 'Impact of Contributory Investor Conduct', 552.
227 Gill and Gupta, 'Principle of Contributory Fault after Yukos', 113.
228 It should be recalled that in *Bear Creek v. Peru* in which Arbitrator Sands argued for the application of contributory fault, there was no finding that the investor's operations caused environmental harm (Section 6.3.4.4.5).

reflect a tribunal's view of the culpability of the parties'.[229] Therefore, the percentage-reduction approach is indeed a valuable method in determining the amount of compensation to be reduced.

It is argued that the criticism of the tribunals' approach to contributory fault should be directed not at the selection of this approach, but at a lack of reasoned explanation for the apportionment of liability between the host state and the investor. Investment arbitration tribunals have not offered any detailed explanation of the grounds for the determination of percentages, but relied on the broad concept of discretion they have in the apportionment of responsibility.[230] However, Hart describes the distinguishing feature of the discretion case, which distinguishes it from arbitrary choice, as that there remains 'a choice to be made' for which 'the factors which we must take into account and conscientiously weigh may themselves be identifiable'.[231] Therefore, while discretion is essential for tribunals' assessment of justice and fairness, which are the justification of contributory fault (see Section 6.4.2), recognised factors to guide that discretion should be explained.[232] In the context of contributory fault, factors that guided the tribunal in determining apportionment must be explained.[233] Specifically, the tribunal's considerations on the relative blameworthiness of the investor against the host state's breach must be explained with reason.

While it is inevitable that the tribunal's reasoning on percentage determination leaves some obscurity, providing reasoned grounds for the reflection of the investor's responsibility in the outcome of the case should indeed be a requirement. It will serve not only to prevent the abuse of discretion, but also enable the application of contributory fault to serve as a way to advance responsible investment in the IIA regime.

6.5 Conclusion

This chapter seeks to clarify the potential ways to materialise the investor's responsibility available in the current framework of IIA-based

229 Ibid., 113.

230 For example, *Occidental* Award, para. 687; *Yukos* Awards, para. 1637; *Copper Mesa* Award, para. 6.102.

231 Hart, 'Discretion', 661.

232 See Virgo, 'Whose Conscience?', 310. See also Lauterpacht, 'Issues of Compensation and Nationality', 250; Elrifai, 'Equity-Based Discretion', 869.

233 Marcoux and Bjorklund, 'Foreign Investors' Responsibilities and Contributory Fault', 899.

dispute settlement mechanisms in the assessment of the investor's principal claims at different phases of proceedings, focusing specifically on the investor's performance-phase environmental misconduct. Regarding the impact of investor responsibility on the investor's claim of 'legitimate expectations', the analysis seeks to reflect the victims' perspectives through the concept of SLO, which is claimed to support the host state's defence based on public interests in certain circumstances.

This study has examined how an investor's responsibility may be materialised in the IIA-based dispute settlement mechanism, through counterclaims and in the host state's defence to the investor's principal claims. Admittedly, even if these attempts are successful, they do not directly redress the harm and injury suffered by the victim.[234] This is a limitation to the current IIA regime. Together with other limitations identified in the previous chapters, this warrants discussion on the ISDS reform. Chapter 7 will consider some ideas for reform of the current regime, focusing on the issues of investor responsibility and the interests of affected local communities and individuals.

[234] Jarrett, *Contributory Fault and Investor Misconduct*, 126.

7

Conclusion

Implications for Reform

7.1 Protection of Responsible Investment: Limitations of the Current Regime

International law has offered protection for foreign investors through international investment agreements (IIAs) without subjecting them to obligations. This makes it possible for a foreign investor to utilise the IIA-based dispute settlement mechanism as a forum where it may pursue its claims without exposing itself to potential claims against itself, even if its conduct has caused damage to the host state, local communities and individuals. Given that it is often difficult to pursue the legal responsibility of transnational corporations (TNCs) through the domestic legal framework (Chapter 2, Section 2.1), there is the risk that TNCs, as foreign investors, may exploit the imbalance between their rights and obligations in the IIA regime to their advantage. Addressing this issue is a condition for the sustainable operation of the regime, whose one-sidedness has become a major source of criticism (Chapter 1, Section 1.4). To this end, the IIA regime must function as a system which protects and advances only responsible investment.

This study has examined the potential of the current IIA-based dispute settlement mechanism for materialising investor responsibility, focusing on the investor's performance-phase misconduct that has resulted in actual or perceived environmental and associated human rights damage. The key conviction informing this study is that, given that this type of investors' conduct always impacts the local people (the victims), any effort to materialise investor responsibility should consider their interests.

The analysis provided in this study has demonstrated that there are different ways to pursue and reflect investor responsibility in the current mechanism which have not been fully utilised. At the same time, however, their limitations have been revealed in terms of the need to both correct asymmetry and reflect the interests of the victims.

With respect to the former, Chapters 4 and 5 demonstrated that many of the stated obstacles that have prevented the successful use of counterclaims can be addressed, and to this extent the asymmetry can be corrected. This having been said, counterclaims, which are reactive to the investor's principal claims, still do not change the structural one-sidedness of the current mechanism.

On the latter, this study has analysed different ways to incorporate the interests and perspectives of the victims into the assessment of the host state's counterclaims and the investor's principal claims. The host state's counterclaim should be denied admissibility in circumstances when allowing such a counterclaim would result in effective deprivation of remedy for the victims (Chapter 3, Section 3.4.2.2). Perspectives of the local community are also relevant when assessing the possible legal effects of investors' voluntary commitments with respect to their business standards and practices (Chapter 5, Section 5.4.1). In the assessment of the investor's principal claim based on the frustration of its legitimate expectations, there are circumstances in which the concept of social licence to operate (SLO), a concept based on local stakeholders' perceptions, should influence the weighing up of the need to protect the host state's public interests as against the need to respect the investor's legitimate expectations (Chapter 6, Section 6.3.4.4).

However, these methods for incorporating victims' interests and perspectives all rely on the host state's action: that is, counterclaims and regulatory actions. The limitation of this approach is that there is no guarantee that the host state will always represent the interest of the victims. As discussed in Chapter 3, Section 3.4.2.2, a conflict of interest may exist between the host state and the victims, especially in situations where the former is jointly liable with the investor for environmental and human rights damage caused to the latter. This may lead to a decision on the part of the host state, when it does not wish to highlight such damage, to refrain from raising counterclaims and invoking an environmental and/or human rights-based defence.[1] From the perspectives of the victims, therefore, the unsurmountable limitation of the current mechanism is that it does not provide a forum within which they may directly claim their interests against the investor and the host state.

[1] Arcuri and Violi, 'Human Rights and Investor-State Dispute Settlement', 582, 591–592; Cotula and Perrone, 'Reforming Investor-State Dispute Settlement', 3; Francioni, 'Access to Justice', 72.

Meanwhile, in the current investor–state dispute settlement (ISDS) reform discussions, reform proposals have been presented to address the issues of the one-sidedness of the IIA-based dispute settlement mechanism and the interests of affected local communities and individuals.[2] This chapter concludes this study by examining the implications of the analysis provided in this study for these reform proposals, and by considering reform options to address the limitations of the current mechanism identified above.

7.2 Providing the Host State's Right to Counterclaims

As a way to address the asymmetry in the IIA regime, this reform option is presented by several countries in the ISDS reform discussions at the UNCITRAL Working Group III (UNCITRAL ISDS reform discussions) (Chapter 3, Section 3.1).[3] Indeed, according to the IIA dataset, the number of IIAs that provide the respondent state's right to raise counterclaims is extremely limited (Chapter 4, Section 4.3.4.1). Given that raising counterclaims has benefits as a way to pursue investor responsibility (Chapter 3, Section 3.2) and that the host state's counterclaims have normative justifications even in circumstances where the claims involve the victims' interests (Chapter 3, Section 3.3), consent to jurisdiction over counterclaims should generally be given, subject to the assessment of admissibility. Since the existing uncertainty regarding questions of jurisdiction and admissibility of counterclaims has led to pessimistic appraisals of the possibility of counterclaims on the part of host states (Chapter 4, Section 4.1), providing a clear and 'tangible' legal basis[4] to the host state's right to counterclaims is certainly a desirable reform option.[5]

Nevertheless, Chapter 4 also demonstrated that the IIAs that should be categorically interpreted to exclude the host state's counterclaims for the lack of consent to the jurisdiction over counterclaims are as follows: (a) those that are interpreted to generally prohibit counterclaims by limiting

[2] The UNCITRAL Working Group III has not closed the door to discussions of substantive aspects of the IIA regime. Langford, Potestà, Kaufmann-Kohler and Behn, 'Special Issue: UNCITRAL and Investment Arbitration Reform', 173.

[3] Counterclaims is included in 'concrete reform options' considered by Working Group III. UNCITRAL, 'Annotated Provisional Agenda', 20 August 2021, UN Doc. A/CN.9/WG.III/WP.207, para. 6. See also Cotula and Neal, 'UNCITRAL Working Group III', 3.

[4] De Luca and Bonfanti, 'Investment and Human Rights', 2.

[5] See Beharry and Kuritzky, 'Going Green: Managing the Environment', 408 (it proposes to explicitly state that 'the term "disputes" signifies both claims and counterclaims' in IIAs).

the scope of the tribunal's jurisdiction or the award of the tribunal (e.g. Article 8(3) of the UK-Venezuela BIT) and (b) those that define investment disputes and investment claims as limited to those concerning the host state's IIA obligations. As demonstrated in Chapter 4, in the IIA dataset, there are forty-four IIAs (out of 1,000 IIAs) that can be interpreted to generally prohibit counterclaims (Figure 4.1). There are 263 IIAs that limit the scope of arbitrable investment disputes to those concerning host states' obligations (Figure 4.3). Given the substantial overlap between these two types of IIAs,[6] it has been observed that, for a majority of IIAs, providing the host state's right to raise counterclaims in IIAs is, although desirable, not a precondition for the finding of such consent.

7.3 Providing Investor Obligations in IIAs

As a way to address the asymmetry issue and to incorporate the concept of responsible investment into the IIA regime, several countries have called for the inclusion of investor obligations in IIAs in the UNCITRAL ISDS reform discussions.[7] Practical implications of this reform option will vary depending on the content and scope of the obligations provided, for which the existing IIAs that provide investor obligations (notwithstanding their being limited in number) will provide guidance. The baseline requirement is the obligation to comply with the host state's laws and regulations.[8] The most extensive obligations found in the third-generation IIAs (see Chapter 2, Section 2.3.2) are the 'hard' obligations (as opposed to those using terms such as 'endeavour' or other soft

[6] See Chapter 4, Section 4.3.4.5.

[7] UNCITRAL, 'Possible Reform of Investor-State Dispute Settlement (ISDS) Submission from the Government of South Africa, Note by the Secretariat', 17 July 2019, UN Doc. A/CN.9/WG.III/WP.176, para. 70; UNCITRAL, 'Possible Reform of Investor-State Dispute Settlement (ISDS) Submission from the Government of Morocco, Note by the Secretariat', 4 March 2019, UN Doc. A/CN.9/WG.III/WP.161, para. 6. For opposition to formulating provisions on investor obligations as a legal basis for counterclaims, see UNCITRAL, 'Possible Reform of Investor–State Dispute Settlement (ISDS) Procedural Rules with Regard to Early Dismissal, Abuse of Process, Security for Costs, Allocation of Costs, and Counterclaims', 2 September 2021, para. 59, available at: https://uncitral.un.org/sites/uncitral.un.org/files/media-documents/uncitral/en/draft_procedural_rules_for_intersessional_final_pdf.pdf (accessed 15 December 2021).

[8] Article 9 of the Agreement on Promotion, Protection and Guarantee of Investments among Member States of the Organization of the Islamic Conference, signed on 5 June 1981, entered into force on 23 September 1986.

obligations) to apply *international* environmental management standards, corporate governance standards, or environmentally sound technologies, even if they are more stringent in their demands than the domestic standards of the host state.[9] Scholars also propose incorporating the principles on business responsibilities under Pillar II the UN Guiding Principles on Business and Human Rights in the IIAs, thereby hardening these soft laws.[10]

A practical implication of providing the baseline requirement of compliance with domestic law is that such provisions may form the legal basis of the host state's counterclaims against the investor, as is the case of *Al-Warraq v. Indonesia*[11] (Chapter 5, Section 5.3.1). Nevertheless, providing this requirement in the relevant IIA is not a condition for the host state's counterclaims because the host state's domestic laws (including its 'rules on the conflict of laws') should always apply to form the basis for the counterclaims (Chapter 4, Section 4.3.4.4 and Chapter 5, Section 5.2).

By contrast, provisions that subject investors to international standards that are higher than domestic standards in the host state have a significant practical impact, as they enable the host state to directly invoke international standards as the basis of its counterclaims. Chapter 5 demonstrated that, even in the absence of such provisions, international standards on business conduct may also generate legal responsibility under domestic law in different ways, and thereby form the basis of counterclaims (Section 5.4.1). However, whether domestic law may produce such results varies between countries. Although there have been important developments on this issue in certain home states of TNCs, a cautious approach may be taken in many other jurisdictions. Providing the fulfilment of international standards as an investor obligation in the relevant IIA would dispel any uncertainty with this regard.

In the context of international standards-based counterclaims, certain cautions should be noted. First, requirements under the international standards need to be clearly specified so as to constrain the interpretative

[9] For example, Article 29(1)(iii) of the 2018 ECOWAS Common Investment Code; Articles 18 and 19 of the 2016 Morocco-Nigeria BIT; Article 14 of the 2012 SADC Model BIT (cited in Chapter 2, Section 2.3.2).

[10] Arcuri, Montanaro and Violi, 'Proposal for a Human Rights'; Jarrett, Puig and Ratner, 'Investor Accountability: Indirect Actions, Direct Actions', 8–9; Choudhury, 'Investor Obligations for Human Rights', 101.

[11] *Hesham Talaat M. Al-Warraq v. Republic of Indonesia*, UNCITRAL, Final Award, 15 December 2014 (*Al-Warraq* Award).

discretion of tribunals.[12] Secondly, the IIA should also provide 'secondary rules' that determine the consequences of a breach of such obligations. As discussed in Chapter 5, Section 5.3.3.1, there is neither treaty nor customary international law on remedies generally applicable to corporations' breach of international obligations. Although Chapter 5 also demonstrated the possibility that domestic laws may serve as a provider of secondary rules for the investor's breach of international obligations (Section 5.3.3.2), secondary rules in the IIA[13] would provide a clearer ground of remedy for investors' international wrongs than through domestic law.

The *Al-Warraq* case also indicates that a breach of IIA provisions on investor obligations may lead to the inadmissibility of the investor's principal claim.[14] However, the existence of such provisions is neither a necessary nor sufficient condition for inadmissibility based on illegality. As discussed in Chapter 6, while investors' serious misconduct has led to this consequence on various grounds such as international public policy, there exists a high threshold for illegality of the investment to constitute a ground of inadmissibility (Section 6.2.2).

Aside from the practical impacts discussed above, the fundamental value of this reform proposal is that it sends a clear message to the participants and audiences of the IIA regime, including states, investors, tribunals, and citizens, that the system recognises the reciprocity of obligations. This will confirm the direction the IIA regime should take: towards a greater recognition of the concept of responsible investment.

7.4 Requiring Exhaustion of Local Remedies as a Precondition for IIA-Based Dispute Settlement Mechanisms

This reform proposal is advanced not only as a way to address the asymmetry of the IIA system[15] but also as an attempt to accord interested

[12] See Jarrett, Puig and Ratner, 'Investor Accountability: Indirect Actions, Direct Actions', 8.

[13] The rules may also lay down principles for the valuation of damages and compensation, which has also been discussed at the UNCITRAL ISDS reform discussions. See UNCITRAL, 'Possible Reform of Investor-State Dispute Settlement (ISDS) Assessment of Damages and Compensation, Note by the Secretariat', available at: https://uncitral.un.org/sites/uncitral.un.org/files/media-documents/uncitral/en/assessment_of_damages_and_compensation.pdf (accessed 15 December 2021).

[14] *Al-Warraq* Award, paras. 631–645.

[15] For example, UNCITRAL, 'Possible Reform of Investor-State Dispute Settlement (ISDS) Submission from the Government of Mali', 17 September 2019, UN Doc. A/CN.9/WG.III/WP.181, Annex, 3.F; UNCITRAL, 'Possible Reform of Investor-State Dispute Settlement

or affected third parties the opportunity to participate in investor–state dispute settlement.[16] It is indeed observed that intervention and joining by interested third parties is permitted in many jurisdictions.[17]

However, Chapter 2 demonstrated that, for various reasons, including the lack of institutional capacity and independence of domestic judicial authorities, pursuance of the TNC's responsibility in the host state's courts is often an unrealistic and ineffective option for the victims (Section 2.1.1). In light of the known cases suggesting corruption and a lack of political independence in the judiciary in the context of TNCs' misconduct (Chapter 3, Section 3.2.1), the extent to which this reform option would contribute to advancing the victims' interests remains unclear.

7.5 Making the IIA-Based Dispute Settlement Mechanism a Forum to Pursue Investors' Responsibility

The most drastic reform proposals for the current system in order to address the issues of asymmetry and third parties' interests are to accord the host states and the third parties (specifically, affected communities and individuals) the right to initiate a claim against investors,[18] and to accord the third parties the right to intervene in the proceedings.[19] These

(ISDS) Submission from the Government of Morocco, Note by the Secretariat', 4 March 2019, UN Doc. A/CN.9/WG.III/WP.161, para. 14.

[16] Erasmus Institute for Public Knowledge, 'An Open Letter to the Chair of UNCITRAL Working Group III and to All Participating States concerning the Reform of the Investor-State Dispute Settlement: Addressing the Asymmetry of ISDS', 13 February 2019 (Open Letter), para. 4, available at: www.eur.nl/en/news/erasmus-institute-public-knowledge (accessed 15 December 2021); Arcuri and Violi, 'Human Rights and Investor-State Dispute Settlement', 592–593; Cotula and Perrone, 'Reforming Investor-State Dispute Settlement', 4; Arcuri and Montanaro, 'Justice for All?', 2821–2822; Van Harten, Kelsey and Schneiderman, 'Phase 2 of the UNCITRAL ISDS Review', 7–10.

[17] Columbia Center on Sustainable Investment, International Institute for Environment and Development, and International Institute for Sustainable Development, 'Third Party Rights in Investor-State Dispute Settlement: Options for Reform, Submission to UNCITRAL Working Group III on ISDS Reform', 15 July 2019, available at: https://uncitral.un.org/sites/uncitral.un.org/files/media-documents/uncitral/en/wgiii_reformoptions_0.pdf.

[18] Arcuri and Violi, 'Human Rights and Investor-State Dispute Settlement', 590; Jarrett, Puig and Ratner, 'Investor Accountability: Indirect Actions, Direct Actions', 11–20.

[19] UNCITRAL, 'Possible Reform of Investor-State Dispute Settlement (ISDS) Submission from the Government of South Africa, Note by the Secretariat', 17 July 2019, UN Doc. A/CN.9/WG.III/WP.176, paras. 52–54; UNCITRAL, 'Possible Reform of Investor-State Dispute Settlement (ISDS) Submission from the Government of Ecuador, Note by the

proposals raise challenging legal questions, including (but not limited to): how to establish the investor's consent to arbitration;[20] how the claims against the investor interact with domestic litigation proceedings;[21] and of tension with the principle of party autonomy.[22]

However, a real issue of such reform options is not these technical challenges but that they amount to a redefinition of the IIA regime, transforming it from a system to promote and protect foreign investment to a system that provides a forum where investors' responsibility is directly pursued. This is the attempt to create the first international dispute settlement forum where TNCs are generally exposed to claims against them and are subject to binding and enforceable awards. Although it is still consent-based, the reform options make investors' investments (or at least their use of the IIA regime) conditional on accepting the jurisdiction of the forum.

As discussed in Chapter 2, Section 2.2, there indeed exists a need to create an international mechanism to hold TNCs accountable for their conduct. Efforts towards this end have been ongoing for several decades. However, so far, the progress has been slow, primarily due to a lack of sufficient political support (Chapter 2, Section 2.2.2). These reform options cited above will certainly face the same issue.[23] Another concern is that these proposals may risk causing 'disengagement from

Secretariat', 17 July 2019, UN Doc. A/CN.9/WG.III/WP.175, paras. 23–26; Open Letter, para. 3; Cotula and Neal, 'UNCITRAL Working Group III'; Coleman et al., 'Third Party Rights in Investor-State Dispute Settlement'; Van Harten, Kelsey and Schneiderman, 'Phase 2 of the UNCITRAL ISDS Review', 3; Jarrett, Puig and Ratner, 'Investor Accountability: Indirect Actions, Direct Actions', 20–26.

20 Scholars argue that many issues concerning the investor's consent to arbitration can be addressed by amending or introducing procedural rules and IIAs. See e.g. Arcuri and Violi, 'Human Rights and Investor-State Dispute Settlement', 590 (to deem the existence of the investor's consent upon admission of the investment in the host state); Jarrett, Puig and Ratner, 'Investor Accountability: Indirect Actions, Direct Actions', 15–16 (providing 'standing offers of arbitration' in IIAs).

21 Cotula and Perrone, 'Reforming Investor-State Dispute Settlement', 4; Jarrett, Puig and Ratner, 'Investor Accountability: Indirect Actions, Direct Actions', 19–20.

22 Outside the IIA regime, it has been argued that third-party intervention over the objection of existing disputing parties may be justified when the good administration of justice and public policy override the principle of party autonomy. Wood and Sthoeger, 'Third-Party Intervention and Involvement', 78 (on arbitration under Part XV and Annex VII of the United Nations Convention on the Law of the Sea); Strong, 'Third Party Intervention and Joinder', 987 (on international commercial arbitration).

23 Jarret, Puig, and Ratner aptly observe that '[t]he outstanding question [of investor accountability in ISDS] is a political one'. Jarrett, Puig and Ratner, 'Investor Accountability: Indirect Actions, Direct Actions', 25.

ISDS'.[24] If the investors start to consider the IIA regime not as a system to protect their legitimate interests but as a threat of actions against them, the regime will lose much of its appeal to them. In turn, the state may lose the incentive to conclude IIAs or join a multilateral IIA.[25] ISDS reform should strike a careful balance between the need to keep its value for the regime's participants, and the need to advance responsible investment.

Based on these considerations, it is suggested here that creating a system for arbitral tribunals or international courts as an international dispute settlement forum addressing TNCs' responsibility is better pursued outside the IIA regime. With this regard, the launch of the Hague Rules on Business and Human Rights Arbitration in 2019 is an important development (Chapter 2, Section 2.2.2.4). Although they are consent-based and apply only to disputes concerning the impact of business activities on human rights, the rules may be used by any type of claimant or respondent, including corporations, individuals, civil society organisations, and states.[26] Steinitz proposes and provides support for the creation of an International Court of Civil Justice as a universally applicable dispute settlement forum with respect to TNCs' responsibility.[27] However, as of the date of writing, discussions at the political level on this matter have not started.

This does not mean that the issue of third parties' interests need not be addressed in the current IIA regime. Investment arbitration and the investment court system (ICS)[28] are by no means the only way to solve investor–state disputes. Among the 'alternative dispute resolution' methods, investor–state mediation has been steadily gaining momentum in the last decade. With this basis, the next section discusses third-party participation in investor–state mediation.

[24] Schill, 'Reforming Investor-State Dispute Settlement', 664.

[25] See Abel, 'Counterclaims Based on International Human Rights Obligations', 85 (in the context of human rights counterclaims).

[26] Center for International Legal Cooperation, 'The Hague Rules on Business and Human Rights Arbitration', Center for International Legal Cooperation, 2019, at 3, available at: www.cilc.nl/cms/wp-content/uploads/2019/12/The-Hague-Rules-on-Business-and-Human-Rights-Arbitration_CILC-digital-version.pdf (accessed 15 December 2021).

[27] Steinitz, *Case for an International Court of Civil Justice*.

[28] As noted in Chapter 1, for the purposes of this study, the ICS refers to both the mechanisms for the investment courts in the recent European Union's (EU) IIAs as well as a Multilateral Investment Court (MIC) (Chapter 1, Section 1.1).

7.6 Promoting Third-Party Participation in Investor–State Mediation

7.6.1 Growing Momentum for Investor–State Mediation

Outside the context of the issue of investor accountability, there has been increasing attention to the use of mediation, which in essence involves a third person assisting the parties in reaching a mutually agreeable solution,[29] as a way to manage investor–state disputes. Developments in the last decade concerning investor–state mediation include: the adoption of the International Bar Association (IBA) Investor–State Mediation Rules by the IBA Council;[30] the adoption of the Guide on Investment Mediation by the Energy Charter Conference (Energy Charter Investment Mediation Guide);[31] the proposal of Mediation Rules by the International Centre for Settlement of Investment Disputes (ICSID);[32] the adoption of the United Nations Convention on International Settlement Agreements Resulting from Mediation[33] and the Model Law on International Commercial Mediation and International Settlement Agreements Resulting from Mediation of the United Nations Commission on International Trade Law;[34] and the increasing references

[29] Franck, 'Using Investor-State Mediation Rules', 71; Wälde, 'Pro-Active Mediation of International Business', 3.

[30] International Bar Association, IBA Rules for Investor-State Mediation, Adopted by a Resolution of the IBA Council, 4 October 2012, available at: www.ibanet.org/MediaHandler?id=C74CE2C9-7E9E-4BCA-8988-2A4DF573192C (accessed 15 December 2021). It is reported that these rules were applied in *Equatorial Guinea v. CMS Energy Corporation and Others*, ICSID Case No. CONC(AF)/12/2. Le Cannu, 'Foundation and Innovation', 466.

[31] The Guide seeks to assist states and investors in deciding whether to use mediation and providing explanations of the mediation process and practical advice for investment mediation. Available at: www.energycharter.org/fileadmin/DocumentsMedia/CCDECS/2016/CCDEC201612.pdf (accessed 15 December 2021). For an overview of this guide, see Carballo Leyda, 'Model Instrument for Management', 681–707.

[32] These are the first institutional procedural rules specifically designed for investor–state mediation. The latest version is available at: https://icsid.worldbank.org/sites/default/files/publications/WP%205-Volume1-ENG-FINAL.pdf (accessed 15 December 2021). For an overview of these rules, see Nitschke, 'The Proposed ICSID Mediation Rules'. See also the 2021 Vienna International Arbitral Centre (VIAC) Rules of Investment Mediation.

[33] United Nations Convention on International Settlement Agreements Resulting from Mediation, GA Res. 73/198, UN GAOR, 73rd Session, Supp. No. 17, 20 December 2018, UN Doc. A/RES/73/198, 20 December 2018, annex A. The Convention entered into force on 12 September 2020.

[34] Ibid. Although the Convention does not define the term 'commercial', the Model Law provides that 'commercial' includes investments (footnote to Article 1(1) of the Convention). It has also been reported that the proposed ICSID Mediation Rules 'have

to mediation in recent IIAs,[35] some of which are accompanied by Annexes that set out detailed mediation rules.[36] In the ISDS reform discussions at the UNCITRAL Working Group III, a large number of states mentioned the use of mediation as a way of addressing cost and duration issues of investor–state dispute settlement or as a dispute prevention measure.[37] Investor–state mediation is considered as part of the reform option of 'dispute prevention and mitigation as well as other means of alternative dispute resolution';[38] and the 'Initial draft on mediation and other forms of alternative dispute resolution (ADR)' (Draft clauses on investor–state mediation)[39] and the 'Guidelines for participants in investor-state mediation'[40] were also recently presented for comments by delegations (until 31 December 2021).

taken the Singapore Convention into consideration'. See Kapoor, 'Singapore Convention Series' (summarising Frauke Nitschke's statement). However, under Article 8 of the Convention, states may make reservations to exclude settlement agreements to which the state, its agencies, or agents of the agencies are parties. See Claxton, 'Compelling Parties to Mediate Investor-State Disputes', 87–88.

35 For example, Article 8.20 of the EU-Canada Comprehensive Economic and Trade Agreement, signed on 30 October 2016. For recent IIAs that provide different forms of reference to mediation, see Nitschke, 'The Proposed ICSID Mediation Rules', 424; UNCITRAL, 'Possible Reform of Investor-State Dispute Settlement (ISDS) Mediation and Other Forms of Alternative Dispute Resolution (ADR), Note by the Secretariat' (Secretariat Note on Mediation and ADR), available at: https://uncitral.un.org/sites/uncitral.un.org/files/media-documents/uncitral/en/draft_clauses_on_mediation.pdf (accessed 15 December 2021) para. 8; Kinnear and Le Cannu, 'Concluding Remarks: ICSID and African States', 547.

36 For example, Annex 10 of the 2018 EU-Singapore Investment Protection Agreement; Annex 10 of the 2019 EU-Viet Nam Investment Protection Agreement.

37 For a list of these submissions, see UNCITRAL, 'Possible Reform of Investor-State Dispute Settlement (ISDS) Note by the Secretariat', 30 July 2019, UN Doc. A/CN.9/WG.III/WP.166.

38 UNCITRAL, 'Possible Reform of Investor–State Dispute Settlement (ISDS) Dispute Prevention and Mitigation – Means of Alternative Dispute Resolution, Note by the Secretariat', 15 January 2020 (Secretariat note on Means of alternative dispute resolution), UN Doc. A/CN.9/WG.III/WP.190.

39 UNCITRAL, 'Possible Reform of Investor-State Dispute Settlement (ISDS) Mediation and Other Forms of Alternative Dispute Settlement, Note by the Secretariat', available at: https://uncitral.un.org/sites/uncitral.un.org/files/media-documents/uncitral/en/draft_clauses_on_mediation.pdf (accessed 15 December 2021).

40 UNCITRAL, 'Possible Reform of Investor-State Dispute Settlement (ISDS) Mediation and Other Forms of Alternative Dispute Settlement, Note by the Secretariat', available at: https://uncitral.un.org/sites/uncitral.un.org/files/media-documents/uncitral/en/draft_guidelines_on_mediation.pdf (accessed 15 December 2021).

7.6.2 *Including Third Parties in Mediation*

Against this background, it is argued that enabling the affected and interested third parties' direct participation in the investor–state mediation process is a feasible reform option that may address the issue of third parties' interests. It does not require a radical reconstruction of IIA-based dispute settlement mechanisms, as mediation is not to replace but to supplement these mechanisms.[41] The voluntary nature of mediation, which requires the agreement and cooperation of the parties in both engagement with the process and in reaching a settlement,[42] will reduce the wariness of and resistance to this option on the part of states and investors. Rather, the flexibility of mediation in terms of both scope (i.e. it does not require the existence of investment disputes)[43] and participants (i.e. it is open to all the relevant stakeholders)[44] may indeed make this option attractive for both host states and investors, for the following reasons.

Seeking constructive solutions that address the concerns of all relevant stakeholders provides opportunities to prevent the escalation of disagreements[45] and to preserve their business relationship for the future.[46] Some states have already established conflict management mechanisms under

[41] Harder, 'Environmental Mediation', 30.

[42] Weeramantry and Chang, 'Investor-State Conciliation and Mediation', 1.

[43] For example, the IBA Investor-State Mediation Rules apply not only to investment-related disputes but also differences, 'which have not yet reached the level of a dispute'. Nitschke, 'IBA's Investor-State Mediation Rules', 126.

[44] Kessedjian, van Aaken, Lie and Mistelis, 'Mediation in Future Investor-State Dispute Settlement', 14; Nitschke, 'The Proposed ICSID Mediation Rules', 427.

[45] Goldberg and Shaw observe that early founders of mediation identify collaboration as 'one of the attractions of mediation'. Goldberg and Shaw, 'Past, Present, and Future of Mediation', 239–240. See also Kubasek and Silverman, 'Environmental Mediation', 546 (noting that litigation 'tends to force parties to take extreme positions').

[46] Preservation of the relationship between the parties is considered to be one of the major benefits of mediation over adjudication in the context of investor–state disputes. See e.g. UNCITRAL, Secretariat Note on Mediation and ADR, para. 5; Titi, 'Mediation and the Settlement', 23; Wälde, 'Efficient Management of Transnational Disputes', 207; Ali and Repousis, 'Investor-State Mediation and the Rise of Transparency', 248; Constain, 'Mediation in Investor-State Dispute Settlement', 26; Dahran and Von Kumberg, 'Investor-State Dispute Settlement Reconceptionalized', 483; Von Kumberg, Lack and Leathes, 'Enabling Early Settlement in Investor-State Arbitration', 133; Dukes, 'What We Know about Environmental Conflict Resolution', 197–199; Claxton, 'Compelling Parties to Mediate Investor-State Disputes', 84; Franck, 'Using Investor-State Mediation Rules', 67; Kessedjian, van Aaken, Lie and Mistelis, 'Mediation in Future Investor-State Dispute Settlement', 11.

their domestic laws[47] and IIAs[48] based on the full recognition of the value of preventing investor–state disputes. For the host state, participation by affected third parties, such as local communities, in the mediation process may also help alleviate, to a certain extent, what are considered to be the major obstacles to settlement for states – the political cost and accountability concerns arising from making a voluntary settlement with the investor.[49] For investors, the value of obtaining community acquiescence or acceptance of the mediation result is significant not only for their continuing business operations but also for maintaining their international business reputation.[50] From the victims' perspective, participating in mediation may have comparative benefits over intervening in investment arbitration and the ICS proceedings, which are '[conducted in a location] far from their locality, expensive and specialising in legal arrangements'.[51] Mediation is more accessible, flexible in terms of interests and arguments to be presented, less costly and shorter in duration.

[47] For example, The Foreign Investment Ombudsman under Korea's 1998 Foreign Investment Promotion Act; Colombia's National Agency for the Legal Defence of the State and Investment Attraction Facilitation System created within the framework of the National Competitiveness System (see www.colombiatrade.com.co/apris (accessed 15 December 2021)); the SICRECI and Special Commission under the Peruvian Act 28933 of 2006 (see Valderrama, 'Investor-State Dispute Prevention'). For states' dispute prevention mechanisms, see Dimitropoulos, 'Investor-State Dispute Settlement Reform'.

[48] For example, An Ombudsman/Joint Committee (National Focal Point) under the Cooperation and Investment Facilitation Agreements (CIFAs) Brazil has concluded since 2015; the Sub-Committee on Business Environment under some of the Japanese Economic Partnership Agreements (EPA) (e.g. Article 14.12 of the 2011 Japan-India EPA. It provides that 'the Sub-Committee may invite representatives of relevant entities other than the Governments of the Parties with the necessary expertise relevant to the issues to be addressed', thereby enabling a dialogue between the relevant stakeholders).

[49] According to a report by Chew, Reed, and Christopher Thomas QC, the desire to avoid responsibility for a settlement and defer decision-making to third-party arbitrators as well as the fear of public criticism are the most significant obstacles to settlement for the state. Chew, Reed and Christopher Thomas, 'Report: Survey on Obstacles', 11–12. See also Secretariat note on Means of alternative dispute resolution, para. 44; Verbist, 'Mediation as an Alternative Method', 777–778; Kessedjian, van Aaken, Lie and Mistelis, 'Mediation in Future Investor-State Dispute Settlement', 13; Claxton, 'Compelling Parties to Mediate Investor-State Disputes', 80; Coe Jr., 'Should Mediation of Investment Disputes Be Encouraged', 348–349; Wälde, 'Efficient Management of Transnational Disputes', 217; Titi, 'Mediation and the Settlement', 37; Dahran and Von Kumberg, 'Investor-State Dispute Settlement Reconceptionalized', 487.

[50] It is observed that seeking consent to the project generally improves 'the reputation of companies in the eyes of civil society, responsible investors, and indigenous groups'. Lehr and Smith, *Implementing a Corporate*, 7.

[51] Cotula and Perrone, 'Reforming Investor-State Dispute Settlement', 4.

Indeed, the possibility of participation by third parties such as local communities and individuals in investor–state mediation is recognised in the ISDS reform discussions at the UNCITRAL Working Group III[52] and by the UN Human Rights Council[53] as a way to allow 'the public interest to be represented in the mediation'.[54] Some scholars also support the inclusion of 'non-disputant' stakeholders in the investor–state mediation process.[55]

Certainly, in the domestic environmental mediation context, it is argued that disputes that turn on questions of basic rights, fundamental and moral values are not suited to mediation, which is more interest- rather than rights- based and cannot set precedents for future disputes.[56] However, as noted in Chapter 2, Section 2.2.2.4, in the international context, mediation has been employed to solve cases[57] that involve environmental and human rights issues by the International Finance Corporation (IFC)/Multilateral Investment Guarantee Agency (MIGA) Compliance Advisory Ombudsman (CAO), and by the National Contact Points for Responsible Business Conduct (NCPs) under the OECD Guidelines for Multinational Enterprises.[58] Welsh and Schneider argue that a 'default' model of mediation that enables the maintenance or improvement of ongoing relationships begins with a focus on interests, yet it should also be supplemented 'with evaluative or directive interventions and consideration of legal rights and norms'.[59]

Although third-party participation in investor–state mediation is always possible, conditional on agreement by both disputing parties, providing mediation rules specifically designed for third-party participation would certainly facilitate such a practice. Although discussions about

[52] Guidelines for participants in investor–state mediation, para. 27.

[53] UN Human Rights Council, 'Report of the Special Rapporteur on the Rights of Indigenous Peoples', 11 August 2016, UN Doc. A/HRC/33/42, para. 84.

[54] Guidelines for participants in investor-state mediation, para. 27.

[55] Coe Jr., 'Should Mediation of Investment Disputes Be Encouraged', 346–347; Güven, 'Investor-State Mediation'; Sharma, 'Mediation of Investor-State Disputes', 354.

[56] Zeinemann, 'Characterization of Public Sector Mediation', 59; English, 'Calming the Waters', 7; Blackburn, 'Environmental Mediation Theory and Practice', 271.

[57] Kressel observes that in the context of environmental mediation, 'site-specific conflict' is more likely to be resolved than 'disputes about general policies'. Kressel, 'Mediation Revisited', 731.

[58] See also Kessedjian, van Aaken, Lie and Mistelis, 'Mediation in Future Investor-State Dispute Settlement', 2 (referring to provisions on mediation in the Hague Rules on Business and Human Rights Arbitration (Article 56)).

[59] Welsh and Schneider, 'Thoughtful Integration of Mediation', 116.

the draft clauses on investor–state mediation are ongoing in the UNCITRAL ISDS reform discussions (see Section 7.6.1), as of the date of writing, they do not specifically address the issue of third-party participation. The following section provides brief insights on the certain elements that could be added to the existing and proposed investor–state mediation rules.

7.6.3 Rules for Third-Party Participation in Investor–State Mediation

7.6.3.1 Inviting the Parties to Consider Third-Party Participation

First, the mediation rules may provide that, when the case at issue involves the interests of third parties who were directly affected by the investment at issue, the mediator(s) shall invite the parties to consider the participation of the third parties in the mediation process at the initial mediation meeting, if not earlier. Such an invitation is expected to encourage the investors to consider possible disadvantages and risks of excluding the third parties, as well as inviting the host state to consider the affected citizens' rights and interests.

To make this more effective, a further ambitious reform proposal would be to introduce a mechanism to request the parties to attend the first mediation session.[60] Among the IIAs that refer to mediation (see Section 7.6.1), a few require mediation and/or consultation and negotiation as a precondition to arbitration.[61] One way to achieve this without amending the existing IIAs is to conclude a multilateral treaty on investor–state mediation, which can be modelled on the method adopted in the Mauritius Convention (the United Nations Convention on Transparency in Treaty-Based Investor–State Arbitration),[62] enabling

[60] See Option 2 of the Draft clauses on investor–state mediation. Welsh and Schneider recommend the inclusion of this requirement, as it would provide a useful opportunity to understand the purposes, advantages, and procedures of mediation. Welsh and Schneider, 'Thoughtful Integration of Mediation', 132.

[61] For example, Article 14.23 of the 2019 Indonesia-Australia FTA; Article 8 of the 2019 Hong Kong-UAE BIT; Article 26(4) of the Investment Agreement for the COMESA Common Investment Area; Article 9.18 of the Comprehensive and Progressive Agreement for Trans-Pacific Partnership. Option 3 of the Draft clauses on investor–state mediation requires the conduct of mediation for a specified period of time as a precondition to arbitration.

[62] The Mauritius convention was drafted to facilitate the application of the UNCITRAL Rules on Transparency in Treaty-based Investor-State Arbitration to the existing IIAs through various means, including by providing that the transparency rules apply where

its application to existing IIAs, and which would include a requirement to mediate, specifically to attend an initial meeting.

While required participation in the first mediation session may be conducive to encouraging the parties to consider the benefits of mediation and third-party participation, the practical benefits of providing a mandatory mediation mechanism as a condition for arbitration may be limited,[63] given the entirely consensual nature of mediation. Mediation lasts 'only as long as the parties wish to continue',[64] and the parties' good faith engagement in the mediation process and efforts towards reaching an agreement cannot be brought by simply requiring mediation as a condition for arbitration.[65] For the same reason, imposing third-party participation over the objection of the parties would be nonsensical. A successful mediation requires the parties' willingness, which is backed by their expectations and trust in the benefits of investor–state mediation and third-party participation.

7.6.3.2 Co-Mediators and Mediator Expertise

Both the IBA Investor–State Mediation Rules and the proposed ICSID Mediation Rules explicitly refer to co-mediators.[66] For environmental mediation in which local communities and individuals participate, co-mediation (or team mediation) should be a rule, for the following reasons. First, this type of mediation requires a set of skills that are very different from those required to solve investor–state disputes. Although this is not the place to comprehensively analyse these skills, they include: skills for the identification of key community individuals, developing community or regional profiles, managing inter-community difference of interests, designing the mediation process, managing group decision processes.[67] A balanced representation of all the interests of a large number of stakeholders is essential for successful conflict resolution

the host state and the investor's home state are parties to the Convention and have not made a relevant reservation (Article 2(1)).

63 Claxton also observes that compulsions to mediate would be practically difficult, as it will be considered to be an infringement on party autonomy or a denial of access to justice. Claxton, 'Compelling Parties to Mediate Investor-State Disputes', 96–97. See also Guidelines for participants in investor–state mediation, para. 32.

64 Welsh and Schneider, 'Thoughtful Integration of Mediation', 125.

65 Titi, 'Mediation and the Settlement', 34.

66 Article 4 of the IBA Investor-State Mediation Rules and Rule 13 of the ICSID Mediation Rules. See also Guidelines for participants in investor–state mediation, para. 14.

67 Blackburn, 'Environmental Mediation Theory and Practice', 272–273.

and justification of the result,[68] and therefore the skill of identifying and involving key community individuals is particularly important.[69] Also important are cultural and language competences in order to communicate with local people[70] – something also necessary for managing internal conflict within communities.[71] If a mediator who has this set of skills works with a mediator who has competency in investor–state disputes[72] as well as knowledge of the subject matter, they can combine different kinds of expertise so as to debrief one another and to supplement each other's knowledge and skill sets.[73] Co-mediation will also alleviate the issue of imbalance in power and resources between the disputing parties, that is, the risk of powerful parties' effectively imposing a 'voluntary agreement' on vulnerable third parties.[74]

It is crucial to have a pool of experienced mediators in the relevant issue areas to establish successful practices.[75] Therefore, designating authorities who appoint mediators in the absence of the parties'

[68] Susskind, 'Environmental Mediation and the Accountability Problem', 14.

[69] For an example of a method for identifying key community individuals, see Moore, *The Mediation Process*, 222.

[70] Consensus Building Institute, NCP Mediation Manual, July 2012, Consensus Building Institute, 44 available at: www.cbi.org/assets/files/CBI_NCP_Mediation_Manual_July2012.pdf (accessed 15 December 2021).

[71] Compliance Advisor Ombudsman, Reflections from Practice Series 1: Representation, 1 January 2018, available at: www.cao-ombudsman.org/resources (accessed 15 December 2021) 8.

[72] Guidelines for participants in investor–state mediation (para. 9) summarises the standards and competency criteria for investor–state mediators in the Energy Charter Investment Mediation Guide and Appendix B to the IBA Investor-State Mediation Rules, and International Mediation Institute Competency Criteria for Investor-State Mediators' (available at: https://imimediation.org/about/who-are-imi/ism-tf/ (accessed 15 December 2021)).

[73] Allen, 'Training Environmental Mediators', 58. For a general advantage of co-mediation, see Coe Jr., 'Concurrent Co-Mediation', 61–78; Constain, 'Mediation in Investor-State Dispute Settlement', 37; NCP Mediation Manual, 52.

[74] For an analysis of the issue of self-representation in mediation, see Nolan-Haley, 'Mediation, Self-Represented Parties, and Access to Justice', 3; Harder, 'Environmental Mediation', 32; Zeinemann, 'Characterization of Public Sector Mediation', 52–53. In the context of community mediation, it is observed that co-mediation 'allows mediators to model collaboration and facilitate transparently, increasing the capacity-building potential of mediation'. Harmon-Darrow et al., 'Defining Inclusive Mediation', 311.

[75] Constain generally observes that 'The lack of a pool of experienced mediators in investment disputes is a challenge for the wider use of this method of dispute resolution'. Constain, 'Mediation in Investor-State Dispute Settlement', 38.

agreement[76] should provide a list of mediators that includes those who have the set of expertise described above.

7.6.3.3 Partially Lifted Confidentiality and Reporting

Confidentiality is one of the hallmarks of mediation. It is necessary for the parties to engage in the mediation with trust and candor.[77] However, as Brown and Winch aptly argue, the 'appropriate level of confidentiality that should apply in mediation' should be determined by referencing to the context of each case within which the confidentiality question is posed.[78] Scholars have identified the need to apply the considerations with respect to 'public confidence, accountability and legitimacy', which underlie the transparency reforms in investment arbitration, to investor–state mediation.[79] When the mediation concerns the cases that directly affect the interests of the third parties, there is a greater demand to lift the confidentiality for its results to be accountable.[80] In domestic environmental mediation practices, confidentiality is lifted to the extent that the public interest and the administration of justice override the aspiration to confidentiality or privacy.[81]

Based on these considerations, it is proposed that in investor–state mediation that involves third-party interests, confidentiality should be lifted to the following extent. First, as the baseline requirement, the fact of the existence of the mediation should be disclosed to the public: This will indeed be a necessary requirement to enable third party participation. Secondly, any settlement agreement should be made available to the public. These are in fact the principles under the IBA Investor–State Mediation Rules, which exclude 'the fact that the parties have agreed to mediate or a settlement resulted from the mediation' from the scope of

[76] Article 4(7) of the IBA Investor-State Mediation Rules (the Permanent Court of Arbitration); Rule 13(4) of the ICSID Mediation Rules (the ICSID Secretary-General); Article 7(2) of the 2021 VIAC Rules of Investment Mediation (the Board). The MIC (or its Secretariat), once established, may also serve as an appointing authority.

[77] Nitschke, 'The Proposed ICSID Mediation Rules', 433; Titi, 'Mediation and the Settlement', 35–36.

[78] Brown and Winch, 'Confidentiality and Transparency Debate', 329.

[79] Shirlow, 'Investor-State Arbitration Meets Mediation'; Sharma, 'Mediation of Investor-State Disputes', 351.

[80] For cases where public access to mediation was discussed, see Goldberg, Sander, Rogers and Cole, *Dispute Resolution: Negotiation, Mediation, Arbitration*, 249–255.

[81] Harrison, 'Environmental Mediation', 89; Ali and Repousis, 'Investor-State Mediation and the Rise of Transparency', 247; English, 'Calming the Waters', 8; Zeinemann, 'Characterization of Public Sector Mediation', 59.

the confidentiality obligation 'unless the parties otherwise agree in writing'.[82] Article 12(4) of the 2021 VIAC Rules of Investment Mediation also lifts confidentiality with respect to the existence of mediation without even subjecting it to the 'unless the parties object' condition.[83] Thirdly, when the mediation is terminated without reaching an agreement, the mediators shall issue a report. On this note, the practice of mediation by NCPs and CAO is suggestive. When a mediation or conciliation carried out by an NCP is closed without an agreement, the NCP issues a statement that describes 'the issues raised, the reasons why the NCP decided that the issues raised merit further examination and the procedures the NCP initiated in assisting the parties'[84] as well as offers recommendations on the implementation of the Guidelines.[85] Both the NCP's statements and the CAO's reports are made available to the public, subject to certain confidentiality requirements.[86]

However, in contrast to the NCPs' statements and the CAO's reports described above, the mediators' report should not include the evaluation of the case. This is because, the purpose of investor–state mediation is different from the processes of NCPs and CAO, which serve as grievance mechanisms based on the complaints received from the investment-affected communities and individuals.[87] Instead, the report should provide the following information: the issues raised; undisputed facts; and a summary of the parties' positions whose disclosure is not objected to by the parties. Such a report will assist subsequent proceedings in identifying the facts and points of disagreement,[88] while protecting the

[82] Article 10(3)(a) of the IBA Investor-State Mediation Rules. See also Draft provision 6 of the Draft clauses on investor–state mediation ('Mutually agreed solutions shall be made publicly available').

[83] By contrast, the proposed ICSID Mediation Rules provide that '[u]nless the parties agree otherwise, the fact that they are mediating or have mediated shall be confidential' (Article 10(2) of the ICSID Mediation Rules).

[84] NCP Mediation Manual, 6.

[85] Maheandiran, 'Calling for Clarity', 218.

[86] OECD, 'OECD Guidelines for Multinational Enterprises', 2011, available at: www.oecd.org/corporate/mne/48004323.pdf (accessed 15 December 2021); Compliance Advisor Ombudsman, 'Operational Guidelines', 2013, World Bank Group, available at: https://documents1.worldbank.org/curated/pt/137211476348756904/pdf/108859-WP-ENGLISH-CAO-Operational-Guidelines-2013-PUBLIC.pdf (accessed 15 December 2021).

[87] OECD Guidelines for Multinational Enterprises (2011) Commentary to IV: Human Rights, para. 46; CAO, Operational Guidelines, 4.

[88] Sharma, 'Mediation of Investor-State Disputes', 357.

confidentiality of the communications between the parties and the mediators. Lastly, when the parties did not consent to third-party participation, this should be noted in the settlement agreement and the report. This will help to raise awareness of issues concerning the interests of the third parties for any subsequent tribunals and for the public at large.

7.6.4 *Establishing Best Practices*

Mediation remains rare in the investor–state dispute context,[89] and as of the date of writing there is no reported case of third-party participation in investor–state mediation. As noted previously, mediation, which is of an entirely voluntary nature, requires the parties' good faith engagement in the mediation process and willingness to collaborate to reach an agreement for its successful operation. To this end, efforts must be made to gain support for this practice. To promote investor–state mediation, international institutions such as the ICSID have conducted capacity-building through training courses for government officials and mediators.[90] The training of mediators should also take into account the skills required for environmental mediation, as discussed above.

In tandem with these efforts, best practices for mediation[91] involving communities and individuals should be developed. The detailed guidance for dispute resolution processes by the CAO[92] and mediation manual by NCPs[93] are suggestive in this regard. With a trust and positive expectations regarding best practices conducted by experienced mediators, states and investors may well start to see the potential value of

[89] UNCITRAL, Secretariat Note on Means of Alternative Dispute Resolution, para. 37.

[90] See e.g. Annex 1 of the Guidelines for participants in investor-state mediation; Nitschke, 'The Proposed ICSID Mediation Rules', 438; Verbist, 'Mediation as an Alternative Method', 774.

[91] See UNCITRAL, 'Summary of the Inter-Sessional Meeting on Investor-State Dispute Settlement (ISDS) Reform Submitted by the People's Republic of China', UN Doc. A/CN.9/WG.III/WP.210, 10 November 2021, para. 35 (stressing the need for providing capacity building and technical assistance to states as well as exchanging best practices for promoting investor-state mediation).

[92] Compliance Advisor Ombudsman, Reflections from Practice Series 1: Getting Started with Dispute Resolution/Representation/Joint Fact Finding, 1 January 2018, available at: www.cao-ombudsman.org/resources (accessed 15 December 2021).

[93] NCP Mediation Manual.

third-party participation in investor–state mediation for them. This may help enhance their willingness to use this mechanism as having the potential to bring a forward-looking, collaborative, and relation-preserving (or building) settlement, which cannot be expected from adversarial dispute settlement mechanisms.

7.7 Concluding Remarks

Responsible investment is a condition for achieving the 2030 Agenda for Sustainable Development, which was unanimously adopted by UN member states in 2015.[94] The recent legislative, judicial, and private sector developments concerning TNCs' due diligence (Chapter 4, Section 4.4.2 and Chapter 5, Section 5.4) and non-financial reporting (Chapter 2, Section 2.2.3.1) as well as governmental investment policy statements[95] suggest that the gap between investment protection and lack of effective regulation of TNCs' conduct has been, and will continue to be, gradually narrowing. However, the gap still exists, and the IIA regime should not provide an opportunity to benefit from the gap. It should operate as a mechanism that protects and advances responsible investment.

The current system has the potential inherent within it to serve this purpose, even though reforms are needed to overcome its limitations. Utilising this potential to reflect investor responsibility in IIA-based dispute settlement mechanisms has a broader impact than achieving

[94] UN General Assembly, 'Transforming Our World: The 2030 Agenda for Sustainable Development', 21 October 2015, UN Doc. A/RES/70/1. See Principles for Responsible Investment, Investing with SDG Outcomes: A Five-Part Framework, Principles for Responsible Investment, 2020, available at: www.unpri.org/download?ac=10795 (accessed 15 December 2021).

[95] For example, OECD, G20 Guiding Principles for Global Investment Policymaking, para. VIII, available at: www.oecd.org/daf/inv/investment-policy/G20-Guiding-Principles-for-Global-Investment-Policymaking.pdf (accessed 15 December 2021); UNCTAD and D-8 Organization for Economic Cooperation, 'The Guiding Principles for Investment Policymaking for the Countries of the D-8 Organization for Economic Corporation, UNCTAD and D-8 Organization for Economic Cooperation', January 2020, available at: https://investmentpolicy.unctad.org/uploaded-files/document/D-8%20Guiding%20Principles%20for%20Investment%20Policymaking%202020.pdf (accessed 15 December 2021); European Commission, 'Q&A: Commission Launches Comprehensive European International Investment Policy', 7 July 2010, European Commission Memo/10/303, available at: https://ec.europa.eu/commission/presscorner/detail/en/MEMO_10_303 (accessed 15 December 2021).

fairness in specific disputes. It will help the IIA regime to obtain trust and acceptance from the participants and audience, which is necessary for its sustainable operation. Moreover, it can impact investors', including TNCs', behaviour and thus help to grow practice based on greater due diligence and responsible business conduct. In this way, materialising investor responsibility in investor–state dispute settlement helps the IIA regime serve the objective of advancing sustainable development.

Appendix

List of IIAs in the IIA Dataset

Germany–United Republic of Tanzania BIT (1965)
Pacific Basin Charter on International Investments (1965)
Germany–Zambia BIT (1966)
Germany–Mali BIT (1977)
Benin–Germany BIT (1978)
Mali–Switzerland BIT (1978)
Netherlands–Senegal BIT (1979)
Bangladesh–United Kingdom BIT (1980)
BLEU–Cameroon BIT (1980)
Cameroon–Romania BIT (1980)
Korea, Republic of–Sri Lanka BIT (1980)
Singapore–Sri Lanka BIT (1980)
Sri Lanka–United Kingdom BIT (1980)
Unified Agreement for the Investment of Arab Capital in the Arab States (1980)
Bangladesh–BLEU BIT (1981)
Bangladesh–Germany BIT (1981)
OIC Investment Agreement (1981)
Belize–United Kingdom BIT (1982)
Cameroon–United Kingdom BIT (1982)
ECGLC Investment Code (1982)
Malaysia–Sri Lanka BIT (1982)
Sri Lanka–Sweden BIT (1982)
ECCAS Treaty (1983)
Finland–Sri Lanka BIT (1983)
France–Nepal BIT (1983)
Haiti–United States of America BIT (1983)
Sweden–Yemen BIT (1983)
CARICOM Negotiation Guidelines for BITs (1984)
Burundi–Germany BIT (1984)
Dominica–Germany BIT (1984)
Netherlands–Sri Lanka BIT (1984)

Asian-African Legal Consultative Committee Revised Draft of Model Agreements (1985)
Austria–Malaysia BIT (1985)
Bangladesh–France BIT (1985)
China–Denmark BIT (1985)
Netherlands–Yemen BIT (1985)
Bangladesh–United States of America BIT (1986)
Cameroon–United States of America BIT (1986)
Antigua and Barbuda–United Kingdom BIT (1987)
Bangladesh–Romania BIT (1987)
Benin–United Kingdom BIT (1987)
BLEU–Malta BIT (1987)
Dominica–United Kingdom BIT (1987)
Jamaica–United Kingdom BIT (1987)
China–Poland BIT (1988)
BLEU–Burundi BIT (1989)
BLEU–Czech Republic BIT (1989)
China Model BIT (1989)
Finland–Russian Federation BIT (1989)
Hungary–Kuwait BIT (1989)
Argentina–United Kingdom BIT (1990)
Australia–Papua New Guinea BIT (1990)
Bangladesh–Italy BIT (1990)
Burundi–United Kingdom BIT (1990)
Congo–United States of America BIT (1990)
Czech Republic–United Kingdom BIT (1990)
Denmark–Turkey BIT (1990)
Albania–Greece BIT (1991)
Algeria–BLEU BIT (1991)
Argentina–Canada BIT (1991)
Argentina–France BIT (1991)
Argentina–Sweden BIT (1991)
Argentina–Switzerland BIT (1991)
Argentina–United States of America BIT (1991)
Australia–Hungary BIT (1991)
Australia–Poland BIT (1991)
Austria–Korea, Republic of BIT (1991)
Bahrain–United Kingdom BIT (1991)
BLEU–Cyprus BIT (1991)
BLEU–Uruguay BIT (1991)
Cape Verde–Netherlands BIT (1991)
Cape Verde–Switzerland BIT (1991)

Denmark–Estonia BIT (1991)
Sri Lanka–United States of America BIT (1991)
Albania–Switzerland BIT (1992)
Albania–Turkey BIT (1992)
Argentina–China BIT (1992)
Argentina–Denmark BIT (1992)
Argentina–Netherlands BIT (1992)
Armenia–United States of America BIT (1992)
Austria–Morocco BIT (1992)
BLEU–Mongolia BIT (1992)
BLEU–Paraguay BIT (1992)
Bolivia, Plurinational State of–China BIT (1992)
Bulgaria–United States of America BIT (1992)
CARICOM–Venezuela FTA (1992)
China–Viet Nam BIT (1992)
Denmark–Ghana BIT (1992)
Denmark–Ukraine BIT (1992)
Finland–Kazakhstan BIT (1992)
France–Viet Nam BIT (1992)
Lithuania–Norway BIT (1992)
Lithuania–Sweden BIT (1992)
Lithuania–Switzerland BIT (1992)
Russian Federation–United States of America BIT (1992)
Singapore–Viet Nam BIT (1992)
Albania–China BIT (1993)
Albania–Croatia BIT (1993)
Albania–Tunisia BIT (1993)
Algeria–France BIT (1993)
Argentina–Armenia BIT (1993)
Argentina–Bulgaria BIT (1993)
Argentina–Finland BIT (1993)
Argentina–Romania BIT (1993)
Armenia–United Kingdom BIT (1993)
Australia–Czech Republic BIT (1993)
Australia–Romania BIT (1993)
Barbados–United Kingdom BIT (1993)
Belarus–Switzerland BIT (1993)
BLEU–Georgia BIT (1993)
Bulgaria–Israel BIT (1993)
Bulgaria–Portugal BIT (1993)
Chile–Finland BIT (1993)
China–United Arab Emirates BIT (1993)

Denmark–Chile BIT (1993)
Denmark–Viet Nam BIT (1993)
Korea, Republic of–Lithuania BIT (1993)
Kyrgyzstan–United States of America BIT (1993)
Moldova, Republic of–United States of America BIT (1993)
Poland–Singapore BIT (1993)
Poland–United Arab Emirates BIT (1993)
United Kingdom–Uzbekistan BIT (1993)
Albania–Bulgaria BIT (1994)
Albania–Czech Republic BIT (1994)
Albania–Netherlands BIT (1994)
Albania–United Kingdom BIT (1994)
Argentina–Croatia BIT (1994)
Argentina–Jamaica BIT (1994)
Argentina–Korea, Republic of BIT (1994)
Armenia–Romania BIT (1994)
Australia–Lao People's Democratic Republic BIT (1994)
Azerbaijan–China BIT (1994)
Bangladesh–Malaysia BIT (1994)
Bangladesh–Netherlands BIT (1994)
Barbados–Germany BIT (1994)
Barbados–Venezuela BIT (1994)
Belarus–Sweden BIT (1994)
Belarus–United Kingdom BIT (1994)
Bosnia and Herzegovina–Malaysia BIT (1994)
Bulgaria–Sweden BIT (1994)
Bulgaria–Turkey BIT (1994)
Cambodia–Malaysia BIT (1994)
Canada–Ukraine BIT (1994)
Chile Model BIT (1994)
China–Egypt BIT (1994)
Ecuador–France BIT (1994)
Estonia–United Kingdom BIT (1994)
Hungary–Ukraine BIT (1994)
Malaysia–Namibia BIT (1994)
Moldova, Republic of–Germany BIT (1994)
Netherlands–Ukraine BIT (1994)
Poland–Viet Nam BIT (1994)
Albania–Denmark BIT (1995)
Albania–France BIT (1995)
Albania–Romania BIT (1995)
Albania–Sweden BIT (1995)

Albania–United States of America BIT (1995)
Argentina–Australia BIT (1995)
Argentina–Israel BIT (1995)
Armenia–Cyprus BIT (1995)
Armenia–France BIT (1995)
Armenia–Iran BIT (1995)
Armenia–Lebanon BIT (1995)
Australia–Peru BIT (1995)
Australia–Philippines BIT (1995)
Austria–Tunisia BIT (1995)
Azerbaijan–Pakistan BIT (1995)
Barbados–Switzerland BIT (1995)
Belarus–Iran, Islamic Republic of BIT (1995)
Belarus–Netherlands BIT (1995)
Brazil–Finland BIT (1995)
Bulgaria–United Kingdom BIT (1995)
Cambodia–Thailand BIT (1995)
Canada–Philippines BIT (1995)
Canada–South Africa BIT (1995)
Canada–Trinidad and Tobago BIT (1995)
Chile–Poland BIT (1995)
China–Oman BIT (1995)
Côte d'Ivoire–UK BIT (1995)
Cuba–South Africa BIT (1995)
Cuba–United Kingdom BIT (1995)
Denmark–Mongolia BIT (1995)
Dominican Republic–Spain BIT (1995)
Estonia–Ukraine BIT (1995)
Finland–Moldova, Republic of BIT (1995)
Korea, Republic of–Tajikistan BIT (1995)
Lao People's Democratic Republic–United Kingdom BIT (1995)
Latvia–United States of America BIT (1995)
Latvia–Viet Nam BIT (1995)
Lithuania–Venezuela BIT (1995)
Moldova, Republic of–Hungary BIT (1995)
Moldova, Republic of–Netherlands BIT (1995)
Oman–United Kingdom BIT (1995)
Romania–United Kingdom BIT (1995)
Sweden–Ukraine BIT (1995)
Switzerland Model BIT (1995)
Albania–Hungary BIT (1996)
Albania–Israel BIT (1996)

Algeria–China BIT (1996)
Algeria–Germany BIT (1996)
Algeria–Jordan BIT (1996)
Algeria–Mali BIT (1996)
Algeria–Qatar BIT (1996)
Armenia–Egypt BIT (1996)
Austria–Hong Kong, China SAR BIT (1996)
Austria–Kuwait BIT (1996)
Austria–Lithuania BIT (1996)
Azerbaijan–Kazakhstan BIT (1996)
Azerbaijan–United Kingdom BIT (1996)
Barbados–Canada BIT (1996)
Barbados–Cuba BIT (1996)
Belarus–Czech Republic BIT (1996)
Belarus–Yugoslavia BIT (1996)
BLEU–Estonia BIT (1996)
BLEU–Latvia BIT (1996)
BLEU–Moldova, Republic of BIT (1996)
BLEU–Romania BIT (1996)
BLEU–Ukraine BIT (1996)
Bolivia, Plurinational State of–Korea, Republic of BIT (1996)
Bosnia and Herzegovina–Iran, Islamic Republic of BIT (1996)
Bulgaria–Viet Nam BIT (1996)
Burkina Faso–Germany BIT (1996)
Cambodia–China BIT (1996)
Cambodia–Singapore BIT (1996)
Cambodia–Switzerland BIT (1996)
Canada–Chile FTA (1996)
Canada–Egypt BIT (1996)
Canada–Panama BIT (1996)
Canada–Venezuela BIT (1996)
China–Mauritius BIT (1996)
China–Zimbabwe BIT (1996)
Croatia–Turkey BIT (1996)
Croatia–United States of America BIT (1996)
Denmark–Pakistan BIT (1996)
Denmark–Tunisia BIT (1996)
Germany–Macedonia, The former Yugoslav Republic of BIT (1996)
Indonesia–Sri Lanka BIT (1996)
Italy–Kenya BIT (1996)
Jordan–Yemen BIT (1996)
Korea, Republic of–Ukraine BIT (1996)

Lao People's Democratic Republic–Sweden BIT (1996)
Lao People's Democratic Republic–Switzerland BIT (1996)
Lebanon–Ukraine BIT (1996)
Macedonia, The former Yugoslav Republic of–Poland BIT (1996)
Moldova, Republic of–United Kingdom BIT (1996)
Netherlands–Uzbekistan BIT (1996)
Nicaragua–United Kingdom BIT (1996)
Slovenia–United Kingdom BIT (1996)
Sri Lanka–Thailand BIT (1996)
Albania–Finland BIT (1997)
Albania–Macedonia BIT (1997)
Albania–Slovenia BIT (1997)
Albania–Yugoslavia BIT (1997)
Algeria–Egypt BIT (1997)
Algeria–Syrian Arab Republic BIT (1997)
Armenia–Canada BIT (1997)
Austria–Bulgaria BIT (1997)
Austria–Chile BIT (1997)
Austria–Croatia BIT (1997)
Azerbaijan–United States of America BIT (1997)
Bangladesh–Philippines BIT (1997)
Bangladesh–Poland BIT (1997)
Belarus–Egypt BIT (1997)
Belarus–Korea, Republic of BIT (1997)
Belarus–Pakistan BIT (1997)
BLEU–Lithuania BIT (1997)
BLEU–Tunisia BIT (1997)
Bulgaria–Kuwait BIT (1997)
Cambodia–Korea, Republic of BIT (1997)
Canada–Croatia BIT (1997)
Canada–Lebanon BIT (1997)
Canada–Thailand BIT (1997)
Canada–Uruguay BIT (1997)
Chad–Morocco BIT (1997)
China Model BIT (1997)
Egypt–Viet Nam BIT (1997)
Finland–Oman BIT (1997)
Jordan–Poland BIT (1997)
Lao People's Democratic Republic–Singapore BIT (1997)
Sweden–Zimbabwe BIT (1997)
Tonga–United Kingdom BIT (1997)
Algeria–Bulgaria BIT (1998)

Algeria–Mozambique BIT (1998)
Algeria–Niger BIT (1998)
Algeria–Turkey BIT (1998)
Antigua and Barbuda–Germany BIT (1998)
Armenia–Italy BIT (1998) (terminated)
Armenia–Switzerland BIT (1998)
Australia–Lithuania BIT (1998)
Australia–Pakistan BIT (1998)
Austria–Mexico BIT (1998)
Azerbaijan–France BIT (1998)
Azerbaijan–Lebanon BIT (1998)
Bangladesh–Indonesia BIT (1998)
Bangladesh–Japan BIT (1998)
Barbados–China BIT (1998)
Belarus–Syrian Arab Republic BIT (1998)
Belize–Cuba BIT (1998)
BLEU–Cuba BIT (1998)
BLEU–Gabon BIT (1998)
BLEU–Kazakhstan BIT (1998)
BLEU–Mexico BIT (1998)
BLEU–Pakistan BIT (1998)
BLEU–Philippines BIT (1998)
BLEU–Uzbekistan BIT (1998)
BLEU–Venezuela BIT (1998)
Bosnia and Herzegovina–Egypt BIT (1998)
Bosnia and Herzegovina–Netherlands BIT (1998)
Bosnia and Herzegovina–Qatar BIT (1998)
Botswana–Switzerland BIT (1998)
Brazil–Netherlands BIT (1998)
Brunei Darussalam–Germany BIT (1998)
Brunei Darussalam–Oman BIT (1998)
Bulgaria–Egypt BIT (1998)
Cambodia Model BIT (1998)
Canada–Costa Rica BIT (1998)
Cape Verde–China BIT (1998)
CARICOM–Dominican Republic FTA (1998)
China–Swaziland BIT (1998)
Croatia Model BIT (1998)
CUTS Model BIT (1998)
Ethiopia–Malaysia BIT (1998)
France–Guatemala BIT (1998)
Gabon–Germany BIT (1998)

Greece–Moldova, Republic of BIT (1998)
Macedonia, The former Yugoslav Republic of–Netherlands BIT (1998)
Malaysia–Turkey BIT (1998)
Malaysia Model BIT (1998)
Mongolia Model BIT (1998)
Russian Federation–Ukraine BIT (1998)
South Africa Model BIT (1998)
Uganda–United Kingdom BIT (1998)
Albania–BLEU BIT (1999)
Algeria–Denmark BIT (1999)
Algeria–Korea, Republic of BIT (1999)
Algeria–Yemen BIT (1999)
Argentina–Greece BIT (1999)
Argentina–New Zealand BIT (1999)
Australia–Fiji Trade Agreement (1999)
Bahrain–China BIT (1999)
Bahrain–Malaysia BIT (1999)
Bahrain–United States of America BIT (1999)
Bangladesh–Korea, Republic of BIT (1999)
Belize–China BIT (1999)
BLEU–Côte d'Ivoire BIT (1999)
BLEU–Egypt BIT (1999)
BLEU–El Salvador BIT (1999)
BLEU–Lebanon BIT (1999)
BLEU–Morocco BIT (1999)
BLEU–North Macedonia BIT (1999)
BLEU–Slovenia BIT (1999)
Bulgaria–Lebanon BIT (1999)
Cambodia–Germany BIT (1999)
Chile–Viet Nam BIT (1999)
China–Qatar BIT (1999)
Czech Republic–Panama BIT (1999)
Denmark–Egypt BIT (1999)
Denmark–United Republic of Tanzania BIT (1999)
El Salvador–United Kingdom BIT (1999)
Iran, Islamic Republic of–Qatar BIT (1999)
Iran, Islamic Republic of–Zimbabwe BIT (1999)
Kenya–United Kingdom BIT (1999)
Korea, Republic of–Qatar BIT (1999)
Lebanon–United Kingdom BIT (1999)
Lithuania–Moldova, Republic of BIT (1999)
Pakistan–Yemen BIT (1999)

Philippines–Turkey BIT (1999)
Taiwan Province of China–Costa Rica BIT (1999)
Taiwan Province of China–Macedonia BIT (1999)
Tajikistan–Viet Nam BIT (1999)
Algeria–Malaysia BIT (2000)
Algeria–Oman BIT (2000)
Algeria–South Africa BIT (2000)
Angola–United Kingdom BIT (2000)
Armenia–Israel BIT (2000)
Austria–Cuba BIT (2000)
Austria–Uzbekistan BIT (2000)
Bahrain–Jordan BIT (2000)
Bangladesh–Uzbekistan BIT (2000)
Belarus–Libya BIT (2000)
Belarus–Singapore BIT (2000)
Belarus–United Arab Emirates BIT (2000)
BLEU–Yemen BIT (2000)
Botswana–China BIT (2000)
Botswana–Germany BIT (2000)
Brunei Darussalam–China BIT (2000)
Bulgaria–Tunisia BIT (2000)
Cambodia–Philippines BIT (2000)
Cameroon–Egypt BIT (2000)
Cotonou Agreement (2000)
Croatia–Zimbabwe BIT (2000)
Denmark Model BIT (2000)
Egypt Model BIT (2000)
Germany–Sri Lanka BIT (2000)
Greece–Mexico BIT (2000)
Indonesia–Qatar BIT (2000)
Malaysia–Saudi Arabia BIT (2000)
Mauritius–Swaziland BIT (2000)
Mongolia–Viet Nam BIT (2000)
Peru Model BIT (2000)
Sierra Leone–United Kingdom BIT (2000)
Thailand–Zimbabwe BIT (2000)
Turkey–Yemen BIT (2000)
Algeria–Kuwait BIT (2001)
Armenia–Austria BIT (2001)
Austria–Belize BIT (2001)
Austria–Egypt BIT (2001)
Austria–Georgia BIT (2001)

Austria–Iran, Islamic Republic of BIT (2001)
Austria–Macedonia BIT (2001)
Austria–Mongolia BIT (2001)
Austria–Oman BIT (2001)
Austria–Saudi Arabia BIT (2001)
Austria–United Arab Emirates BIT (2001)
Bangladesh–Iran, Islamic Republic of BIT (2001)
Belarus–Croatia BIT (2001)
Belarus–Kuwait BIT (2001)
Belarus–Qatar BIT (2001)
Belize–El Salvador BIT (2001)
Benin–Chad BIT (2001)
Benin–Ghana BIT (2001)
Benin–Mali BIT (2001)
Benin–Netherlands BIT (2001)
BLEU–Burkina Faso BIT (2001)
BLEU–Comoros BIT (2001)
BLEU–Croatia BIT (2001)
BLEU–Zambia BIT (2001)
Bolivia, Plurinational State of–Paraguay BIT (2001)
Bosnia and Herzegovina–Kuwait BIT (2001)
Bosnia and Herzegovina–Pakistan BIT (2001)
Bosnia and Herzegovina–Slovenia BIT (2001)
Burkina Faso–Chad BIT (2001)
Burkina Faso–Ghana BIT (2001)
Burkina Faso–Mauritania BIT (2001)
Burundi–Comoros BIT (2001)
Cambodia–Croatia BIT (2001)
Cambodia–Viet Nam BIT (2001)
Cameroon–Mauritania BIT (2001)
Chad–Mali BIT (2001)
Chad–Mauritius BIT (2001)
China–Myanmar BIT (2001)
Costa Rica–Ecuador BIT (2001)
Croatia–Moldova, Republic of BIT (2001)
Cuba–Denmark BIT (2001)
Cuba–Qatar BIT (2001)
Denmark–Ethiopia BIT (2001)
Denmark–Kuwait BIT (2001)
Denmark–Kyrgyzstan BIT (2001)
Denmark–Uganda BIT (2001)
Eritrea–Uganda BIT (2001)

Finland Model BIT (2001)
Finland–Qatar BIT (2001)
France–Venezuela BIT (2001)
France–Zimbabwe BIT (2001)
Gabon–Lebanon BIT (2001)
Gambia–Ukraine BIT (2001)
Greece Model BIT (2001)
Guatemala–Netherlands BIT (2001)
Honduras–Netherlands BIT (2001)
Iran Model BIT (2001)
Korea, Republic of–Panama BIT (2001)
OPEC Fund Model BIT (2001)
Portugal–Uzbekistan BIT (2001)
Albania–Ukraine BIT (2002)
Algeria–EC Association Agreement (2002)
Algeria–Nigeria BIT (2002)
Armenia–Qatar BIT (2002)
Australia–Egypt BIT (2002)
Australia–Sri Lanka BIT (2002)
Austria–Libya BIT (2002)
Austria–Philippines BIT (2002)
Bahrain–Belarus BIT (2002)
Bahrain–Thailand BIT (2002)
Bangladesh–Thailand BIT (2002)
Belarus–Jordan BIT (2002)
Belize–Netherlands BIT (2002)
Benin Model BIT (2002)
Bosnia and Herzegovina– China BIT (2002)
Bosnia and Herzegovina–Portugal BIT (2002)
Bosnia and Herzegovina–Spain BIT (2002)
Bosnia and Herzegovina–Turkey FTA (2002)
Bosnia and Herzegovina–Ukraine BIT (2002)
Bosnia and Herzegovina–United Kingdom BIT (2002)
Burundi Model BIT (2002)
China–Côte d'Ivoire BIT (2002)
Dominican Republic–Morocco BIT (2002)
Finland–Namibia BIT (2002)
France–Zambia BIT (2002)
Gambia–United Kingdom BIT (2002)
Ghana–India BIT (2002)
Hungary–Uzbekistan BIT (2002)
Iceland–Lithuania BIT (2002)

Jordan–Lithuania BIT (2002)
Kyrgyzstan–Moldova, Republic of BIT (2002)
Libya–South Africa BIT (2002)
Mauritius Model BIT (2002)
Oman–Ukraine BIT (2002)
Russian Federation–Yemen BIT (2002)
Sweden Model BIT (2002)
Thailand Model BIT (2002)
United Kingdom–Viet Nam BIT (2002)
Albania–Montenegro-Serbia FTA (2003)
Albania–Spain BIT (2003)
Algeria–Austria BIT (2003)
Algeria–Sweden BIT (2003)
Australia–Singapore FTA (2003)
Austria–Namibia BIT (2003)
Austria–Yemen BIT (2003)
Azerbaijan–Finland BIT (2003)
Bahrain–Singapore BIT (2003)
Belarus–Yemen BIT (2003)
Bolivia Model BIT (2003)
Bosnia and Herzegovina–Moldova, Republic of BIT (2003)
Bosnia and Herzegovina–Switzerland BIT (2003)
Bulgaria–Singapore BIT (2003)
Bulgaria–Thailand BIT (2003)
Cambodia–Netherlands BIT (2003)
China–Germany BIT (2003)
China–Guyana BIT (2003)
Czech Republic–Guatemala BIT (2003)
Denmark–Morocco BIT (2003)
Israel Model BIT (2003)
Israel–Mongolia BIT (2003)
Italy Model BIT (2003)
Jamaica–Korea, Republic of BIT (2003)
Japan–Viet Nam BIT (2003)
Kazakhstan–Pakistan BIT (2003)
Kenya Model BIT (2003)
Korea, Republic of–Oman BIT (2003)
Korea, Republic of–Viet Nam BIT (2003)
Lao People's Democratic Republic–Myanmar BIT (2003)
Malta–Turkey BIT (2003)
Namibia–Viet Nam BIT (2003)
Netherlands–Zambia BIT (2003)

Spain–Uzbekistan BIT (2003)
Uganda Model BIT (2003)
Ukraine–United Arab Emirates BIT (2003)
United Kingdom–Vanuatu BIT (2003)
Afghanistan–Turkey BIT (2004)
Albania–Moldova, Republic of BIT (2004)
Algeria–Portugal BIT (2004)
Algeria–Switzerland BIT (2004)
Armenia–Finland BIT (2004)
Australia–Thailand FTA (2004)
Australia–United States of America FTA (2004)
Austria–Ethiopia BIT (2004)
Azerbaijan–BLEU BIT (2004)
Azerbaijan–Greece BIT (2004)
Bahrain–United States of America FTA (2004)
Bangladesh–Singapore BIT (2004)
Barbados–Mauritius BIT (2004)
Belarus–Denmark BIT (2004)
Belarus–Oman BIT (2004)
Benin–Lebanon BIT (2004)
BLEU–Serbia BIT (2004)
BLEU–United Arab Emirates BIT (2004)
Bosnia and Herzegovina–Denmark BIT (2004)
Botswana–China BIT (2004)
Burkina Faso–Korea, Republic of BIT (2004)
CAFTA-DR (2004)
CARICOM–Costa Rica FTA (2004)
Chad–Lebanon BIT (2004)
Congo–South Africa BIT (2004)
Croatia–Oman BIT (2004)
Dominican Republic–Switzerland BIT (2004)
Finland–Ukraine BIT (2004)
Gabon–Morocco BIT (2004)
Germany–Libya BIT (2004)
Hungary–Yemen BIT (2004)
Iceland–Lebanon BIT (2004)
Israel–Serbia BIT (2004)
Lebanon–Turkey BIT (2004)
Mozambique–United Kingdom BIT (2004)
Pakistan–Tajikistan BIT (2004)
Afghanistan–Germany BIT (2005)
Armenia–Latvia BIT (2005)

Armenia–Netherlands BIT (2005)
Australia–Turkey BIT (2005)
Azerbaijan–Latvia BIT (2005)
Bangladesh–Viet Nam BIT (2005)
Belarus–Slovakia BIT (2005)
BLEU–China BIT (2005)
BLEU–Guatemala BIT (2005)
BLEU–Madagascar BIT (2005)
BLEU–Mauritius BIT (2005)
BLEU–Nicaragua BIT (2005)
BLEU–Peru BIT (2005)
BLEU–Uganda BIT (2005)
Cyprus–Montenegro BIT (2005)
Finland–Guatemala BIT (2005)
Finland–Serbia BIT (2005)
Finland–Zambia BIT (2005)
Georgia–Lithuania BIT (2005)
Germany–Timor-Leste BIT (2005)
Germany–Yemen BIT (2005)
Guinea–Morocco BIT (2005)
Italy–Sudan BIT (2005)
Macedonia, The former Yugoslav Republic of–Spain BIT (2005)
Serbia–Switzerland BIT (2005)
United States of America–Uruguay BIT (2005)
Agreement on amendment of and accession to the Central European Free Trade Agreement (2006)
Albania–Poland BIT (2006)
Albania–Turkey FTA (2006)
Algeria–Finland BIT (2006)
Armenia–Lithuania BIT (2006)
Armenia–Sweden BIT (2006)
Austria–Guatemala BIT (2006)
Azerbaijan–Lithuania BIT (2006)
Azerbaijan–United Arab Emirates BIT (2006)
Bahrain–BLEU BIT (2006)
Bahrain–Italy BIT (2006)
Belarus–Finland BIT (2006)
Belarus–Slovenia BIT (2006)
BLEU–Botswana BIT (2006)
BLEU–Ethiopia BIT (2006)
Bulgaria–Korea, Republic of BIT (2006)
Dominican Republic–Italy BIT (2006)

Egypt–Ethiopia BIT (2006)
France Model BIT (2006)
Guatemala–Israel BIT (2006)
Madagascar–South Africa BIT (2006)
Mexico–Spain BIT (2006)
Moldova, Republic of–Spain BIT (2006)
Albania–Lithuania BIT (2007)
Algeria–Netherlands BIT (2007)
Azerbaijan–Hungary BIT (2007)
Azerbaijan–Korea, Republic of BIT (2007)
Bahrain–Czech Republic BIT (2007)
Bahrain–Germany BIT (2007)
Bahrain–Netherlands BIT (2007)
BLEU–Qatar BIT (2007)
BLEU–Rwanda BIT (2007)
Brunei Darussalam–Japan BIT (2007)
Bulgaria–Oman BIT (2007)
Bulgaria–Qatar BIT (2007)
Burundi–Netherlands BIT (2007)
Cambodia–Japan BIT (2007)
Denmark–Indonesia BIT (2007)
Djibouti–France BIT (2007)
Finland–Mongolia BIT (2007)
France–Kenya BIT (2007)
France–Seychelles BIT (2007)
Gabon–South Africa BIT (2007)
Korea, Republic of–Kyrgyzstan BIT (2007)
Investment Agreement for the COMESA Common Investment Area (2007)
Oman–Singapore BIT (2007)
United Arab Emirates–Uzbekistan BIT (2007)
South Africa–Sudan BIT (2007)
Albania–Bosnia and Herzegovina BIT (2008)
Algeria–Mauritania BIT (2008)
Angola–Portugal BIT (2008)
Australia–Chile FTA (2008)
Austria Model BIT (2008)
Belarus–Mexico BIT (2008)
Bosnia and Herzegovina–Slovakia BIT (2008)
Botswana Model BIT (2008)
Cambodia–Czech Republic BIT (2008)
Canada-Colombia FTA (2008)
Canada–Peru FTA (2008)

CARIFORUM-EC Economic Partnership Agreement (2008)
Congo–Spain BIT (2008)
Cyprus–Qatar BIT (2008)
Czech Republic–Syrian Arab Republic BIT (2008)
Czech Republic–Yemen BIT (2008)
ECOWAS Supplementary Act on Investments (2008)
Egypt–Iceland BIT (2008)
Ethiopia–South Africa BIT (2008)
Finland–Montenegro BIT (2008)
Germany Model BIT (2008)
Ghana Model BIT (2008)
Japan–Uzbekistan BIT (2008)
Madagascar–Switzerland BIT (2008)
Mexico Model BIT (2008)
Moldova, Republic of–Slovakia BIT (2008)
United Kingdom Model BIT (2008)
Albania–FETA FTA (2009)
APTA Investment Agreement (2009)
ASEAN–Australia New Zealand FTA (AANZFTA) (2009)
ASEAN–China Free Trade Area (2009)
ASEAN Comprehensive Investment Agreement (2009)
Azerbaijan–Syrian Arab Republic BIT (2009)
Bangladesh–India BIT (2009)
Barbados–BLEU BIT (2009)
Belarus–Saudi Arabia BIT (2009)
BLEU–Colombia BIT (2009)
BLEU–Panama BIT (2009)
Burundi–Kenya BIT (2009)
Canada–Jordan BIT (2009)
China–Mali BIT (2009)
China Model BIT (2009)
Czech Republic–Zimbabwe BIT (2009)
Denmark–Montenegro BIT (2009)
Estonia–Viet Nam BIT (2009)
Ethiopia–United Kingdom BIT (2009)
Finland–Nepal BIT (2009)
Finland–Panama BIT (2009)
Georgia–Kuwait BIT (2009)
Libya–Turkey BIT (2009)
Macedonia, The former Yugoslav Republic of Model BIT (2009)
Montenegro–Qatar BIT (2009)
Oman–Netherlands BIT (2009)

Saint Vincent and the Grenadines–Taiwan Province of China BIT (2009)
South Africa–Zimbabwe BIT (2009)
Turkey Model BIT (2009) (replaced)
United Arab Emirates–Viet Nam BIT (2009)
Albania–Cyprus BIT (2010)
Armenia–Kuwait BIT (2010)
Austria–Kazakhstan BIT (2010)
Austria–Tajikistan BIT (2010)
Azerbaijan–Estonia BIT (2010)
BLEU–Montenegro BIT (2010)
Canada–Panama FTA (2010)
Canada–Slovakia BIT (2010)
Chile-Malaysia FTA (2010)
Colombia–United Kingdom BIT (2010)
Congo–Libya BIT (2010)
Estonia–Jordan BIT (2010)
Estonia–Moldova, Republic of BIT (2010)
EU–Korea, Republic of FTA (2010)
France–Iraq BIT (2010)
Gambia–Taiwan Province of China BIT (2010)
Guatemala Model BIT (2010)
Hong Kong, China SAR–Kuwait BIT (2010)
Israel–Ukraine BIT (2010)
Malta–Montenegro BIT (2010)
Malta–Serbia BIT (2010)
Kazakhstan–Serbia BIT (2010)
Korea, Republic of–Peru FTA (2010)
Macedonia, The former Yugoslav Republic of–Montenegro BIT (2010)
Russian Federation–Singapore BIT (2010)
Switzerland–Trinidad and Tobago BIT (2010)
Albania–Malta BIT (2011)
Albania–Qatar BIT (2011)
Australia–New Zealand Investment Protocol (2011)
Azerbaijan–Czech Republic BIT (2011)
Azerbaijan–Montenegro BIT (2011)
Azerbaijan–Serbia BIT (2011)
Azerbaijan–Turkey BIT (2011)
Bahrain–Turkmenistan BIT (2011)
Bangladesh–United Arab Emirates BIT (2011)
Bosnia and Herzegovina–San Marino BIT (2011)
Canada–Kuwait BIT (2011)
China–Uzbekistan BIT (2011)

Colombia–Japan BIT (2011)
Colombia Model BIT (2011)
Czech Republic–Sri Lanka BIT (2011)
EFTA–Montenegro FTA (2011)
Equatorial Guinea–Russian Federation BIT (2011)
Estonia–Kazakhstan BIT (2011)
Estonia–United Arab Emirates BIT (2011)
India–Japan EPA (2011)
India–Lithuania BIT (2011)
India–Malaysia FTA (2011)
Indonesia–Serbia BIT (2011)
Japan–Papua New Guinea BIT (2011)
Kenya–Slovakia BIT (2011)
Kuwait–Pakistan BIT (2011)
Lithuania–Macedonia, The former Yugoslav Republic of BIT (2011)
Macedonia, The former Yugoslav Republic of–Qatar BIT (2011)
Nigeria–Turkey BIT (2011)
Oman–Viet Nam BIT (2011)
Portugal–Senegal BIT (2011)
Portugal–United Arab Emirates BIT (2011)
United Republic of Tanzania–Turkey BIT (2011)
Albania–Azerbaijan BIT (2012)
Albania–San Marino BIT (2012)
Algeria–Serbia BIT (2012)
Armenia–Iraq BIT (2012)
Australia–Malaysia FTA (2012)
Bahrain–Mexico BIT (2012)
Bangladesh–Turkey BIT (2012)
Burkina Faso Model BIT (2012)
CACM–EU Association Agreement (2012)
Cameroon–Turkey BIT (2012)
Canada–China BIT (2012)
Chile–China Supplementary Agreement on Investment (2012)
Chile–Hong Kong FTA (2012)
Colombia–Ecuador–EU–Peru Trade Agreement (2012)
EU–Iraq Cooperation Agreement (2012)
EU–Viet Nam Framework PCA (2012)
Gabon–Turkey BIT (2012)
GCC–Peru Framework Agreement (2012)
GCC–United States Framework Agreement (2012)
Investment Promotion and Protection Agreement between Japan, Korea, Republic of and China (2012)

Iraq–Japan BIT (2012)
Japan–Kuwait BIT (2012)
Kazakhstan–Macedonia, The former Yugoslav Republic of BIT (2012)
Kenya–Mauritius BIT (2012)
Malaysia–San Marino BIT (2012)
Moldova, Republic of–Qatar BIT (2012)
Montenegro–Turkey BIT (2012)
Montenegro–United Arab Emirates BIT (2012)
Morocco–Viet Nam BIT (2012)
Nicaragua–Russian Federation BIT (2012)
Oman–United Republic of Tanzania BIT (2012)
Pakistan–Turkey BIT (2012)
Russian Federation–Zimbabwe BIT (2012)
SADC Model BIT (2012)
Switzerland–Tunisia BIT (2012)
US Model BIT (2012)
ANZTEC (2013)
Austria–Nigeria BIT (2013)
Benin–Canada BIT (2013)
Benin–United Arab Emirates BIT (2013)
Bosnia and Herzegovina–EFTA FTA (2013)
Cameroon–Korea, Republic of BIT (2013)
Canada–Honduras FTA (2013)
Canada–United Republic of Tanzania BIT (2013)
Chile–Thailand FTA (2013)
China–Iceland FTA (2013)
China–Switzerland FTA (2013)
China–United Republic of Tanzania BIT (2013)
Colombia–Korea, Republic of FTA (2013)
Djibouti–Turkey BIT (2013)
EFTA–Costa Rica–Panama FTA (2013)
Gambia–Turkey BIT (2013)
Guatemala–Russian Federation BIT (2013)
Guatemala–Trinidad and Tobago BIT (2013)
Guinea–Turkey BIT (2013)
India–United Arab Emirates BIT (2013)
Japan–Mozambique BIT (2013)
Japan–Myanmar BIT (2013)
Japan–Saudi Arabia BIT (2013)
Kuwait–Kenya BIT (2013)
Kuwait–Mauritius BIT (2013)
Kuwait–Mexico BIT (2013)

Libya–United States TIFA (2013)
Mauritius–Turkey BIT (2013)
Mexico–Turkey BIT (2013)
Morocco–Serbia BIT (2013)
Myanmar–United States TIFA (2013)
Netherlands–United Arab Emirates BIT (2013)
New Zealand–Taiwan Province of China ECA (2013)
Serbia–United Arab Emirates BIT (2013)
Singapore–Taiwan Province of China EPA (2013)
Turkey–Benin BIT (2013)
US–CARICOM TIFA (2013)
ASEAN–India Investment Agreement (2014)
Australia–Japan EPA (2014)
Australia–Korea, Republic of FTA (2014)
Bahrain–Pakistan BIT (2014)
Bahrain–Russian Federation BIT (2014)
Belarus–Cambodia BIT (2014)
Burkina Faso–Singapore BIT (2014)
Cameroon–Canada BIT (2014)
Canada–Côte d'Ivoire BIT (2014)
Canada–Korea, Republic of FTA (2014)
Canada–Mali BIT (2014)
Canada–Nigeria BIT (2014)
Canada–Senegal BIT (2014)
Canada–Serbia BIT (2014)
Colombia–Turkey BIT (2014)
ECOWAS–US TIFA (2014)
Egypt–Mauritius BIT (2014)
Georgia–Switzerland BIT (2014)
Greece–Kuwait BIT (2014)
Greece–United Arab Emirates BIT (2014)
Israel–Myanmar BIT (2014)
Kenya–Korea, Republic of BIT (2014)
Kenya–Qatar BIT (2014)
Kenya–Turkey BIT (2014)
Kenya–United Arab Emirates BIT (2014)
Kyrgyzstan–United Arab Emirates BIT (2014)
Mali–Morocco BIT (2014)
Malaysia–Turkey FTA (2014)
Moldova, Republic of–Montenegro BIT (2014)
Serbia Model BIT (2014)
Sudan–Turkey BIT (2014)

Turkey–Viet Nam BIT (2014)
Andorra–United Arab Emirates BIT (2015)
Australia–China FTA (2015)
Azerbaijan–San Marino BIT (2015)
Bahrain–Bangladesh BIT (2015)
Brazil–Colombia BIT (2015)
Brazil–Malawi BIT (2015)
Brazil Model BIT (2015)
Burkina Faso–Canada BIT (2015)
Cambodia-Russian Federation BIT (2015)
Canada–Guinea BIT (2015)
China–Turkey BIT (2015)
Denmark–Macedonia, The former Yugoslav Republic BIT (2015)
Eurasian Economic Union–Viet Nam FTA (2015)
Guatemala–Turkey BIT (2015)
Guinea-Bissau–Morocco BIT (2015)
Japan–Mongolia EPA (2015)
Japan–Oman BIT (2015)
Japan–Ukraine BIT (2015)
Japan–Uruguay BIT (2015)
Korea, Republic of–Turkey Investment Agreement (2015)
Korea, Republic of–Viet Nam FTA (2015)
Kuwait–Kyrgyzstan BIT (2015)
Mauritius–United Arab Emirates BIT (2015)
Norway Model BIT (2015)
Singapore–Turkey FTA (2015)
Thailand–United Arab Emirates BIT (2015)
Argentina–Qatar BIT (2016)
Armenia–United Arab Emirates BIT (2016)
Austria–Kyrgyzstan BIT (2016)
Azerbaijan Model BIT (2016)
Cambodia–Hungary BIT (2016)
Canada–Hong Kong, China SAR BIT (2016)
Canada–Mongolia BIT (2016)
CETA (2016)
Chile–Hong Kong, China SAR BIT (2016)
Côte d'Ivoire–Turkey BIT (2016)
Czech Republic Model BIT (2016)
Ethiopia–United Arab Emirates BIT (2016)
EU-Kazakhstan Enhanced Partnership and Cooperation Agreement (2016)
Ghana–Turkey BIT (2016)
India Model BIT (2016)

Iran, Islamic Republic of–Japan BIT (2016)
Iran, Islamic Republic of–Singapore BIT (2016)
Iran, Islamic Republic of–Slovakia BIT (2016)
Jordan–Turkey BIT (2016)
Kenya–Japan BIT (2016)
Mexico–United Arab Emirates BIT (2016)
Moldova, Republic of–Turkey BIT (2016)
Morocco–Nigeria BIT (2016)
Morocco–Russian Federation BIT (2016)
Morocco–Rwanda BIT (2016)
Nigeria–Singapore BIT (2016)
Nigeria–United Arab Emirates BIT (2016)
Russian Federation Model BIT (2016)
Rwanda–Turkey BIT (2016)
Slovakia–United Arab Emirates (2016)
Somalia–Turkey BIT (2016)
Armenia–EU Comprehensive and Enhanced Partnership Agreement (2017)
ASEAN–Hong Kong, China SAR Investment Agreement (2017)
Belarus–Sudan BIT (2017)
Burundi–Turkey BIT (2017)
Chad–Turkey BIT (2017)
China–Georgia FTA (2017)
Colombia Model BIT (2017)
Colombia–United Arab Emirates BIT (2017)
Ethiopia–Qatar BIT (2017)
Hungary–Tajikistan BIT (2017)
Israel–Japan BIT (2017)
Moldova, Republic of–United Arab Emirates BIT (2017)
Mozambique–Turkey BIT (2017)
PACER Plus (2017)
Pacific Agreement on Closer Economic Relations Plus (2017)
Qatar–Singapore BIT (2017)
Rwanda–United Arab Emirates BIT (2017)
Turkey–Ukraine BIT (2017)
Turkey–Uzbekistan BIT (2017)
Argentina–Japan BIT (2018)
Argentina–United Arab Emirates BIT (2018)
Armenia–Japan BIT (2018)
Armenia–Korea, Republic of BIT (2018)
Australia–Peru FTA (2018)
Belarus–India BIT (2018)
Belarus–Turkey BIT (2018)

Brazil–Ethiopia BIT (2018)
Brazil–Guyana BIT (2018)
Brazil–Suriname BIT (2018)
Cambodia–Turkey BIT (2018)
Canada–Moldova, Republic of BIT (2018)
Central America–Korea, Republic of FTA (2018)
Comprehensive and Progressive Agreement for Trans-Pacific Partnership (CPTPP) (2018)
Congo–Morocco BIT (2018)
Ecuador–EFTA FTA (2018)
EFTA States–Indonesia EPA (2018)
EU–Singapore Investment Protection Agreement (2018)
Indonesia–Singapore BIT (2018)
Japan–Jordan BIT (2018)
Japan–United Arab Emirates BIT (2018)
Kazakhstan–Singapore BIT (2018)
Kazakhstan–United Arab Emirates BIT (2018)
Lithuania–Turkey BIT (2018)
Mali–Turkey BIT (2018)
Mali–United Arab Emirates BIT (2018)
Mauritania–Turkey BIT (2018)
Serbia–Turkey BIT (2018)
Singapore–Sri Lanka FTA (2018)
Turkey–State of Palestine BIT (2018)
USMCA (2018)
Armenia–Singapore BIT (2019)
Australia–Hong Kong, China SAR Investment Agreement (2019)
Australia–Indonesia CEPA (2019)
Australia–Uruguay BIT (2019)
BLEU Model BIT (2019)
Brazil–Morocco BIT (2019)
Brazil–United Arab Emirates BIT (2019)
Burkina Faso–Turkey BIT (2019)
Cabo Verde–Hungary BIT (2019)
CARIFORUM–United Kingdom Economic Partnership Agreement (2019)
ESA–United Kingdom EPA (2019)
EU–Viet Nam Investment Protection Agreement (2019)
Hong Kong, China SAR–United Arab Emirates BIT (2019)
India–Kyrgyzstan BIT (2019)
Israel–United Kingdom Trade and Partnership Agreement (2019)
Korea, Republic of–United Kingdom FTA (2019)
Korea, Republic of–Uzbekistan BIT (2019)

Lebanon–United Kingdom Association Agreement (2019)
Morocco Model BIT (2019)
Myanmar–Singapore BIT (2019)
Netherlands Model BIT (2019)
SACU and Mozambique–United Kingdom EPA (2019)
Slovakia Model BIT (2019)
Tunisia–United Kingdom Association Agreement (2019)

BIBLIOGRAPHY

Abadie, Pauline. 'A New Story of David and Goliath: The Alien Tort Claims Act Gives Victims of Environmental Injustice in the Developing World a Viable Claim against Multinational Corporations' (2004) 34(3) *Golden Gate Law Review* 745–796.

Abel, Patrick. 'Counterclaims Based on International Human Rights Obligations of Investors in International Investment Arbitration: Fallacies and Potentials of the 2016 ICSID *Urbaser v. Argentina* Award' (2018) 1 *Brill Open Law* 61–90.

Abramchayev, Liliya. 'A Social Contract Argument for the State's Duty to Protect from Private Violence' (2004) 18(3) *Journal of Civil Rights and Economic Development* 849–874.

Addo, Michael K. 'Human Rights and Transnational Corporations: An Introduction', in Michael K. Addo (ed.), *Human Rights Standards and the Responsibility of Transnational Corporations* (The Hague: Kluwer Law International, 1999), 3–37.

Adeola, Francis O. 'Environmental Injustice and Human Rights Abuse: The States, MNCs, and Repression of Minority Groups in the World System' (2001) 8(1) *Human Ecology* 39–59.

Adeyeye, Adefolake. 'Corporate Responsibility in International Law: Which Way to Go?' (2007) 11 *Singapore Year Book of International Law* 141–161.

Aftab, Yousuf. 'The Intersection of Law and Corporate Social Responsibility: Human Rights Strategy and Litigation Readiness for Extractive-Sector Companies', 60th Annual Rocky Mountain Mineral Law Institute (2014), 1–30.

Ahmed, Farrah and Perry, Adam. 'The Coherence of the Doctrine of Legitimate Expectations' (2014) 73(1) *Cambridge Law Journal* 61–85.

Alexis, Gwendolyn Yvonne. 'Global Sullivan Principles', in Nevin Cohen and Paul Robbins (eds.), *Green Business: An A-to-Z Guide* (Thousand Oaks, CA: Sage, 2011), 279–281.

Al Faruque, Abdullah. 'Mapping the Relationship between Investment Protection and Human Rights' (2010) 11(4) *Journal of World Investment & Trade* 539–560.

Alford, Roger P. 'The Future of Human Rights Litigation after *Kiobel*' (2014) 89(4) *Notre Dame Law Review* 1749–1772.

'Human Rights after *Kiobel*: Choice of Law and the Rise of Transnational Tort Litigation' (2014) 63(5) *Emory Law Journal* 1089–1162.

Ali, Shahla F. and Repousis, Odysseas G. 'Investor–State Mediation and the Rise of Transparency in International Investment Law: Opportunity or Threat?' (2018) 45(2) *Denver Journal of International Law* 225–249.

Allen, John C. 'Training Environmental Mediators: A Community-Based Approach', in J. Walton Blackburn and Willa Marie Bruce (eds.), *Mediating Environmental Conflicts: Theory and Practice* (Westport, CT: Quorum Books, 1995), 49–59.

Alschner, Wolfgang and Skougarevskiy, Dmitriy. 'Convergence and Divergence in the Investment Treaty Universe: Scoping the Potential for Multilateral Consolidation' (2017) 8(2) *Trade, Law, and Development* 152–183.

Alvarez, José E. 'Are Corporations "Subjects" of International Law?' (2011) 9(1) *Santa Clara Journal of International Law* 1–36.

'Is Investor–State Arbitration "Public"?' (2016) 7(3) *Journal of International Dispute Settlement* 534–576.

Amado, Jose Daniel, Kern, Jackson Shaw and Rodriguez, Martin Doe. *Arbitrating the Conduct of International Investors* (Cambridge: Cambridge University Press, 2018), Chapters 1, 2, 5.

Amel-Zadeh, Amir and Serafeim, George. 'Why and How Investors Use ESG Information: Evidence from a Global Survey' (2018) 74(3) *Financial Analyst Journal* 87–103.

American Law Institute, *Restatement of the Law, Third, Torts: Liability for Physical and Emotional Harm* (St. Paul, MN: American Law Institute Publishers, 2010).

Amianto, Lodovico. 'The Role of "Unclean Hands" Defences in International Investment Law' (2019–2020) 6(1) *McGill Journal of Dispute Resolution* 1–37.

Ancelin, Julien. 'À-propos de la "théorie des mains propres": Observations sur les sentences arbitrales Yukos de la Cour Permanente d'Arbitrage du 18 juillet 2014' (2015) LXI *Annuaire Français de droit international* 831–856.

Anderson, Michael R. 'Human Rights Approaches to Environmental Protection: An Overview', in Alan Boyle and Michael R. Anderson (eds.), *Human Rights Approaches to Environmental Protection* (Oxford: Clarendon Press, 1996), 71–87.

'Transnational Corporations and Environmental Damage: Is Tort Law the Answer?' (2002) 41(3) *Washburn Law Journal* 399–426.

Andreoni, James and Levinson, Anik. 'The Simple Analytics of the Environmental Kuznets Curve' (2001) 80(2) *Journal of Public Economics* 269–286.

Andrews, Neil. *Contract Law* (Cambridge: Cambridge University Press, 2011), Part II.

Anning, Molly. 'Counterclaims Admissibility in Investment Arbitration: The Case of Environmental Disputes', in Julien Chaisse, Leïla Choukroune and Sufian Jusoh (eds.), *Handbook of International Investment Law and Policy* (Singapore: Springer, 2019), 1277–1325.

Anton, Donald K. and Shelton, Dinah L. *Environmental Protection and Human Rights* (Cambridge: Cambridge University Press, 2011), Chapter 1.

Antonopoulos, Constantine. *Counterclaims before the International Court of Justice* (Berlin: Springer, 2011).

Anzilotti, Dionisio. 'La demande reconventionnelle en procédure internationale' (1930) 57(4) *Journal du Droit International* 857–877.

Arcuri, Alessandra and Montanaro, Francesco. 'Justice for All? Protecting the Public Interest in Investment Treaties' (2018) 59(8) *Boston College Law Review* 2791–2824.

Arcuri, Alessandra and Violi, Federica. 'Human Rights and Investor–State Dispute Settlement: Changing (Almost) Everything, So That Everything Stays the Same?' (2019) 3 *Diritti umani e diritto internazionale* 579–596.

Arcuri, Alessandra, Montanaro, Francesco and Violi, Federica. 'Proposal for a Human Rights – Compatible International Investment Agreement: Arbitration for All', OHCHR, 2018.

Aristova, Ekaterina. 'Tort Litigation against Transnational Corporations in the English Courts: The Challenge of Jurisdiction' (2018) 14(2) *Utrecht Law Review* 1–21.

Ascensio, Hervé. 'Les activités normatives des entreprises multinationals', in Laurence Dubin, Pierre Bodeau-Livinec, Jean-Louis Iten and Vincent Tomkiewicz (eds.), *L'entreprise multinationale et le droit international* (Paris: Pedone, 2017), 265–278.

Atanasova, Dafina, Martínez Benoit, Carlos Adrián and Ostřanský, Josef. 'Counterclaims in Investor–State Dispute Settlement (ISDS) under International Investment Agreements (IIAs)' (2012) Trade and Investment Law Clinic Papers 1–60.

Augenstein, Daniel. 'Torture as Tort? Transnational Tort Litigation for Corporate-Related Human Rights Violations and the Human Right to a Remedy' (2018) 18(3) *Human Rights Law Review* 593–612.

Augenstein, Daniel and Kinley, David. 'Beyond the 100 Acre Wood: In Which International Human Rights Law Finds New Ways to Tame Global Corporate Power' (2015) 19(6) *International Journal of Human Rights* 828–848.

Baade, Björnstjern. 'Due Diligence and the Duty to Protect Human Rights', in Heike Krieger, Anne Peters and Leonhard Kreuzer (eds.), *Due Diligence in the International Legal Order* (Oxford: Oxford University Press, 2020), 92–109.

Baba, Sofiane and Raufflet, Emmanuel. 'L'acceptabilité sociale: une notion en consolidation' (2015) 19(3) *Management International/International Management/Gestiòn Internacional* 98–114.

Backer, Larry Catá. 'On the Evolution of the United Nations' "Protect-Respect-Remedy" Project: The State, the Corporation and Human Rights in a Global Governance Context' (2010) 9(1) *Santa Clara Journal of International Law* 37–80.

Baetens, Freya. 'Procedural Issues Relating to Shared Responsibility in Arbitral Proceedings' (2013) 4(2) *Journal of International Dispute Settlement* 319–341.

Baez, Cristina, Dearing, Michele, Delatour, Margaret and Dixon, Christine. 'Multinational Enterprises and Human Rights' (2000) 8(1) *University of Miami International & Comparative Law Review* 183–338.

Baiashvili, Tamar and Gattini, Luca. 'Impact of FDI on Economic Growth: The Role of Country Income Levels and Institutional Strength' (2020) EIB Working Paper 2020/02.

Balcerzak, Filip. *Investor-State Arbitration and Human Rights* (Leiden: Brill NIjhoff, 2017), Chapters 2, 3.

Baltag, Crina. 'Reforming the ISDS System: In Search of a Balanced Approach' (2019) 12(2) *Contemporary Asia Arbitration Journal* 279–312.

'The Role of *Amici Curiae* in Light of Recent Developments in Investment Treaty Arbitration: Legitimizing the System?' (2020) 35(1–2) *ICSID Review* 279–310.

Baltag, Crina and Dautaj, Ylli. 'Investors, States, and Arbitrators in the Crosshairs of International Investment Law and Environmental Protection' (2019) 3(1) *International Investment Law and Arbitration* 1–77.

Banifatemi, Yas. 'The Law Applicable in Investment Treaty Arbitration', in Katia Yannaca-Small (ed.), *Arbitration under International Investment Agreements* (Oxford: Oxford University Press, 2010), 191–210.

Bantekas, Ilias. 'Corporate Social Responsibility in International Law' (2004) 22(2) *Boston University International Law Journal* 309–348.

Bassiouni, M. Cherif. 'A Functional Approach to "General Principles of International Law"' (1990) 11(3) *Michigan Journal of International Law* 768–818.

Baxi, Upendra. 'Geographies of Injustice: Human Rights at the Alter of Convenience', in Craig Martin Scott (ed.), *Torture as Tort: Comparative Perspectives on the Development of Transnational Human Rights Litigation* (Oxford: Hart Publishing, 2001), 197–212.

Beckers, Anna. *Enforcing Corporate Social Responsibility Codes: On Global Self-Regulation and National Private Law* (Oxford: Hart Publishing, 2015), Chapters 3, 4.

'Regulating Corporate Regulators through Contract Law? The Case of Corporate Social Responsibility Codes of Conduct' (2016) MWP 2016/12

Max Weber Programme, available at: https://cadmus.eui.eu/bitstream/handle/1814/41485/MWP_2016_12.pdf?sequence=4.

Bederman, David J. 'Contributory Fault and State Responsibility' (1990) 30(2) *Vanderbilt Journal of International Law* 335–370.

Beharry, Christina L. and Kuritzky, Melinda E. 'Going Green: Managing the Environment through International Investment Arbitration' (2015) 30(3) *American University International Law Review* 383–429.

Bellia, Anthony J. and Clark, Bradford R. 'The Alien Tort Statute and the Law of Nations' (2011) 78(2) *University of Chicago Law Review* 445–552.

Ben Hamida, Walid. 'L'arbitrage Etat-investisseur cherche son équilibre perdu: Dans quelle mersure l'Etat peut introduire des demandes reconventionnelles contre l'investisseur privé?' (2005) 7(4) *International Law FORUM du droit international* 261–272.

Bennouna, Mohamed. 'Experts before the International Court of Justice: What for?' (2018) 9(3) *Journal of International Dispute Settlement* 345–351.

Besson, Samantha. *La due diligence en droit international* (Leiden: Brill Nijhoff, 2021), Chapitre IV.

Beuscher, J. H. 'The Use of Experts by the Courts' (1941) 54(7) *Harvard Law Review* 1105–1127.

Bhatt, Kinnari and Erdem Türkelli, Gamze. 'OECD National Contact Points as Sites of Effective Remedy: New Expressions of the Role and Rule of Law within Market Globalization?' (2021) 6(3) *Business and Human Rights Journal* 423–448.

Bilchitz, 'David. 'Introduction: Putting Flesh on the Bone – What Should a Business and Human Rights Treaty Look Like?', in Surya Deva and David Bilchitz (eds.), *Building a Treaty on Business and Human Rights: Context and Contours* (Cambridge: Cambridge University Press, 2017), 1–24.

Binder, Christina and Hofbauer, Jane A. 'Case Study: *Burlington Resources Inc. v Ecuador/Kichwa Indigenous People of Sarayaku v Ecuador*' (2016) Committee on the Implementation of the Rights of Indigenous Peoples of the International Law Association, available at: http://dx.doi.org/10.2139/ssrn.2810062.

Bjorklund, Andrea K. 'The Role of Counterclaims in Rebalancing Investment Law' (2013) 17(2) *Lewis & Clark Law Review* 461–480.

Bjorklund, Andrea K. and Vanhonnaeker, Lukas. 'Article 42', in Julien Fouret, Rémy Gerbay and Gloria M. Alvarez (eds.), *The ICSID Convention, Regulations and Rules: A Practical Commentary* (Cheltenham: Edward Elgar, 2019), 347–369.

'Yukos: The Clean Hands Doctrine Revisited' (2015) 9(2) *Diritti umani e diritto internazionale* 365–385.

Blackaby, Nigel and Wilbraham, Alex. 'Practical Issues Relating to the Use of Expert Evidence in Investment Treaty Arbitration' (2016) 31(3) *ICSID Review* 655–669.

Blackburn, J. Walton. 'Environmental Mediation Theory and Practice: Challenges, Issues, and Needed Research and Theory Development', in J. Walton Blackburn and Willa Marie Bruce (eds.), *Mediating Environmental Conflicts: Theory and Practice* (Westport, CT: Quorum Books, 1995), 267–279.

Blanton, Shannon Lindsey and Blanton, Robert G. 'A Sectoral Analysis of Human Rights and FDI: Does Industry Type Matter?' (2009) 53(2) *International Studies Quarterly* 469–493.

Blowfield, Michael and Murray, Alan, *Corporate Social Responsibility*, 4th ed. (Oxford: Oxford University Press, 2019), Chapter 2.

Bodansky, Daniel. 'Legitimacy in International Law and International Relations', in Jeffrey L. Dunoff and Mark A. Pollack (eds.), *Interdisciplinary Perspectives on International Law and International Relations: The State of the Art* (Cambridge: Cambridge University Press, 2013), 321–342.

Bodansky, Daniel and Crook, John R. 'Introduction and Overview' (2002) 96(4) *American Journal of International Law* 773–791.

Boisson de Chazournes, Laurence. 'Environmental Protection and Investment Arbitration: Yin and Yang?' (2017) 10 *Anuario Colombiano de Derecho Internacional, Bogotá* 371–399.

'The Principle of Compétence de la Compétence in International Adjudication and Its Role in an Era of Multiplication of Courts and Tribunals', in Mahnoush H. Arsanjani, Jacob Katz Cogan, Robert D. Sloane and Siegfried Wiessner (eds.), *Looking to the Future: Essays in Honor of W. Michael Reisman* (Leiden: Martinus Nijhoff, 2010), 1027–1064.

Boisson de Chazournes, Laurence, Mbengue, Makane Moise, Das, Rukmini and Gros, Guillaume. 'One Size does not Fit All – Uses of Experts before International Courts and Tribunals: An Insight into the Practice' (2018) 9 (3) *Journal of International Dispute Settlement* 477–505.

Bonfanti, Angelica. 'Applying Corporate Social Responsibility to Foreign Investment: Failures and Prospects', in Tullio Treves, Francesco Seatzu and Seline Trevisanut (eds.), *Foreign Investment, International Law and Common Concerns* (Abingdon: Routledge, 2014), 230–246.

Bonnitcha, Jonathan. *Substantive Protection under Investment Treaties: A Legal and Economic Analysis* (Cambridge: Cambridge University Press, 2014), Chapters 4, 5.

Borchard, Edwin. 'Protection of Citizens Abroad and Change of Original Nationality' (1934) 20(4) *Yale Law Journal* 359–392.

Born, Gary and Forrest, Stephanie. '*Amicus Curiae* Participation in Investment Arbitration' (2019) 34(3) *ICSID Review* 626–665.

Boscariol, John W., Taborda, Ashley and Zaccaria, Melina. 'Mitigating Risk Exposure to Forced Labour in the Supply Chain: Part II – Canada's Response to Forced Labour', McCarthy Tétrault, 2 November 2021, available at: www.mccarthy.ca/en/insights/blogs/terms-trade/mitigating-risk-exposure-forced-labour-supply-chain-part-ii-canadas-response-forced-labour#_ftn16.

Bose, Debadatta. '*David R Aven v Costa Rica*: The Confluence of Corporations, Public International Law and International Investment Law' (2020) 35(1–2) *ICSID Review* 20–28.

Bottini, Gabriel. 'Legality of Investments under ICSID Jurisprudence', in Michael Waibel, Asha Kaushal, Liz Kyo-Hwa Chung and Claire Balchin (eds.), *The Backlash against Investment Arbitration* (Alphen aan den Rijn: Kluwer Law International, 2010), 297–314.

Boutilier, Robert G. 'Frequently Asked Questions about the Social Licence to Operate' (2014) 32(4) *Impact Assessment and Project Appraisal* 263–272.

Boutilier, Robert G., Black, Leeora D. and Thomson, Ian. 'From Metaphor to Management Tool: How the Social License to Operate Can Stabilise the Socio-political Environment for Business' (2012) *International Mine Management 2012 Proceedings* 227–237.

Boyle, Alan. 'Human Rights and the Environment: Where Next?' (2012) 23(3) *European Journal of International Law* 613–642.

'Human Rights or Environmental Rights? A Reassessment' (2006) 18(3) *Fordham Environmental Law Review* 470–511.

'Some Reflections on the Relationship of Treaties and Soft Law' (1999) 48(4) *International & Comparative Law Quarterly* 901–913.

Bravin, Mark N. and Kaplan, Alex B. 'Arbitrating Closely Related Counterclaims at ICSID in the Wake of Spyridon Roussalis v. Romania' (2012) 9(4) *Transnational Dispute Management* 1–11.

Brierly, James Leslie. *The Law of Nations: An Introduction to the International Law of Peace*, 6th ed. (Oxford: Clarendon Press, 1963), Chapter VI.

Bronckers, M. 'Is Investor-State Dispute Settlement (ISDS) Superior to Litigation before Domestic Courts? An EU View on Bilateral Trade Agreements' (2015) 18(3) *Journal of International Economic Law* 655–677.

Brower, Charles N. and Schill, Stephan W. 'Is Arbitration a Threat or a Boon to the Legitimacy of International Investment Law?' (2009) 9(2) *Chicago Journal of International Law* 471–498.

Brown, Chester. 'The Protection of Legitimate Expectations as a "General Principle of Law": Some Preliminary Thoughts' (2009) 6(1) *Transnational Dispute Management* 1–10.

Brown, Chester and Winch, Phoebe. 'The Confidentiality and Transparency Debate in Commercial and Investment Mediation', in Catharine Titi and Katia Fach Gómez (eds.), *Mediation in International Commercial and Investment Disputes* (Oxford: Oxford University Press, 2019), 321–341.

Bubrowski, Helene. 'Balancing IIA Arbitration through the Use of Counterclaims', in Armand de Mestral and Céline Lévesque (eds.), *Improving International Investment Agreements* (Abingdon: Routledge, 2013), 212–246.

Buhmann, Karin. 'Corporate Social Responsibility: What Role for Law? Some Aspects of Law and CSR' (2006) 6(2) *Corporate Governance* 188–202.

'Public Regulators and CSR: The "Social Licence to Operate" in Recent United Nations Instruments on Business and Human Rights and the Juridification of CSR' (2016) 136(4) *Journal of Business Ethics* 699–714.

Bungenberg, Marc and Reinisch, August. *From Bilateral Arbitral Tribunals and Investment Courts to a Multilateral Investment Court: Options Regarding the Institutionalization of Investor-State Dispute Settlement* (Berlin: Springer Open, 2018).

Burda, Julien. 'Le consentement aux demandes reconventionnelles dans le cadre du CIRDI à la lumière de la sentence *Spyridon Roussalis contre Roumanie*' (2003) 3(1) *Revue d'arbitrage et de médiation* 25–51.

Burke-White, William W. and von Staden, Andreas. 'The Need for Public Law Standards of Review in Investor-State Arbitrations', in Stephan W. Schill (ed.), *International Investment Law and Comparative Public Law* (Oxford: Oxford University Press, 2010), 689–720.

'Private Litigation in a Public Law Sphere: The Standard of Review in Investor-State Arbitrations' (2010) 35(2) *Yale Journal of International Law* 283–346.

Butler, Lisa F. '*Parens Patriae* Representation in Transnational Crisis: The Bhopal Tragedy' (1987) 17(1) *California Western International Law Journal* 175–207.

Buur, Lars, Nystrand, Malin J. and Pedersen, Rasmus Hundsbæk. 'The Political Economy of Land and Natural Resource Investments in Africa: An Analytical Framework' (2017) *Danish Institute for International Studies Working Paper 2017*:2, 1–48.

Calamita, N. Jansen. 'The Challenge of Establishing a Multilateral Investment Tribunal at ICSID' (2017) 32(3) *ICSID Review* 611–624.

Campbell, Christopher. 'House of Cards: The Relevance of Legitimate Expectations under Fair and Equitable Treatment Provisions in Investment Treaty Law' (2013) 30(4) *Journal of International Arbitration* 361–379.

Carballo Leyda, Alejandro. 'Model Instrument for Management of Investment Disputes', in Julien Chaisse, Leïla Choukroune and Sufian Jusoh (eds.), *Handbook of International Investment Law and Policy* (Singapore: Springer, 2021), 681–707.

Caron, David D. 'The Nature of the Iran-United States Claims Tribunal and the Evolving Structure of International Dispute Resolution' (1990) 84(1) *American Journal International Law* 104–156.

Carroll, Archie B. 'A History of Corporate Social Responsibility: Concepts and Practices', in Andrew Crane, Dirk Matten, Abagail McWilliams, Jeremy Moon and Donald S. Siegel (eds.), *The Oxford Handbook of Corporate Social Responsibility* (Oxford: Oxford University Press, 2008), 19–45.

Cazala, Julien. 'Le respect des droits de l'homme comme justification de la violation d'un traité d'investissement', in Walid Ben Hamida and Frédérique Coulée (eds.), *Convergences et contradictions du droit des investissements et des droits de l'homme: une approche contentieuse* (Paris: Pedone, 2017), 333–355.

Chen, Richard C. 'A Contractual Approach to Investor-State Regulatory Disputes' (2015) 40(2) *Yale Journal of International Law* 295–336.

Cheng, Bin. *General Principles of Law as Applied by International Courts and Tribunals* (London: Stevens, 1953), Chapter 14.

Chetail, Vincent. 'The Legal Personality of Multinational Corporations, State Responsibility and Due Diligence: The Way Forward', in Denis Alland, Vincent Chetail, Olivier de Frouville and Jorge E. Viñuales (eds.), *Unity and Diversity of International Law: Essays in Honour of Prof, Pierre-Marie Dupuy* (Leiden: Martinus Nijhoff, 2014), 105–130.

Chew, Seraphina, Reed, Lucy and Thomas QC, J. Christopher. 'Report: Survey on Obstacles to Settlement of Investor-State Disputes' (2018) NUS Centre for International Law Research Paper No. 18/01; NUS Law Working Paper No. 2018/022.

Choudhury, Barnali. 'Investor Obligations for Human Rights' (2020) 35(1–2) *ICSID Review* 82–104.

'The Role of Soft Law Corporate Responsibilities in Defining Investor Obligations in International Investment Agreements', in Jean Ho and Mavluda Sattorova (eds.), *Investors' International Law* (Oxford: Hart, 2021), 151–168.

Churchill, Robin R. 'Environmental Rights in Existing Human Rights Treaties', in Alan Boyle and Michael R. Anderson (eds.), *Human Rights Approaches to Environmental Protection* (Oxford: Clarendon Press, 1996), 89–108.

Clapham, Andrew. *Human Rights Obligations of Non-State Actors* (Oxford: Oxford University Press, 2006), Chapters 1, 2.

Human Rights in the Private Sphere (Oxford: Oxford University Press, 1996), Chapter 4.

Clapp, Jennifer. 'Transnational Corporations and Global Environmental Governance', in Peter Dauvergne (ed.), *Handbook of Global Environmental Politics* (Cheltenham: Edward Elgar, 2005), 284–297.

Claxton, James M. 'Compelling Parties to Mediate Investor-State Disputes: No Pressure, No Diamonds?' (2020) 20(1) *Pepperdine Dispute Resolution Law Journal* 78–100.

Coe Jr., Jack. 'Concurrent Co-Mediation: Toward a More Collaborative Centre of Gravity in Investor-State Dispute Resolution', in Catharine Titi and Katia Fach Gómez (eds.), *Mediation in International Commercial and Investment Disputes* (Oxford: Oxford University Press, 2019), 61–78.

'Should Mediation of Investment Disputes Be Encouraged, and, If So, by Whom and How?' (2009) 3 *Contemporary Issues in International Arbitration and Mediation: The Fordham Papers* 339–357.

Coleman, Jesse, Johnson, Lise, Güven, Brooke, Cotula, Lorenzo and Berger, Thierry. 'Third Party Rights in Investor-State Dispute Settlement: Options for Reform' (2019) Submission to UNCITRAL Working Group III on ISDS Reform, contributed by Columbia Center on Sustainable Investment (CCSI), International Institute for Environment and Development (IIED), and International Institute for Sustainable Development (IISD), available at: https://uncitral.un.org/sites/uncitral.un.org/files/media-documents/uncitral/en/wgiii_reformoptions_0.pdf.

Constain, Silvia. 'Mediation in Investor-State Dispute Settlement: Government Policy and the Changing Landscape' (2014) 29(1) *ICSID Review* 25–40.

Cordero-Moss, Giuditta. 'International Arbitration and the Quest for the Applicable Law' (2008) 8(3) *Global Jurist* 1–42.

'Why Arbitration Needs Conflict of Laws Rules', Kluwer Arbitration Blog, 17 October 2018.

Corkin, Joseph. 'Misappropriating Citizenship: The Limits of Corporate Social Responsibility', in Nina Boeger, Rachel Murray and Charlotte Villiers (eds.), *Perspectives on Corporate Social Responsibility* (Cheltenham: Edward Elgar, 2008), 39–62.

Cosbey, Aaron, Maennling, Nicolas, Geipe, Jeff, Mann, Howard, Toledano, Perrinem and Brauch, Martin Dietrich. 'Mining a Mirage? Reassessing the Shared-Value Paradigm in Light of the Technological Advances in the Mining Sector', International Institute for Sustainable Development, September 2016.

Cottier, Thomas, Echandi, Roberto, Leal-Arcas, Rafael, Liechti, Rachel and Payosova, Tetyana. 'The Principle of Proportionality in International Law: Foundations and Variations' (2017) 18(4) *Journal of World Investment & Trade* 628–672.

Cotula, Lorenzo. '(Dis)integration in Global Resource Governance: Extractivism, Human Rights, and Investment Treaties' (2020) 23(2) *Journal of International Economic Law* 431–454.

Cotula, Lorenzo and Neal, Terrence. 'UNCITRAL Working Group III: Can Reforming Procedures Rebalance Investor Rights and Obligations?' (2019) *Investment Policy Brief* No. 15, 1–5.

Cotula, Lorenzo and Perrone, Nicolas M. 'Investors' International Law and Its Asymmetries: The Case of Local Communities', in Jean Ho and Mavluda Sattorova (eds.), *Investors' International Law* (Oxford: Hart, 2021), 71–88.

'Reforming Investor-State Dispute Settlement: What about Third-Party Rights?' (2019) IIED Briefing 1–4.

Cotula, Lorenzo and Schröder, Mika. *Community Perspectives in Investor-State Arbitration* (2017) IIED Land, Investment and Rights Series, available at: https://pubs.iied.org/sites/default/files/pdfs/migrate/12603IIED.pdf.

Craig, Paul P. 'Substantive Legitimate Expectations in Domestic and Community Law' (1996) 55(2) *Cambridge Law Journal* 289–312.

Crawford, James. *Brownlie's Principles of Public International Law*, 9th ed. (Oxford: Oxford University Press, 2019), Chapter 31.

'The ILC's Articles on Responsibility of States for Internationally Wrongful Acts: A Retrospect' (2002) 96(4) *American Journal of International Law* 874–890.

'Treaty and Contract in Investment Arbitration' (2008) 24(3) *Arbitration International* 351–374.

Crawford, James and Olleson, Simon. 'The Application of the Rules of State Responsibility', in Marc Bungenberg, Jörn Griebel, Stephan Hobe and August Reinisch (eds.), *International Investment Law: A Handbook* (Baden-Baden: Nomos, 2015), 411–441.

Crow, Kevin and Lorenzoni Escobar, Lina. 'International Corporate Obligations, Human Rights, and the Urbaser Standard: Breaking New Ground?' (2017) 144 *Beiträge zum Transnationalen Wirtschaftsrecht* 1–31.

Custer, Lawrence B. 'The Origins of the Doctrine of *Parens Patriae*' (1978) 27(2) *Emory Law Journal* 195–208.

Dahlsrud, Alexander. 'How Corporate Social Responsibility Is Defined: An Analysis of 37 Definitions' (2008) 15(1) *Corporate Social Responsibility Environment Management* 1–13.

Dahran, M. R. and Von Kumberg, Wolf. 'Investor-State Dispute Settlement Reconceptionalized: Regulation of Disputes, Standards and Mediation' (2017) 17(2) *Pepperdine Dispute Resolution Law Journal* 467–496.

Đajić, Sanja. 'Mapping the Good Faith Principle in International Investment Arbitration: Assessment of Its Substantive and Procedural Value' (2012) 46(3) *Zbornik Radova* 207–234.

Dalhuisen, Hendrik and Guzman, Andrew T. 'The Applicable Law in Foreign Investment Disputes' (2014) 8(2) *World Arbitration and Mediation Review* 229–250.

Daly, Brooks W. and Poon, Fiona. 'Technical and Legal Experts in International Investment Disputes', in Chiara Giorgetti (ed.), *Litigating International Investment Disputes: A Practitioner's Guide* (Leiden: Brill Nijhoff, 2014), 323–374.

Dani, Mojtaba and Akhtar-Khavari, Afshin. 'Rethinking the Use of Deference in Investment Arbitration: New Solutions against the Perception of Bias' (2018) 22(1) *UCLA Journal of International Law and Foreign Affairs* 37–69.

Danic, Olivia. 'Droit international des investissements, droits de l'homme, droit de l'environnement', in Charles Leben (ed.), *Droit international des investissements et de l'arbitrage transnational* (Paris: Pedone, 2015), 531–579.

Danis-Fatôme, Anne and Viney, Geneviève. 'La responsabilité civile dans la loi relative au devoir de vigilance des sociétés mères et des entreprises donneuses d'ordre' (2017) 28 *Recueil Dalloz* 1610–1618.

Daoud, Emmanuel and Le Corre, Clarisse. 'Arrêt Erika: marée verte sur le droit de la responsabilité civile et pénale des compagnies pétrolières' (2012) 122 *Le Lamy droit pénal des affaires* 1–7.

Dasgupta, Susmita, Laplante, Benoit, Wang, Hua and Wheeler, David, 'Confronting the Environmental Kuznets Curve' (2002) 16(1) *Journal of Economic Perspectives* 147–168.

Davis, Seth and Whytock, Christopher A. 'State Remedies for Human Rights' (2018) 98(2) *Boston University Law Review* 397–484.

De Brabandere, Eric. *Investment Treaty Arbitration as Public International Law* (Cambridge: Cambridge University Press, 2014), Chapter 2.

De Castro, Gregorio. 'Corporate Social Responsibility and Restructuring in the EU: A Historical Overview of Recent Developments', in International Institute for Labour Studies, *Governance, International Law & Corporate Social Responsibility* (Geneva: ILO, 2008), 129–154.

De Jonge, Alice. *Transnational Corporations and International Law: Accountability in the Global Business Environment* (Cheltenham: Edward Elgar, 2011), Chapter 8.

De Luca, Anna and Baltag, Crina. 'Counterclaims in Investment Arbitration: Reflections on UNCITRAL WG III Reform', Kluwer Arbitration Blog, 5 November 2021.

De Luca, Anna and Bonfanti, Angelica. 'Investment and Human Rights: Is There an Elephant in the Room?' (2020) 282 *Columbia FDI Perspectives* 1–3.

De Ly, Filip, Friedman, Mark and Brozolo, Luca Radicati Di. 'International Law Association International Commercial Arbitration Committee's Report and Recommendations on "Ascertaining the Contents of the Applicable Law in International Commercial Arbitration"' (2010) 26(2) *Arbitration International* 193–220.

De Nanteuil, Arnaud. 'Counterclaims in Investment Arbitration: Old Questions, New Answers?' (2018) 17(2) *The Law & Practice of International Courts and Tribunals* 374–392.

De Schutter, Olivier. 'La responsabilité des Etats dans le contrôle des sociétés transnationales: vers une Convention internationale sur la lutte contre les atteintes aux droits de l'homme commises par les sociétés transnationales', in Emmanuel Decaux (ed.), *La responsabilité des entreprises multinationales en matière de droits de l'homme* (Bruxelles: Bruylant, 2010), 19–100.

'Transnational Corporations as Instruments of Human Development', in Philip Alston and Mary Robinson (eds.), *Human Rights and Development: Towards Mutual Reinforcement* (Oxford: Oxford University Press, 2005), 403–444.

Deacon, Robert T. and Norman, Catherine S. 'Does the Environmental Kuznets Curve Describe How Individual Countries Behave?' (2006) 82(2) *Land Economics* 291–315.

Decaux, Emmanuel. 'Présentation', in Emmanuel Decaux (ed.), *La responsabilité des entreprises multinationales en matière de droits de l'homme* (Bruxelles: Bruylant, 2010), 11–17.

Deumier, Pascale. 'Les codes de conduite des entreprises et l'effectivité des droits de l'Homme', in Laurence Boy, Jean-Baptiste Racine and Fabrice Siiriainen (eds.), *Droit économique et droits de l'Homme* (Belgium: Larcier, 2009), 671–696.

Deva, Surya. 'International Investment Agreements and Human Rights: Assessing the Role of the UN's Business and Human Rights Regulatory Initiatives', in Julien Chaisse, Leïla Choukroune and Sufian Jusoh (eds.), *Handbook of International Investment Law and Policy* (Singapore: Springer, 2021), 1733–1758.

Diehl, Alexandra. *The Core Standard of International Investment Protection: Fair and Equitable Treatment* (Alphen aan den Rijn: Kluwer Law International, 2012), Chapter 6.

Diel-Gligor, Katharina and Hennecke, Rudolf. 'Investment in Accordance with the Law', in Marc Bungenberg, Jörn Griebel, Stephan Hobe and August Reinisch (eds.), *International Investment Law: A Handbook* (Baden-Baden: Nomos, 2015), 566–576.

DiMascio, Nicholas and Pauwelyn, Joost. 'Nondiscrimination in Trade and Investment Treaties: Worlds Apart or Two Sides of the Same Coin?' (2008) 102(1) *American Journal of International Law* 48–89.

Dimitropoulos, Georgios. 'Investor-State Dispute Settlement Reform and Theory of Institutional Design' (2018) 9(4) *Journal of International Dispute Settlement* 535–569.

Dimsey, Mariel. 'Article 4: Submission by a Third Person', in Dimitrij Euler, Markus Gehring and Maxi Scherer (eds.), *Transparency in International Investment Arbitration: A Guide to the UNCITRAL Rules on Transparency in Treaty-Based Investor-State Arbitration* (Cambridge: Cambridge University Press, 2015), 128–195.

Dodge, William S. 'Breaking the Public Law Taboo' (2002) 43(1) *Harvard International Law Journal* 161–236.

'*Jesner v. Arab Bank*: The Supreme Court Preserves the Possibility of Human Rights Suits Against U.S. Corporations', UC Davis School of Law Faculty Blogs, 26 April 2018.

'Local Remedies under NAFTA Chapter 11', in Emmanuel Gaillard and Frédéric Bachand (eds.), *Fifteen Years of NAFTA Chapter 11 Arbitration* (Huntington, NY: Juris, 2011), 37–56.

Dolzer, Rudolf. 'Fair and Equitable Treatment: Today's Contours' (2013) 12(1) *Santa Clara Journal of International Law* 7–34.

'The Impact of International Investment Treaties on Domestic Administrative Law' (2005) 37(4) *New York Journal of International Law and Politics* 953–972.

Dolzer, Rudolf and Schreuer, Christoph. *Principles of International Investment Law* (Oxford: Oxford University Press, 2008), Chapter X.

Dörr, Oliver, 'Article 32: Supplementary Means of Interpretation', in Oliver Dörr and Kirsten Schmalenbach (eds.), *Vienna Convention on the Law of Treaties: A Commentary* (Heidelberg: Springer, 2012), 571–586.

Douglas, Zachary. 'The Enforcement of Environmental Norms in Investment Treaty Arbitration', in Pierre-Marie Dupuy and Jorge E. Viñuales (eds.), *Harnessing Foreign Investment to Promote Environmental Protection: Incentives and Safeguards* (Cambridge: Cambridge University Press, 2013), 415–444.

'The Hybrid Foundations of Investment Treaty Arbitration' (2003) 74(1) *British Yearbook of International Law* 151–289.

The International Law of Investment Claims (Cambridge: Cambridge University Press, 2009), Chapters 1–6.

'International Responsibility for Domestic Adjudication: Denial of Justice Deconstructed' (2014) 63(4) *International & Comparative Law Quarterly* 867–900.

'Other Specific Regimes of Responsibility: Investment Treaty Arbitration and ICSID: Investment Treaty Arbitration and ICSID', in James Crawford, Alain Pellet and Simon Olleson (eds.), *The Law of International Responsibility* (Oxford: Oxford University Press, 2010), 815–842.

'The Plea of Illegality in Investment Treaty Arbitration' (2014) 29(1) *ICSID Review* 155–186.

Drimmer, Jonathan and Torrance, Michael. 'CSR Risk Management and Due Diligence', in Rae Lindsay and Roger Martella (eds.), *Corporate Responsibility, Sustainable Business: Environmental, Social and Governance Frameworks for the 21st Century* (Alphen aan den Rijn: Kluwer Law International, 2020), 611–627.

Dubin, Laurence. 'L'entreprise multinationale, de la fragmentation à la reconstruction par le droit international', in Laurence Dubin, Pierre Bodeau-Livinec, Jean-Louis Iten and Vincent Tomkiewicz (eds.), *L'entreprise multinationale et le droit international* (Paris: Pedone, 2017), 13–51.

Dudas, Stefan. 'Treaty Counterclaims under the ICSID Convention', in Crina Baltag (ed.), *ICSID Convention after 50 Years: Unsettled Issues* (Alphen aan den Rijn: Kluwer Law International, 2017), 385–405.

Dugard, John. 'Diplomatic Protection and Human Rights: The Draft Articles of the International Law Commission' (2005) 24(1) *Australian Yearbook of International Law* 75–91.

Duggal, Kabir A. N. and van de Ven, Laurens H. 'The 2019 Netherlands Model BIT: Riding the New Investment Treaty Waves' (2019) 35(3) *Arbitration International* 347–374.

Dukes, E. Franklin. 'What We Know about Environmental Conflict Resolution: An Analysis Based on Research' (2004) 22(1–2) *Conflict Resolution Quarterly* 191–220.

Dumberry, Patrick. 'The Clean Hands Doctrine as a General Principle of International Law' (2020) 21(4) *Journal of World Investment & Trade* 489–527.

'L'entreprise, sujet de droit international? Retour sur la question à la lumière des développements récents du droit international des investissements' (2004) 108(1) *Revue générale de droit international public* 103–121.

A Guide to General Principles of Law in International Investment Arbitration (Oxford: Oxford University Press, 2020), Chapters 1, 3, 4.

'The Protection of Investors' Legitimate Expectations and the Fair and Equitable Treatment Standard under NAFTA Article 1105' (2014) 31(1) *Journal of International Arbitration* 47–74.

'State of Confusion: The Doctrine of Clean Hands in Investment Arbitration after the Yukos Award' (2016) 17(2) *Journal of World Investment & Trade* 229–259.

Dumberry, Patrick and Dumas-Aubin, Gabrielle. 'When and How Allegations of Human Rights Violations Can Be Raised in Investor-State Arbitration' (2012) 13(3) *Journal of World Investment & Trade* 349–372.

Dupuy, Florian and Dupuy, Pierre-Marie. 'What to Expect from Legitimate Expectations? A Critical Appraisal and Look into the Future of the "Legitimate Expectations" Doctrine in International Investment Law', in Mohamed Abdel Raouf, Philippe Leboulanger and Nassib G. Ziadé (eds.), *Festschrift Ahmed Sadek El-Kosheri: From the Arab World to the Globalization of International Law* (Alphen aan den Rijn: Wolters Kluwer Law & Business, 2015), 273–298.

Earnest, David L. 'The Duty of Arbitrators to Delimitate between Jurisdiction and Admissibility in Investor-State Arbitration' (2018) 17(1) *The Law & Practice of International Courts and Tribunals* 135–144.

Easterbrook, Frank and Fischel, Daniel. 'Limited Liability and the Corporation' (1985) 52(1) *Chicago Law Review* 89–117.

Eccles, Robert G. and Klimenko, Svetlana. 'The Investor Revolution: Shareholders Are Getting Serious about Sustainability', *Harvard Business Review*, May–June 2019.

Elrifai, Silke Noa. 'Equity-Based Discretion and the Anatomy of Damages Assessment in Investment Treaty Law' (2017) 34(5) *Journal of International Arbitration* 835–888.

Endicott, Martin. 'Remedies in Investor-State Arbitration: Restitution, Specific Performance and Declaratory Awards', in Philippe Kahn and Thomas W. Wälde (eds.), *Les aspects nouveaux du droit des investissements internationaux/New aspects of international investment law* (Leiden/Boston: Martinus Nijhoff, 2007), 517–552.

English, Alexander. 'Calming the Waters: Environmental Mediation and Water Resources Disputes' (2017) 47(1) *Texas Environmental Law Journal* 1–16.

Enneking, Liesbeth. 'Crossing the Atlantic? The Political and Legal Feasibility of European Foreign Direct Liability Cases' (2009) 40(4) *George Washington International Law Review* 903–938.

Foreign Direct Liability and Beyond: Exploring the Role of Tort Law in Promoting International Corporate Social Responsibility and Accountability (The Hague: Eleven International Publishing, 2012), Chapter 9.

Eroglu, Muzaffer. *Multinational Enterprises and Tort Liabilities* (Cheltenham: Edward Elgar, 2008), Chapters 5, 7.

Erwin, Patrick M. 'Corporate Codes of Conduct: The Effects of Code Content and Quality on Ethical Performance' (2011) 99(4) *Journal of Business Ethics* 535–548.

Esty, Daniel C. 'The World Trade Organization's Legitimacy Crisis' (2002) 1(1) *World Trade Review* 7–22.

Evans, Kimberly. 'Foreign Portfolio and Direct Investment: Complementarity, Differences and Integration' (2002) Paper prepared on the OECD Global forum on international investment in Shanghai, available at: www.oecd.org/investment/investmentfordevelopment/2764407.pdf.

Fahner, Johannes Hendrik. 'The Conundrum of Contributory Fault in Investment Arbitratin: From Causation to Apportionment, Book Review of Jarrett Martin, *Contributory Fault and Investor Misconduct in Investment Arbitration* (CUP 2019)' (2021) 37(3) *Arbitration International* 769–780.

Judicial Deference in International Adjudication: A Comparative Analysis (Oxford: Hart, 2020), Chapter 3.

Farmer, Susan Beth. 'More Lessons from the Laboratories: *Cy Pres* Distributions in *Parens Patriae* Antitrust Actions Brought by State Attorneys General' (1999) 68(2) *Fordham Law Review* 361–406.

Fatoux, François. 'La différenciation normative selon les activités', in Emmanuel Decaux (ed.), *La responsabilité des entreprises multinationales en matière de droits de l'homme* (Bruxelles: Bruylant, 2010), 155–160.

Fenton, Ruth. 'A Civil Matter for a Common Expert: How Should Parties and Tribunals Use Experts in International Commercial Arbitration?' (2006) 6(2) *Pepperdine Dispute Resolution Law Journal* 279–293.

Fernandez-Feijoo, Belen, Romero, Silvia and Ruiz, Silvia. 'Effect of Stakeholders' Pressure on Transparency of Sustainability Reports within the GRI Framework' (2014) 122(1) *Journal of Business Ethics* 53–63.

Fitzmaurice, Gerald. 'The General Principles of International Law Considered from the Standpoint of the Rule of Law' (1957) 92 *Recueil des Cours* 1–227, Chapter VII.

Flett, James. 'When Is an Expert Not an Expert?' (2018) 9(3) *Journal of International Dispute Settlement* 352–360.

Fontanelli, Filippo. *Jurisdiction and Admissibility in Investment Arbitration: The Practice and the Theory* (Leiden: Brill, 2017), Part B.

Foster, Caroline E. 'New Clothes for the Emperor? Consultation of Experts by the International Court of Justice' (2014) 5(1) *Journal of International Dispute Settlement* 139–173.

Foster, George K. 'Investors, States, and Stakeholders: Power Asymmetries in International Investment and the Stabilizing Potential of Investment Treaties' (2013) 17(2) *Lewis & Clark Law Review* 361–422.

Francioni, Francesco. 'Access to Justice, Denial of Justice and International Investment Law' (2009) 20(3) *European Journal of International Law* 729–747.

'International Human Rights in an Environmental Horizon' (2010) 21(2) *European Journal of International Law* 41–55.

Franck, Susan D. 'The Legitimacy Crisis in Investment Treaty Arbitration: Privatizing Public International Law through Inconsistent Decisions' (2005) 73(4) *Fordham Law Review* 1521–1625.

'Using Investor-State Mediation Rules to Promote Conflict Management: An Introductory Guide' (2014) 29(1) *ICSID Review* 66–89.

Franck, Thomas M. *Fairness in International Law and Institutions* (Oxford: Clarendon Press, 1995), Chapters 1, 2.

Fredman, Sandra. *Human Rights Transformed: Positive Rights and Positive Duties* (Oxford: Oxford University Press, 2008), Introduction, Chapter 3.

French, Duncan. 'Treaty Interpretation and the Incorporation of Extraneous Legal Rules' (2006) 55(2) *International & Comparative Law Quarterly* 281–314.

Frey, Barbara A. 'The Legal and Ethical Responsibilities of Transnational Corporations in the Protection of International Human Rights' (1997) 6(1) *Minnesota Journal of Global Trade* 153–188.

Friedman, Mark W. and Popova, Ina C. 'Can State Counterclaims Salvage Investment Arbitration?' (2014) 8(2) *World Arbitration and Mediation Review* 139–179.

Fry, James D. 'International Human Rights Law in Investment Arbitration: Evidence of International Law's Unity' (2007) 18(1) *Duke Journal of Comparative & International Law* 77–149.

Gaillard, Emmanuel. 'L'avenir des traités de protection des investissements', in Charles Leben (ed.), *Droit international de l'investissement et de l'arbitrage transnational* (Paris: Pedone, 2015), 1037–1041.

Gaillard, Emmanuel and Banifatemi, Yas. 'The Meaning of "and" in Article 42(1), Second Sentence, of the Washington Convention: The Role of International Law in the ICSID Choice of Law Process' (2003) 18(2) *ICSID Review* 375–411.

Gaja, Giorgio. 'The Position of Individuals in International Law: An ILC Perspective' (2010) 21(1) *European Journal of International Law* 11–14.

Galindo, Alvaro and Elsisi, Ahmed. 'Non-Disputing Parties' Rights in Investor-State Dispute Settlement: The Application of the Monetary Gold Principle', in Katia Fach Gómez (ed.), *Private Actors in International Investment Law* (Cham: Springer, 2021), 175–190.

Galvão Teles, Patrícia. 'The Impact and Influence of the Articles on State Responsibility on the Work of the International Law Commission and Beyond', European Journal of International Law Talk!, 3 August 2021.

García-Sánchez, Isabel-María, Hussain, Nazim, Martínez-Ferrero, Jennifer and Ruiz-Barbadillo, Emiliano. 'Impact of Disclosure and Assurance Quality of Corporate Sustainability Reports on Access to Finance' (2019) 26(4) *Corporate Social Responsibility and Environmental Management* 832–848.

Gardiner, Richard. *Treaty Interpretation* (Oxford: Oxford University Press, 2008), Chapter 8.

Garner, Bryan A. (editor in chief), *Black's Law Dictionary*, 11th ed. (St. Paul, MN: Thomson Reuters, 2019).

Garsten, Bryan. 'Representative Government and Popular Sovereignty', in Ian Shapiro, Susan C. Stokes, Elisabeth Jean Wood and Alexander S. Kirshner (eds.), *Political Representation* (Cambridge: Cambridge University Press, 2009), 90–109.

Gathii, James Thuo. 'Understanding Tanzania's Termination of Its BIT with the Netherlands in Context', AfronomicsLaw, 1 April 2019, available at: www.afronomicslaw.org/2019/04/01/understanding-tanzanias-termination-of-its-bit-with-the-netherlands-in-context.

Gaukrodger, David. 'Business Responsibilities and Investment Treaties' (2021) OECD Working Papers on International Investment 2021/02, 1–128.

Gazzini, Tarcisio. 'General Principles of Law in the Field of Foreign Investment' (2009) 10(1) *Journal of World Investment & Trade* 103–119.

George, James Paul. 'Defining *Filartiga*: Characterizing International Torture Claims in United States Courts' (1984) 3(1) *Dickinson Journal of International Law* 1–42.

Ghouri, Ahmad Ali. 'On Genealogy of Proposals to Reform Investor-State Arbitration' (2014) 11(1) *Transnational Dispute Management* 1–11.

Gill, Judith and Gupta, Rishab. 'The Principle of Contributory Fault after Yukos' (2015) 9(2) *Dispute Resolution International* 93–114.

Ginsburg, Tom. 'International Substitutes for Domestic Institutions: Bilateral Investment Treaties and Governance' (2005) 25(1) *International Review of Law & Economics* 107–123.

Giorgetti, Chiara. 'Hulley Enterprises Ltd. (Cyprus) v. Russian Federation, Yukos Universal Ltd. (Isle of Man) v. Russian Federation, Veteran Petroleum Ltd.

(Cyprus) v. Russian Federation' (2015) 109(2) *American Journal of International Law* 387–393.

Giuliani, Elisa and Macchi, Chiara. 'Multinational Corporations' Economic and Human Rights Impacts on Developing Countries: A Review and Research Agenda' (2014) 38(2) *Cambridge Journal of Economics* 479–517.

Glinski, Carola. 'Corporate Codes of Conduct: Moral or Legal Obligation?', in Doreen McBarnet, Aurora Voiculescu and Tom Campbell (eds.), *The New Corporate Accountability: Corporate Social Responsibility and the Law* (Cambridge: Cambridge University Press, 2007), 119–147.

Goldberg, Stephen B., Sander, Frank E. A., Rogers, Nancy H. and Cole, Sarah Rudolph. *Dispute Resolution: Negotiation, Mediation, Arbitration, and Other Processes*, 7th ed. (New York: Wolters Kluwer, 2020), Chapter 5.

Goldberg, Stephen B. and Shaw, Margaret L. 'The Past, Present, and Future of Mediation as Seen through the Eyes of Some of Its Founders' (2010) 26(2) *Negotiation Journal* 237–253.

Goldhaber, Michael D. 'Corporate Human Rights Litigation in Non-U.S. Courts: A Comparative Scorecard' (2013) 3(1) *University of California Irvine Law Review* 126–149.

Goldstein, Itay and Razin, Assaf. 'Foreign Direct Investment vs Foreign Portfolio Investment' (2005) NBER Working Paper No. 11047.

Goldstein, Itay, Razin, Assaf and Tong, Hui. 'Liquidity, Institutional Quality and the Composition of International Equity Flows' (2010) NBER Working Paper No. 15727.

Gordon, Kathryn and Pohl, Joachim. 'Environmental Concerns in International Investment Agreements: A Survey' (2011) 1 *OECD Working Papers on International Investment* 9–14.

Gouiffès, Laurent and Ordonez, Mellisa. 'Jurisdiction and Admissibility: Are We Closer to a Line in the Sand?' (2015) 31(1) *Arbitration International* 107–122.

Gourgourinis, Anastasios. 'Fair and Equitable Treatment in International Investment Law: The Art of Watching Out for Both the "Elephants" and the "Fleas" in the (Normative) "Room" of Investment Protection' (2015) 16(2) *Journal of World Investment & Trade* 335–359.

'The Nature of Investor's Rights under Investment Treaties: A Comment on Paparinskis' "Investment Treaty Arbitration and the (New) Law of State Responsibility"', European Journal of International Law Talk!, 22 October 2013.

Grehan, Kevin J. 'Comparative Negligence' (1981) 81(8) *Columbia Law Review* 1668–1701.

Grisel, Florian. 'The Sources of Foreign Investment Law', in Zachary Douglas, Joost Pauwelyn and Jorge E. Viñuales (eds.), *The Foundations of*

International Investment Law: Bringing Theory into Practice (Oxford: Oxford University Press, 2014), 214–233.

Grossman, Nienke. 'The Normative Legitimacy of International Courts' (2013) 86(1) *Temple Law Review* 61–106.

Grušić, Uglješa. 'Responsibility in Groups of Companies and the Future of International Human Rights and Environmental Litigation' (2015) 74(1) *Cambridge Law Journal* 30–34.

Gunningham, Neil, Kagan, Robert A. and Thornton, Dorothy. 'Social License and Environmental Protection: Why Businesses Go beyond Compliance' (2004) 29(2) *Law & Social Inquiry* 307–341.

Guntrip, Edward. 'A Host State Human Rights Counterclaim in Investment Arbitration' (2018) Crowd-Drafting: Designing a Human Rights-Compatible International Investment Agreement, Session at the United Nations Forum on Business and Human Rights 2018.

Güven, Brooke Skartvedt. 'Investor-State Mediation: An Opportunity to Advance Sustainable Outcomes' (2020) CCSI, available at: https://ccsi.columbia.edu/news/investor-state-mediation-opportunity-advance-sustainable-outcomes.

Haas, Ernst B. 'Why Collaborate? Issue-Linkage and International Regimes' (1980) 32(3) *World Politics* 357–405.

Haftel, Yoram Z. and Thompson, Alexander. 'When Do States Renegotiate Investment Agreements? The Effect of Arbitration' (2018) 13(1) *The Review of International Organizations* 25–48.

Hakimi, Monica. 'State Bystander Responsibility' (2010) 21(2) *European Journal of International Law* 341–385.

Hamamoto, Shotaro. 'Protection of the Investor's Legitimate Expectations: Intersection of a Treaty Obligation and a General Principle of Law', in Wenhua Shan and Jinyuan Su (eds.), *China and International Investment Law: Twenty Years of ICSID Membership* (Leiden: Brill Nijhoff, 2015), 141–169.

Hamann, Andrea. 'The Use of Ex Curia Experts in International Litigation: Why the WTO Dispute Settlement Cannot Serve to Improve ICJ Practice', in Hélène Ruiz Fabri (ed.), *International Law and Litigation: A Look into Procedure* (Baden-Baden: Nomos, 2019), 107–146.

Hamdani, Khalil and Ruffing, Lorraine. 'Lessons from the UN Centre on Transnational Corporations for the Current Treaty Initiative', in Surya Deva and David Bilchitz (eds.), *Building a Treaty on Business and Human Rights: Context and Contours: Context and Contours* (Cambridge: Cambridge University Press, 2017), 27–47.

Handl, Gunther F., Reisman, W. Michael, Simma, Bruno, Dupuy, Pierre-Marie and Chinkin, Christine. 'A Hard Look at Soft Law' (1988) 82 *Proceedings of the Annual Meeting (American Society of International Law)* 371–395.

Hanna, Gabrielle J. 'The Helicopter State: Misuse of *Parens Patriae* Unconstitutionally Precludes Individual and Class Claims' (2017) 92(4) *Washington Law Review* 1955–1990.

Hansen, Robin F. 'Parallel Proceedings in Investor-State Treaty Arbitration: Responses for Treaty-Drafters, Arbitrators and Parties' (2010) 73(4) *Modern Law Review* 523–550.

Happold, Matthew and Radović, Relja. 'The ECOWAS Court of Justice as an Investment Tribunal' (2018) 19(1) *Journal of World Investment & Trade* 95–117.

Harder, Jennifer. 'Environmental Mediation: The Promise and the Challenge' (1995) 19(1) *Environs: Environmental Law and Policy Journal* 29–43.

Harmon-Darrow, Caroline, Charkoudian, Lorig, Ford, Tracee, Ennis, Michele and Bridgeford, Erricka. 'Defining Inclusive Mediation: Theory, Practice, and Research' (2020) 37(4) *Conflict Resolution Quarterly* 305–324.

Harrison, James. 'Environmental Counterclaims in Investor-State Arbitration' (2016) 17(3) *Journal of World Investment & Trade* 479–488.

Harrison, John. 'Environmental Mediation: The Ethical and Constitutional Dimension' (1997) 9(1) *Journal of Environmental Law* 79–102.

Hart, H. L. A. *The Concept of Law* (Oxford: Clarendon Law Series, 1961), Chapter V.

'Discretion' (2013) 127(2) *Harvard Law Review* (written in 1956) 652–665.

Hartka, Margaret. 'The Role of International Law in Domestic Courts: Will the Legal Procrastination End?' (1990) 14(1) *Maryland Journal of International Law* 99–125.

Haynes, Jason. 'The Evolving Nature of the Fair and Equitable Treatment (FET) Standard: Challenging Its Increasing Pervasiveness in Light of Developing Countries' Concerns – The Case for Regulatory Rebalancing' (2013) 14(1) *Journal of World Investment & Trade* 114–146.

'The Shifting Pendulum: Foreign Investors' Liability under Canada's Common Law for Breaches of Customary International Law' (2021) 36(3) *Canadian Journal of Law and Society / Revue Canadienne Droit et Société* 447–465.

Hedley, R. Alan. 'Transnational Corporations and Their Regulation: Issues and Strategies' (1999) 40(2) *International Journal of Comparative Sociology* 215–230.

Heiskanen, Veijo. 'Ménage à trois? Jurisdiction, Admissibility and Competence in Investment Treaty Arbitration' (2014) 29(1) *ICSID Review* 231–246.

Helleringer, Geneviève and Garcia, Kiteri. 'Le rayonnement des droits de l'Homme et des droits fondamentaux en droit privé' (2014) 66(2) *Revue internationale de droit comparé, Études de droit contemporain. Contributions françaises au 19e Congrès international de droit comparé (Vienne, 20 – 26 juillet 2014)* 283–336.

Henckels, Caroline. 'Legitimate Expectations and the Rule of Law in International Investment Law' (2020) available at: https://papers.ssrn.com/sol3/papers.cfm?abstract_id=3409086.

Proportionality and Deference in Investor-State Arbitration: Balancing Investment Protection and Regulatory Autonomy (Cambridge: Cambridge University Press, 2015), Chapters 1, 2.

'Protecting Regulatory Autonomy through Greater Precision in Investment Treaties: The TPP, CETA, and TTIP' (2016) 19(1) *Journal of International Economic Law* 27–50.

Hepburn, Jarrod. *Domestic Law in International Investment Arbitration* (Oxford: Oxford University Press, 2017), Chapters 5–7.

Higgins, Rosalyn. *Problems and Process: International Law and How We Use It* (Oxford: Clarendon Press, 1994), Chapter 3.

Hilson, Gavin. 'Corporate Social Responsibility in the Extractive Industries: Experiences from Developing Countries' (2012) 37(2) *Resources Policy* 131–137.

Hindelang, Steffen. 'Restitution and Compensation: Reconstructing the Relationship in Investment Treaty Law', in Rainer Hofmann and Christian J. Tams (eds.), *International Investment Law and General International Law: From Clinical Isolation to Systemic Integration?* (Baden-Baden: Nomos, 2011), 161–199.

Ho, Jean. 'International Law's Opportunities for Investor Accountability', in Jean Ho and Mavluda Sattorova (eds.), *Investors' International Law* (Oxford: Hart, 2021), 13–44.

Hodgson, Mélida and Stewart, Melissa. 'Experts in Investor-State Arbitration: The Tribunal as Gatekeeper' (2018) 9(3) *Journal of International Dispute Settlement* 453–463.

Hoffmann, Anne K. 'Counterclaims in Investment Arbitration' (2013) 28(2) *ICSID Review* 438–453.

'Counterclaims: *Spyridon Roussalis v. Romania*, ICSID Case No. ARB/06/01', in Meg Kinnear, Geraldine R. Fischer, Jara Mínguez Almeida, Luisa Fernanda Torres and Mairée Uran Bidegain (eds.), *Building International Investment Law: The First 50 Years of ICSID* (Alphen aan den Rijn: Kluwer Law International, 2015), 505–520.

Igbokwe, Virtus Chitoo. 'Determination, Interpretation and Application of Substantive Law in Foreign Investment Treaty Arbitrations' (2006) 23(4) *Journal of International Arbitration* 267–300.

Ishikawa, Tomoko. 'Counterclaims and the Rule of Law in Investment Arbitration' (2019) 113 *American Journal of International Law Unbound* 33–37.

'Intervention: Investment Arbitration', in Hélène Ruiz Fabri (ed.), *Max Planck Encyclopedia of International Procedural Law* (Oxford: Oxford University Press, 2019).

Iten, Jean-Louis. 'Les rattachements de l'entreprise multinationale: le point de vue du droit international public', in Laurence Dubin, Pierre Bodeau-Livinec, Jean-Louis Iten and Vincent Tomkiewicz (eds.), *L'entreprise multinationale et le droit international* (Paris: Pedone, 2017), 99–113.

Jacur, Francesca Romanin. 'Remarks on the Role of *Ex Curia* Scientific Experts in International Environmental Disputes', in Nerina Boschiero, Cesare Pitea, Chiara Ragni and Tullio Scovazzi (eds.), *International Courts and the Development of International Law: Essays in Honour of Tullio Treves* (The Hague: Asser Press, 2013), 441–455.

Jaeger, Kathleen. 'Environmental Claims under the Alien Tort Statute' (2010) 28(2) *Berkeley Journal of International Law* 519–536.

Jägers, Nicola. *Corporate Human Rights Obligations: In Search of Accountability* (Cambridge: Intersentia, 2002), Chapters I, VI.

Jamali, Dima. 'The CSR of MNC Subsidiaries in Developing Countries: Global, Local, Substantive or Diluted?' (2010) 93(Suppl. 2) *Journal of Business Ethics* 181–200.

Jana, Andrés. 'Reparation in Investment Treaty Arbitration' (2016) 110 *Proceedings of the Annual Meeting (American Society of International Law)* 288–292.

Janis, Mark W. 'The Doctrine of Forum Non Conveniens and the Bhopal Case' (1987) 34(2) *Netherlands International Law Review* 192–203.

Jarrett, Martin. *Contributory Fault and Investor Misconduct in Investment Arbitration* (Cambridge: Cambridge University Press, 2019), Chapters 1, 3–6.

'Responding to Investor Misconduct: The Line between Lawful and Unlawful Responses and Apportionment in Cases of Unlawful Responses', in Jean Ho and Mavluda Sattorova (eds.), *Investors' International Law* (Oxford: Hart, 2021), 169–191.

Jarrett, Martin, Puig, Sergio and Ratner, Steven. 'Investor Accountability: Indirect Actions, Direct Actions by States, and Direct Actions by Individuals' (2021) Academic Forum on ISDS Concept Paper 2021/1, 1–26.

Javillier, Jean-Claude. 'Corporate Social Responsibility and Law: Synergies Are Needed for Sustainable Development', in International Institute for Labour Studies, *Governance, International Law & Corporate Social Responsibility* (Geneva: ILO, 2008) 37–62.

Jaworek, Małgorzata and Kuzel, Marcin. 'Transnational Corporations in the World Economy: Formation, Development and Present Position' (2015) 4(1) *Copernican Journal of Finance & Accounting* 55–70.

Jenkins, Rhys. 'Globalization, Corporate Social Responsibility and Poverty' (2005) 81(3) *International Affairs* 525–540.

Jenks, C. Wilfred. 'The Interpretation and Application of Municipal Law by the Permanent Court of International Justice' (1938) 19 *British Yearbook of International Law* 67–103.

Jennings, Robert and Watts, Arthur (eds.). *Oppenheim's International Law: Volume I: Peace*, 9th ed. (London: Longman, 1992), Chapter 1, Section 21.

Jijelava, David and Vanclay, Frank. 'Legitimacy, Credibility and Trust as the Key Components of a Social Licence to Operate: An Analysis of BP's Projects in Georgia' (2017) 140(3) *Journal of Cleaner Production* 1077–1086.

Johnson, Jennifer L. 'Public-Private-Public Convergence: How the Private Actor Can Shape Public International Labor Standards' (1998) 24(1) *Brooklyn Journal of International Law* 291–356.

Johnson, Lise and Guven, Brooke Skartvedt. 'The Settlement of Investment Disputes: A Discussion of Democratic Accountability and the Public Interest', *Investment Treaty News*, 13 March 2017.

Joshi, Riddhi Dhananjay and Gurpur, Shashikala. 'The Silent Spring of Human Rights in Investment Arbitration: *Jurisprudence Constante* through Case-Law Trajectory' (2020) 36(4) *Arbitration International* 557–570.

Jouannet, Emmanuel. 'L'impossible protection des droits du tiers par la Cour internationale de justice dans les affaires de délimitation maritime', in Laurent Lucchini and Jean-Pierre Quéneudec (eds.), *La mer et son droit: Mélanges offerts à Laurent Lucchini et Jean-Pierre Quéneudec* (Paris: Pedone, 2003), 315–341.

Juarsa, Nyoman Indra and Persian, Yanuarda Yudo. 'Corporate Social Responsibility in International Economic Law Perspective' (2015) 2(2) *Brawijaya Law Journal* 84–102.

Kaeb, Caroline. 'Emerging Issues of Human Rights Responsibility in the Extractive and Manufacturing Industries: Patterns and Liability Risks' (2008) 6(2) *Northwestern Journal of International Human Rights* 327–353.

Kaldunski, Marcin. 'Principle of Clean Hands and Protection of Human Rights in International Investment Arbitration' (2015) 4(2) *Polish Review of International and European Law* 69–101.

Kalicki, Jean E. 'Counterclaims by States in Investment Arbitration', *Investment Treaty News*, 14 January 2013.

Kamminga, Menno T. and Zia-Zarifi, Saman. 'Liability of Multinational Corporations under International Law: An Introduction', in Menno T. Kamminga and Saman Zia Zarifi (eds.), *Liability of Multinational Corporations under International Law* (The Hague: Kluwer Law International, 2000), 1–15.

Kang, Kaiser. 'Innovative but Insufficient? The Investment Court System (ICS) in the EU-Vietnam Investment Protection Agreement (EVIPA)', European Institute for Asian Studies, 17 August 2021.

Kantor, Mark. 'The Impact of Contributory Investor Conduct: Only with Difficulty Commensurable', in Meg Kinnear, Geraldine R. Fischer, Jara Mínguez Almeida, Luisa Fernanda Torres and Mairée Uran Bidegain (eds.), *Building International Investment Law: The First 50 Years of ICSID* (Alphen aan den Rijn: Kluwer Law International, 2015), 533–553.

Kapoor, Surya. 'Singapore Convention Series: How Does the Singapore Mediation Convention Affect International Dispute Resolution? ISDS Perspective', Kluwer Mediation Blog, 15 November 2019.

Karavias, Markos. *Corporate Obligations under International Law* (Oxford: Oxford University Press, 2014), Chapters I–III.

Kaufmann-Kohler, Gabrielle. 'The Arbitrator and the Law: Does He/She Know It? Apply It? How? And a Few More Questions' (2005) 21(4) *Arbitration International* 631–638.

Kaufmann-Kohler, Gabrielle and Potestà, Michele. 'The Composition of a Multilateral Investment Court and of an Appeal Mechanism for Investment Awards', CIDS Supplemental Report, 2017, available at: http://dx.doi.org/10.2139/ssrn.3457310.

Investor-State Dispute Settlement and National Courts: Current Framework and Reform Options (Cham: Springer, 2020).

Kendra, Thomas. 'State Counterclaims in Investment Arbitration: A New Lease of Life?' (2013) 29(4) *Arbitration International* 575–606.

Kerbrat, Yann. 'Les manifestations de la notion d'entreprise multinationale en droit international', in Laurence Dubin, Pierre Bodeau-Livinec, Jean-Louis Iten and Vincent Tomkiewicz (eds.), *L'entreprise multinationale et le droit international* (Paris: Pedone, 2017), 57–69.

Kessedjian, Catherine. 'Transnational Public Policy', in Albert Jan van den Berg (ed.), *International Arbitration 2006: Back to Basics?* (Alphen aan den Rijn: Kluwer Law International, 2007), 857–870.

Kessedjian, Catherine, van Aaken, Anne, Lie, Runar and Mistelis, Loukas. 'Mediation in Future Investor-State Dispute Settlement' (2020) Academic Forum on ISDS Concept Paper 2020/16.

Kethireddy, Srinath Reddy. 'Still the Law of Nations: Legitimate Expectations and the Sovereigntist Turn in International Investment Law' (2019) 44(2) *Yale Journal of International Law* 315–354.

Khoury, Stéfanie and Whyte, David. 'Sidelining Corporate Human Rights Violations: The Failure of the OECD's Regulatory Consensus' (2019) 18(4) *Journal of Human Rights* 363–381.

Kingsbury, Benedict and Schill, Stephan. 'Investor-State Arbitration as Governance: Fair and Equitable Treatment, Proportionality and the Emerging Global Administrative Law' (2009) IILJ Working Paper 2009/6 (Global Administrative Law Series), 1–53.

Kingsbury, Benedict, Krisch, Nico and Stewart, Richard. 'The Emergence of Global Administrative Law' (2005) 68(3–4) *Law & Contemporary Problems* 15–62.

Kinley, David and Tadaki, Junko. 'From Talk to Walk: The Emergence of Human Rights Responsibilities for Corporations at International Law' (2004) 44(4) *Virginia Journal International Law* 931–1024.

Kinnear, Meg. 'ICSID in the Twenty-First Century: An Interview with Meg Kinnear' (2010) 104 *American Society of International Law Proceedings* 413–434.

Kinnear, Meg and Le Cannu, Paul-Jean. 'Concluding Remarks: ICSID and African States Leading International Investment Law Reform' (2019) 34(2) *ICSID Review* 542–551.

Kinney, Eleanor D. 'The International Human Right to Health: What Does This Mean for Our Nation and World?' (2001) 34(4) *Indiana Law Review* 1457–1475.

Kjos (Veenstra-Kjos), Hege Elisabeth. *Applicable Law in Investor-State Arbitration: The Interplay between National and International Law* (Oxford: Oxford University Press, 2013), Chapters 2, 4, and 6.

'Counterclaims by Host States in Investment Treaty Arbitration' (2007) 4(4) *Transnational Dispute Management* 1–48.

Klabbers, Jan. *An Introduction to International Institutional Law*, 2nd ed. (Cambridge: Cambridge University Press, 2009), Chapter 3.

Kläger, Roland. *'Fair and Equitable Treatment' in International Investment Law* (Cambridge: Cambridge University Press, 2011), Chapter 4.

Knight, Christopher R. 'International Human Rights Litigation after *Bauman*: The Viability of Veil Piercing to Hale Foreign Parent Corporations into U.S. Courts' (2016) 41(2) *University of Dayton Law Review* 214–260.

Knox, John H. 'Human Rights, Environmental Protection, and the Sustainable Development Goals' (2015) 24(3) *Washington International Law Journal* 517–536.

Knox, John H. and Pejan, Ramin. 'Introduction', in John H. Knox and Ramin Pejan (eds.), *The Human Right to a Healthy Environment* (Oxford: Oxford University Press, 2018), 1–16.

Koh, Harold Hongju, 'Transnational Legal Process', (1996) 75(1) *Nebraska Law Review* 181–207.

'Transnational Public Law Litigation' (1991) 100(8) *Yale Law Journal* 2347–2402.

Kolk, Ans and van Tulder, Rob. 'Setting New Global Rules? TNCs and Codes of Conduct' (2005) 14(3) *Transnational Corporations* 1–28.

Kordos, Marcel and Vojtovic, Sergej. 'Transnational Corporations in the Global World Economic Environment' (2016) 230 *Procedia Social and Behavioral Sciences* 150–158.

Kotuby Jr., Charles T. and Sobota, Luke A. *General Principles of Law and International Due Process: Principles and Norms Applicable in Transnational Disputes* (New York: Oxford University Press, 2017), Chapters 1–2.

Krajewski, Markus. 'The State Duty to Protect against Human Rights Violations through Transnational Business Activities' (2017) 23 *Deakin Law Review* 13–40.

Krajewski, Markus, Tonstad, Kristel and Wohltmann, Franziska. 'Mandatory Human Rights Due Diligence in Germany and Norway: Stepping, or Striding, in the Same Direction?' (2021) 6(3) *Business and Human Rights Journal* 1–9.

Krasner, Stephen D. 'Structural Causes and Regime Consequences: Regimes as Intervening Variables', in Stephen D. Krasner (ed.), *International Regimes* (Ithaca, NY: Cornell University Press 1983), 1–22.

Kreindler, Richard. 'Corruption in International Investment Arbitration: Jurisdiction and the Unclean Hands Doctrine', in Kaj Hobér, Annette Magnusson and Marie Öhrström (eds.), *Between East and West: Essays in Honour of Ulf Franke* (Huntington, NY: Juris, 2010), 309–328.

Kressel, Kenneth. 'Mediation Revisited', in Morton Deutsch, Peter T. Coleman and Eric C. Marcus (eds.), *The Handbook of Conflict Resolution: Theory and Practice*, 2nd ed. (San Francisco: Jossey-Bass, 2011), 726–756.

Kriebaum, Ursula. 'Human Rights of the Population of the Host State in International Investment Arbitration' (2009) 10(5) *Journal of World Investment & Trade* 653–677.

'Investment Arbitration – Illegal Investments', in Christian Klausegger et al. (eds.), *Austrian Arbitration Yearbook 2010* (Vienna: C. H. Beck, Stämpfli & Manz, 2010), 307–335.

'Is the European Court of Human Rights an Alternative to Investor-State Arbitration?', in Pierre-Marie Dupuy, Ernst-Ulrich Petersmann and Francesco Francioni (eds.), *Human Rights in International Investment Law and Arbitration* (Oxford: Oxford University Press, 2009), 219–245.

Kryvoi, Yaraslau (Yarik). 'Counterclaims in Investor-State Arbitration' (2012) 21(2) *Minnesota Journal of International Law* 216–252.

'Economic Crimes in International Investment Law' (2018) 67(3) *International & Comparative Law Quarterly* 577–605.

'Piercing the Corporate Veil in International Arbitration' (2010–2011) 1(2) *Global Business Law Review* 169–186.

Kubasek, Nancy and Silverman, Gary. 'Environmental Mediation' (1988) 26(3) *American Business Law Journal* 533–556.

Kurtz, Jürgen. 'On Foreign Investor "Privilege" and the Limits of the Law: A Reply to Ivar Alvik' (2020) 31(1) *European Journal of International Law* 313–319.

Kusek, Peter and Silva, Andrea. 'What Matters to Investors in Developing Countries: Findings from the Global Investment Competitiveness Survey', in *Global Investment Competitiveness Report 2017/2018: Foreign Investor Perspectives and Policy Implications* (Washington, DC: The World Bank, 2017), 19–49.

Laborde, Gustavo. 'The Case for Host State Claims in Investment Arbitration' (2010) 1(1) *Journal of International Dispute Settlement* 97–122.

Lahlou, Yasmin, Willard, Rainbow and Craven, Meredith. 'The Rise of Environmental Counterclaims in Mining Arbitration', in Jason Fry and Louis-Alexis Bret (eds.), *The Guide to Mining Arbitration* (Global Arbitration Review, 2019), 51–67, available at: www.litigationboutique.com/uploads/files/Canada.pdf.

Lalive, Pierre. 'Transnational (or Truly International) Public Policy and International Arbitration', in Pieter Sanders (ed.), *Comparative Arbitration Practice and Public Policy in Arbitration* (Deventer, Netherlands: Kluwer Law International, 1987), 258–318.

Lalive, Pierre and Halonen, Laura. 'On the Availability of Counterclaims in Investment Treaty Arbitration', in Alexander J. Bělohlávek and Naděžda Rozehnalová (eds.), *Rights of the Host States within the System of International Investment Protection: Czech Yearbook of International Law*, Volume II (Huntington, NY: Juris, 2011), 141–156.

Lamb, Sophie, Harrison, Daniel and Hew, Jonathan. 'Recent Developments in the Law and Practice of Amicus Briefs in Investor-State Arbitration' (2017) 5(2) *Indian Journal of Arbitration Law* 72–92.

Langford, Malcolm and Behn, Daniel. 'Managing Backlash: The Evolving Investment Treaty Arbitrator?' (2018) 29(2) *European Journal of International Law* 551–580.

Langford, Malcolm, Potestà, Michele, Kaufmann-Kohler, Gabrielle and Daniel Behn. 'Special Issue: UNCITRAL and Investment Arbitration Reform: Matching Concerns and Solutions: An Introduction' (2020) 21(2–3) *Journal of World Investment & Trade* 167–187.

Laryea, Emmanuel T. 'Legitimate Expectations in Investment Treaty Law: Concept and Scope of Application', in Julien Chaisse, Leïla Choukroune and Sufian Jusoh (eds.), *Handbook of International Investment Law and Policy* (Singapore: Springer, 2021), 97–120.

Lauterpacht, Eli. 'Issues of Compensation and Nationality in the Taking of Energy Investments' (1990) 8(1–4) *Journal of Energy & Natural Resources Law* 241–250.

Le Cannu, Paul-Jean. 'Foundation and Innovation: The Participation of African States in the ICSID Dispute Resolution System' (2018) 33(2) *ICSID Review* 456–500.

Lee, Thomas H. 'The Supreme Court of the United States as Quasi-International Tribunal: Reclaiming the Court's Original and Exclusive Jurisdiction over Treaty-Based Suits by Foreign States Against States' (2004) 104(7) *Columbia Law Review* 1765–1885.

Legum, Barton and Petculescu, Ioana. 'GATT Article XX and International Investment Law', in Roberto Echandi and Pierre Sauve (eds.), *Prospects in International Investment Law and Policy: World Trade Forum* (Cambridge: Cambridge University Press, 2013), 340–362.

Lehr, Amy K. and Smith, Gare A. *Implementing a Corporate Free, Prior, and Informed Consent Policy: Benefits and Challenges* (Foley Hoag eBook, 2010), available at: https://foleyhoag.com/-/media/files/foley%20hoag/publications/ebooks%20and%20whitepapers/2010/implementing%20a%20corporate%20free%20prior%20and%20informed%20consent%20policy%20benefits%20and%20challenges%200710.ashx.

Lehtonen, Markku, Kojo, Matti, Jartti, Tuija, Litmanen, Tapio and Kari, Mika. 'The Roles of the State and Social Licence to Operate? Lessons from Nuclear Waste Management in Finland, France, and Sweden' (2020) 61 *Energy Research & Social Science* 1–12.

Leikin, Eric, Gadodia, Stuti and Loudon, Charles. 'The State Doesn't Strike Back After All: India's Final Model BIT Takes the Bite out of Investor Obligations and Eliminates State Counterclaims' (2018) 15(2) *Transnational Dispute Management* 1–21.

Leinhardt, Stephanie B. 'Some Thoughts on Foreign Investors' Responsibilities to Respect Human Rights' (2013) 10(1) *Transnational Dispute Management* 1–26.

Lemos, Margaret H. 'Aggregate Litigation Goes Public: Representative Suits by State Attorneys General' (2012) 126(2) *Harvard Law Review* 486–549.

Levashova, Yulia. 'Fair and Equitable Treatment and Investor's Due Diligence under International Investment Law' (2020) 67(2) *Netherlands International Law Review* 233–255.

Lévesque, Céline. 'The Inclusion of GATT Article XX Exceptions in IIAs: A Potentially Risky Policy', in Roberto Echandi and Pierre Sauvé (eds.), *Prospects in International Investment Law and Policy: World Trade Forum* (Cambridge: Cambridge University Press, 2013), 363–370.

Lim, Alwyn and Tsutsui, Kiyoteru. 'Globalization and Commitment in Corporate Social Responsibility: Cross-National Analyses of Institutional and Political-Economy Effects' (2012) 77(1) *American Sociology Review* 69–98.

Lim, Chin Leng, Ho, Jean and Paparinskis, Martins. *International Investment Law and Arbitration* (Cambridge: Cambridge University Press, 2018), Chapter 19.

Linderfalk, Ulf. 'Who Are "the Parties"? Article 31, Paragraph 3(c) of the 1969 Vienna Convention and the "Principle of Systemic Integration" Revisited' (2008) 55(3) *Netherlands International Law Review* 343–364.

Lindroos, Anja and Mehling, Michael. 'Dispelling the Chimera of "Self-Contained Regimes" International Law and the WTO' (2005) 16(5) *European Journal of International Law* 857–877.

Llamzon, Aloysius P. *Corruption in International Investment Arbitration* (Oxford: Oxford University Press, 2014), Chapter 6.

'*Yukos Universal Limited (Isle of Man) v The Russian Federation*: The State of the "Unclean Hands" Doctrine in International Investment Law: Yukos as Both Omega and Alpha' (2015) 30(2) *ICSID Review* 315–325.

Llamzon, Aloysius and Sinclair, Anthony. 'Investor Wrongdoing in Investment Arbitration: Standards Governing Issues of Corruption, Fraud, Misrepresentation and Other Investor Misconduct', in Albert Jan van den Berg (ed.), *Legitimacy: Myths, Realities, Challenges* (Alphen aan den Rijn: Kluwer Law International, 2015), 451–530.

Lopez, Carlos. 'Human Rights Legal Liability for Business Enterprises: The Role of an International Treaty', in Surya Deva and David Bilchitz (eds.), *Building a Treaty on Business and Human Rights: Context and Contours* (Cambridge: Cambridge University Press, 2017), 299–317.

Lorz, Ralph Alexander and Busch, Manuel. 'Investment in Accordance with the Law: Specifically Corruption', in Marc Bungenberg, Jörn Griebel, Stephan Hobe and August Reinisch (eds.), *International Investment Law: A Handbook* (Baden-Baden: Nomos, 2015), 577–589.

Loucaides, Loukis. 'Environmental Protection through the Jurisprudence of the European Convention on Human Rights' (2004) 75(1) *British Yearbook of International Law* 249–267.

Loutit, Jennifer, Mandelbaum, Jacqueline and Szoke-Burke, Sam. 'Emerging Practices in Community Development Agreements' (2016) 7(1) *Journal of Sustainable Development Law and Policy* 64–96.

Lowe, Vaughan. 'Corporations as International Actors and International Law Makers' (2004) 13 *The Italian Yearbook of International Law* 23–38.

Lowenfeld, Andreas F. 'Public Law in the International Arena: Conflict of Laws, International Law, and Some Suggestions for Their Interaction' (1979-II) 163 *Recueil Des Cours* 321–428.

Mach, Tomáš. 'Legitimate Expectations as Part of the FET Standard: An Overview of a Doctrine Shaped by Arbitral Awards in Investor-State Claims' (2018) *ELTE Law Journal 2018/1*, 105–121.

MacKay, William R. 'Parens Patriae as Basis for Provincial Standing in Judicial Review of Federal Decisions' (2008) 45(4) *Alberta Law Review* 961–988.

MacLeod, Sorcha. 'The United Nations, Human Rights and Transnational Corporations: Challenging the International Legal Order', in Nina Boeger, Rachel Murray and Charlotte Villiers (eds.), *Perspectives on Corporate Social Responsibility* (Cheltenham: Edward Elgar, 2008), 64–84.

Magnus, Ulrich and Martin-Casals, Miquel. 'Comparative Conclusions', in Ulrich Magnus and Miquel Martin-Casals (eds.), *Unification of Tort Law: Contributory Negligence* (The Hague: Kluwer Law International, 2004), 259–290.

Maheandiran, Bernadette. 'Calling for Clarity: How Uncertainty Undermines the Legitimacy of the Dispute Resolution System under the OECD Guidelines for Multinational Enterprises' (2015) 20 *Harvard Negotiation Law Review* 205–244.

Malintoppi, Loretta and Haeri, Hussein. 'The Non-Disputing State Party in Investment Arbitration: An Interested Player or the Third Man Out?', in David D. Caron, Stephan W. Schill, Abby Cohen Smutny and Epaminontas E. Triantafilou (eds.), *Practising Virtue: Inside International Arbitration* (Oxford: Oxford University Press, 2015), 565–583.

Mann, Frederick. *Further Studies in International Law* (Oxford: Oxford University Press, 1990), Chapter 14.

Mann, Howard. 'Investment Agreements and the Regulatory State: Can Exceptions Clauses Create a Safe Haven for Governments?' (2007) IISD Background Papers for the Developing Country Investment Negotiators' Forum, 2–23.

Marboe, Irmgard. *Calculation of Compensation and Damages in International Investment Law* (Oxford: Oxford University Press, 2009), Chapter 3.

Marceau, Gabrielle Z. and Hawkins, Jennifer K. 'Experts in WTO Dispute Settlement' (2012) 3(3) *Journal of International Dispute Settlement* 493–507.

Marcoux, Jean-Michel. 'Transnational Public Policy as an International Practice in Investment Arbitration' (2019) 10(3) *Journal of International Dispute Settlement* 496–515.

Marcoux, Jean-Michel and Bjorklund, Andrea K. 'Foreign Investors' Responsibilities and Contributory Fault in Investment Arbitration' (2020) 69(4) *International & Comparative Law Quarterly* 877–905.

Marcoux, Jean-Michel and Newcombe, Andrew. '*Bear Creek Mining Corporation v Republic of Peru*: Two Sides of a "Social License" to Operate' (2018) 33(3) *ICSID Review* 653–659.

Mares, Radu. 'Liability within Corporate Groups: Parent Companies' Accountability for Subsidiary Human Rights Abuses', in Surya Deva and David Birchall (eds.), *Research Handbook on Human Rights and Business* (Cheltenham: Edward Elgar, 2020), 446–470.

Marquais, Olivier. 'Faute contributive et calcul des dommages dans les arbitrages d'investissement', Arbitrage International, 9 September 2015.

Márquez, Daniel Iglesias. 'Legal Avenues for Holding Multinational Corporations Liable for Environmental Damages in a Globalized World' (2015) 2(3) *ARACÊ – Direitos Humanos em Revista* 58–74.

Matten, Dirk and Moon, Jeremy. '"Implicit" and 'Explicit' CSR: A Conceptual Framework for a Comparative Understanding of Corporate Social Responsibility' (2008) 33(2) *Academy of Management Review* 404–424.

Mbengue, Makane Moise. 'Les obligations des investisseurs étrangers', in Laurence Dubin, Pierre Bodeau-Livinec, Jean-Louis Iten and Vincent Tomkiewicz (eds.), *L'entreprise Multinationale et le droit international* (Paris: Pedone, 2017), 295–337.

Mbengue, Makane Moïse and Schacherer, Stefanie. 'Africa and the Rethinking of International Investment Law about the Elaboration of the Pan-African Investment Code', in Anthea Roberts, Paul B. Stephan, Pierre-Hugues Verdier and Mila Versteeg (eds.), *Comparative International Law* (Oxford: Oxford University Press, 2017), 547–569.

'Evolution of International Investment Agreements in Africa: Features and Challenges of Investment Law "Africanization"', in Julien Chaisse, Leïla Choukroune and Sufian Jusoh (eds.), *Handbook of International Investment Law and Policy* (Singapore: Springer, 2021), 2597–2618.

McBarnet, Doreen. 'Corporate Social Responsibility Beyond Law, Through Law, for Law: The New Corporate Accountability', in Doreen McBarnet, Aurora Voiculescu and Tom Campbell (eds.), *The New Corporate Accountability: Corporate Social Responsibility and the Law* (Cambridge: Cambridge University Press, 2007), 9–56.

McBarnet, Doreen and Kurkchiyan, Marina. 'Corporate Social Responsibility through Contractual Control? Global Supply Chains and "Other-Regulation"', in Doreen McBarnet, Aurora Voiculescu and Tom Campbell (eds.), *The New Corporate Accountability: Corporate Social Responsibility and the Law* (Cambridge: Cambridge University Press, 2007), 59–92.

McBarnet, Doreen and Schmidt, Patrick. 'Corporate Accountability through Creative Enforcement: Human Rights, the Alien Tort Claims Act and the Limits of Legal Impunity', in Doreen McBarnet, Aurora Voiculescu and Tom Campbell (eds.), *The New Corporate Accountability: Corporate Social Responsibility and the Law* (Cambridge: Cambridge University Press, 2007), 148–176.

McBeth, Adam. 'Crushed by an Anvil: A Case Study on Responsibility for Human Rights in the Extractive Sector' (2008) 11(1) *Yale Human Rights & Development Law Journal* 127–166.

McConnaughay, Philip J. 'Reviving the "Public Law Taboo" in International Conflict of Laws' (1999) 35(2) *Stanford Journal of International Law* 255–312.

McCorquodale, Robert. 'Corporate Social Responsibility and International Human Rights Law' (2009) 87(2) *Journal of Business Ethics* 385–400.

McCorquodale, Robert and Smit, Lise. 'Human Rights, Responsibilities and Due Diligence', in Surya Deva and David Bilchitz (eds.), *Building a Treaty on Business and Human Rights: Context and Contours* (Cambridge: Cambridge University Press, 2017), 216–237.

McCrudden, Christopher. 'Corporate Social Responsibility and Public Procurement', in Doreen McBarnet, Aurora Voiculescu and Tom Campbell (eds.), *The New Corporate Accountability: Corporate Social Responsibility and the Law* (Cambridge: Cambridge University Press, 2007), 93–118.

McLachlan, Campbell. 'Investment Treaties and General International Law' (2008) 57(2) *International & Comparative Law Quarterly* 361–401.

'The Principle of Systemic Integration and Art 31(3)(c) of the Vienna Convention' (2005) 54(2) *International & Comparative Law Quarterly* 279–320.

McLachlan, Campbell, Shore, Laurence and Weiniger, Matthew. *International Investment Arbitration: Substantive Principles*, 2nd ed. (Oxford: Oxford University Press, 2017), Chapters 6–7.

Mendelson, Nina A. 'A Control-Based Approach to Shareholder Liability for Corporate Torts' (2002) 102(5) *Columbia Law Review* 1203–1303.

Merrill, Thomas W. 'Golden Rules for Transboundary Pollution' (1997) 46(5) *Duke Law Journal* 931–1019.

Merrills, John G. 'Environmental Rights', in Daniel Bodansky, Jutta Brunnée and Ellen Hey (eds.), *The Oxford Handbook of International Environmental Law* (Oxford: Oxford University Press, 2007), 663–680.

Miles, Cameron A. 'Corruption, Jurisdiction and Admissibility in International Investment Claims' (2012) 3(2) *Journal of International Dispute Settlement* 329–369.

Millennium Ecosystem Assessment, *Ecosystems and Human Well-Being: A Framework for Assessment* (Washington, DC: Island Press, 2003).

Mitra, Trisha. 'Relevance of Domestic Court Decisions to the Merits in Investment Arbitration', in Julien Chaisse, Leïla Choukroune and Sufian Jusoh (eds.), *Handbook of International Investment Law and Policy* (Singapore: Springer, 2021), 1103–1121.

Moffat, Kieren, Lacey, Justine, Zhang, Airong and Leipold, Sina. 'The Social Licence to Operate: A Critical Review' (2016) 89(5) *Forestry* 477–488.

Mollengarden, Zachary and Zamir, Noam. 'The Monetary Gold Principle: Back to Basics' (2021) 115(1) *American Journal of International Law* 41–77.

Moloo, Rahim. 'A Comment on the Clean Hands Doctrine in International Law' (2010) *Inter Alia: University of Durham Student Law Journal* 39–51.

Moloo, Rahim and Khachaturian, Alex. 'The Compliance with the Law Requirement in International Investment Law' (2011) 34(6) *Fordham International Law Journal* 1473–1501.

Montt, Santiago. *State Liability in Investment Treaty Arbitration: Global Constitutional and Administrative Law in the BIT Generation* (Oxford: Hart, 2009), Chapters 5–6.

Moore, Christopher W. *The Mediation Process: Practical Strategies for Resolving*, 4th ed. (San Francisco: Jossey-Bass, 2014), Part Two.

Moran, Theodore H. 'The United Nations and Transnational Corporations: A Review and a Perspective' (2009) 18(2) *Transnational Corporations* 91–112.

Morgera, Elisa. *Corporate Accountability in International Environmental Law* (Oxford: Oxford University Press, 2009), Chapters 1–3.

Mortenson, Julian Davis. 'The *Travaux* of *Travaux*: Is the Vienna Convention Hostile to Drafting History?' (2013) 107(4) *American Journal of International Law* 780–822.

Mosca, Fabrizio and Civera, Chiara. 'The Evolution of CSR: An Integrated Approach' (2017) 1 *Symphonya* 16–35.

Motte-Baumvol, Julia. 'Le comportement de l'investisseur', in Walid Ben Hamida and Frédérique Coulée (eds.), *Convergences et contradictions du droit des investissements et des droits de l'homme: une approche contentieuse* (Paris: Pedone, 2017), 197–225.

Mouawad, Caline and Beess und Chrostin, Jessica. 'The Illegality Objection in Investor-State Arbitration' (2021) 37(1) *Arbitration International* 57–95.

Mowery, Lauren A. 'Earth Rights, Human Rights–Can International Environmental Human Rights Affect Corporate Accountability?' (2002) 13(2) *Fordham Environmental Law Review* 343–373.

Muchlinski, Peter. '"Caveat Investor"?: The Relevance of the Conduct of the Investor under the Fair and Equitable Treatment Standard' (2006) 55(3) *International & Comparative Law Quarterly* 527–558.

'Limited Liability and Multinational Enterprises: A Case for Reform?' (2010) 34 (5) *Cambridge Journal of Economics* 915–928.

Multinational Enterprises and the Law, 2nd ed. (Oxford: Oxford University Press, 2007), Chapter 1.

'Towards a Coherent International Investment System: Key Issues in the Reform of International Investment Law', in Roberto Echandi and Pierre Sauvé (eds.), *Prospects in International Investment Law and Policy* (Cambridge: Cambridge University Press, 2013) 411–442.

Murphy, Sean D. 'Counter-Claims Article 80 of the Rules', in Andreas Zimmermann, Christian J. Tams, Karin Oellers-Frahm and Christian Tomuschat (eds.), *The Statute of the International Court of Justice: A Commentary*, 3rd ed. (Oxford: Oxford University Press, 2019), 1104–1134.

Mushkat, Roda. 'Corporate Social Responsibility, International Law, and Business Economics: Convergences and Divergences' (2012) 12(1) *Oregon Review of International Law* 55–76.

Nahman, Anton and Antrobus, Geoff. 'The Environmental Kuznets Curve: A Literature Survey' (2005) 73(1) *South African Journal of Economics* 105–120.

Nappert, Sophie. 'Mammoth Arbitrations: The Yukos Awards of 18 July 2014' (2015) 12(5) *Transnational Dispute Management* 1–35.

Nardin, Michel. 'Is There a Future for Tribunal-Appointed Experts?' (2019) 37(1) *ASA Bulletin* 48–63.

Narine, Marcia. 'Disclosing Disclosure's Defects: Addressing Corporate Irresponsibility for Human Rights Impacts' (2015) 47(1) *Columbia Human Rights Law Review* 84–150.

Nedumpara, James J. and Laddha, Aditya. 'Human Rights and Environmental Counterclaims in Investment Treaty Arbitration', in Julien Chaisse, Leïla Choukroune and Sufian Jusoh (eds.), *Handbook of International Investment Law and Policy* (Singapore: Springer, 2021), 1831–1849.

Newcombe, Andrew. 'General Exceptions in International Investment Agreements', in Marie-Claire Cordonier Segger, Markus W. Gehring and Andrew Newcombe (eds.), *Sustainable Development in World Investment Law* (Alphen aan den Rijn: Kluwer Law International, 2011), 351–370.

'Investor Misconduct: Jurisdiction, Admissibility or Merits?', in Chester Brown and Kate Miles (eds.), *Evolution in Investment Treaty Law and Arbitration* (Cambridge: Cambridge University Press, 2011), 187–200.

Newcombe, Andrew and Marcoux, Jean-Michel. '*Hesham Talaat M. Al-Warraq v Republic of Indonesia*: Imposing International Obligations on Foreign Investors' (2015) 30(3) *ICSID Review* 525–532.

Newman, Dwight G. 'Be Careful What You Wish For: Why Some Versions of "Social Licence" Are Unlicensed and May Be Anti-Social' (2014) *Macdonald-Laurier Institute Publication Commentary* 1–9.

Neyret, Laurent. 'L'affaire Erika: moteur d'évolution des responsabilités civile et pénale' (2010) 1 *Recueil Dalloz* 2238–2246.

Nitschke, Frauke. 'The IBA's Investor-State Mediation Rules and the ICSID Dispute Settlement Framework' (2014) 29(1) *ICSID Review* 112–132.

'The Proposed ICSID Mediation Rules' (2021) 17(2) *University of St. Thomas Law Journal* 422–454.

Nogales, Francisco S. 'The NAFTA Environmental Framework, Chapter 11 Investment Provisions, and the Environment' (2002) 8(1) *Annual Survey International & Comparative Law* 97–149.

Nolan-Haley, Jacqueline. 'Mediation, Self-Represented Parties, and Access to Justice: Getting There from Here' (2018) 87 *Fordham Law Review Online* 1–11.

Nowak, Manfred and Januszewski, Karolina Miriam. 'Non-State Actors and Human Rights', in Math Noortmann, August Reinisch and Cedric Ryngaert (eds.), *Non-State Actors in International Law* (Oxford: Hart, 2017), 113–161.

Nowrot, Karsten. 'Obligation of Investors', in Marc Bungenberg, Jörn Griebel, Stephan Hobe and August Reinisch (eds.), *International Investment Law* (Baden-Baden: Nomos, 2015), 1154–1185.

Nwauche, Enyinna S. 'The ECOWAS Community Court of Justice and the Horizontal Application of Human Rights' (2013) 13(1) *African Human Rights Law Journal* 30–54.

Obersteiner, Thomas. '"In Accordance with Domestic Law" Clauses: How International Investment Tribunals Deal with Allegations of Unlawful Conduct of Investors' (2014) 31(2) *Journal of International Arbitration* 265–288.

O'Brien, Clair Methven. 'The Home State Duty to Regulate the Human Rights Impacts of TNCs Abroad: A Rebuttal' (2018) 3(1) *Business and Human Rights Journal* 47–73.

Ogbodo, S. Gozie. 'An Overview of the Challenges Facing the International Court of Justice in the 21st Century' (2012) 18(1) *Annual Survey of International & Comparative Law* 93–114.

Okowa, Phoebe. 'Issues of Admissibility and the Law on International Responsibility', in Malcolm D. Evans (ed.), *International Law*, 5th ed. (Oxford: Oxford University Press, 2018), 450–483.

Ong, David M. 'Locating the "Environment" within Corporate Social Responsibility: Continuing Problems of Legal Definition and Representation', in Nina Boeger, Rachel Murray and Charlotte Villiers (eds.), *Perspectives on Corporate Social Responsibility* (Cheltenham: Edward Elgar, 2008), 186–223.

'Regulating Environmental Responsibility for the Multinational Oil Industry: Continuing Challenges for International Law' (2015) 11(2) *International Journal of Law in Context* 153–173.

Orrego Vicuña, Francisco. 'Interim Report on "The Changing Law of Nationality of Claims"', Report of the Sixty-Ninth Conference Held in London, 25–29 July 2000, London, International Law Association, 631–648.

Oshionebo, Evaristus. *Mineral Mining in Africa: Legal and Fiscal Regimes* (London: Routledge, 2021), Chapter 1.

Ostřanský, Josef. 'An Exercise in Equivocation: A Critique of Legitimate Expectations as a General Principle of Law under the Fair and Equitable Treatment Standard', in Andrea Gattini, Attila Tanzi and Filippo Fontanelli (eds.), *General Principles of Law and International Investment Arbitration* (Leiden: Brill Nijhoff, 2018), 344–377.

Owen, John R. and Kemp, Deanna. 'Social Licence and Mining: A Critical Perspective' (2013) 38(1) *Resources Policy* 29–35.

Paine, Joshua. 'Standard of Review (Investment Arbitration)', in Hélène Ruiz Fabri (ed.), *Max Planck Encyclopedia of International Procedural law* (Oxford: Oxford University Press, 2019).

Palchetti, Paolo. 'Litigating Member State Responsibility: The Monetary Gold Principle and the Protection of Absent Organizations' (2015) 12(2) *International Organizations Law Review* 468–483.

Palombo, Dalia. 'The Duty of Care of the Parent Company: A Comparison between French Law, UK Precedents and the Swiss Proposals' (2019) 4(2) *Business and Human Rights Journal* 265–286.

Paparinskis, Martins. 'Inherent Powers of ICSID Tribunals: Broad and Rightly So', in Todd J. Weiler and Ian A. Laird (eds.), *Investment Treaty Arbitration and International Law*, volume 5 (Huntington, NY: Juris, 2012), 11–42.

The International Minimum Standard and Fair and Equitable Treatment (Oxford: Oxford University Press, 2013), Chapters 6, 7, 9.

'Investment Treaty Arbitration and the (New) Law of State Responsibility' (2013) 24(2) *European Journal of International Law* 617–647.

Parance, Béatrice. 'L'influence du droit international de l'environnement sur les entreprises multinationals, à propos de la proposition de loi française relative au devoir de vigilance des entreprises', in Laurence Dubin, Pierre Bodeau-Livinec, Jean-Louis Iten and Vincent Tomkiewicz (eds.), *L'entreprise multinationale et le droit international* (Paris: Pedone, 2017), 279–294.

Parker, Christine. 'Meta-Regulation: Legal Accountability for Corporate Social Responsibility', in Doreen McBarnet, Aurora Voiculescu and Tom Campbell (eds.), *The New Corporate Accountability: Corporate Social Responsibility and the Law* (Cambridge: Cambridge University Press, 2007), 207–237.

Parlett, Kate. 'Parties' Engagement with Experts in International Litigation' (2018) 9(3) *Journal of International Dispute Settlement* 440–452.

Parra, Antonio R. 'Applicable Law in Investor-State Arbitration' (2009) 6(1) *Transnational Dispute Management* 1–15.

Partiti, Enrico. 'Polycentricity and Polyphony in International Law: Interpreting the Corporate Responsibility to Respect Human Rights' (2021) 70(1) *International & Comparative Law Quarterly* 133–164.

Pathak, Harshad. 'Consenting to Counterclaims under the ICSID Convention' (2019) 19(1) *Pepperdine Dispute Resolution Law Journal* 101–125.

Pauker, Saar A. 'Admissibility of Claims in Investment Treaty Arbitration' (2018) 34(1) *Arbitration International* 1–78.

Paulsson, Jan. 'Jurisdiction and Admissibility', in Gerald Aksen (ed.), *Global Reflections on International Law, Commerce and Dispute Resolution: Liber Amicorum in Honour of Robert Briner* (Paris: ICC Publishing, 2005), 601–617.

Paulsson, Jan and Petrochilos, Georgios. 'Revision of the UNCITRAL Arbitration Rules: A Report,' 2006, UNCITRAL Law Library, 347.918 P385.

Pauwelyn, Joost. *Conflict of Norms in Public International Law: How WTO Law Relates to other Rules of International Law* (Cambridge: Cambridge University Press, 2003), Chapter 3.

'The Role of Public International Law in the WTO: How Far Can We Go?' (2001) 95(3) *American Journal of International Law* 535–578.

'The Use of Experts in WTO Dispute Settlement' (2002) 51(2) *International & Comparative Law Quarterly* 325–364.

Pearsall, Patrick W. and Heath, J. Benton. 'Causation and Injury in Investor-State Arbitration', in Christina L. Beharry (ed.), *Contemporary and Emerging Issues on the Law of Damages and Valuation in International Investment Arbitration* (Leiden/Boston: Brill Nijhoff, 2018), 85–110.

Pellet, Alain. 'Le Projet d'articles de la C.D.I. sur la protection diplomatique, une codification pour (presque) rien', in Marcelo G. Kohen (ed.), *Promoting*

Justice, Human Rights and Conflict Resolution through International Law, Liber Amicorum Lucius Caflisch (Leiden: Nijhoff, 2006), 1133–1155.

Peloso, Margaret and Hunt, Travis. 'Corporate Social Responsibility Reporting', in Rae Lindsay and Roger Martella (eds.), *Corporate Responsibility, Sustainable Business: Environmental, Social and Governance Frameworks for the 21st Century* (Alphen aan den Rijn: Kluwer Law International, 2020), 125–172.

Peña, Susana C. Mijares. 'Human Rights Violations by Canadian Companies Abroad: Choc v Hudbay Minerals Inc.' (2014) 5(1) *Western Journal of Legal Studies* 1–19.

Pentikäinen, Merja. 'Changing International "Subjectivity" and Rights and Obligations under International Law – Status of Corporations' (2012) 8(1) *Utrecht Law Review* 145–154.

Peralta, Raúl F. Zúñiga. 'The Judicialisation of the Social License to Operate: Criteria for International Investment Law' (2021) 22(1) *Journal of World Investment & Trade* 92–128.

Percival, Robert V. 'Liability for Environmental Harm and Emerging Global Environmental Law' (2010) 25(1) *Maryland Journal of International Law* 37–63.

Pereira de Andrade, Priscila and Monebhurrun, Nitish. 'Mapping Investor's Environmental Commitments and Obligations', in Jean Ho and Mavluda Sattorova (eds.), *Investors' International Law* (Oxford: Hart, 2021), 263–290.

Perrone, Nicolás M. 'The International Investment Regime and Local Populations: Are the Weakest Voices Unheard?' (2016) 7(3) *Transnational Legal Theory* 383–405.

'Taking Local Expectations Seriously: A Fresh Start for Foreign Investment Governance?', in John D. Haskell and Akbar Rasulov (eds.), *New Voices and New Perspectives in International Economic Law* (Cham: Springer, 2020), 113–131.

Peters, Anne. 'Corruption as a Violation of International Human Rights' (2018) 29(4) *European Journal of International Law* 1251–1287.

Peterson, Luke Eric and Gray, Kevin R. 'International Human Rights in Bilateral Investment Treaties and in Investment Treaty Arbitration' (2003) A Research Paper Prepared by the IISD for the Swiss Department of Foreign Affairs, available at: www.iisd.org/publications/pub.aspx?id=577.

Pigrau, Antoni, Borràs, Susana, Manzano, Jordi Jariai and Cardesa-Salzmann, Antonio. 'Legal Avenues for EJOs to Claim Environmental Liability' (2012) 4 *Environmental Justice Organisation Liabilities and Trade Report* 1–98.

Pomson, Ori. 'Does the Monetary Gold Principle Apply to International Courts and Tribunals Generally?' (2019) 10(1) *Journal of International Dispute Settlement* 88–125.

Pomson, Ori and Horowitz, Yonatan. 'Humanitarian Intervention and the Clean Hands Doctrine in International Law' (2015) 48(2) *Israel Law Review* 219–252.

Popova, Ina C. and Poon, Fiona. 'From Perpetual Respondent to Aspiring Counterclaimant? State Counterclaims in the New Wave of Investment Treaties' (2015) 2(2) *BCDR International Arbitration Review* 223–260.

Porterfield, Matthew C. 'Exhaustion of Local Remedies in Investor-State Dispute Settlement: An Idea Whose Time Has Come?' (2015) 41 *Yale Journal of International Law Online* 1–11.

Potestà, Michele. 'Legitimate Expectations in Investment Treaty Law: Understanding the Roots and the Limits of a Controversial Concept' (2013) 28(1) *ICSID Review* 88–122.

Potestà, Michele and Kaufmann-Kohler, Gabrielle. 'Can the Mauritius Convention Serve as a Model for the Reform of Investor-State Arbitration in Connection with the Introduction of a Permanent Investment Tribunal or an Appeal Mechanism? – Analysis and Roadmap', 2016, available at: http://dx.doi.org/10.2139/ssrn.3455511.

Poulton, Ed, Kryvoi, Yarik, Finkel, Ekaterina and Bednarz, Janek. 'Empirical Study: Corporate Restructuring and Investment Treaty Protections', BIICL and Baker McKenzie, 2020, available at: www.biicl.org/documents/89_biicl-baker-mckenzie-corporate-restructuring-and-investment-treaty-protections-2020.pdf.

Puig, Sergio and Shaffer, Gregory. 'Imperfect Alternatives: Institutional Choice and the Reform of Investment Law' (2018) 112(3) *American Journal of International Law* 361–409.

Puma, Giuseppe. 'Human Rights and Investment Law: Attempts at Harmonization through a Difficult Dialogue between Arbitrators and Human Rights Tribunals', in Maurizio Arcari and Louis Balmond (eds.), *Judicial Dialogue in the International Legal Order: Between Pluralism and Legal Certainty* (Napoli: Editoriale Scientifica, 2014), 193–243.

Radi, Yannick. 'The "Human Nature" of International Investment Law' (2013) 10(1) *Transnational Dispute Management* 1–26.

Ramasastry, Anita. 'Corporate Social Responsibility versus Business and Human Rights: Bridging the Gap between Responsibility and Accountability' (2015) 14(2) *Journal of Human Rights* 237–259.

Ranjan, Prabhash. 'Investor Obligations in Investment Treaties: Missing Text or a Matter of Application?', in Jean Ho and Mavluda Sattorova (eds.), *Investors' International Law* (Oxford: Hart, 2021), 125–149.

Ranjan, Prabhash and Anand, Pushkar. 'The 2016 Model Indian Bilateral Investment Treaty: A Critical Deconstruction' (2017) 38(1) *Northwestern Journal of International Law & Business* 1–54.

Ratner, Steven R. 'Corporations and Human Rights: A Theory of Legal Responsibility' (2001) 111(3) *Yale Law Journal* 443–545.

Redgwell, Catherine. 'Life, The Universe and Everything: A Critique of Anthropocentric Rights', in Alan Boyle and Michael R. Anderson (eds.), *Human Rights Approaches to Environmental Protection* (Oxford: Clarendon Press, 1996), 71–87.

Reinisch, August. 'Jurisdiction and Admissibility in International Investment Law' (2017) 16(1) *The Law & Practice of International Courts and Tribunals* 21–43.

'Will the EU's Proposal Concerning an Investment Court System for CETA and TTIP Lead to Enforceable Awards?: The Limits of Modifying the ICSID Convention and the Nature of Investment Arbitration' (2016) 19(4) *Journal of International Economic Law* 761–786.

Reisman, Diana A. A. 'Apportioning Fault for Performance Corruption in Investment Arbitration' (2021) 37(1) *Arbitration International* 1–19.

Reisman, W. Michael. 'International Investment Arbitration and ADR: Married but Best Living Apart' (2009) 24(1) *ICSID Review* 185–192.

'The Regime for *Lacunae* in the ICSID Choice of Law Provision and the Question of Its Threshold' (2000) 15(2) *ICSID Review* 362–381.

Renneboog, Luc, Ter Horst, Jenke and Zhang, Chendi. 'Socially Responsible Investment Funds', in Güler Aras and David Crowther (eds.), *A Handbook of Corporate Governance and Social Responsibility* (Farnham: Gower, 2010), 395–412.

Ripinsky, Sergey and Williams, Kevin. *Damages in International Investment Law* (London: British Institute of International and Comparative Law, 2008), Chapter 8.

Risso, Giorgio and Amato, Anna Chiara. 'Pleas of Illegality and the Application of Domestic Law in Investment Treaty Arbitration' (2020) 9(1) *Cambridge International Law Journal* 96–116.

Rivas, José Antonio. 'ICSID Treaty Counterclaims: Case Law and Treaty Evolution' (2014) 11(1) *Transnational Dispute Management* 1–45.

Roberts, Anthea. 'Clash of Paradigms: Actors and Analogies Shaping the Investment Treaty System' (2013) 107(1) *American Journal of International Law* 45–94.

'Incremental, Systemic and Paradigmatic Reform of Investor-State Arbitration' (2018) 112(3) *American Journal of International Law* 410–432.

'Power and Persuasion in Investment Treaty Interpretation: The Dual Role of States' (2010) 104(2) *American Journal of International Law* 179–225.

Rodrik, Dani. *Has Globalization Gone Too Far?* (Washington, DC: Institute of International Economics, 1997), Chapter 5.

Roe, Thomas and Happold, Matthew. *Settlement of Investment Disputes under the Energy Charter Treaty* (Cambridge: Cambridge University Press, 2011), Chapter 3.

Rolland, Sonia E. and Trubek, David M. 'Legal Innovation in Investment Law: Rhetoric and Practice in the South' (2017) 39(2) *University of Pennsylvania Journal of International Law* 355–434.

Roorda, Lucas and Ku, Julian G. 'Applying International Law to Corporations: The Limits to the Lessons Offered by the United States Experience with the Alien Tort Statute', in Jean Ho and Mavluda Sattorova (eds.), *Investors' International Law* (Oxford: Hart, 2021), 213–234.

Roorda, Lucas and Leader, Daniel Leader. 'Okpabi v Shell and Four Nigerian Farmers v Shell: Parent Company Liability Back in Court' (2021) 6(2) *Business and Human Rights Journal* 368–376.

Rose-Ackerman, Susan. 'Judicial Independence and Corruption', in Transparency International (ed.), *Global Corruption Report 2007: Corruption in Judicial Systems* (Cambridge: Cambridge University Press, 2007), 15–24.

Rosenberg, Kim. 'Practical and Innovative Use of Experts' (2018–2019) 13(4) *Construction Law International* 20–26.

Rosenfeld, Friedrich. 'Arbitral Praeliminaria – Reflections on the Distinction between Admissibility and Jurisdiction after *BG v. Argentina*' (2016) 29(1) *Leiden Journal of International Law* 137–154.

Rudall, Jason. 'The Tribunal with a Toolbox: On *Perenco v Ecuador*, Black Gold and Shades of Green' (2020) 11(3) *Journal of International Dispute Settlement* 485–500.

Ruggie, John Gerard. 'Business and Human Rights: The Evolving International Agenda', (2007) 101(4) *American Journal of International Law* 819–840.

Just Business: Multinational Corporations and Human Rights (New York: W. W. Norton, 2013), Chapter Two.

'Multinationals as Global Institution: Power, Authority and Relative Autonomy' (2018) 12(3) *Regulation & Governance* 317–333.

Obstacles to Justice and Redress for Victims of Corporate Human Rights Abuse (Oxford: Oxford Pro Bono Publico, 2008), Introduction.

Rühmkorf, Andreas. *Corporate Social Responsibility, Private Law and Global Supply Chains: Corporations, Globalisation and the Law series* (Cheltenham: Edward Elgar, 2015), Chapter 5.

Rusk, Dean. 'A Comment on *Filartiga v. Pena-Irala*' (1981) 11(2) *Georgia Journal of International and Comparative Law* 311–316.

Sabahi, Borzu. *Compensation and Restitution in Investor-State Arbitration: Principles and Practice* (Oxford: Oxford University Press, 2011), Chapter 7.

Sabahi, Borzu and Duggal, Kabir. '*Occidental Petroleum v Ecuador (2012)*: Observations on Proportionality, Assessment of Damages and Contributory Fault' (2013) 28 (2) *ICSID Review* 279–290.

Sabahi, Borzu, Duggal, Kabir and Birch, Nicholas. 'Principles Limiting the Amount of Compensation', in Christina L. Beharry (eds.), *Contemporary and Emerging Issues on the Law of Damages and Valuation in International Investment Arbitration* (Leiden/Boston: Brill Nijhoff, 2018), 325–346.

Sachs, Klaus and Schmidt-Ahrendts, Nils. 'Protocol on Expert Teaming: A New Approach to Expert Evidence', in Albert Jan van den Berg (ed.), *Arbitration*

Advocacy in Changing Times (Alphen aan den Rijn: Kluwer Law International, 2011), 135–148.

Sachs, Noah M. 'Beyond the Liability Wall: Strengthening Tort Remedies in International Environmental Law' (2008) 55(4) *UCLA Law Review* 837–904.

Sadowski, Wojciech. 'Yukos and Contributory Fault' (2015) 12(5) *Transnational Dispute Management* 1–36.

Salas-Fouksmann, Olivier. 'Corporate Liability of Energy/Natural Resources Companies at National Law for Breach of International Human Rights Norms' (2013) 2(1) *UCL Journal of Law and Jurisprudence* 201–229.

Sands, Philippe, Peel, Jacqueline, Fabra, Adriana and MacKenzie, Ruth. *Principles of International Environmental Law*, 4th ed. (Cambridge: Cambridge University Press, 2018), Chapter 5.

Sanger, Andrew. 'Transnational Corporate Responsibility in Domestic Courts: Still Out of Reach?' (2019) 113 *American Journal International Law Unbound* 4–9.

Sasson, Monique. *Substantive Law in Investment Treaty Arbitration: The Unsettled Relationship between International and Municipal Law*, 2nd ed. (Alphen aan den Rijn: Kluwer Law International, 2017), Introduction, Chapters 1, 4, 6.

Sattorova, Mavluda. 'The Foreign Investor as a Good Citizen: Investor Obligations to do Good', in Jean Ho and Mavluda Sattorova (eds.), *Investors' International Law* (Oxford: Hart, 2021), 45–69.

Sauvant, Karl P. 'The Negotiations of the United Nations Code of Conduct on Transnational Corporations: Experience and Lessons Learned' (2015) 16(1) *Journal of World Investment & Trade* 11–87.

Sauvant, Karl P. and Ünüvar Güneş, 'Can Host Countries Have Legitimate Expectations?' (2016) 183 *Columbia FDI Perspectives* 1–4.

Savadogo, Louis. 'Le recours des juridictions internationales à des experts' (2004) 50 *Annuaire français de droit international* 231–258.

Schepel, Harm. *The Constitution of Private Governance: Product Standards in the Regulation of Integrating Markets* (Oxford: Hart, 2005), Chapters 1, 10.

Scherer, Maxi, Bruce, Stuart and Reschke, Juliane. 'Environmental Counterclaims in Investment Treaty Arbitration' (2021) 36(2) *ICSID Review* 413–440.

Schill, Stephan W. 'Deference in Investment Treaty Arbitration: Re-conceptualizing the Standard of Review' (2012) 3(3) *Journal of International Dispute Settlement* 577–607.

'"Fair and Equitable Treatment" as an Embodiment of the Rule of Law', in Rainer Hofmann and Christian Tams (eds.), *The International Convention on the Settlement of Investment Disputes (ICSID): Taking Stock after 40 Years* (Baden-Baden: Nomos, 2007), 31–72.

'General Principles of Law and International Investment Law', in Tarcisio Gazzini and Eric De Brabandere (eds.), *International Investment Law: The Sources of Rights and Obligations* (Leiden: Martinus Nijhoff, 2018), 133–181.

'Illegal Investments in International Arbitration' (2012) 11(2) *The Law & Practice of International Courts and Tribunals* 281–323.

'Reforming Investor-State Dispute Settlement: A (Comparative and International) Constitutional Law Framework' (2017) 20(3) *Journal of International Economic Law* 649–672.

Schill, Stephan W. and Djanic, Vladislav. 'International Investment Law and Community Interests', in Eyal Benvenisti and Georg Nolte (eds.), *Community Interests Across International Law* (Oxford: Oxford University Press, 2018), 221–248.

Schlesinger, Rudolf B. 'Research on the General Principles of Law Recognized by Civilized Nations' (1957) 51(4) *American Journal of International Law* 734–753.

Schreuer, Christoph H. 'Jurisdiction and Applicable Law in Investment Treaty Arbitration' (2014) 1(1) *McGill Journal of Dispute Resolution* 1–25.

'Why Still ICSID?' (2012) 9(3) *Transnational Dispute Management* 1–7.

Schreuer, Christoph H., Malintoppi, Loretta, Reinisch, August and Sinclair, Anthony. *The ICSID Convention: A Commentary*, 2nd ed. (Cambridge: Cambridge University Press, 2009), Articles 42, 46.

Schwartz, Gary T. 'Contributory and Comparative Negligence: A Reappraisal' (1978) 87(4) *Yale Law Journal* 697–727.

Scott, Craig. 'Multinational Enterprises and Emergent Jurisprudence on Violations of Economic, Social and Cultural Rights', in Asbjørn Eide, Catarina Krause and Allan Rosas (eds.), *Economic, Social and Cultural Rights: A Textbook*, 2nd ed. (Dordrecht: Martinus Nijhoff, 2001), 563–595.

Seck, Sara L. and Ogunranti, Akinwumi. 'Accountability: Legal Risks and Remedies', in Rae Lindsay and Roger Martella (eds.), *Corporate Responsibility, Sustainable Business: Environmental, Social and Governance Frameworks for the 21st Century* (Alphen aan den Rijn: Kluwer Law International, 2020), 587–609.

Seif, Isabella. 'Business and Human Rights in International Investment Law: Empirical Evidence', in Julien Chaisse, Leïla Choukroune and Sufian Jusoh (eds.), *Handbook of International Investment Law and Policy* (Singapore: Springer, 2021), 1759–1782.

Senogles, Geoffrey. 'Some Views from the Crucible: The Perspective of an Expert Witness on the Adversarial Principle' (2018) 9(3) *Journal of International Dispute Settlement* 361–366.

Shamir, Ronen. 'Between Self-Regulation and the Alien Tort Claims Act: On the Contested Concept of Corporate Social Responsibility' (2004) 38(4) *Law & Society Review* 635–664.

Shan, Wenhua and Feng, Yunya. 'A Trinity Analytical Framework for ISDS Reform' (2018) 112 *American Journal of International Law Unbound* 244–248.

Shany, Yuval. 'Jurisdiction and Admissibility', in Cesare P. R. Romano, Karen J. Alter and Yuval Shany (eds.), *The Oxford Handbook of International Adjudication* (Oxford: Oxford University Press, 2014), 779–805.

Shao, Xuan. 'Environmental and Human Rights Counterclaims in International Investment Arbitration: At the Crossroads of Domestic and International Law' (2021) 24(1) *Journal of International Economic Law* 157–179.

Sharma, Rajesh. 'Mediation of Investor-State Disputes: Should It Be Transparent?' (2020) 13(2) *Contemporary Asia Arbitration Journal* 349–364.

Sharma, Uma Jitendra. 'What's Past Is Prologue: Revisiting Proportionality in Investor-State Arbitration' (2018–2019) 36 *Singapore Law Review* 152–185.

Sharpe, Jeremy K. and Jacob, Marc. 'Counterclaims and State Claims', in Christina L. Beharry (ed.), *Contemporary and Emerging Issues on the Law of Damages and Valuation in International Investment Arbitration* (Leiden/Boston: Brill Nijhoff, 2018), 347–368.

Shelton, Dinah. 'Human Rights, Environmental Rights, and the Right to Environment', (1991) 28(1) *Stanford Journal of International Law* 103–138.

Sherman III, John F. 'Beyond CSR: The Story of the UN Guiding Principles on Business and Human Rights', in Rae Lindsay and Roger Martella (eds.), *Corporate Responsibility, Sustainable Business: Environmental, Social and Governance Frameworks for the 21st Century* (Alphen aan den Rijn: Kluwer Law International, 2020), 473–503.

Shihata, Ibrahim F. I. and Parra, Antonio R. 'The Experience of the International Centre for Settlement of Investment Disputes' (1999) 14(2) *ICSID Review* 299–361.

Shirlow, Esmé. 'Investor-State Arbitration Meets Mediation: Potential Problems?', Kluwer Arbitration Blog, 30 September 2020.

Judging at the Interface: Deference to State Decision-Making Authority in International Adjudication (Cambridge: Cambridge University Press, 2021), Chapters 4, 5.

Shrivastava, Ankur. 'Category-wise Analysis of Awarded Cases Related to Compensation to the Bhopal Gas Victims', *Legal Services India*, available at: www.legalservicesindia.com/article/750/Category-wise-Analysis-of-Awarded-Cases-related-to-compensation-to-the-Bhopal-Gas-Victims.html.

Shue, Henry. *Basic Rights*, 2nd ed. (Princeton, NJ: Princeton University Press, 1996), Chapter 2.

Simma, Bruno. 'Foreign Investment Arbitration: A Place for Human Rights?' (2011) 60(3) *International & Comparative Law Quarterly* 573–596.

'Self-Contained Regimes' (1985) 26 *Netherlands Yearbook of International Law* 111–136.

Simma, Bruno and Pulkowski, Dirk. 'Of Planets and the Universe: Self-contained Regimes in International Law' (2006) 17(3) *European Journal of International Law* 483–529.

Simmons, Joshua B. 'Valuation in Investor-State Arbitration: Toward a More Exact Science' (2012) 30(1) *Berkeley Journal of International Law* 196–250.

Simons, Penelope. 'The Value-Added of a Treaty to Regulate Transnational Corporations', in Surya Deva and David Bilchitz (eds.), *Building a Treaty on Business and Human Rights: Context and Contours* (Cambridge: Cambridge University Press, 2017), 48–78.

Skinner, Gwynne. 'Beyond Kiobel: Providing Access to Judicial Remedies for Corporate Accountability for Violations of International Human Rights Norms by Transnational Corporations in a New (Post-Kiobel) World' (2014) 46(1) *Columbia Human Rights Law Review* 158–265.

'Parent Company Accountability: Ensuring Justice for Human Rights Violations', The International Corporate Accountability Roundtable, 2015, available at: www.bhrinlaw.org/documents/pcap-report-2015.pdf.

Skinner, Gwynne, McCorquodale, Robert and Shutter, Olivier De. 'The Third Pillar. Access to Judicial Remedies for Human Rights Violations by Transnational Business', ICAR-CORE-ECCJ, December 2013.

Sloss, David. 'Treaty Enforcement in Domestic Courts: A Comparative Analysis', in David Sloss (ed.), *The Role of Domestic Courts in Treaty Enforcement: A Comparative Study* (Cambridge: Cambridge University Press, 2009), 1-60.

'Using International Court of Justice Advisory Opinions to Adjudicate Secessionist Claims' (2001) 42(2) *Santa Clara Law Review* 357–390.

Sloss, David and Van Alstine, Michael. 'International Law in Domestic Courts', in Wayne Sandholtz and Christopher A. Whytock (eds.), *Research Handbook on the Politics of International Law* (Cheltenham: Edward Elgar, 2017), 79–115.

Snodgrass, Elizabeth. 'Protecting Investors' Legitimate Expectations – Recognizing and Delimiting a General Principle' (2006) 21(1) *ICSID Review* 1–58.

Söderlund, Christer and Burova, Elena. 'Is There Such a Thing as Admissibility in Investment Arbitration?' (2018) 33(2) *ICSID Review* 525–559.

Sohn, Louis B. and Baxter, R. R. 'Responsibility of States for Injuries to the Economic Interests of Aliens: II. Draft Convention on the International Responsibility of States for Injuries to Aliens' (1961) 55(3) *American Journal of International Law* 548–584.

Sornarajah, Muthucumaraswamy. *The International Law on Foreign Investment*, 4th ed. (Cambridge: Cambridge University Press 2017), Chapters 1–4, 8.

Resistance and Change in the International Law on Foreign Investment (Cambridge: Cambridge University Press, 2015), Chapters 1, 5–7.

Spar, Debora. 'Foreign Investment and Human Rights' (1999) 42(1) *Challenge* 55–80.

Sparks, Tom. 'Reassessing State Consent to Jurisdiction: The Indispensable Third Party Principle before the ICJ' (2020) Max Planck Institute, MPIL Research Paper Series No. 2020-22.

Spears, Suzanne A. 'Corporate Responsibility and National and International Legal Frameworks', in Rae Lindsay and Roger Martella (eds.), *Corporate Responsibility, Sustainable Business: Environmental, Social and Governance Frameworks for the 21st Century* (Alphen aan den Rijn: Kluwer Law International, 2020), 557–586.

'The Quest for Policy Space in a New Generation of International Investment Agreements' (2010) 13(4) *Journal of International Economic Law* 1037–1075.

Spieler, Paula. 'The La Oroya Case: The Relationship between Environmental Degradation and Human Rights Violations' (2010) 18(1) *Human Rights Brief* 19–23.

Spiermann, Ole. 'Applicable Law', in Peter Muchlinski, Federico Ortino and Christoph Schreuer (eds.), *The Oxford Handbook of International Investment Law* (Oxford: Oxford University Press, 2008), 89–118.

St John, Taylor. *The Rise of Investor-State Arbitration: Politics, Law, and Unintended Consequences* (Oxford: Oxford University Press, 2018), Chapter 8.

Steiner, Richard. 'Double Standard: Shell Practices in Nigeria Compared with International Standards to Prevent and Control Pipeline Oil Spills and the Deepwater Horizon Oil Spill', Friends of the Earth Netherlands, November 2010, available at: www.foei.org/wp-content/uploads/2014/01/20101109-rapport-Double-Standard.pdf.

Steingruber, Andrea Marco. '*Antoine Goetz and others v Republic of Burundi*: Consent and Arbitral Tribunal Competence to Hear Counterclaims in Treaty-Based ICSID Arbitrations' (2013) 28(2) *ICSID Review* 291–300.

'Some Remarks on Veijo Heiskanen's Note "Ménage à trois? Jurisdiction, Admissibility and Competence in Investment Treaty Arbitration"' (2014) 29(3) *ICSID Review* 675–689.

Steinitz, Maya. *The Case for an International Court of Civil Justice* (Cambridge: Cambridge University Press, 2019).

Stephens, Beth. 'Corporate Liability: Enforcing Human Rights through Domestic Litigation' (2001) 24(3) *Hastings International and Comparative Law Review* 401–414.

'Translating *Filártiga*: A Comparative and International Law Analysis of Domestic Remedies for International Human Rights Violations' (2002) 27 (1) *Yale Journal of International Law* 1–58.

Stephens-Chu, Gisele. 'Is It Always All about the Money? The Appropriateness of Non-Pecuniary Remedies in Investment Treaty Arbitration' (2014) 30(4) *Arbitration International* 661–686.

Stern, David, Common, Michael S. and Barbier, Edward. 'Economic Growth and Environmental Degradation: The Environmental Kuznets Curve and Sustainable Development' (1996) 24(7) *World Development* 1151–1160.

Stern, Marc J. 'Coercion, Voluntary Compliance and Protest: The Role of Trust and Legitimacy in Combating Local Opposition to Protected Areas' (2008) 35(3) *Environmental Conservation* 200–210.

Stone Sweet, Alec. 'Investor-State Arbitration: Proportionality's New Frontier' (2010) 4(1) *Law & Ethics of Human Rights* 46–76.

Stoyanova, Vladislava. 'Common Law Tort of Negligence as a Tool for Deconstructing Positive Obligations under the European Convention on Human Rights' (2019) 24(5) *International Journal of Human Rights* 632–655.

Strebel, Felix D. 'The Enforcement of Foreign Judgements and Foreign Public Law' (1999) 21(1) *Loyola of Los Angeles International and Comparative Law Journal* 55–130.

Strong, Stacie I. 'Third Party Intervention and Joinder as of Right in International Arbitration: An Infringement of Individual Contract Rights or a Proper Equitable Measure?' (1998) 31(4) *Vanderbilt Journal of Transnational Law* 915–996.

Šturma, Pavel. 'Public Goods and International Investment Law: Does the New Generation of IIAs Better Protect Human Rights?' (2018) 1 *Brill Open Law* 5–15.

Sullivan, Rory and Hachez, Nicolas. 'Human Rights Norms for Business: The Missing Piece of the Ruggie Jigsaw – The Case of Institutional Investors', in Radu Mares (ed.), *The UN Guiding Principles on Business and Human Rights: Foundations and Implementation* (Leiden: Martinus Nijhoff, 2012), 217–244.

Susskind, Lawrence. 'Environmental Mediation and the Accountability Problem' (1981) 6(1) *Vermont Law Review* 1–48.

Svoboda, Ondřej. 'Coming of Age: The System of OECD 1 National Contact Points for Responsible 2 Business Conduct in Its 20 Years', in Marc Bungenberg et al. (eds.), *European Yearbook of International Economic Law*, volume 11 (Berlin: Springer, 2020), 31–54.

'Investors' Responsibilities beyond Investment Treaties: A Workaround to Balance the Investment Protection Regime' (2020) 11 *Czech Yearbook of Public & Private International Law* 462–474.

Symeonides, Symeon C. *Codifying Choice of Law Around the World: An International Comparative Analysis* (Oxford: Oxford University Press, 2014), Chapter 2.

Tams, Christian J. *Enforcing Obligations Erga Omnes in International Law* (Cambridge: Cambridge University Press, 2005), Chapter 1.

Tanaka, Yoshifumi. *The Peaceful Settlement of International Disputes* (Cambridge: Cambridge University Press, 2018), Chapter 7.

Taylor, Prudence E. 'From Environmental to Ecological Human Rights: A New Dynamic in International Law?' (1998) 10(2) *Georgetown International Environmental Law Review* 309–398.

Thi-Huyen Dinh, Trang, Vo, Duc Hong, Vo, Anh The and Nguyen, Thang Cong. 'Foreign Direct Investment and Economic Growth in the Short Run and Long Run: Empirical Evidence from Developing Countries' (2019) 12(4) *Journal of Risk and Financial Management* 176–187.

Thienel, Tobias. 'Third States and the Jurisdiction of the International Court of Justice: The Monetary Gold Principle' (2014) 57 *German Yearbook of International Law* 322–353.

Thirlway, Hugh. 'The International Court of Justice', in Malcolm D. Evans (ed.), *International Law*, 5th ed. (Oxford: Oxford University Press, 2018), 573–600.

Thomas, Margaret S. '*Parens Patriae* and the States' Historic Police Power' (2016) 69(4) *SMU Law Review* 759–810.

Titi, Catharine. 'Mediation and the Settlement of International Investment Disputes: Between Utopia and Realism', in Catharine Titi and Katia Fach Gómez (eds.), *Mediation in International Commercial and Investment Disputes* (Oxford: Oxford University Press, 2019), 21–38.

Toope, Stephen J. 'Formality and Informality', in Ellen Hey, Jutta Brunnée and Daniel Bodansky (eds.), *The Oxford Handbook of International Environmental Law* (Oxford: Oxford University Press, 2007), 107–124.

Mixed International Arbitration: Studies in Arbitration between States and Private Persons (Cambridge: Grotius, 1990), Chapter III.

Toral, Mehmet and Schultz, Thomas. 'The State, a Perpetual Respondent in Investment Arbitration? Some Unorthodox Considerations', in Michael Waibel, Asha Kaushal, Kyo-Hwa Chung and Claire Balchin (eds.), *The Backlash against Investment Arbitration* (Alphen aan den Rijn: Kluwer Law International, 2009), 577–602.

Tudor, Ioana. *The Fair and Equitable Treatment Standard in the International Law of Foreign Investment* (Oxford: Oxford University Press, 2008), Chapter 7.

Tully, Stephen (ed.). *International Documents on Corporate Responsibility* (Cheltenham: Edward Elgar, 2005), Chapter 2.

Uff, Alexander. 'La réparation du dommage et la place du règlement transactionnel, point de vue des praticiens', in Laurence Dubin, Pierre Bodeau-Livinec, Jean-Louis Iten and Vincent Tomkiewicz (eds.), *L'entreprise multinationale et le droit international* (Paris: Pedone, 2017), 483–507.

Urdaneta, Juan Felipe Merizalde. 'Proportionality, Contributory Negligence and Other Equity Considerations in Investment Arbitration', in Todd J. Weiler and Ian A. Laird (eds.), *Investment Treaty Arbitration and International Law*, volume 8 (Huntington, NY: Juris, 2015), 301–325.

Uribe, Mariano de Alba. 'Drawing the Line: Addressing Allegations of Unclean Hands in Investment Arbitration' (2015) 12(1) *Brazilian Journal of International Law* 322–338.

Vadi, Valentina. 'The Migration of Constitutional Ideas to Regional and International Economic Law: The Case of Proportionality' (2015) 35(3) *Northwestern Journal of International Law & Business* 557–589.

Vagts, Detlev F. 'The Multinational Enterprise: A New Challenge for Transnational Law' (1970) 83(4) *Harvard Law Review* 739–792.

Valderrama, Carlos José. 'Investor-State Dispute Prevention: The Perspective of Peru', in Catherine Titi (ed.), *European Yearbook of International Economic Law Special Issue: Public Actors in International Investment Law* (Berlin: Springer, 2021), 117–133.

Vallat, Julie. 'Les apports de la responsabilité sociétale des entreprises (RSE), point de vue des enterprises', in Laurence Dubin, Pierre Bodeau-Livinec, Jean-Louis Iten and Vincent Tomkiewicz (eds.), *L'entreprise multinationale et le droit international* (Paris: Pedone, 2017), 477–482.

van Aaken, Anne and Lehmann, Tobias. 'Sustainable Development and International Investment Law: An Harmonious View from Economics', in Roberto Echandi and Pierre Sauvé (eds.), *Prospects in International Investment Law and Policy* (Cambridge: Cambridge University Press, 2013), 317–339.

van den Beukel, Jilles and Geuns, Lucia van. 'Groningen Gas: The Loss of a Social License to Operate' (2019) *Hague Centre for Strategic Studies* 1–21.

van der Heijden, Paul F. et al. (eds.), '3 Inter-American Court of Human Rights: *The Standing of Legal Entities in the Inter-American Human Rights System*, Advisory Opinion OC-22/16, 26 February 2016' (2017) 3 *International Labor Rights Case Law* 29–38.

van Dam, Cees. 'Tort Law and Human Rights: Brothers in Arms on the Role of Tort Law in the Area of Business and Human Rights' (2011) 2(3) *Journal of European Tort Law* 221–254.

Van Damme, Isabelle. 'The Assessment of Expert Evidence in International Adjudication' (2018) 9(3) *Journal of International Dispute Settlement* 401–410.

Van Harten, Gus. *Investment Treaty Arbitration and Public Law* (Oxford: Oxford University Press, 2008), Chapter I.

Van Harten, Gus, and Loughlin, Martin. 'Investment Treaty Arbitration as a Species of Global Administrative Law' (2006) 17(1) *European Journal of International Law* 121–150.

Van Harten, Gus, Kelsey, Jane and Schneiderman, David. 'Phase 2 of the UNCITRAL ISDS Review: Why "Other Matters" Really Matter' (2019) *Osgoode Legal Studies Research Paper* 1–15.

Van Loo, Relinde. 'The Rise and Fall of the Dutch Groningen Gas Field', E&C Consultants, 16 August 2018, available at: www.eecc.eu/blog/groningen-gas-field.

Van Putten, Ingrid E., Cvitanovic, Christopher, Fulton, Elizabeth, Lacey, Justine and Kelly, Rachel. 'The Emergence of Social Licence Necessitates Reforms in Environmental Regulation' (2018) 23(3) *Ecology and Society* 1–11.

Vandevelde, Kenneth J. 'Sustainable Liberalism and the International Investment Regime' (1998) 19(2) *Michigan Journal International Law* 373–399.

Vastardis, Anil Yilmaz and Chambers, Rachel. 'Overcoming the Corporate Veil Challenge: Could Investment Law Inspire the Proposed Business and Human Rights Treaty?' (2018) 67(2) *International & Comparative Law Quarterly* 389–423.

Vaypan, Grigory. 'Choosing among the Shades of Nuance: The Discourse of Proportionality in International Law' (2015) 15(2) *Global Jurist* 237–259.

Vázquez, Carlos Manuel. 'Alien Tort Claims and the Status of Customary International Law' (2012) 106(3) *American Journal of International Law* 531–546.

'Choice-of-Law as Geographic Scope Limitation', in Chiara Giorgetti and Natalie Klein (eds.), *Resolving Conflicts in the Law: Essays in Honour of Lea Brilmayer* (Leiden: Brill Nijhoff, 2020), 42–77.

'Customary International Law as U.S. Law: A Critique of the Revisionist and Intermediate Positions and a Defense of the Modern Position' (2011) 86(4) *Notre Dame Law Review* 1495–1634.

'Direct vs. Indirect Obligations of Corporations under International Law' (2005) 43(3) *Columbia Journal of Transnational Law* 927–960.

'Jurisdiction and Choice of Law for Non-Contractual Obligations Part I: Hemispheric Approaches to Jurisdiction and Applicable Law for Non-Contractual Civil Liability', Organization of American States Permanent Council 62nd Regular Session, Rio de Janeiro, 10–21 March 2003.

Verbist, Herman. 'Mediation as an Alternative Method to Settle Investor-State Disputes', in Julien Chaisse, Leïla Choukroune and Sufian Jusoh (eds.), *Handbook of International Investment Law and Policy* (Singapore: Springer, 2021), 759–786.

Vermeer-Künzli, A. 'As If: The Legal Fiction in Diplomatic Protection' (2007) 18 (1) *European Journal of International Law* 37–68.

Viñuales, Jorge E. 'International Investment Law and Natural Resource Governance' (2015) E15Initiative. Geneva: International Centre for Trade and Sustainable Development (ICTSD) and World Economic Forum, 2015. www.e15initiative.org/ (accessed 15 December 2021).

'Investor Diligence in Investment Arbitration: Sources and Arguments' (2017) 32(2) *ICSID Review* 346–370.

Foreign Investment and the Environment in International Law (Cambridge: Cambridge University Press, 2012), Chapters 1, 5.

Virgo, Graham. 'Whose Conscience? Unconscionability in the Common Law of Obligations', in Andrew Robertson and Michael Tilbury (eds.), *Divergencies in Private Law* (Oxford: Hart, 2016), 293–320.

Vohryzek-Griest, Ana. 'State Counterclaims in Investor-State Disputes: A History of 30 Years of Failure' (2009) 15 *International Law: Revista Colombiana de Derecho Internacional* 83–124.

von Bogdandy, Armin and Venzke, Ingo. *In Whose Name?: A Public Law Theory of International Adjudication* (Oxford: Oxford University Press, 2014), Chapter 4.

von Kumberg, Wolf, Lack, Jeremy and Leathes, Michael. 'Enabling Early Settlement in Investor-State Arbitration: The Time to Introduce Mediation Has Come' (2014) 29(1) *ICSID Review* 133–141.

von Staden, Andreas. 'Deference or No Deference, That Is the Question: Legitimacy and Standards of Review in Investor-State Arbitration', *Investment Treaty News*, 19 July 2012.

'The Democratic Legitimacy of Judicial Review beyond the State: Normative Subsidiarity and Judicial Standards of Review' (2012) 10(4) *International Journal of Constitutional Law* 1023–1049.

von Wobeser, Claus. 'The Arbitral Tribunal-Appointed Expert' (2007) 4(3) *Transnational Dispute Management* 1–11.

Vurro, Clodia. 'The Evolutionary Path of the Concept of CSR', in Francesco Perrini, Stefano Pogutz and Antonio Tencati (eds.), *Developing Corporate Social Responsibility: A European Perspective* (Cheltenham: Edward Elgar, 2006), 54–71.

Wagner, Markus. 'Regulatory Space in International Trade Law and International Investment Law' (2014) 36(1) *University of Pennsylvania Journal of International Law* 1–87.

Waibel, Michael. 'Investment Arbitration: Jurisdiction and Admissibility', in Marc Bungenberg, Jörn Griebel, Stephan Hobe and August Reinisch (eds.), *International Investment Law: A Handbook* (Baden-Baden: Nomos, 2015), 1212–1287.

Wälde, Thomas W. 'Efficient Management of Transnational Disputes: Mutual Gain by Mediation or Joint Loss in Litigation' (2006) 22(2) *Arbitration International* 205–232.

'Pro-Active Mediation of International Business and Investment Disputes Involving Long-Term Contracts: From Zero-Sum Litigation to Efficient Dispute Management' (2004) 1(2) *Transnational Dispute Management* 1–10.

Wälde, Thomas and Kolo, Abba. 'Environmental Regulation, Investment Protection and "Regulatory Taking" in International Law' (2001) 50(4) *International & Comparative Law Quarterly* 811–848.

Ward, Halina. 'Corporate Social Responsibility in Law and Policy', in Nina Boeger, Rachel Murray and Charlotte Villiers (eds.), *Perspectives on Corporate Social Responsibility* (Cheltenham: Edward Elgar, 2008), 8–38.

'Legal Issues in Corporate Citizenship' (2003) Paper Prepared for the Swedish Partnership for Global Responsibility, available at: https://pubs.iied.org/sites/default/files/pdfs/migrate/16000IIED.pdf.

Ward, Peter. 'Tort Cause of Action' (1956) 42(1) *Cornell Law Review* 28–58.

Webb, Philippa, '*Forum non conveniens*: Recent Developments at the Intersection of Public and Private International Law', in Chiara Giorgetti and Natalie

Klein (eds.), *Resolving Conflicts in the Law: Essays in Honour of Lea Brilmayer* (Leiden: Brill Nijhoff, 2020), 78–97.

Weeramantry, Romesh and Chang, Brian. 'Investor-State Conciliation and Mediation' (2021) *Oxford Bibliography Online* 1–25.

Wehland, Hanno. 'Jurisdiction and Admissibility in Proceedings under the ICSID Convention and the ICSID Additional Facility Rules', in Crina Baltag (ed.), *ICSID Convention after 50 Years: Unsettled Issues* (Alphen aan den Rijn: Kluwer Law International, 2017), 227–247.

Weil, Prosper. 'Towards Relative Normativity in International Law?' (1983) 77(3) *American Journal of International Law* 413–442.

Weiler, Todd. 'Balancing Human Rights and Investor Protection: A New Approach for a Different Legal Order' (2004) 27(2) *Boston College International and Comparative Law Review* 429–452.

Weissbrodt, David and Kruger, Muria. 'Norms on the Responsibilities of Transnational Corporations and Other Business Enterprises with Regard to Human Rights' (2003) 97(4) *American Journal of International Law* 901–922.

Welsh, Nancy A. and Schneider, Andrea K. 'The Thoughtful Integration of Mediation into Bilateral Investment Treaty Arbitration' (2013) 18 *Harvard Negotiation Law Review* 71–144.

Wettstein, Florian. *Multinational Corporations and Global Justice: Human Rights Obligations of a Quasi-Governmental Institution* (Stanford, CA: Stanford Business Books, 2009), Part III.

Whitsitt, Elizabeth and Bankes, Nigel. 'The Evolution of International Investment Law and Its Application to the Energy Sector' (2013) 51(2) *Alberta Law Review* 207–247.

Wildhaber, Luzius. 'Some Aspects of the Transnational Corporation in International Law' (1980) 27(1) *Netherlands International Law Review* 79–88.

Wittich, Stephan. 'Domestic Courts and the Content and Implementation of State Responsibility' (2013) 26(3) *Leiden Journal of International Law* 643–665.

Wongkaew, Teerawat. *Protection of Legitimate Expectations in Investment Treaty Arbitration* (Cambridge: Cambridge University Press, 2019).

'Specific Approval Requirement in Investment Treaties: A Pursuit of Legitimate Policy Objectives', in Julien Chaisse, Leïla Choukroune and Sufian Jusoh (eds.), *Handbook of International Investment Law and Policy* (Singapore: Springer, 2021), 71–96.

Wood, Michael and Sthoeger, Eran. 'Third-Party Intervention and Involvement in Inter-State Arbitration', in Helene Ruiz Fabri et al. (eds.), *A Bridge over Troubled Waters: Dispute Resolution in the Law of International Watercourses and the Law of the Sea* (Leiden: Brill Nijhoff, 2020), 61–82.

Wouters, Jan and Chanet, Leen. 'Corporate Human Rights Responsibility: A European Perspective' (2008) 6(2) *Northwestern Journal of International Human Rights* 262–302.

Yamamoto, Hiroko, Ramesh, Shreya and Seelmann-Eggebert, Sebastian. '*Perenco Ecuador v Republic of Ecuador Lessons from Perenco*: Tribunal-Appointed Experts and Avoiding Double Recovery' (2020) 35(3) *ICSID Review* 459–467.

Yates, Brian F. and Horvath, Celesa L. 'Social License to Operate: How to Get It, and How to Keep It' (2013) *2013 Pacific Energy Summit Working Papers*, available at: www.nbr.org/wp-content/uploads/pdfs/programs/PES_2013_summitpaper_Yates_Horvath.pdf.

Yotova, Rumiana. 'Challenges in the Identification of the "General Principles of Law Recognized by Civilized Nations": The Approach of the International Court' (2017) University of Cambridge Faculty of Law Research Paper No. 38.

Zamir, Noam. 'The Applicability of the Monetary Gold Principle in International Arbitration' (2017) 33(4) *Arbitration International* 523–538.

Zarsky, Lyuba. 'Global Reach: Human Rights and Environment in the Framework of Corporate Accountability', in Lyuba Zarsky (ed.), *Human Rights and the Environment: Conflicts and Norms in a Globalizing World* (London: Earthscan, 2012), 31–56.

Zeinemann, Robert. 'The Characterization of Public Sector Mediation' (2001) 24(2) *Environs: Environmental Law and Policy Journal* 49–64.

Zerk, Jennifer. 'Corporate Liability for Gross Human Rights Abuses: Towards a Fairer and More Effective System of Domestic Law Remedies' (2012) A Report Prepared for the Office of the UN High Commissioner for Human Rights, available at: www.ohchr.org/Documents/Issues/Business/DomesticLawRemedies/StudyDomesticeLawRemedies.pdf.

Zerk, Jennifer A. 'Corporate Social Responsibility and International Law: Where Are We Now, and Where Are We Headed?', in Rae Lindsay and Roger Martella (eds.), *Corporate Responsibility, Sustainable Business: Environmental, Social and Governance Frameworks for the 21st Century* (Alphen aan den Rijn: Kluwer Law International, 2020), 173–203.

Multinationals and Corporate Social Responsibility: Limitations and Opportunities in International Law (Cambridge: Cambridge University Press, 2006), Chapters 1, 4, and 5.

Zeyl, Trevor. 'Charting the Wrong Course: The Doctrine of Legitimate Expectations in investment Treaty Law' (2011) 49(1) *Alberta Law Review* 203–235.

Zomorrodi, Ahmad and Zhou, Xiaoyan. 'Impact of FDI on Environmental Quality of China' (2017) 4(1) *International Journal of Business, Economics and Management* 1–15.

INDEX

For EU product safety concerns, contact us at Calle de José Abascal, 56–1°,
28003 Madrid, Spain or eugpsr@cambridge.org.

www.ingramcontent.com/pod-product-compliance
Lightning Source LLC
LaVergne TN
LVHW052245200926
848481LV00002B/275

* 9 7 8 1 0 0 9 0 7 7 0 3 3 *